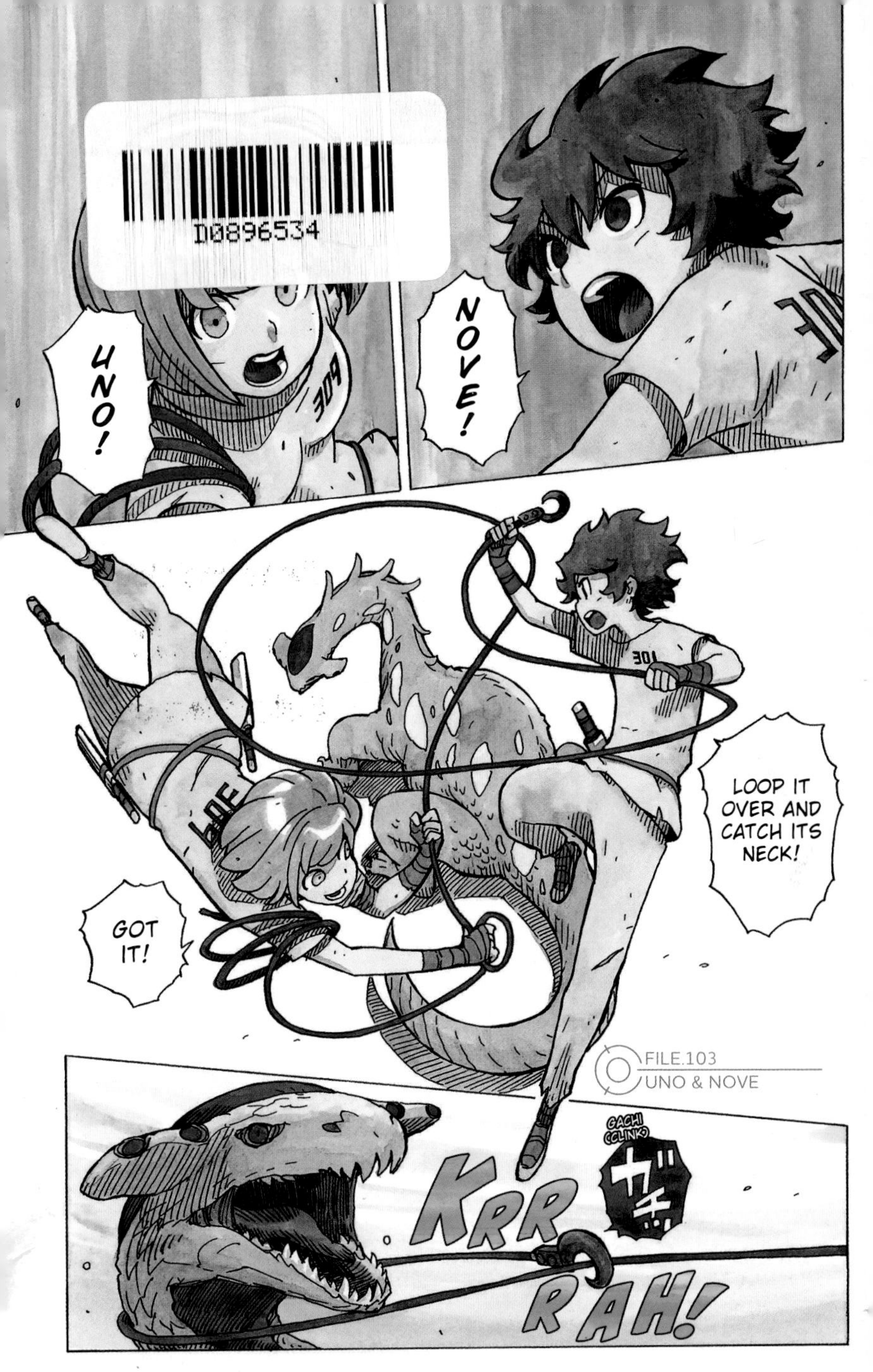
NOVE!
UNO!
LOOP IT OVER AND CATCH ITS NECK!
GOT IT!
FILE.103
UNO & NOVE
GACHI (CLINK)
KRR RAH!

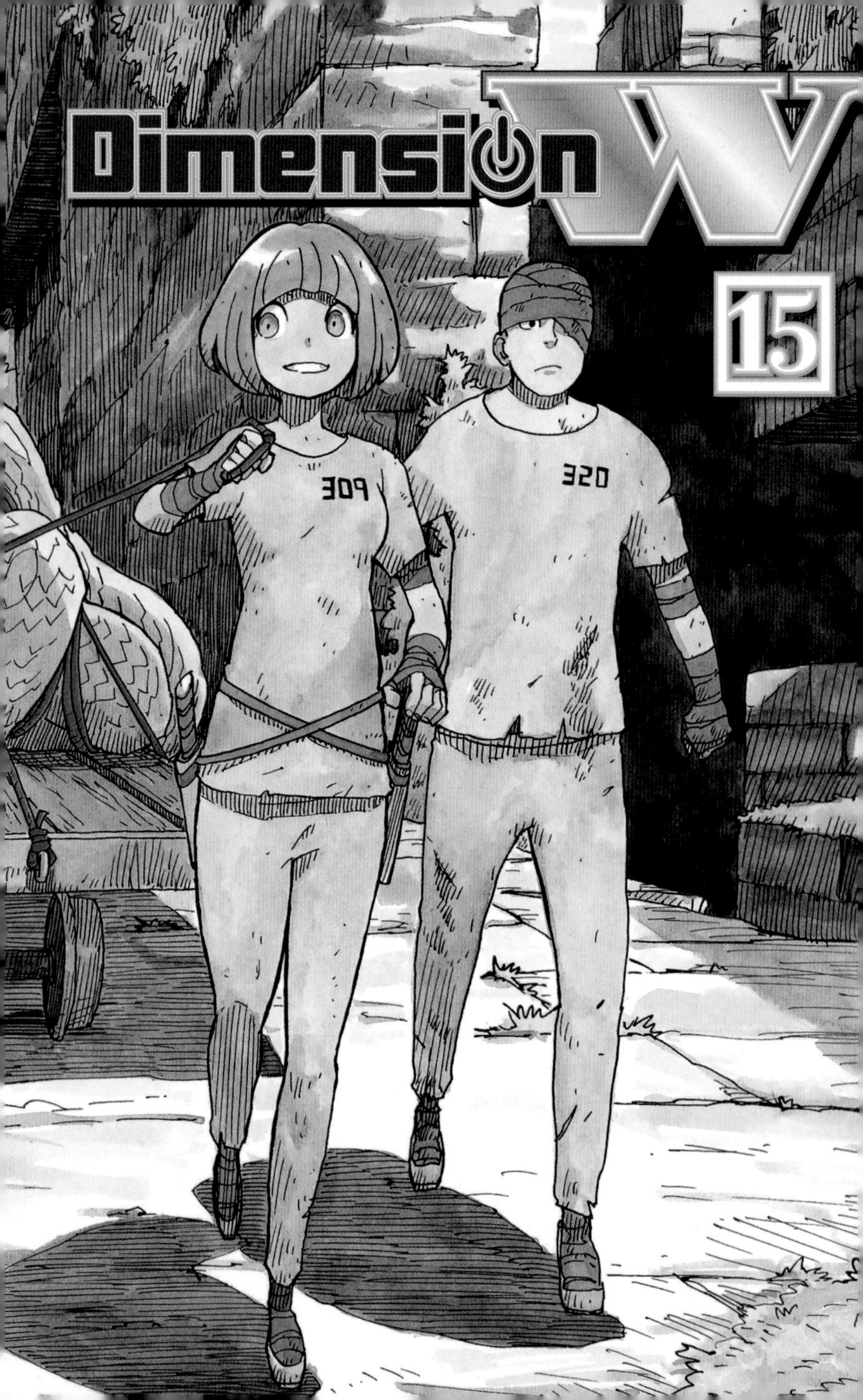
Dimension W
15
309
320

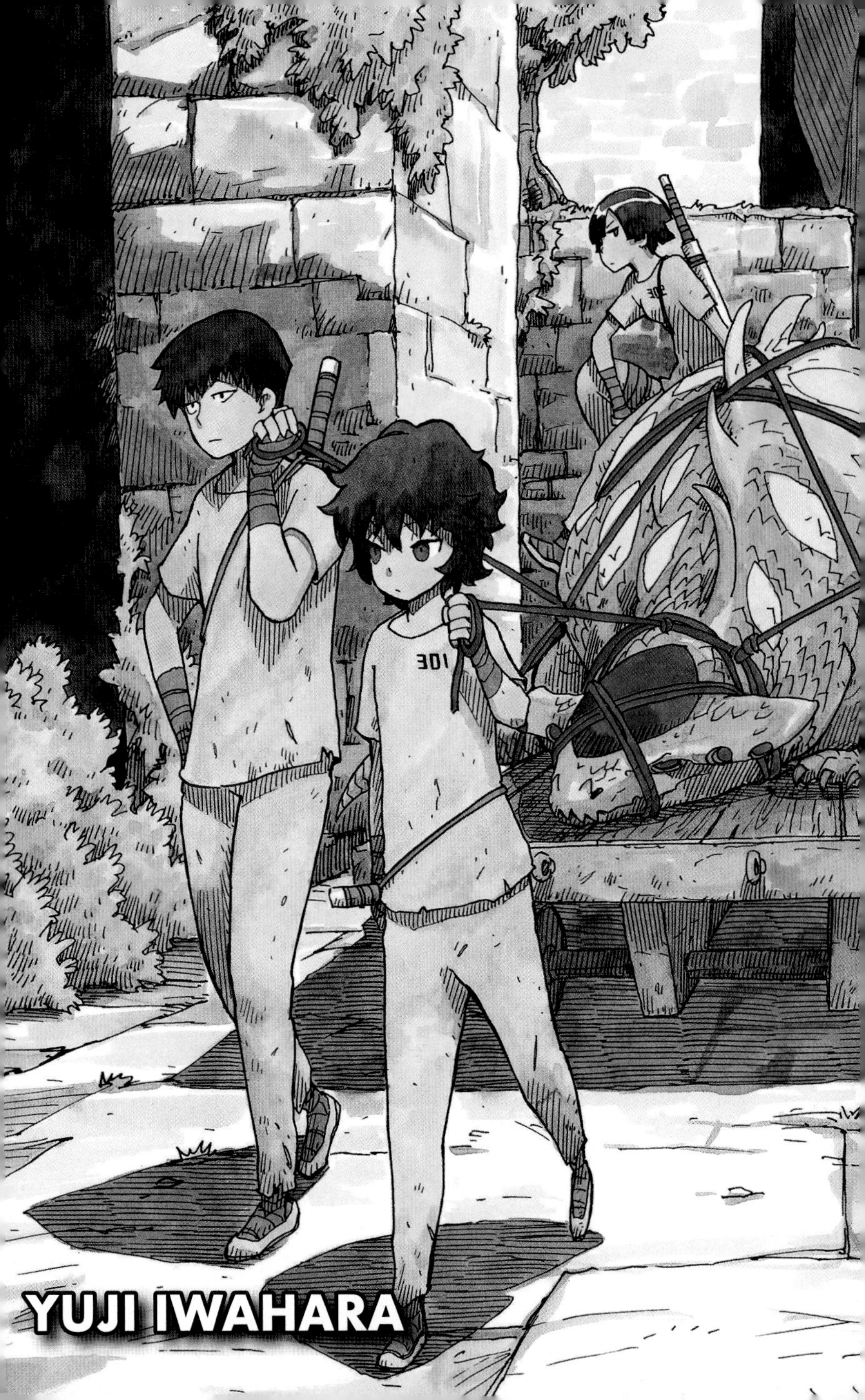
YUJI IWAHARA

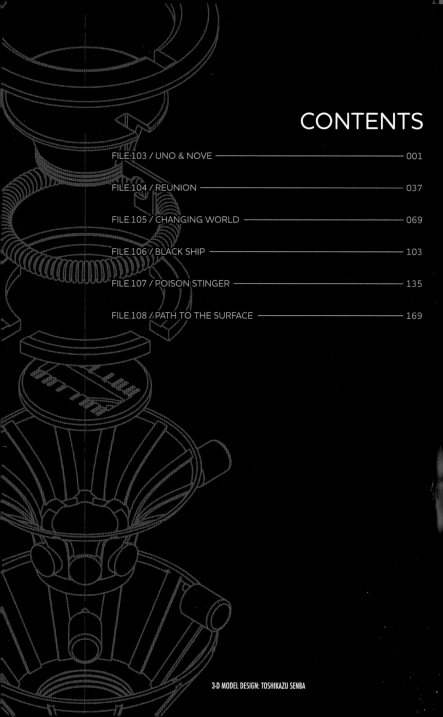

CONTENTS

3-D MODEL DESIGN: TOSHIKAZU SENBA

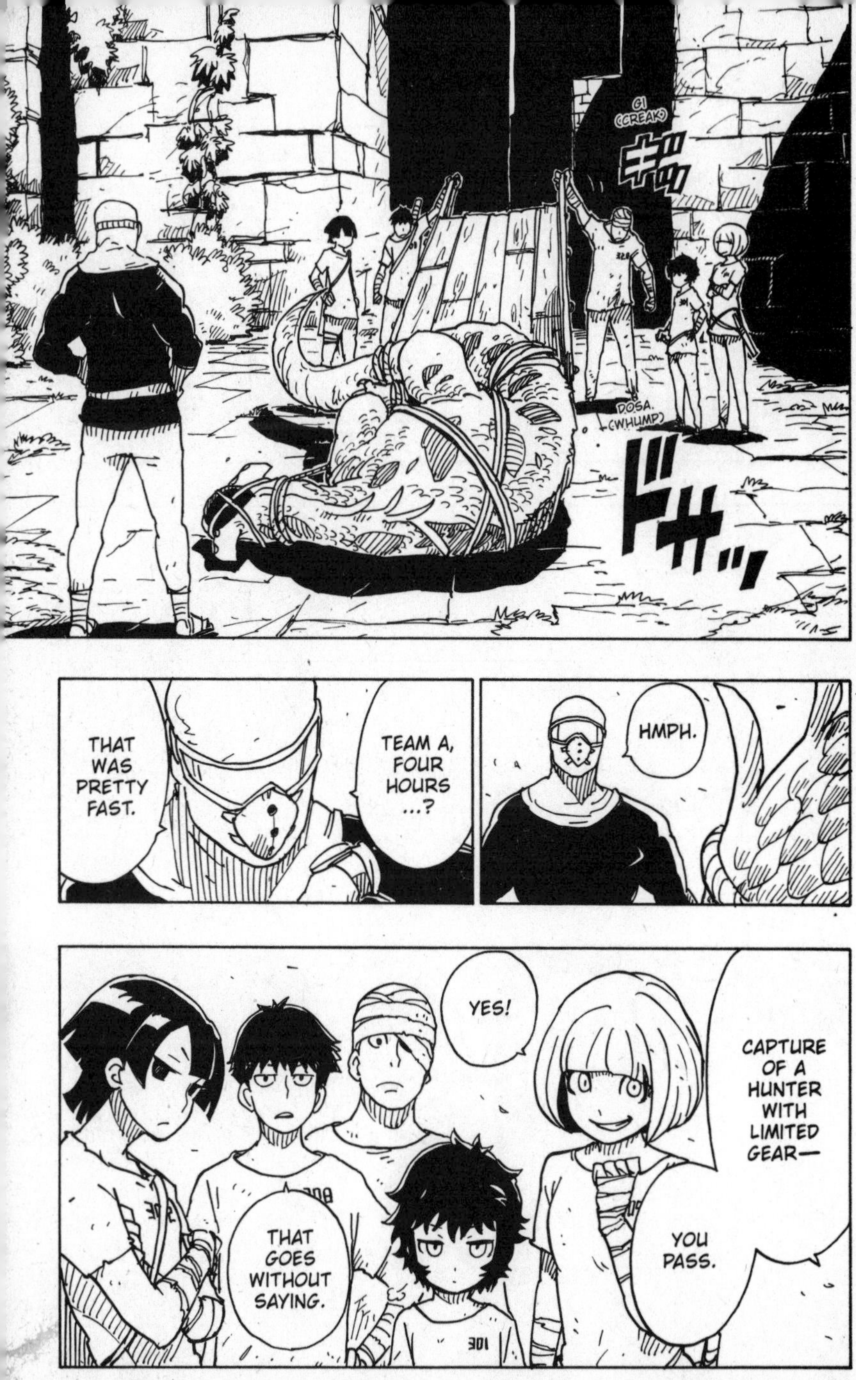
GI (CREAK)
ギッ
DOSA. (WHUMP)
ドサッ
HMPH.
TEAM A, FOUR HOURS ...?
THAT WAS PRETTY FAST.
CAPTURE OF A HUNTER WITH LIMITED GEAR—
YOU PASS.
YES!
THAT GOES WITHOUT SAYING.

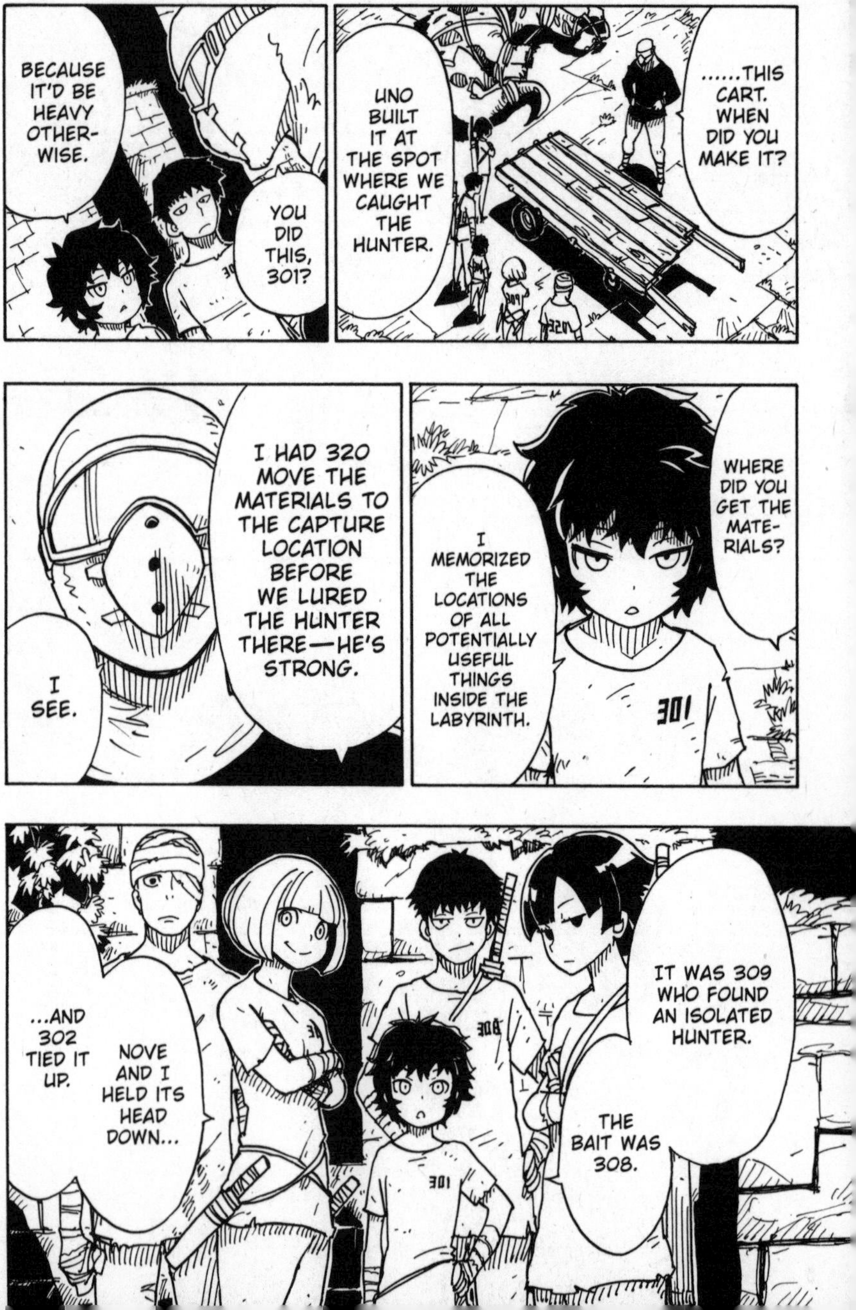
......THIS CART. WHEN DID YOU MAKE IT?
UNO BUILT IT AT THE SPOT WHERE WE CAUGHT THE HUNTER.
YOU DID THIS, 301?
BECAUSE IT'D BE HEAVY OTHER-WISE.
WHERE DID YOU GET THE MATE-RIALS?
I MEMORIZED THE LOCATIONS OF ALL POTENTIALLY USEFUL THINGS INSIDE THE LABYRINTH.
I HAD 320 MOVE THE MATERIALS TO THE CAPTURE LOCATION BEFORE WE LURED THE HUNTER THERE—HE'S STRONG.
I SEE.
IT WAS 309 WHO FOUND AN ISOLATED HUNTER.
THE BAIT WAS 308.
NOVE AND I HELD ITS HEAD DOWN...
...AND 302 TIED IT UP.

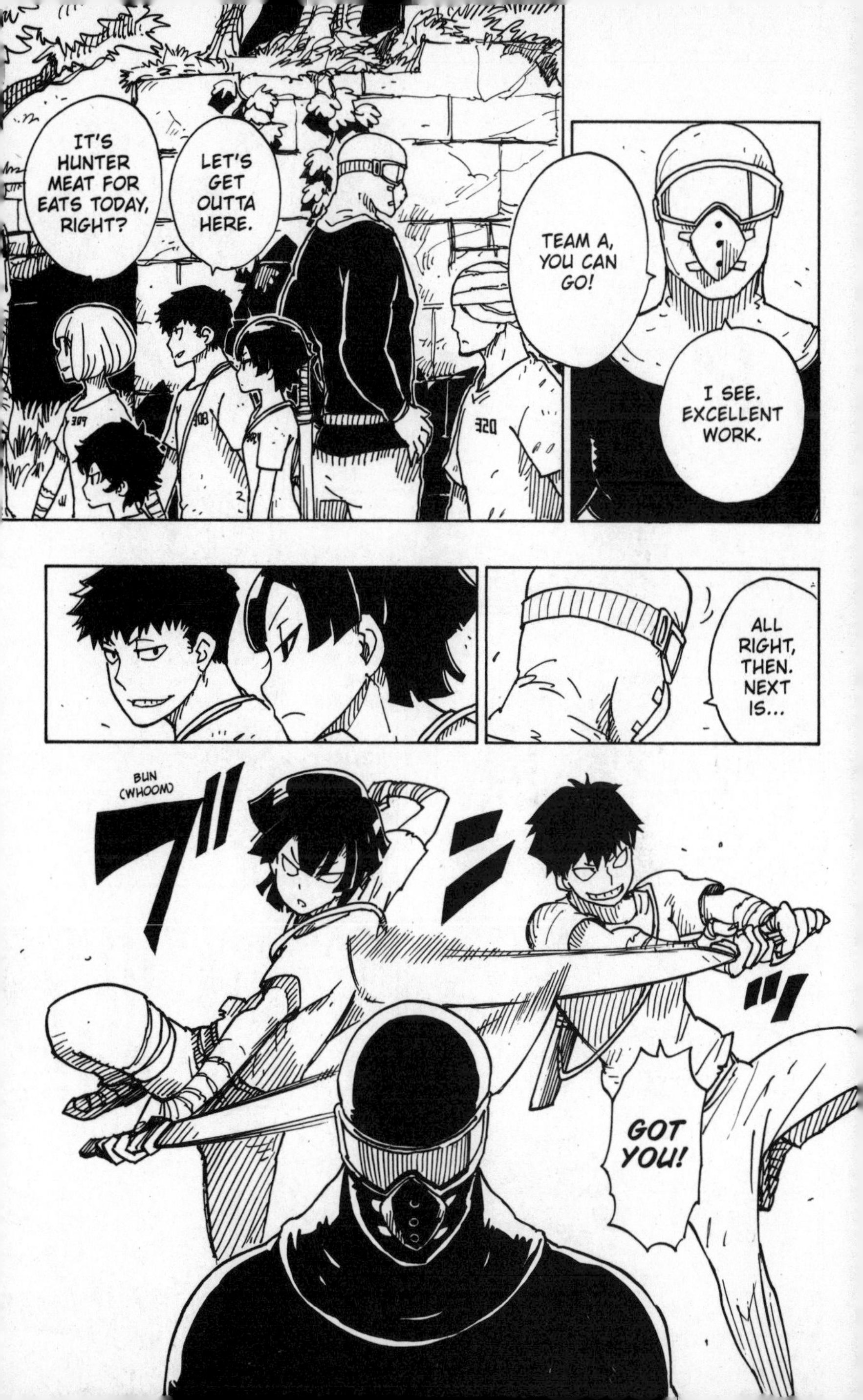

TEAM A, YOU CAN GO!
I SEE. EXCELLENT WORK.
LET'S GET OUTTA HERE.
IT'S HUNTER MEAT FOR EATS TODAY, RIGHT?
ALL RIGHT, THEN. NEXT IS...
BUN (WHOOM)
GOT YOU!

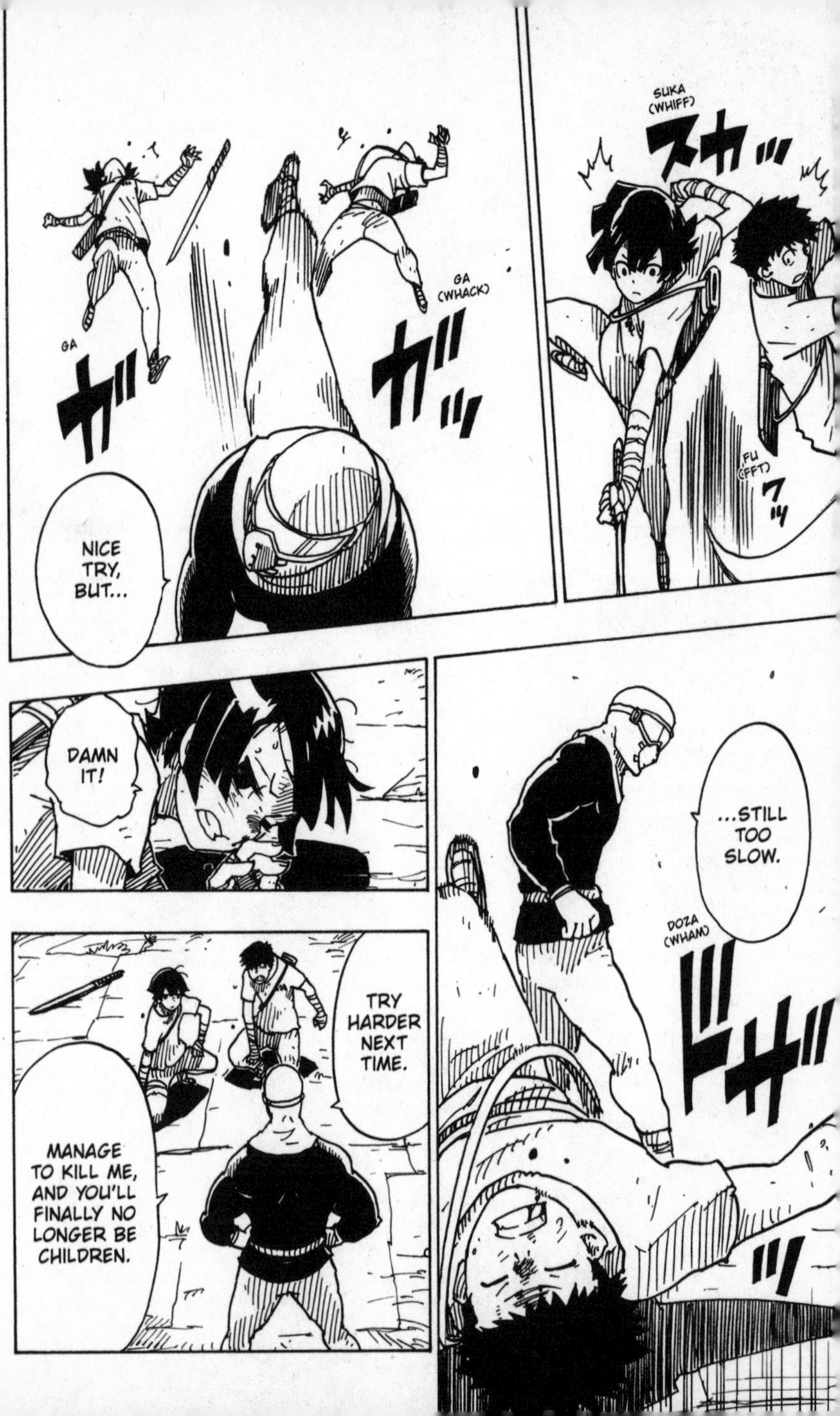
SUKA (WHIFF)
スカッ
FU (FFT)
フッ
GA (WHACK)
ガッ
GA
ガッ
NICE TRY, BUT...
...STILL TOO SLOW.
DOZA (WHAM)
ドザッ
DAMN IT!
TRY HARDER NEXT TIME.
MANAGE TO KILL ME, AND YOU'LL FINALLY NO LONGER BE CHILDREN.

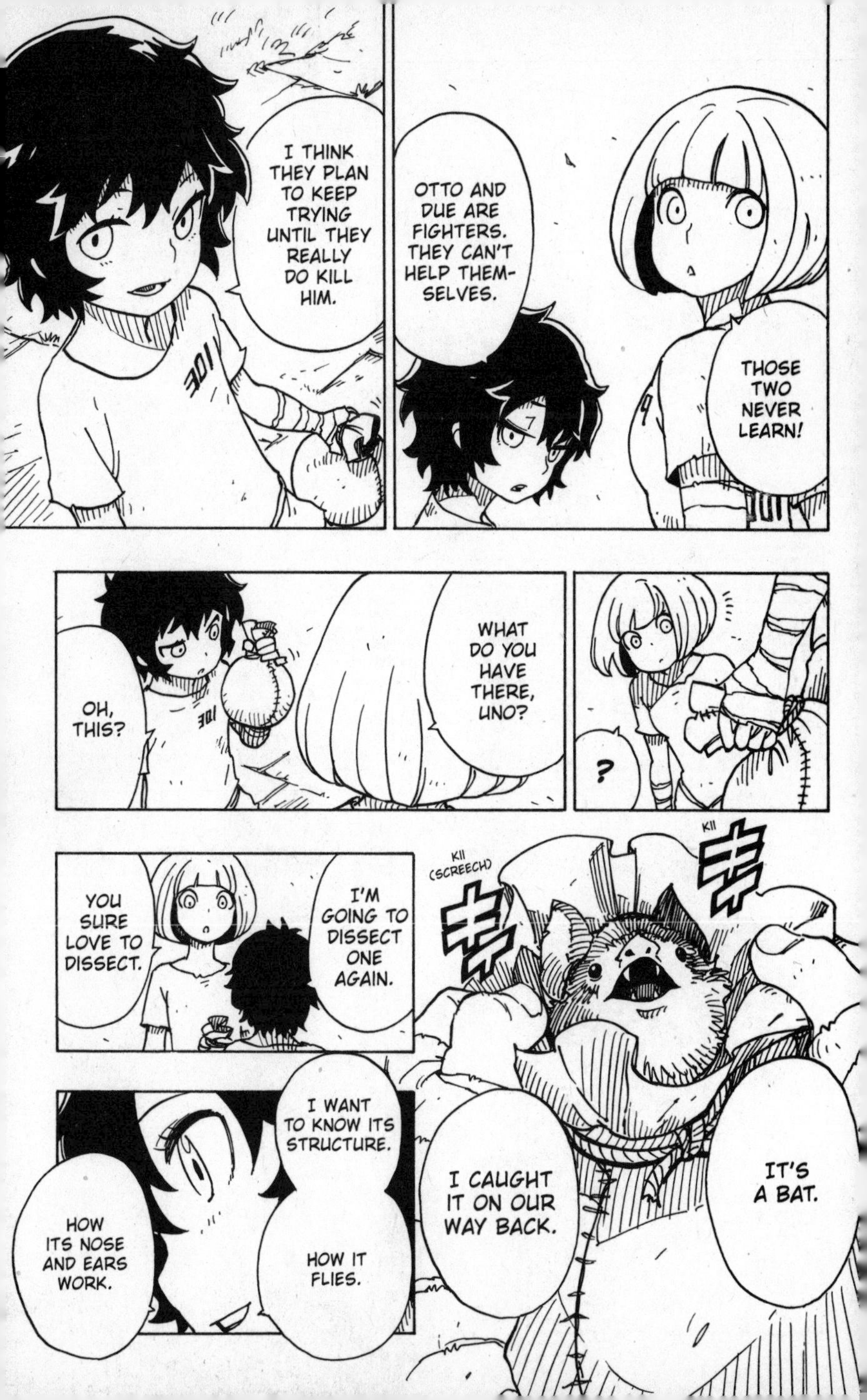

THOSE TWO NEVER LEARN!
OTTO AND DUE ARE FIGHTERS. THEY CAN'T HELP THEM-SELVES.
I THINK THEY PLAN TO KEEP TRYING UNTIL THEY REALLY DO KILL HIM.
?
WHAT DO YOU HAVE THERE, UNO?
OH, THIS?
KII
KII (SCREECH)
IT'S A BAT.
I CAUGHT IT ON OUR WAY BACK.
I'M GOING TO DISSECT ONE AGAIN.
YOU SURE LOVE TO DISSECT.
I WANT TO KNOW ITS STRUCTURE.
HOW IT FLIES.
HOW ITS NOSE AND EARS WORK.

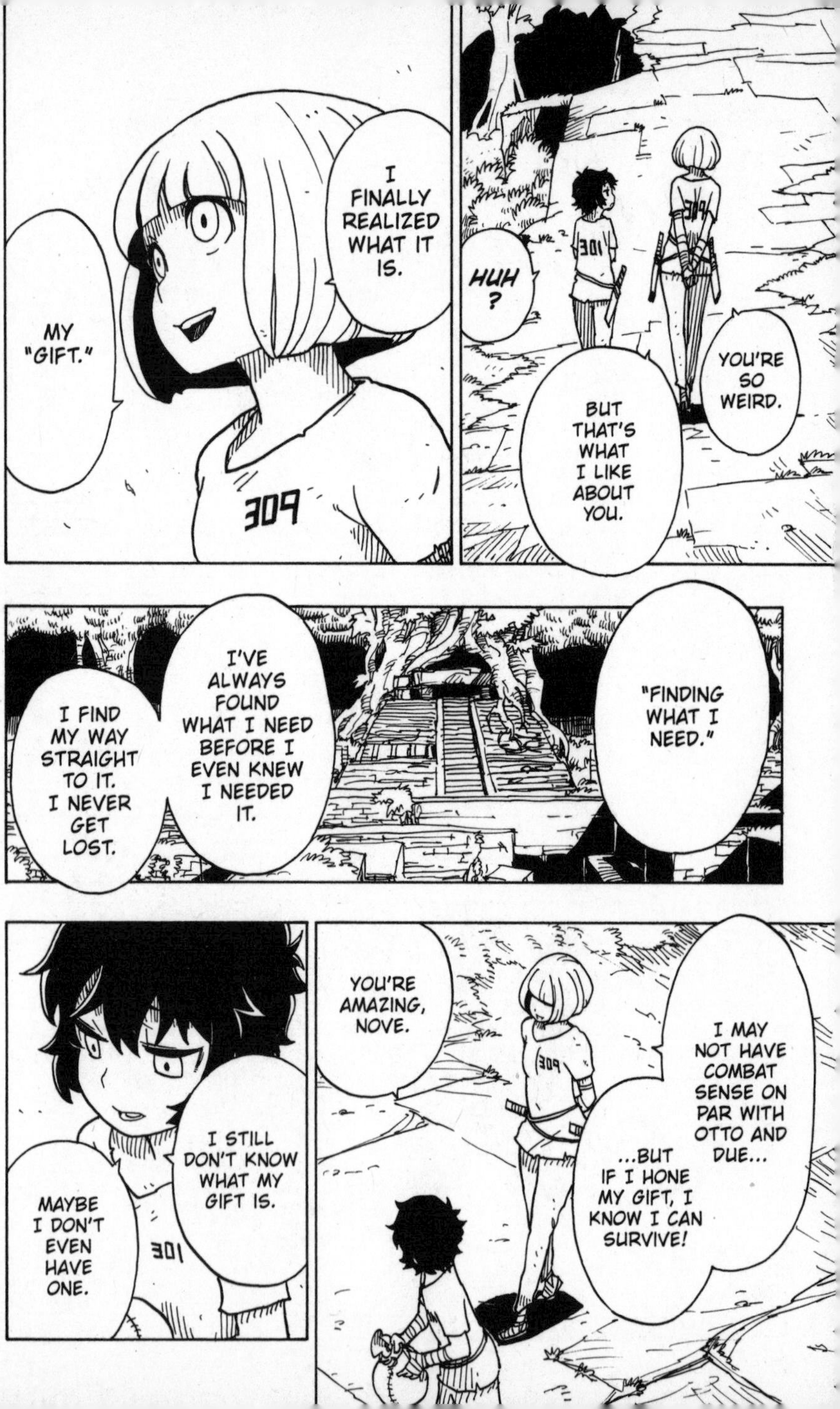
HUH?
YOU'RE SO WEIRD.
BUT THAT'S WHAT I LIKE ABOUT YOU.
I FINALLY REALIZED WHAT IT IS.
MY "GIFT."
"FINDING WHAT I NEED."
I'VE ALWAYS FOUND WHAT I NEED BEFORE I EVEN KNEW I NEEDED IT.
I FIND MY WAY STRAIGHT TO IT. I NEVER GET LOST.
I MAY NOT HAVE COMBAT SENSE ON PAR WITH OTTO AND DUE...
...BUT IF I HONE MY GIFT, I KNOW I CAN SURVIVE!
YOU'RE AMAZING, NOVE.
I STILL DON'T KNOW WHAT MY GIFT IS.
MAYBE I DON'T EVEN HAVE ONE.

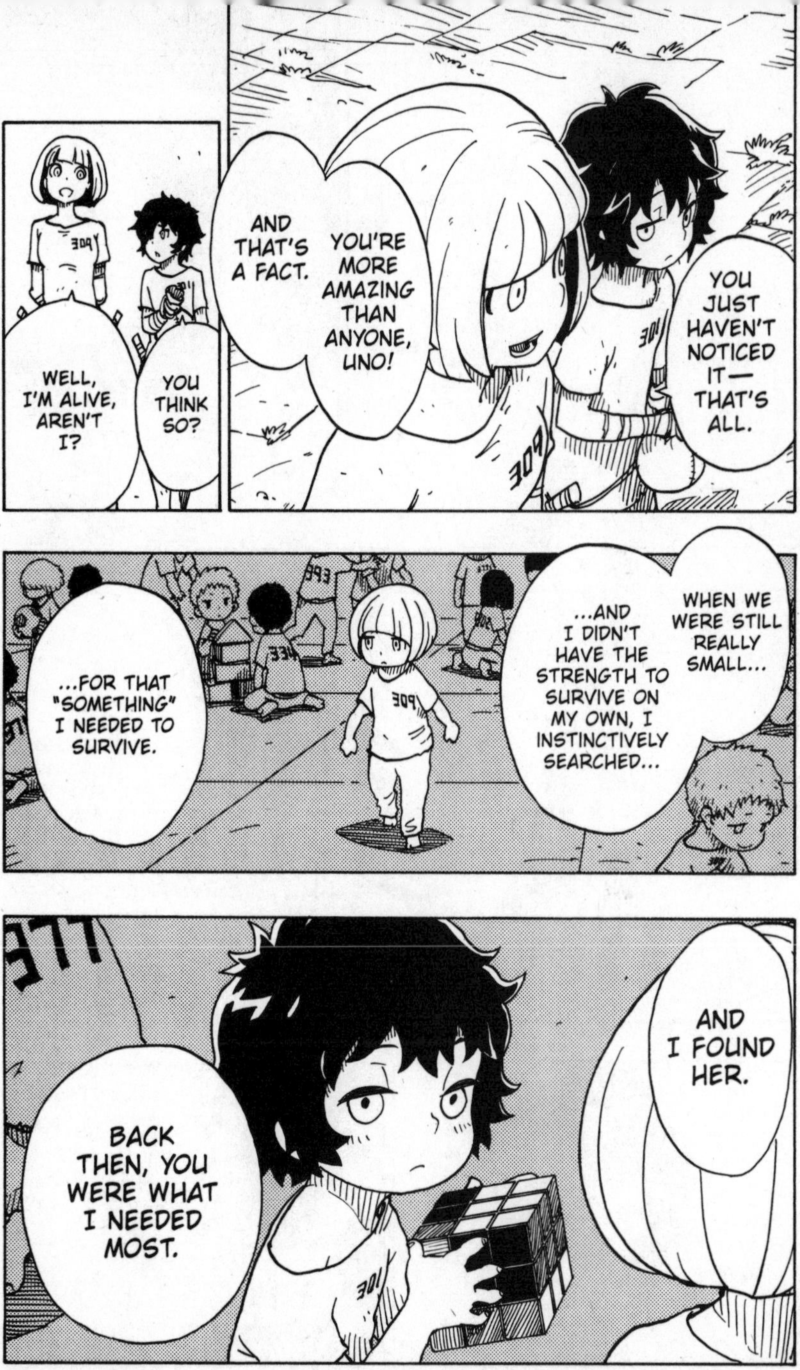
YOU JUST HAVEN'T NOTICED IT— THAT'S ALL.
YOU'RE MORE AMAZING THAN ANYONE, UNO!
AND THAT'S A FACT.
YOU THINK SO?
WELL, I'M ALIVE, AREN'T I?
WHEN WE WERE STILL REALLY SMALL...
...AND I DIDN'T HAVE THE STRENGTH TO SURVIVE ON MY OWN, I INSTINCTIVELY SEARCHED...
...FOR THAT "SOMETHING" I NEEDED TO SURVIVE.
AND I FOUND HER.
BACK THEN, YOU WERE WHAT I NEEDED MOST.

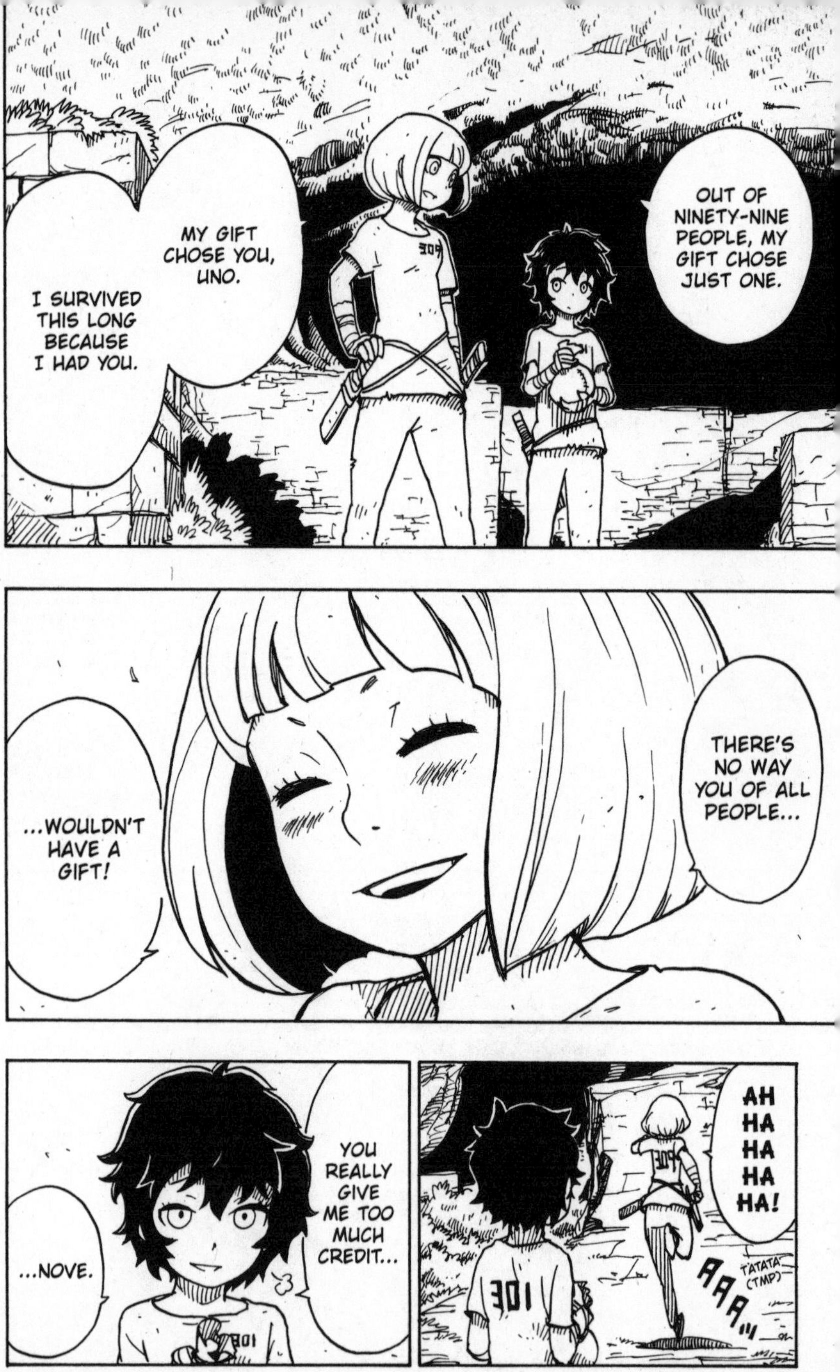
OUT OF NINETY-NINE PEOPLE, MY GIFT CHOSE JUST ONE.
MY GIFT CHOSE YOU, UNO.
I SURVIVED THIS LONG BECAUSE I HAD YOU.
THERE'S NO WAY YOU OF ALL PEOPLE...
...WOULDN'T HAVE A GIFT!
AH HA HA HA HA!
TATATA (TMP)
YOU REALLY GIVE ME TOO MUCH CREDIT...
...NOVE.

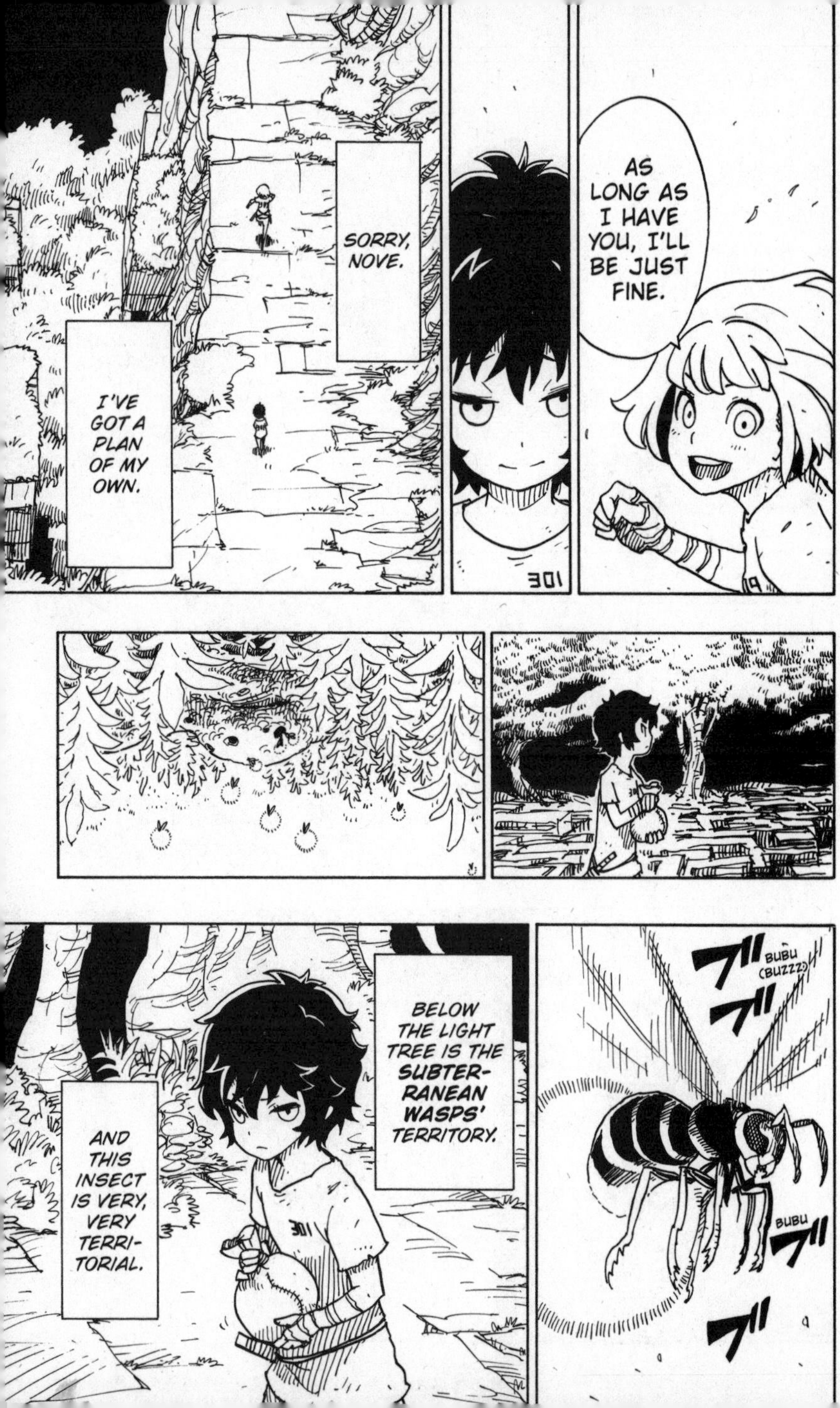
AS LONG AS I HAVE YOU, I'LL BE JUST FINE.
SORRY, NOVE.
I'VE GOT A PLAN OF MY OWN.
BUBU (BUZZZ)
BUBU
BELOW THE LIGHT TREE IS THE SUBTERRANEAN WASPS' TERRITORY.
AND THIS INSECT IS VERY, VERY TERRITORIAL.

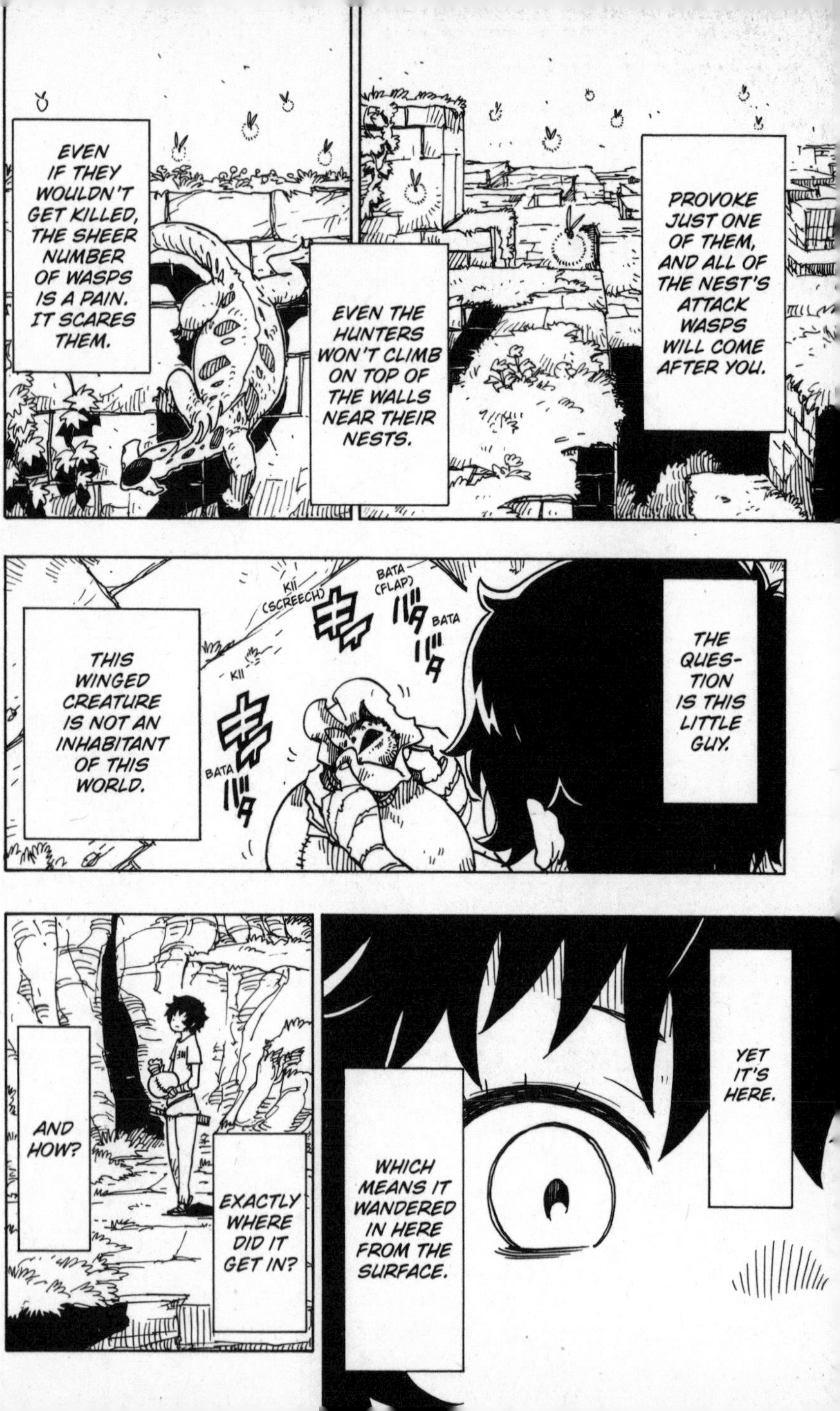
PROVOKE JUST ONE OF THEM, AND ALL OF THE NEST'S ATTACK WASPS WILL COME AFTER YOU.
EVEN THE HUNTERS WON'T CLIMB ON TOP OF THE WALLS NEAR THEIR NESTS.
EVEN IF THEY WOULDN'T GET KILLED, THE SHEER NUMBER OF WASPS IS A PAIN. IT SCARES THEM.
THE QUESTION IS THIS LITTLE GUY.
BATA (FLAP)
BATA
KII (SCREECH)
KII
BATA
THIS WINGED CREATURE IS NOT AN INHABITANT OF THIS WORLD.
YET IT'S HERE.
WHICH MEANS IT WANDERED IN HERE FROM THE SURFACE.
EXACTLY WHERE DID IT GET IN?
AND HOW?

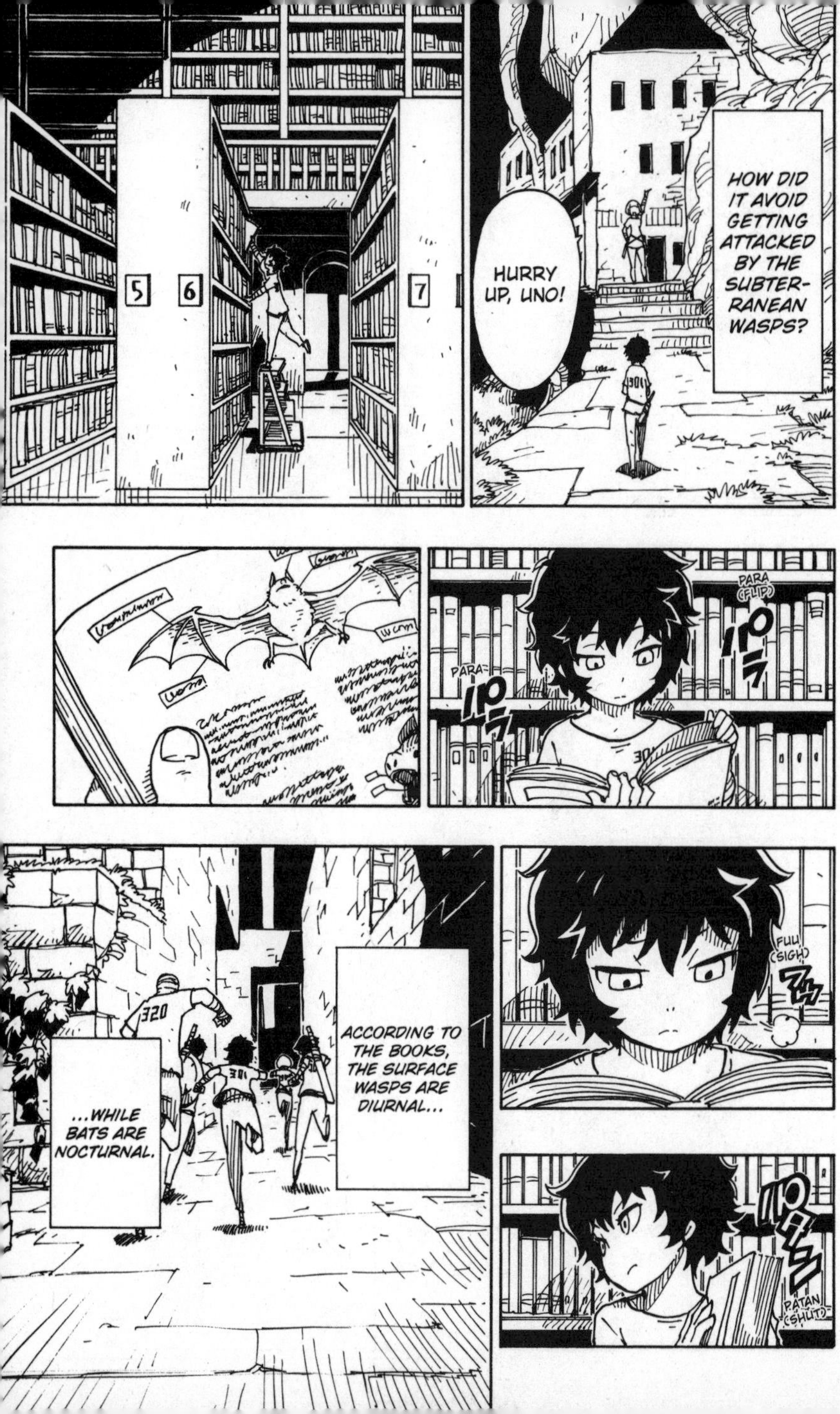
HOW DID IT AVOID GETTING ATTACKED BY THE SUBTER-RANEAN WASPS?
HURRY UP, UNO!
5
6
7
PARA (FLIP)
PARA
FUU (SIGH)
PATAN (SHUT)
ACCORDING TO THE BOOKS, THE SURFACE WASPS ARE DIURNAL...
...WHILE BATS ARE NOCTURNAL.

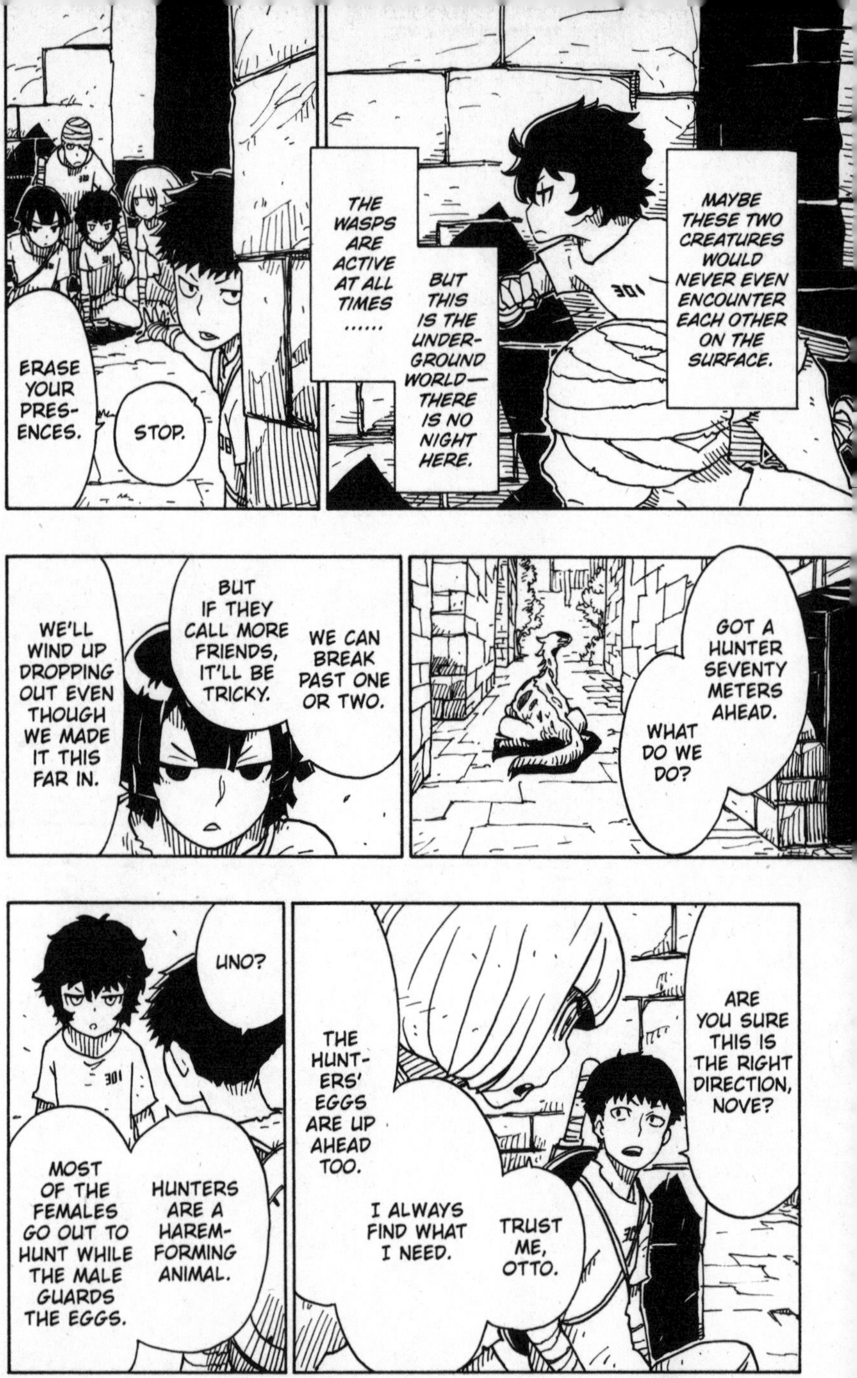
MAYBE THESE TWO CREATURES WOULD NEVER EVEN ENCOUNTER EACH OTHER ON THE SURFACE.
THE WASPS ARE ACTIVE AT ALL TIMES……
BUT THIS IS THE UNDERGROUND WORLD—THERE IS NO NIGHT HERE.
STOP.
ERASE YOUR PRESENCES.
GOT A HUNTER SEVENTY METERS AHEAD.
WHAT DO WE DO?
WE CAN BREAK PAST ONE OR TWO.
BUT IF THEY CALL MORE FRIENDS, IT'LL BE TRICKY.
WE'LL WIND UP DROPPING OUT EVEN THOUGH WE MADE IT THIS FAR IN.
ARE YOU SURE THIS IS THE RIGHT DIRECTION, NOVE?
THE HUNTERS' EGGS ARE UP AHEAD TOO.
TRUST ME, OTTO.
I ALWAYS FIND WHAT I NEED.
UNO?
HUNTERS ARE A HAREM-FORMING ANIMAL.
MOST OF THE FEMALES GO OUT TO HUNT WHILE THE MALE GUARDS THE EGGS.

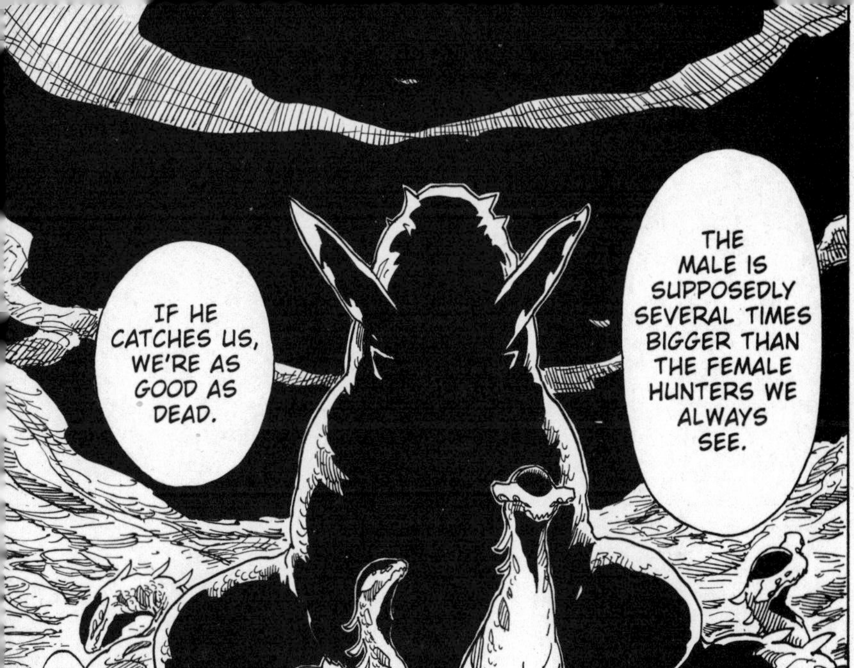
THE MALE IS SUPPOSEDLY SEVERAL TIMES BIGGER THAN THE FEMALE HUNTERS WE ALWAYS SEE.
IF HE CATCHES US, WE'RE AS GOOD AS DEAD.

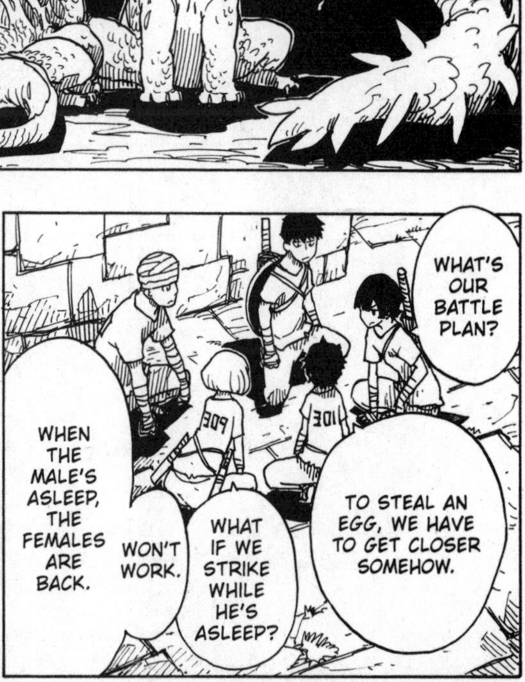
WHAT'S OUR BATTLE PLAN?
TO STEAL AN EGG, WE HAVE TO GET CLOSER SOMEHOW.
WHAT IF WE STRIKE WHILE HE'S ASLEEP?
WON'T WORK.
WHEN THE MALE'S ASLEEP, THE FEMALES ARE BACK.

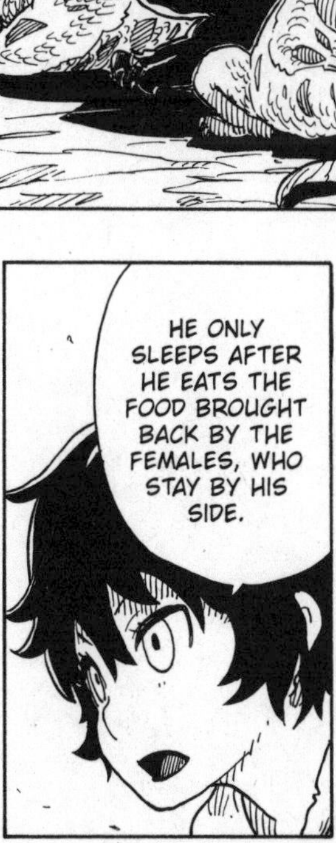
HE ONLY SLEEPS AFTER HE EATS THE FOOD BROUGHT BACK BY THE FEMALES, WHO STAY BY HIS SIDE.

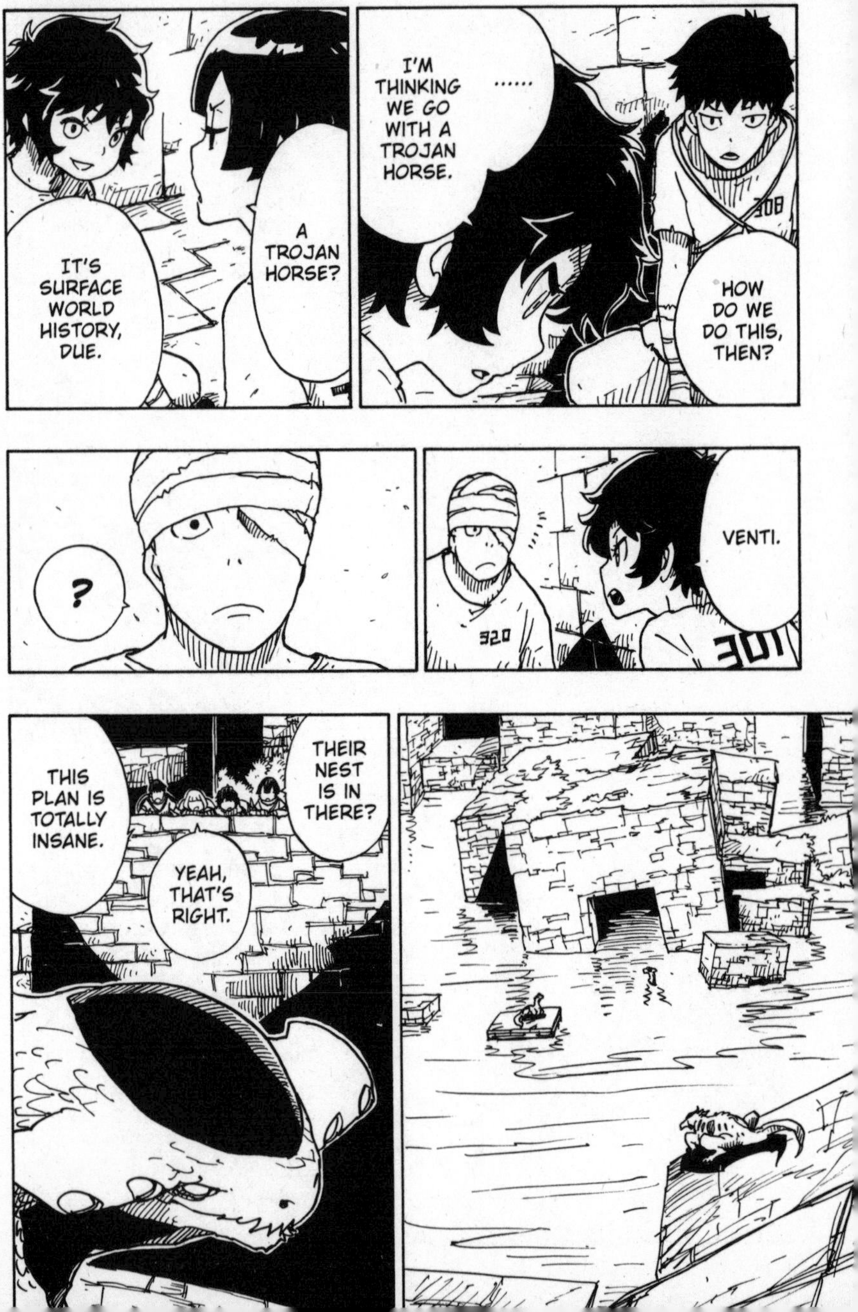
HOW DO WE DO THIS, THEN?
......
I'M THINKING WE GO WITH A TROJAN HORSE.
A TROJAN HORSE?
IT'S SURFACE WORLD HISTORY, DUE.
VENTI.
?
THEIR NEST IS IN THERE?
YEAH, THAT'S RIGHT.
THIS PLAN IS TOTALLY INSANE.

YURA
(LIFT)

NOSHI
(CLUMBER)

NOSHI

BY NORMAL RULES, IT'S IMPOSSIBLE.

BUT VENTI ISN'T NORMAL. HE CAN PULL IT OFF.

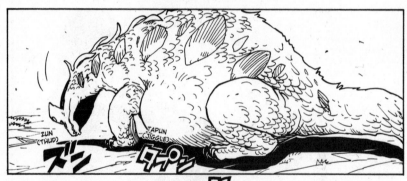

ZUN
(THUD)

TAPUN
(JIGGLE)

ZUNUN
(LURCH)

GUNYURU
(SQUELCH)

......

ZUNUN

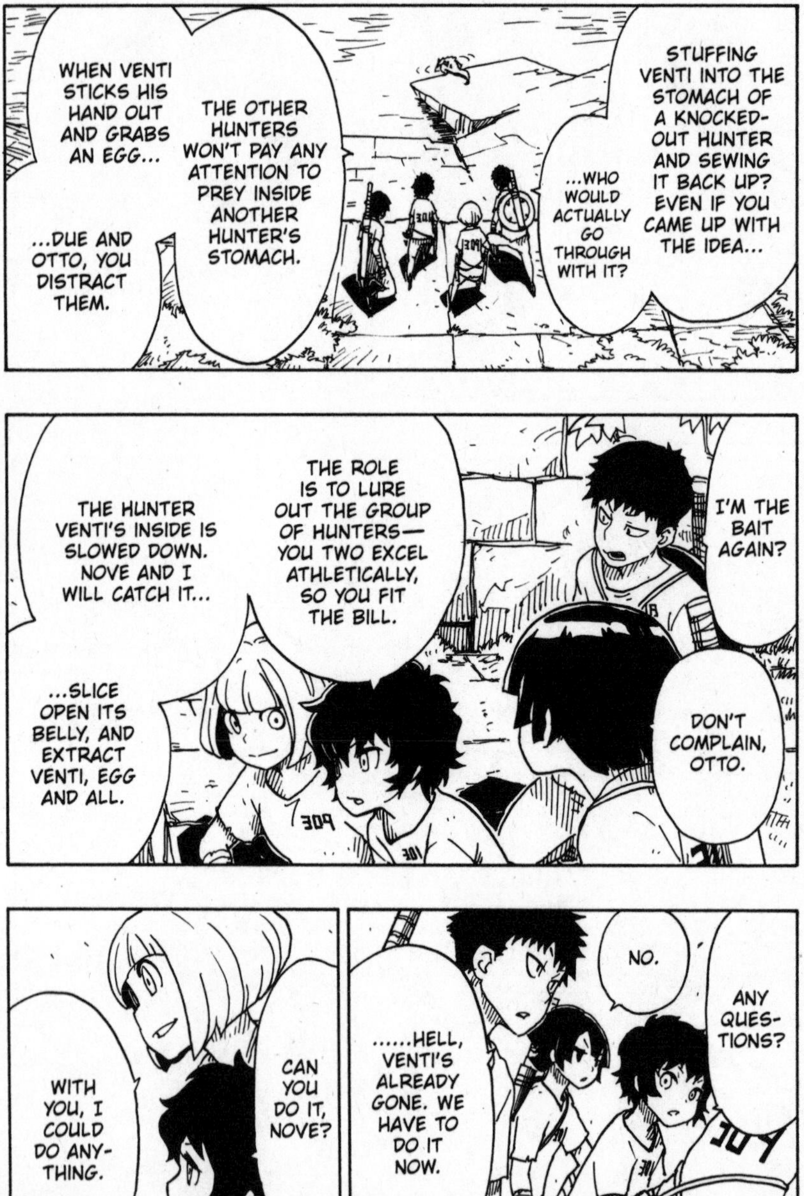
STUFFING VENTI INTO THE STOMACH OF A KNOCKED-OUT HUNTER AND SEWING IT BACK UP? EVEN IF YOU CAME UP WITH THE IDEA...
...WHO WOULD ACTUALLY GO THROUGH WITH IT?
THE OTHER HUNTERS WON'T PAY ANY ATTENTION TO PREY INSIDE ANOTHER HUNTER'S STOMACH.
WHEN VENTI STICKS HIS HAND OUT AND GRABS AN EGG...
...DUE AND OTTO, YOU DISTRACT THEM.
I'M THE BAIT AGAIN?
DON'T COMPLAIN, OTTO.
THE ROLE IS TO LURE OUT THE GROUP OF HUNTERS—YOU TWO EXCEL ATHLETICALLY, SO YOU FIT THE BILL.
THE HUNTER VENTI'S INSIDE IS SLOWED DOWN. NOVE AND I WILL CATCH IT...
...SLICE OPEN ITS BELLY, AND EXTRACT VENTI, EGG AND ALL.
ANY QUES-TIONS?
NO.
......HELL, VENTI'S ALREADY GONE. WE HAVE TO DO IT NOW.
CAN YOU DO IT, NOVE?
WITH YOU, I COULD DO ANY-THING.

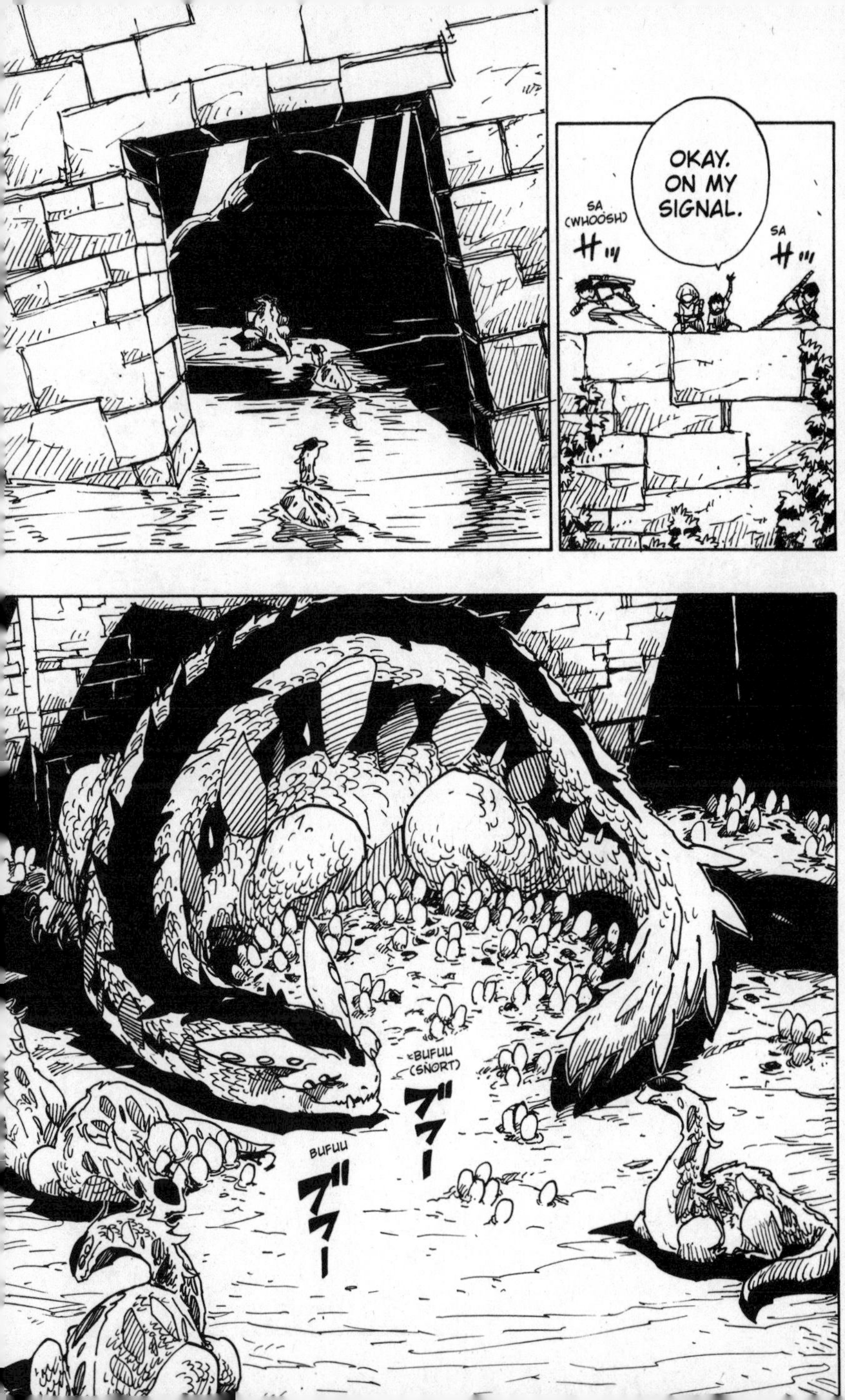
OKAY. ON MY SIGNAL.
SA
SA (WHOOSH)
BUFUU (SNORT)
BUFUU

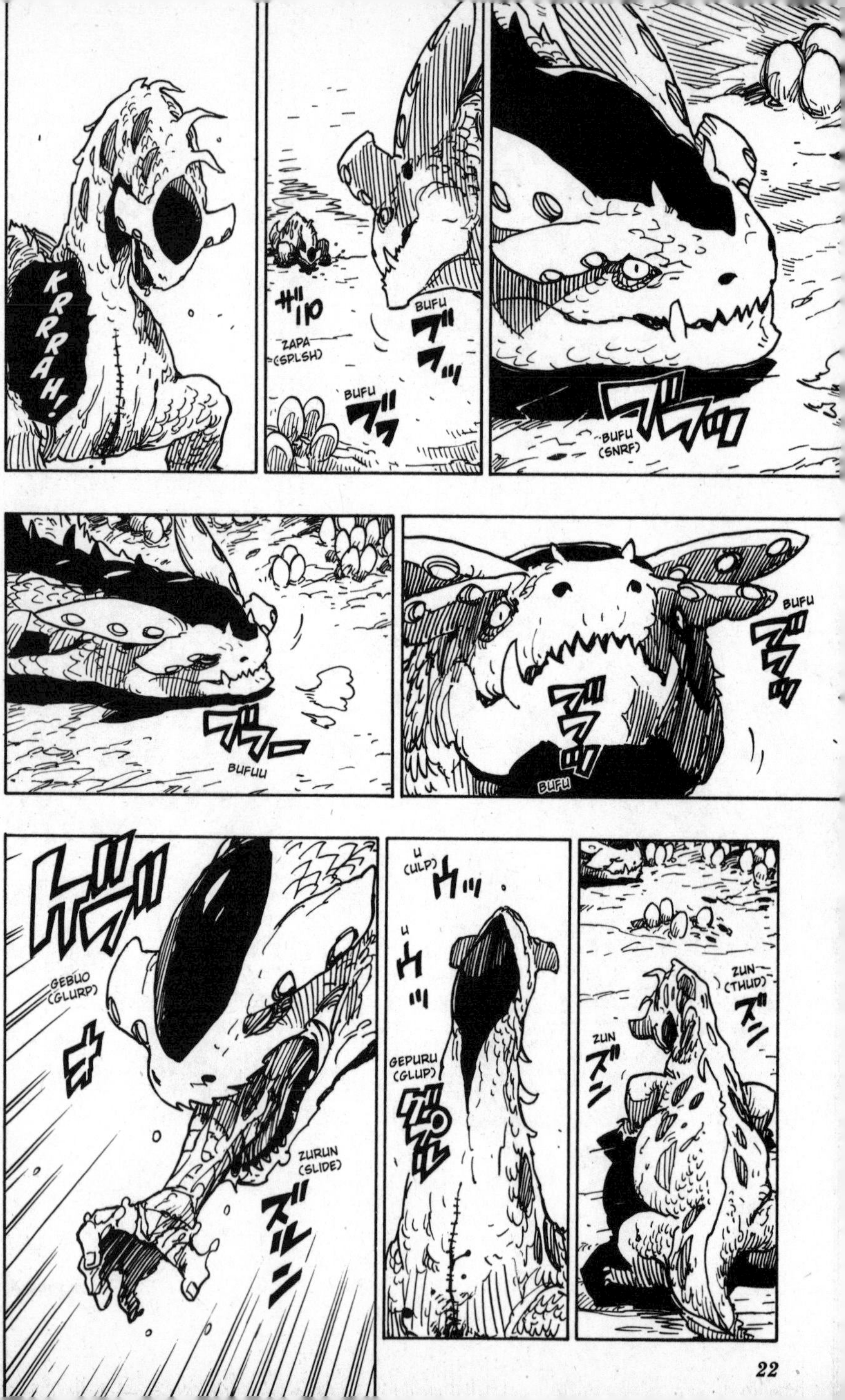
BUFU (SNRF)
ZAPA (SPLSH)
BUFU
BUFU
KRRRAH!
BUFU
BUFU
BUFUU
ZUN (THUD)
ZUN
U (ULP)
U
GEPURU (GLUP)
GEBUO (GLURP)
ZURUN (SLIDE)

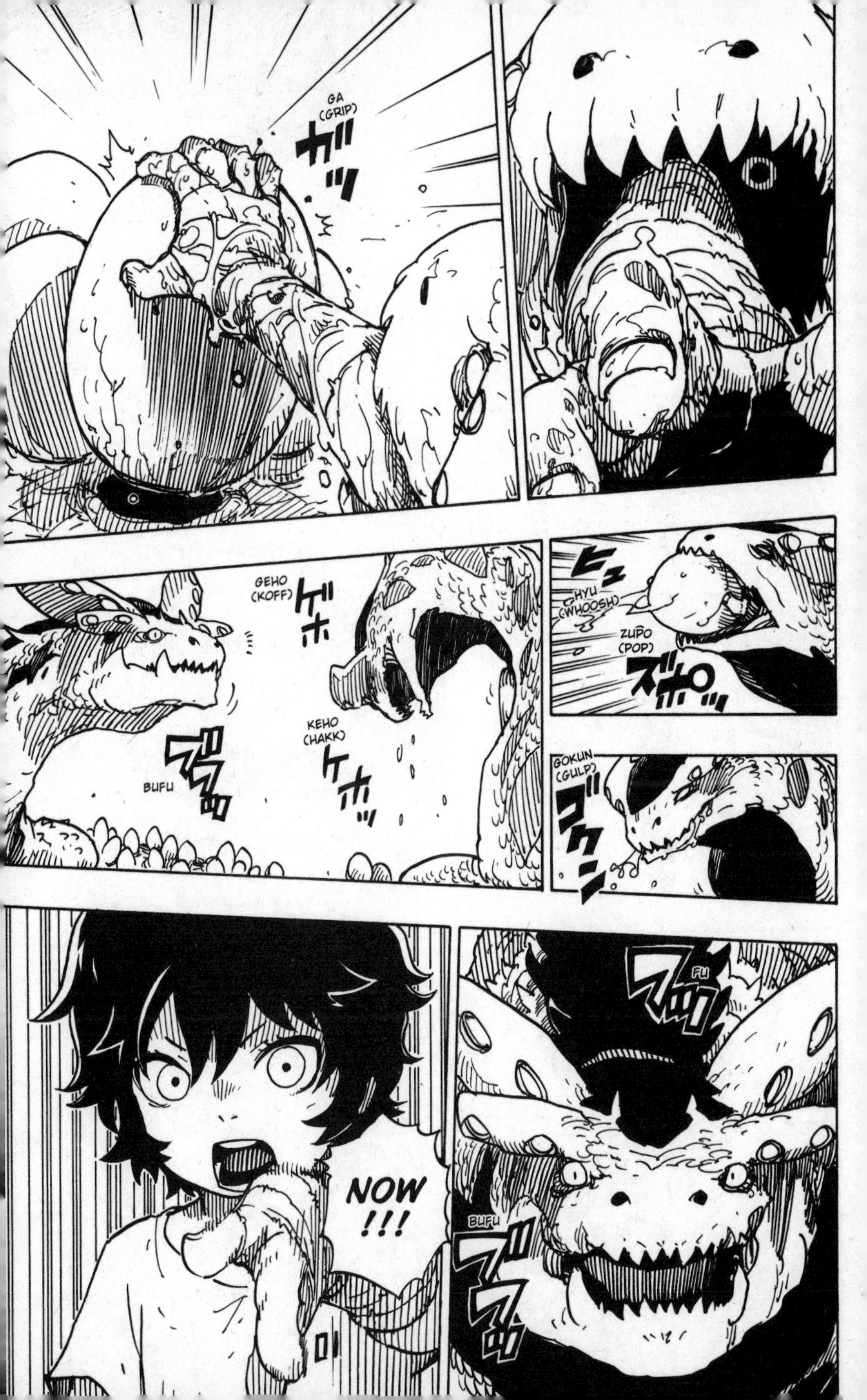
GA (GRIP)
HYU (WHOOSH)
ZUPO (POP)
GOKUN (GULP)
GEHO (KOFF)
KEHO (HAKK)
BUFU
FU
BUFU
NOW!!!

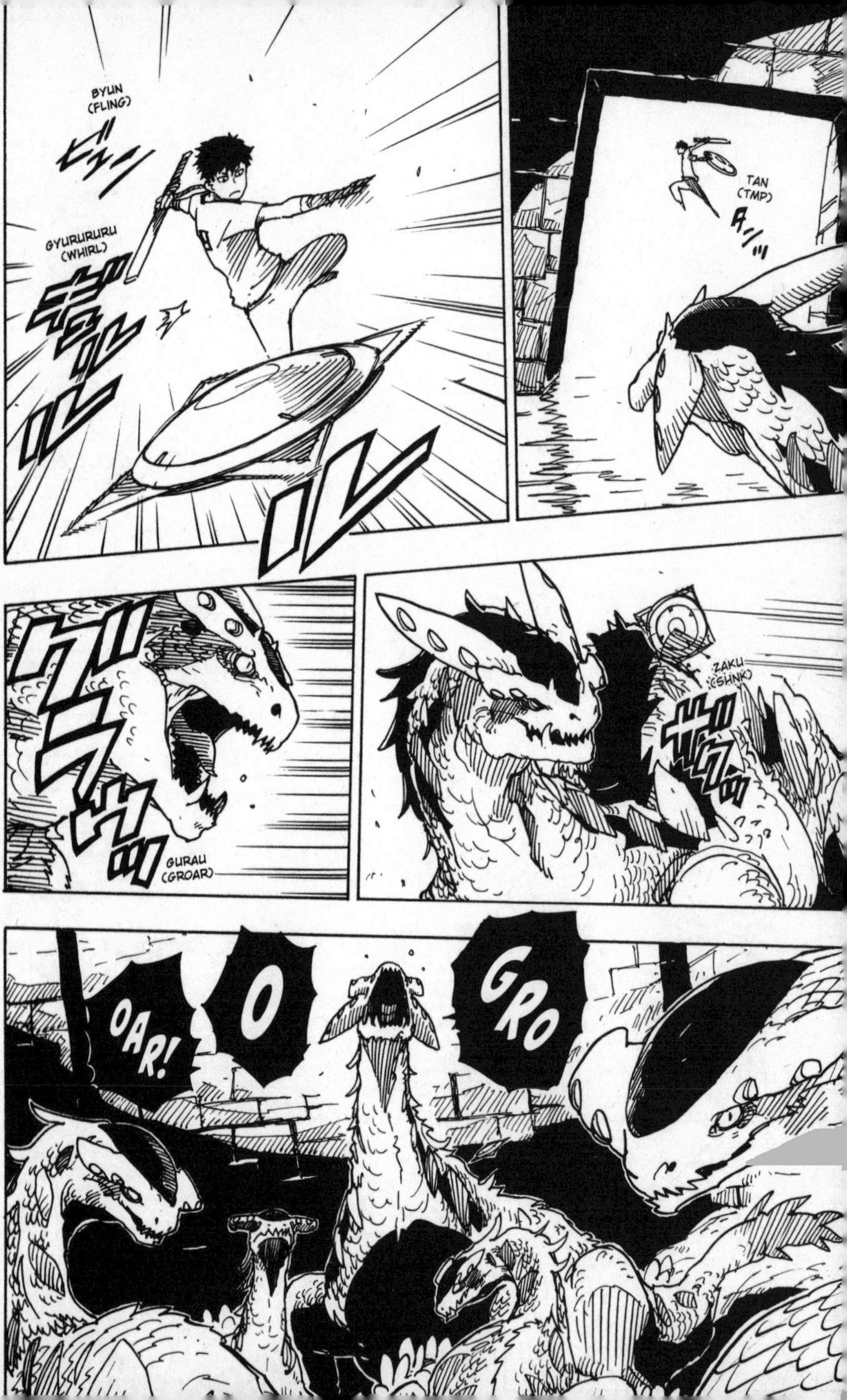
TAN
(TMP)
BYUN
(FLING)
GYURURURU
(WHIRL)
ZAKU
(SHNK)
GURAU
(GROAR)
GRO
O
OAR!

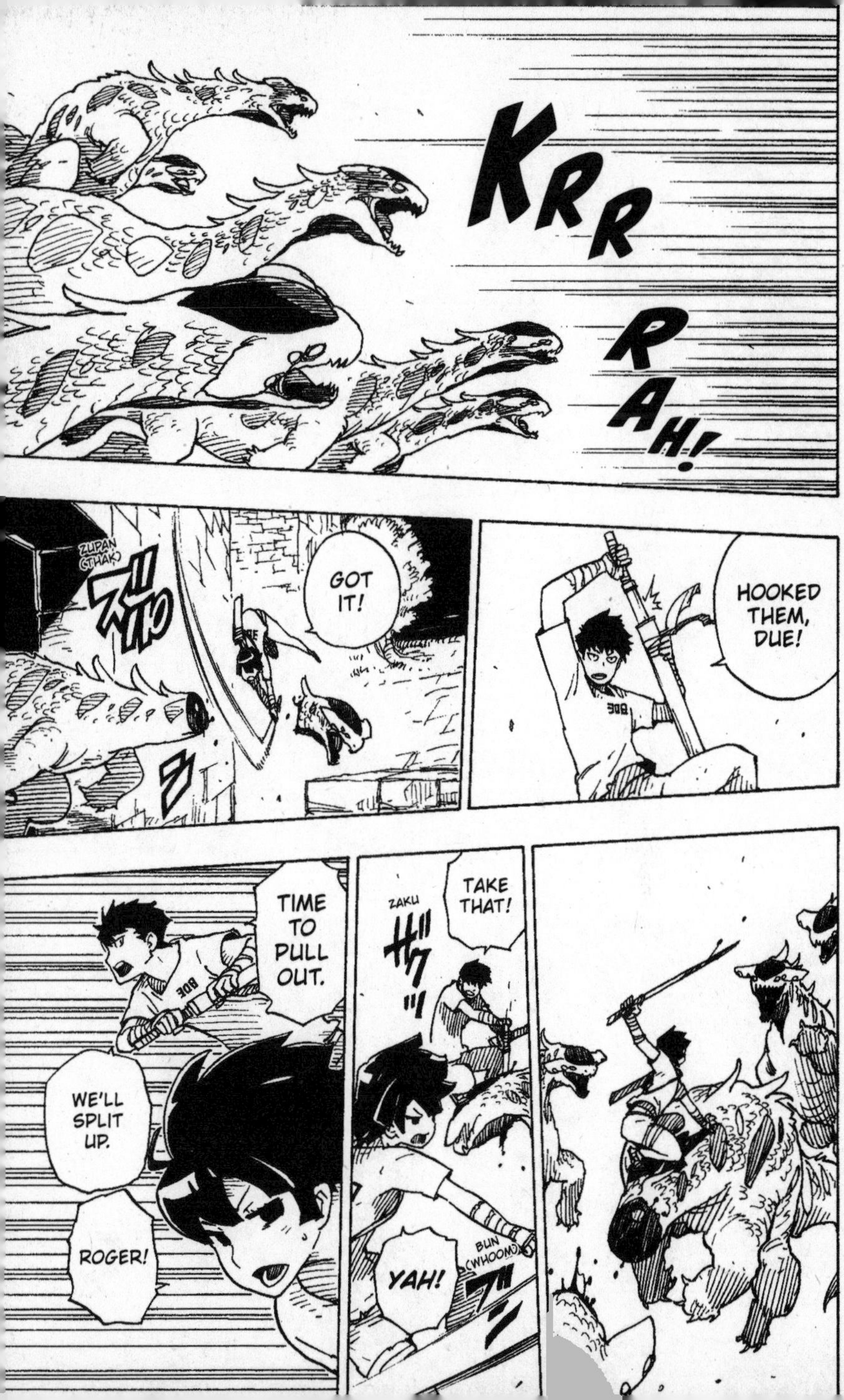
KRRRAH!
HOOKED THEM, DUE!
GOT IT!
ZUPAN (THAK)
TAKE THAT!
ZAKU
BUN (WHOOM)
YAH!
TIME TO PULL OUT.
WE'LL SPLIT UP.
ROGER!

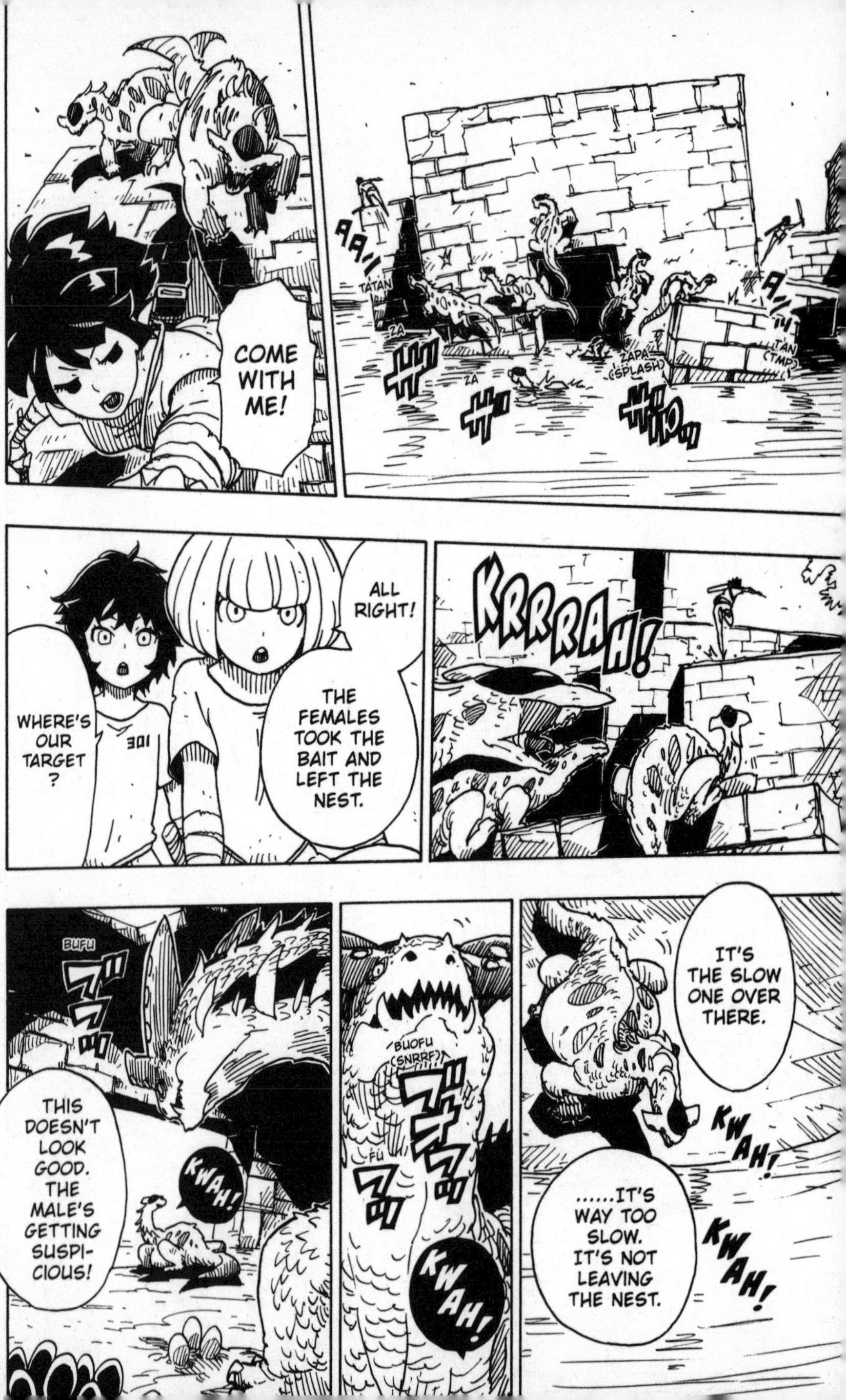
TAN (TMP)
ZAPA (SPLASH)
TATAN
ZA
ZA
COME WITH ME!
KRRRAH!
ALL RIGHT!
THE FEMALES TOOK THE BAIT AND LEFT THE NEST.
WHERE'S OUR TARGET?
IT'S THE SLOW ONE OVER THERE.
KWAH!
KWAH!
......IT'S WAY TOO SLOW. IT'S NOT LEAVING THE NEST.
BUOFU (SNRRF)
FU
KWAH!
BUFU
KWAH!
THIS DOESN'T LOOK GOOD. THE MALE'S GETTING SUSPICIOUS!

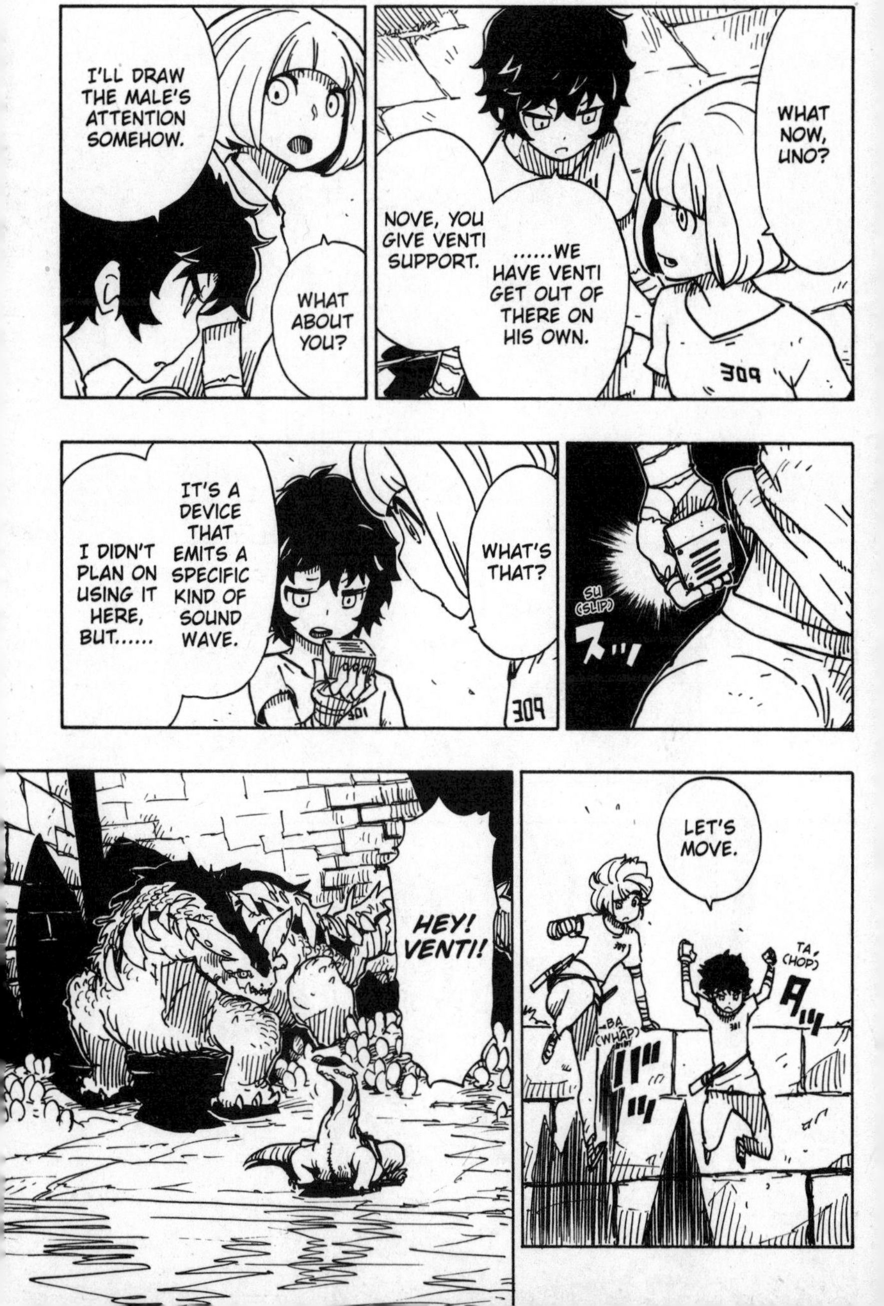
WHAT NOW, UNO?
......WE HAVE VENTI GET OUT OF THERE ON HIS OWN.
NOVE, YOU GIVE VENTI SUPPORT.
WHAT ABOUT YOU?
I'LL DRAW THE MALE'S ATTENTION SOMEHOW.
SU (SLIP)
スッ
WHAT'S THAT?
IT'S A DEVICE THAT EMITS A SPECIFIC KIND OF SOUND WAVE.
I DIDN'T PLAN ON USING IT HERE, BUT......
LET'S MOVE.
TA (HOP)
タッ
BA (WHAP)
バッ
HEY! VENTI!

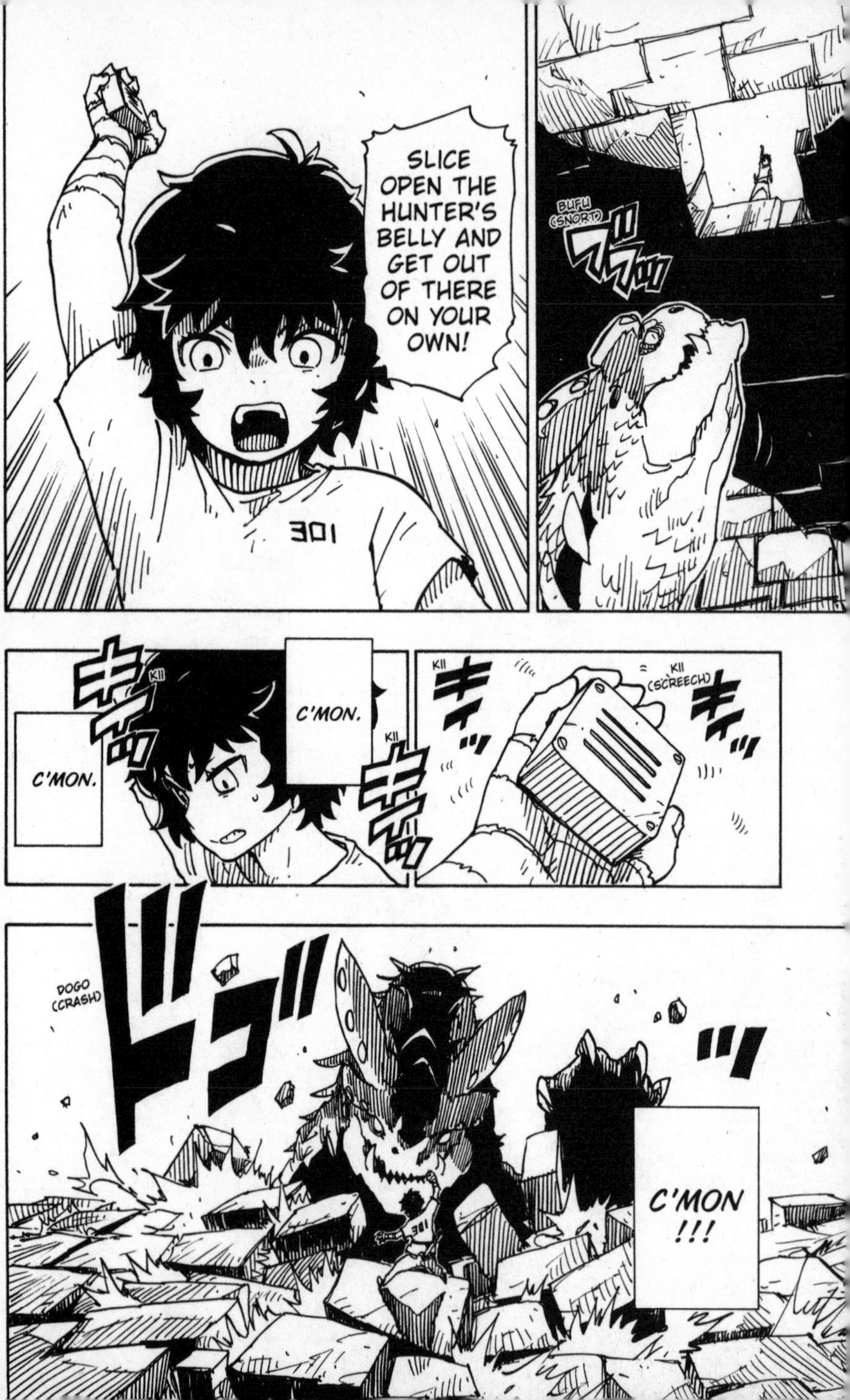
BUFU (SNORT)
SLICE OPEN THE HUNTER'S BELLY AND GET OUT OF THERE ON YOUR OWN!
KII (SCREECH)
KII
C'MON.
KII
KII
C'MON.
DOGO (CRASH)
C'MON!!!

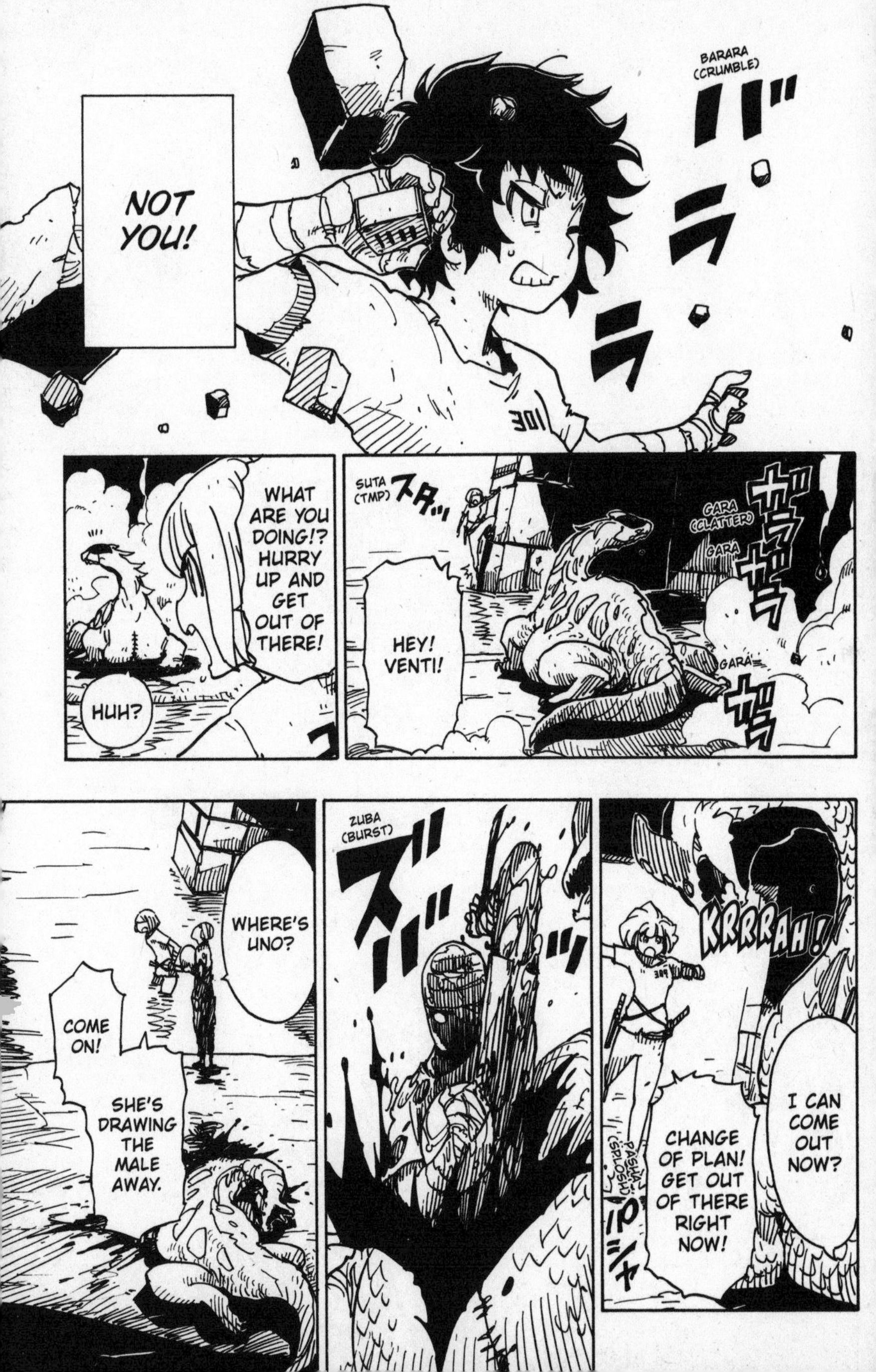

BARARA (CRUMBLE)
NOT YOU!
GARA (CLATTER)
GARA
SUTA (TMP)
HEY! VENTI!
GARA
WHAT ARE YOU DOING!? HURRY UP AND GET OUT OF THERE!
HUH?
KRRRAH!
I CAN COME OUT NOW?
CHANGE OF PLAN! GET OUT OF THERE RIGHT NOW!
PASHA (SPLOSH)
ZUBA (BURST)
WHERE'S UNO?
COME ON!
SHE'S DRAWING THE MALE AWAY.

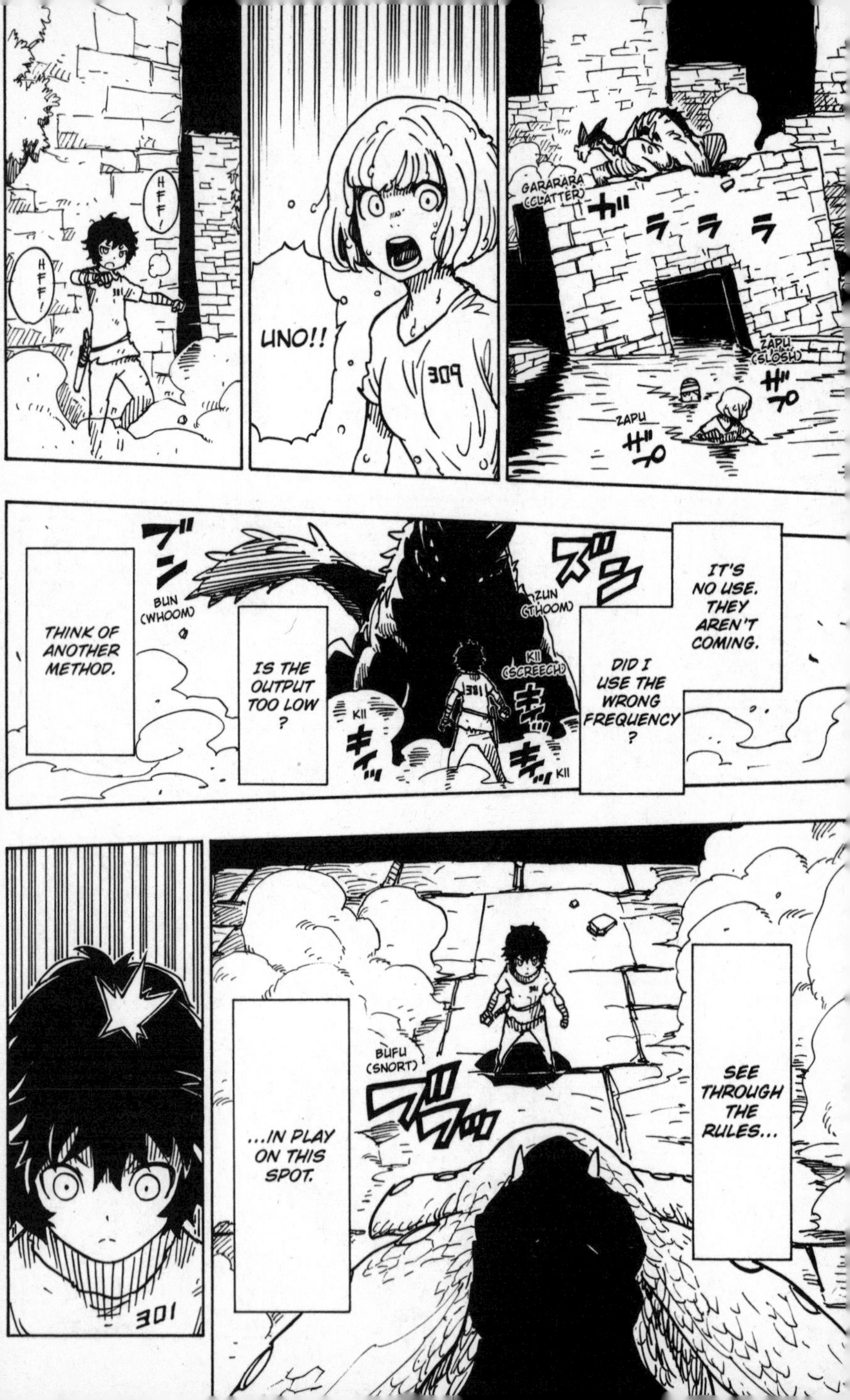
GARARARA (CLATTER)
ZAPU (SLOSH)
ZAPU
UNO!!
HFF!
HFF!
IT'S NO USE. THEY AREN'T COMING.
DID I USE THE WRONG FREQUENCY?
ZUN (THOOM)
KII (SCREECH)
KII
KII
IS THE OUTPUT TOO LOW?
BUN (WHOOM)
THINK OF ANOTHER METHOD.
SEE THROUGH THE RULES...
BUFU (SNORT)
...IN PLAY ON THIS SPOT.

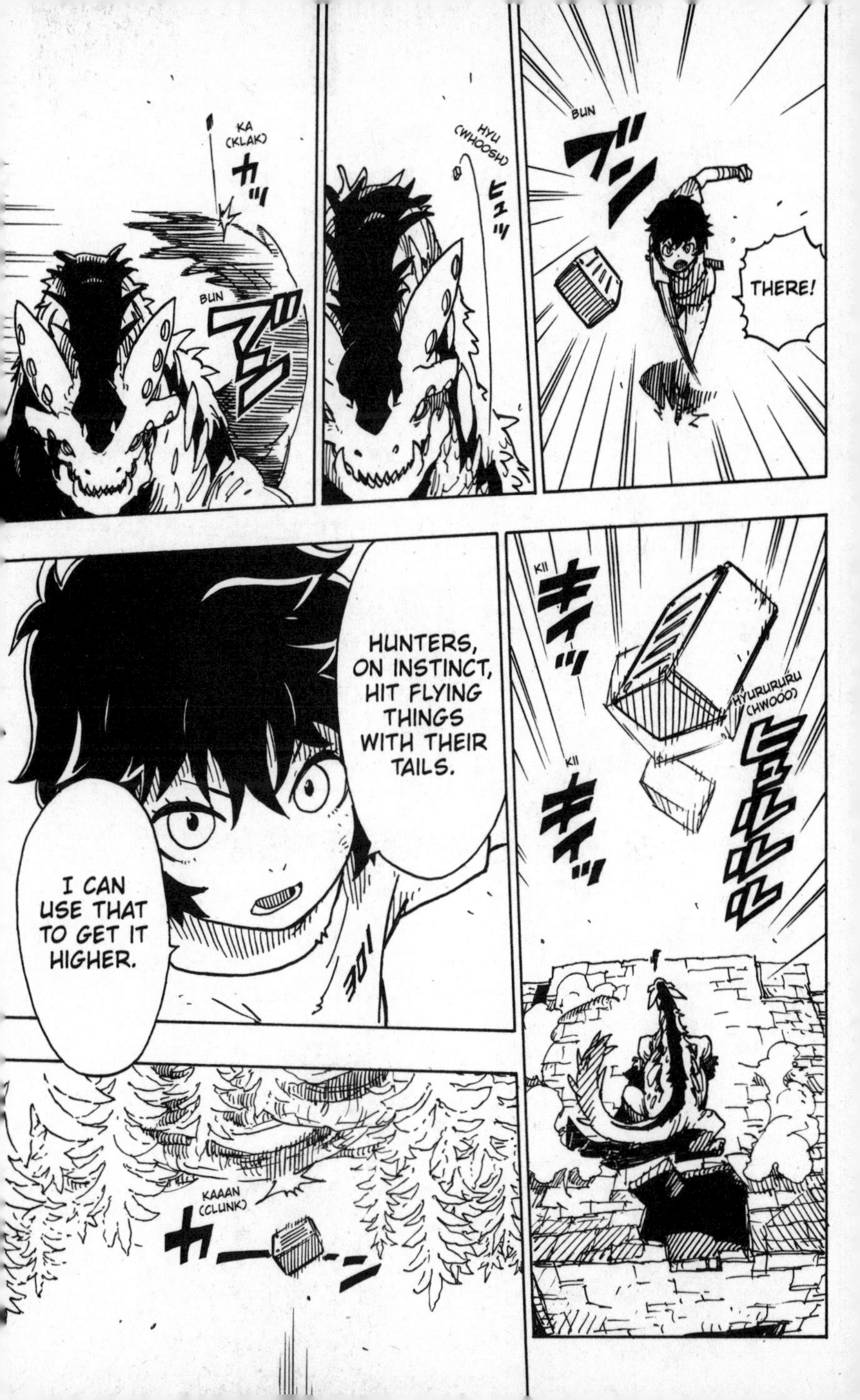

BUN
ブン
THERE!
HYU (WHOOSH)
ヒュッ
KA (KLAK)
カッ
BUN
ブン
KII
キイッ
HYURURURU (WHOOO)
ヒュルルル
KII
キイッ
HUNTERS, ON INSTINCT, HIT FLYING THINGS WITH THEIR TAILS.
I CAN USE THAT TO GET IT HIGHER.
KAAAN (CLUNK)
カーン

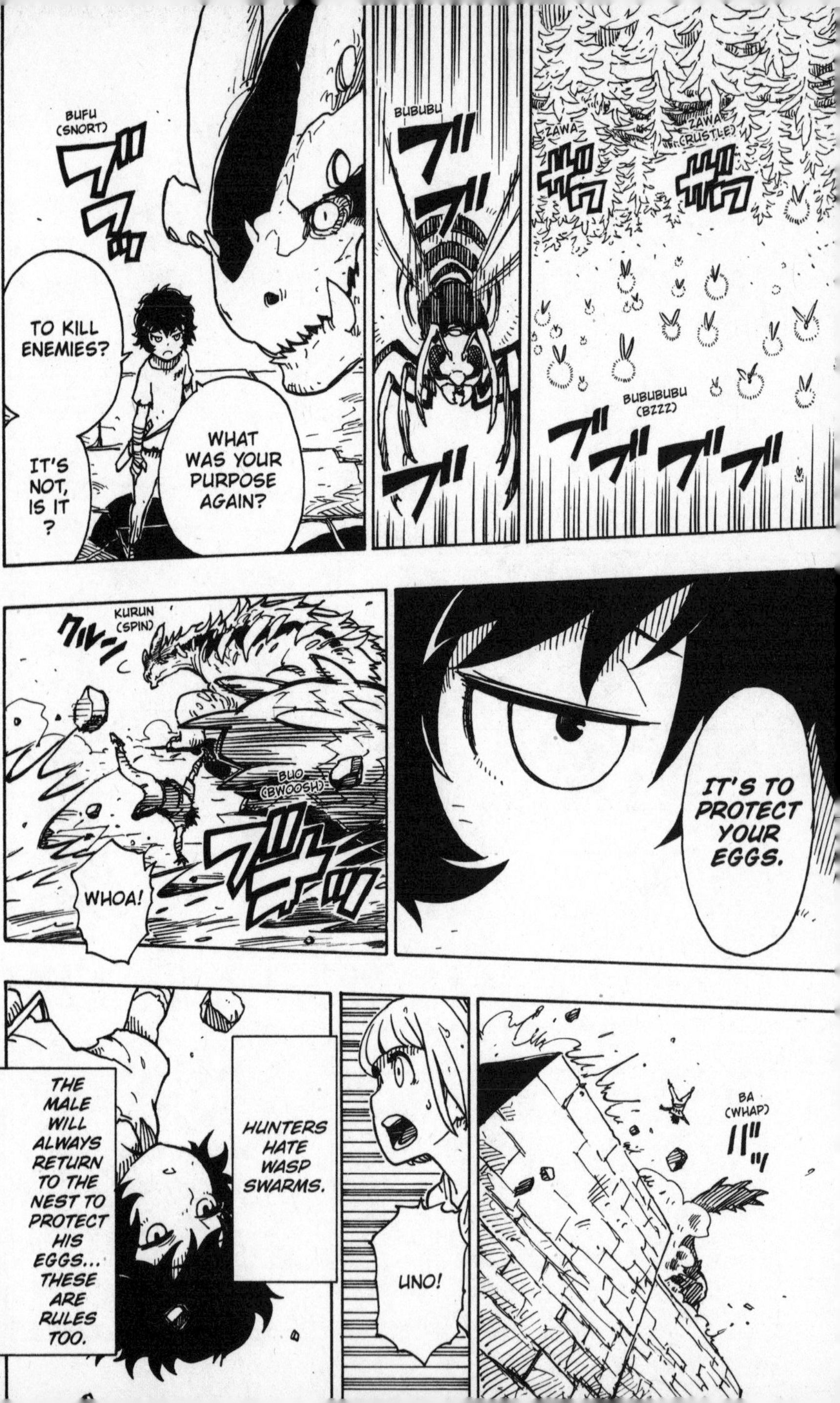
ZAWA
ZAWA (RUSTLE)
BUBUBUBU (BZZZ)
BUBUBU
BUFU (SNORT)
TO KILL ENEMIES?
IT'S NOT, IS IT?
WHAT WAS YOUR PURPOSE AGAIN?
IT'S TO PROTECT YOUR EGGS.
KURUN (SPIN)
BUO (BWOOSH)
WHOA!
BA (WHAP)
UNO!
HUNTERS HATE WASP SWARMS.
THE MALE WILL ALWAYS RETURN TO THE NEST TO PROTECT HIS EGGS... THESE ARE RULES TOO.

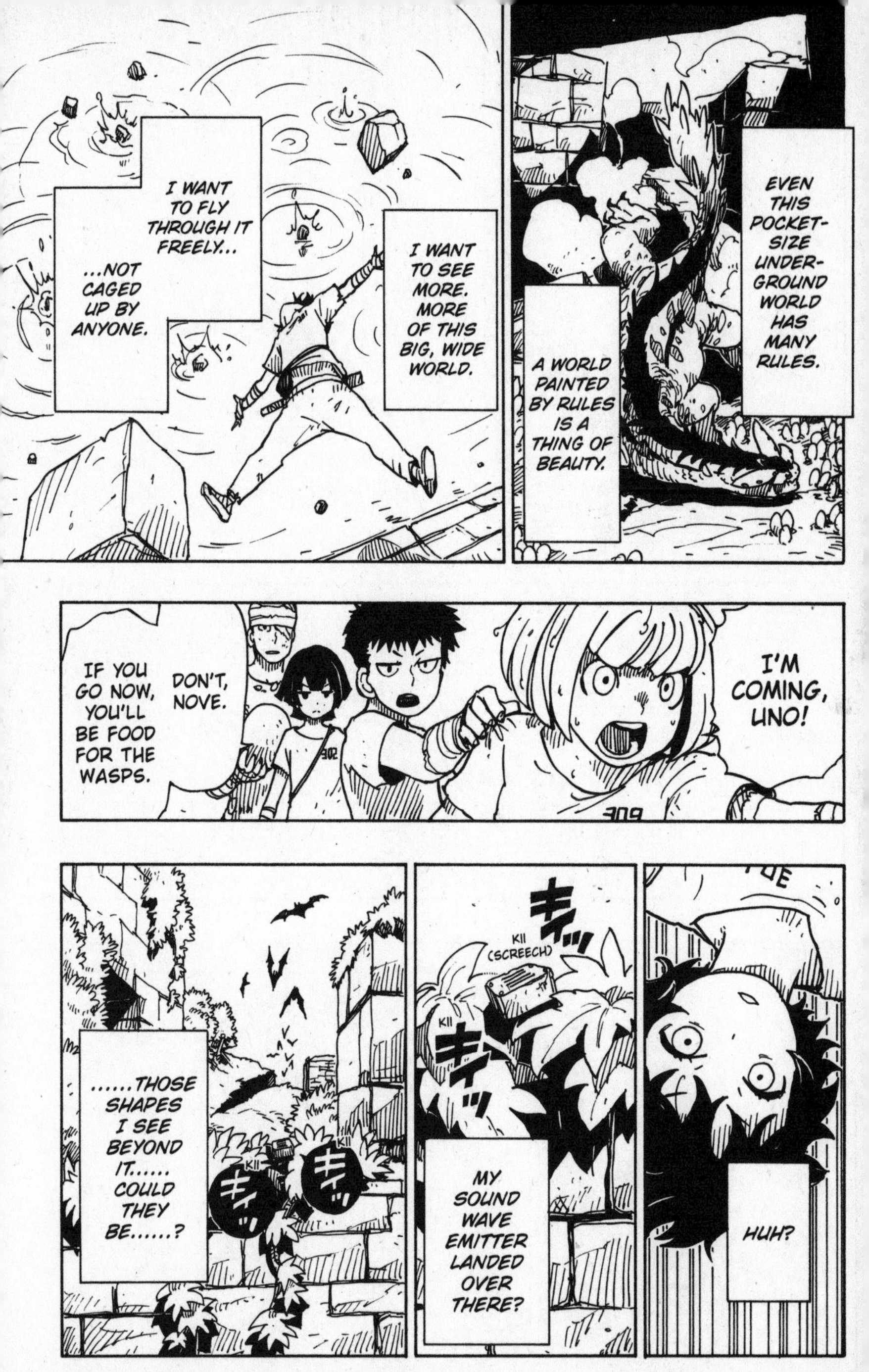
EVEN THIS POCKET-SIZE UNDER-GROUND WORLD HAS MANY RULES.
A WORLD PAINTED BY RULES IS A THING OF BEAUTY.
I WANT TO SEE MORE. MORE OF THIS BIG, WIDE WORLD.
I WANT TO FLY THROUGH IT FREELY...
...NOT CAGED UP BY ANYONE.
I'M COMING, UNO!
DON'T, NOVE.
IF YOU GO NOW, YOU'LL BE FOOD FOR THE WASPS.
HUH?
キッ
KII (SCREECH)
キッ
KII
MY SOUND WAVE EMITTER LANDED OVER THERE?
キッ
KII
キッ
KII
......THOSE SHAPES I SEE BEYOND IT...... COULD THEY BE......?

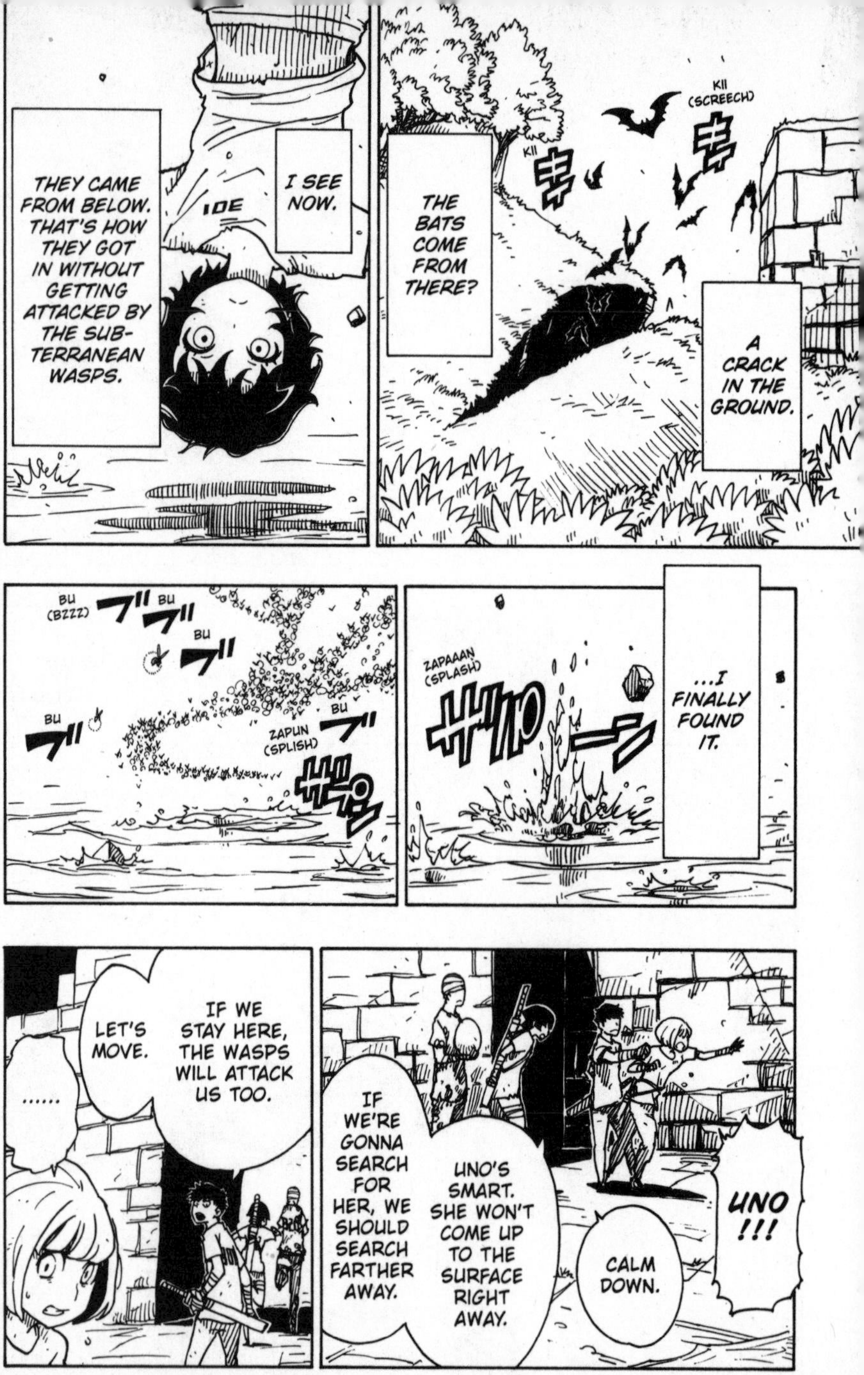
KII (SCREECH)
A CRACK IN THE GROUND.
THE BATS COME FROM THERE?
KII
I SEE NOW.
THEY CAME FROM BELOW. THAT'S HOW THEY GOT IN WITHOUT GETTING ATTACKED BY THE SUB-TERRANEAN WASPS.
IDE
...I FINALLY FOUND IT.
ZAPAAAN (SPLASH)
BU (BZZZ)
BU
BU
BU
ZAPUN (SPLISH)
BU
UNO!!!
CALM DOWN.
UNO'S SMART. SHE WON'T COME UP TO THE SURFACE RIGHT AWAY.
IF WE'RE GONNA SEARCH FOR HER, WE SHOULD SEARCH FARTHER AWAY.
IF WE STAY HERE, THE WASPS WILL ATTACK US TOO.
LET'S MOVE.
......

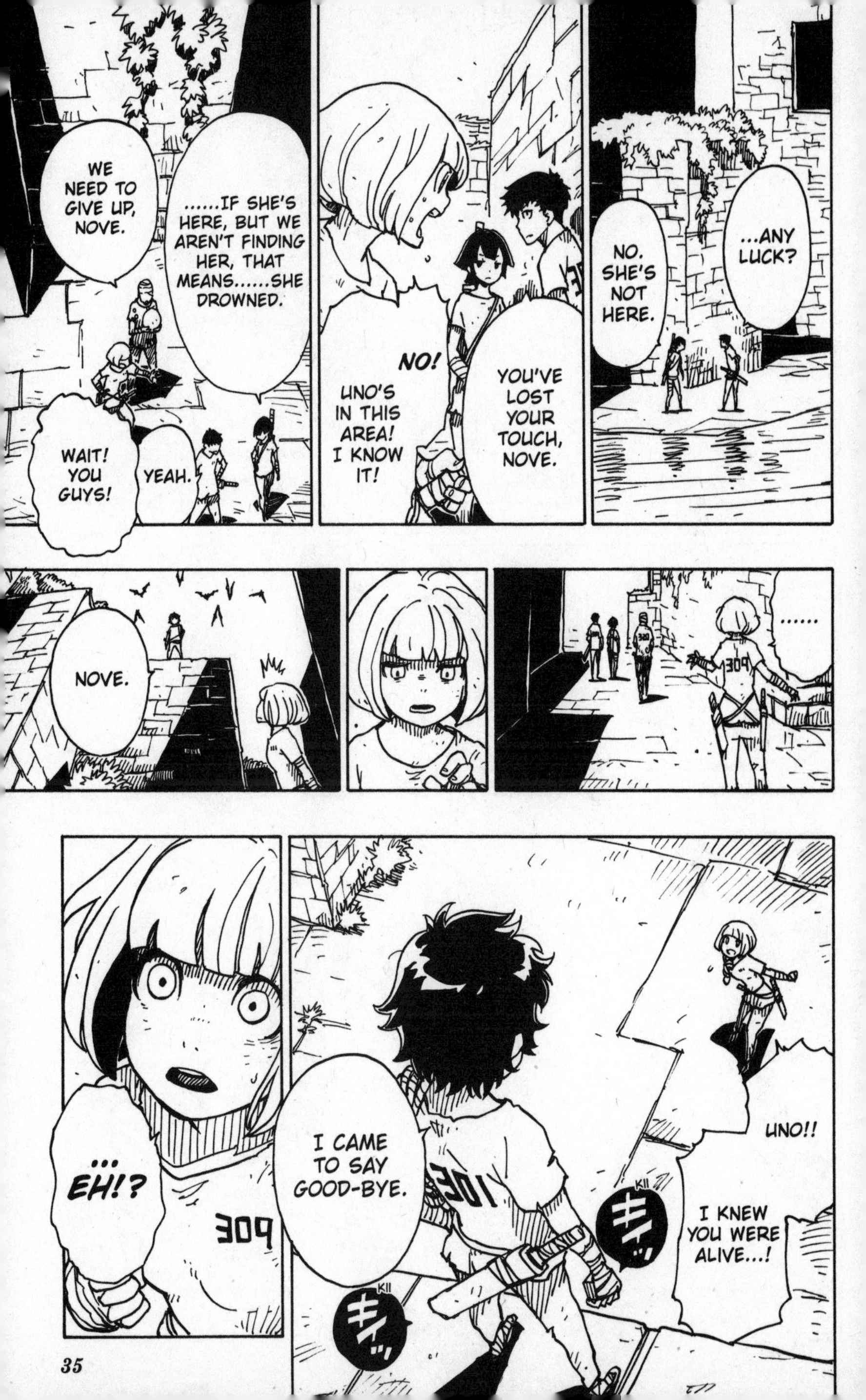
...ANY LUCK?
NO. SHE'S NOT HERE.
YOU'VE LOST YOUR TOUCH, NOVE.
NO!
UNO'S IN THIS AREA! I KNOW IT!
......IF SHE'S HERE, BUT WE AREN'T FINDING HER, THAT MEANS......SHE DROWNED.
WE NEED TO GIVE UP, NOVE.
YEAH.
WAIT! YOU GUYS!
......
NOVE.
UNO!!
I KNEW YOU WERE ALIVE...!
KII
I CAME TO SAY GOOD-BYE.
KII
...EH!?

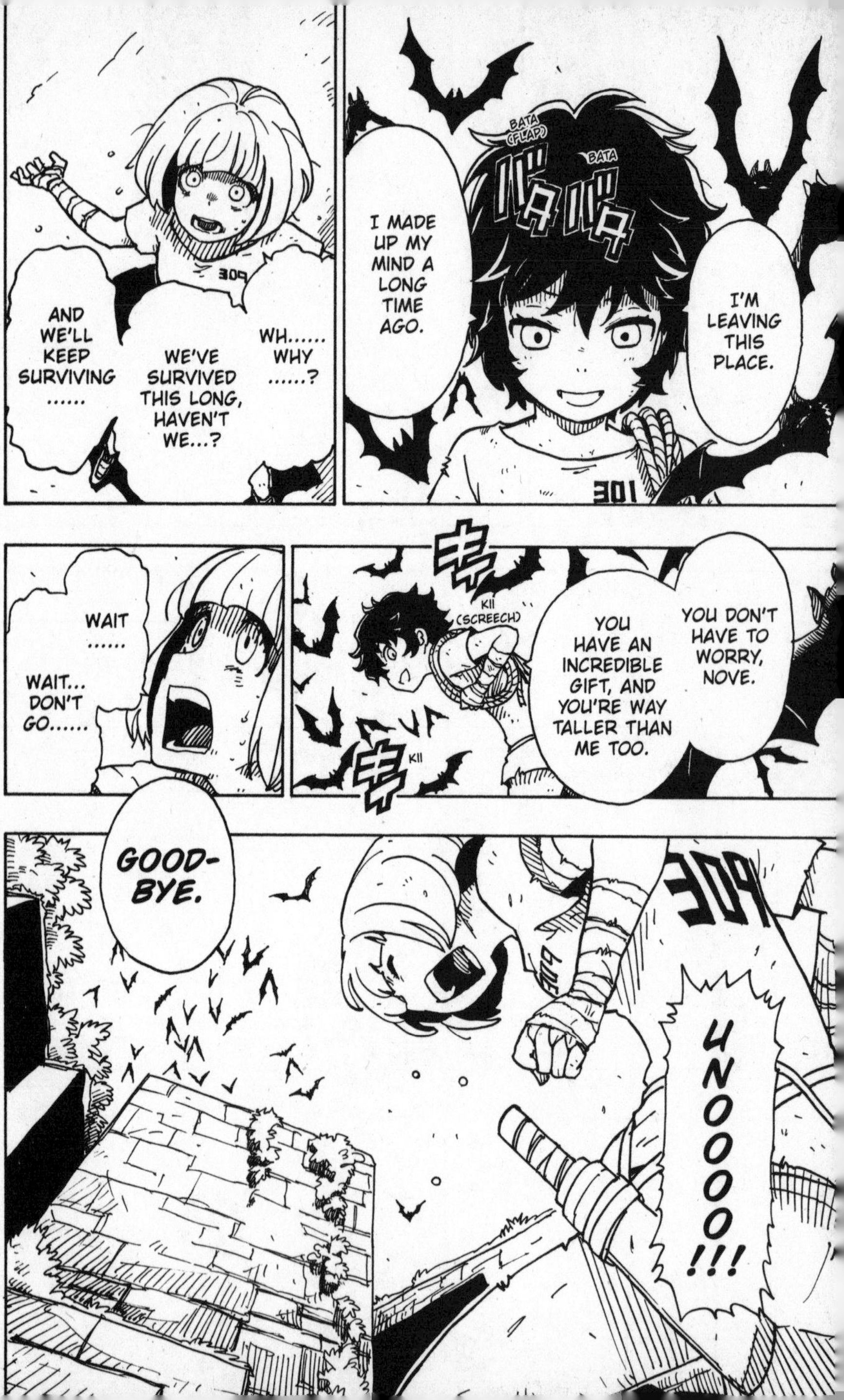
BATA (FLAP) BATA
I'M LEAVING THIS PLACE.
I MADE UP MY MIND A LONG TIME AGO.
WH...... WHY ......?
WE'VE SURVIVED THIS LONG, HAVEN'T WE...?
AND WE'LL KEEP SURVIVING ......
YOU DON'T HAVE TO WORRY, NOVE.
YOU HAVE AN INCREDIBLE GIFT, AND YOU'RE WAY TALLER THAN ME TOO.
KII (SCREECH)
KII
WAIT ......
WAIT... DON'T GO......
GOOD-BYE.
UNOOOOO!!!

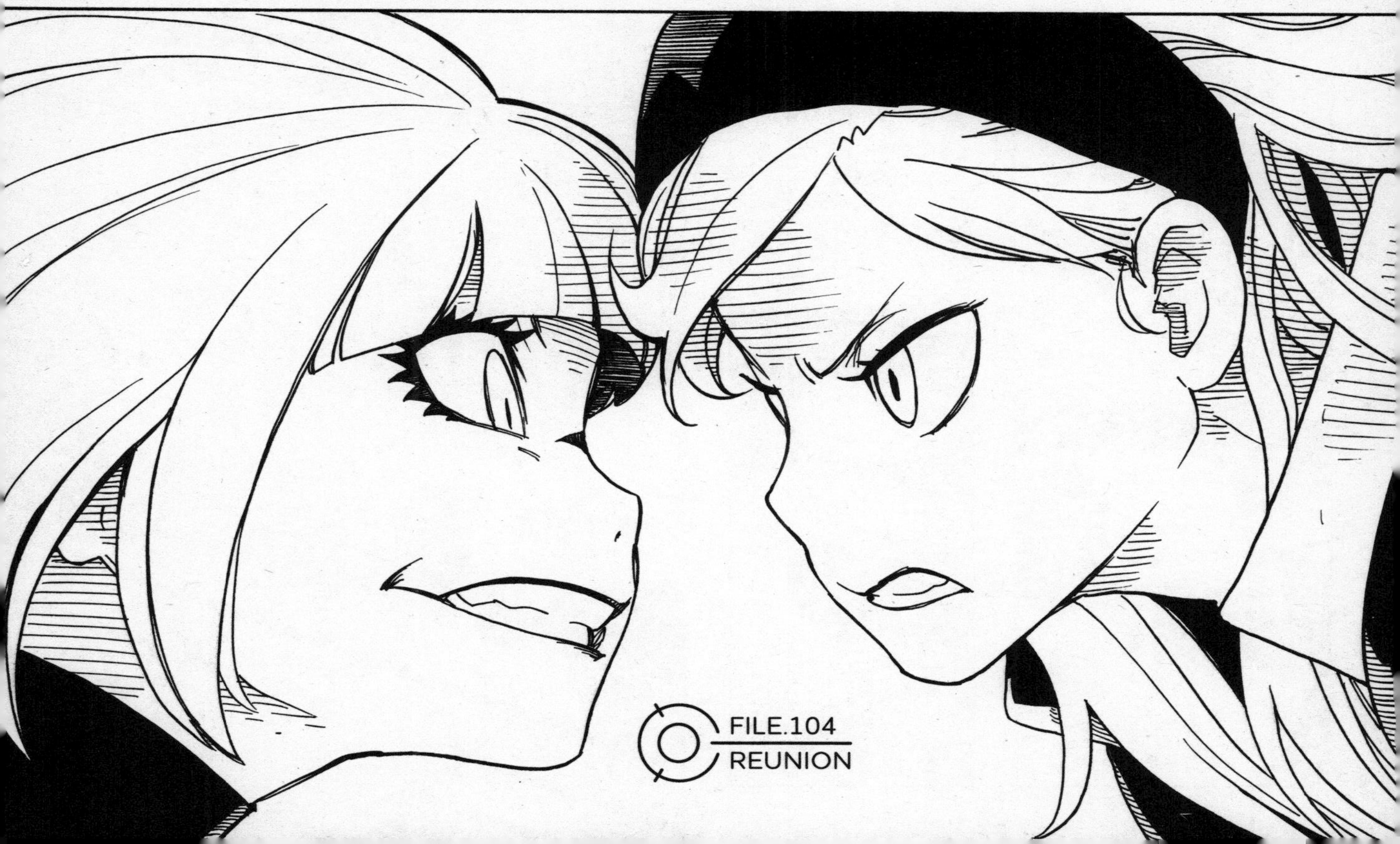
FILE.104
REUNION

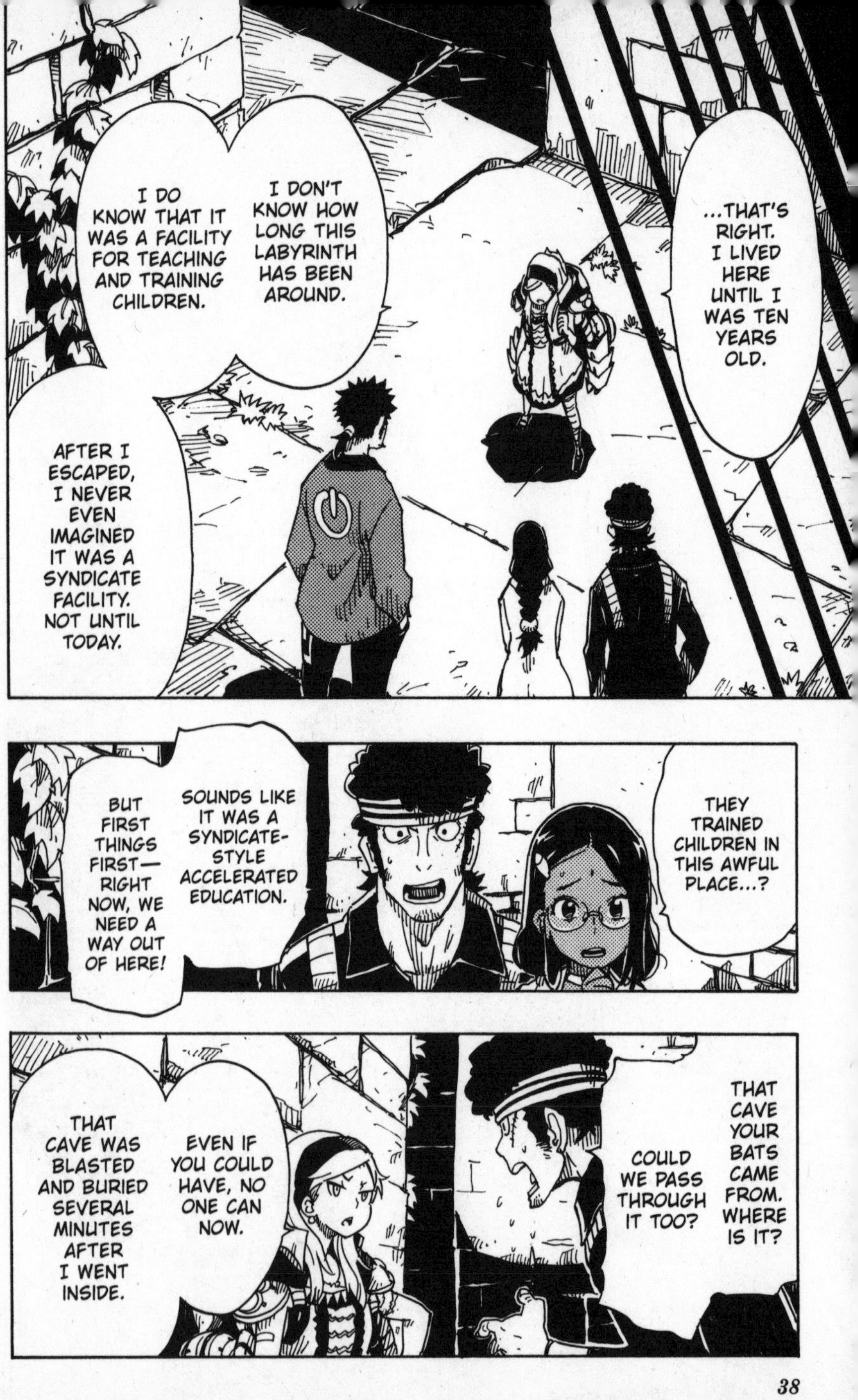
...THAT'S RIGHT. I LIVED HERE UNTIL I WAS TEN YEARS OLD.
I DON'T KNOW HOW LONG THIS LABYRINTH HAS BEEN AROUND.
I DO KNOW THAT IT WAS A FACILITY FOR TEACHING AND TRAINING CHILDREN.
AFTER I ESCAPED, I NEVER EVEN IMAGINED IT WAS A SYNDICATE FACILITY. NOT UNTIL TODAY.
THEY TRAINED CHILDREN IN THIS AWFUL PLACE...?
SOUNDS LIKE IT WAS A SYNDICATE-STYLE ACCELERATED EDUCATION.
BUT FIRST THINGS FIRST—RIGHT NOW, WE NEED A WAY OUT OF HERE!
THAT CAVE YOUR BATS CAME FROM. WHERE IS IT?
COULD WE PASS THROUGH IT TOO?
EVEN IF YOU COULD HAVE, NO ONE CAN NOW.
THAT CAVE WAS BLASTED AND BURIED SEVERAL MINUTES AFTER I WENT INSIDE.

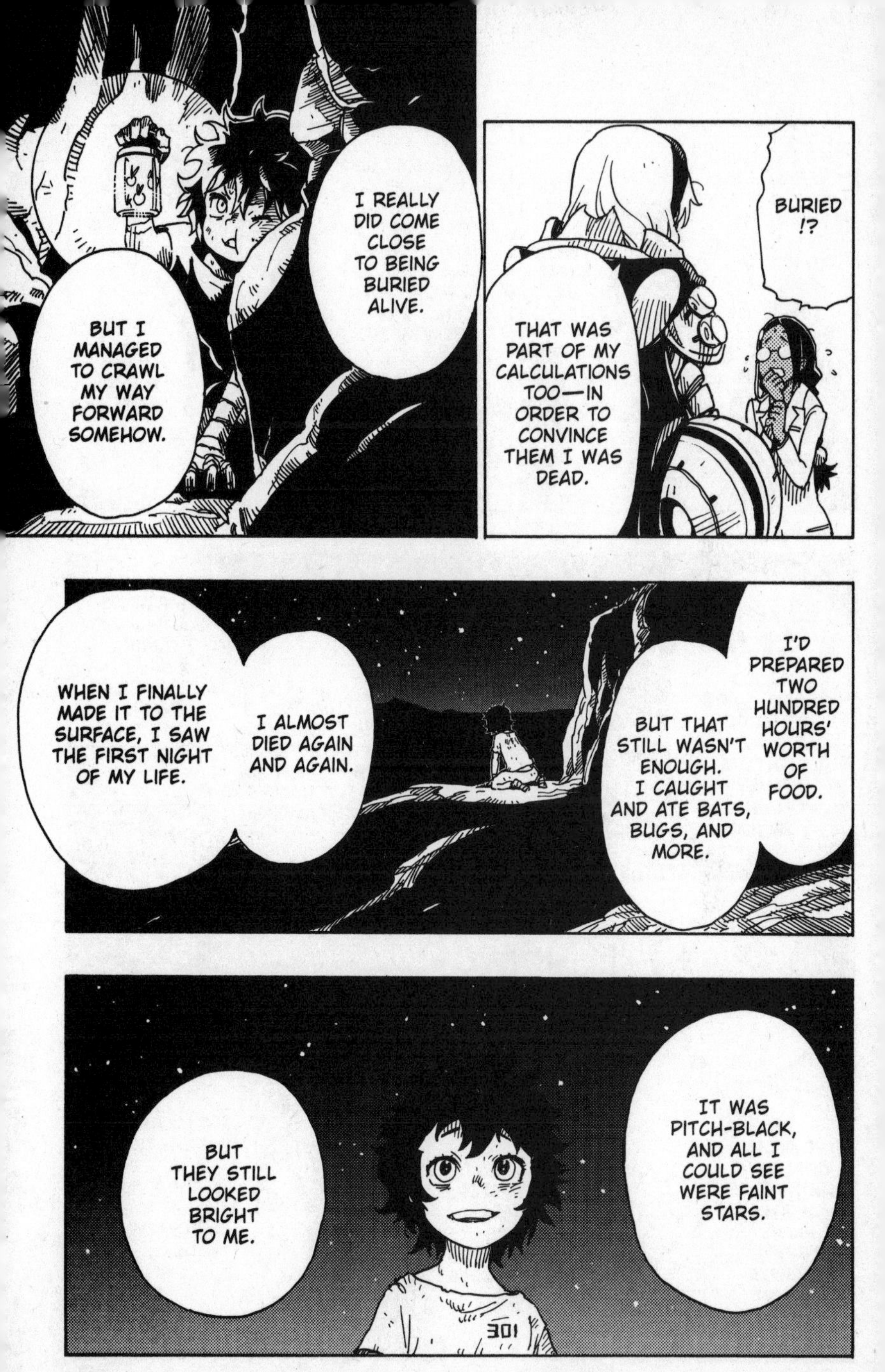
BURIED !?
THAT WAS PART OF MY CALCULATIONS TOO—IN ORDER TO CONVINCE THEM I WAS DEAD.
I REALLY DID COME CLOSE TO BEING BURIED ALIVE.
BUT I MANAGED TO CRAWL MY WAY FORWARD SOMEHOW.
I'D PREPARED TWO HUNDRED HOURS' WORTH OF FOOD.
BUT THAT STILL WASN'T ENOUGH. I CAUGHT AND ATE BATS, BUGS, AND MORE.
I ALMOST DIED AGAIN AND AGAIN.
WHEN I FINALLY MADE IT TO THE SURFACE, I SAW THE FIRST NIGHT OF MY LIFE.
IT WAS PITCH-BLACK, AND ALL I COULD SEE WERE FAINT STARS.
BUT THEY STILL LOOKED BRIGHT TO ME.

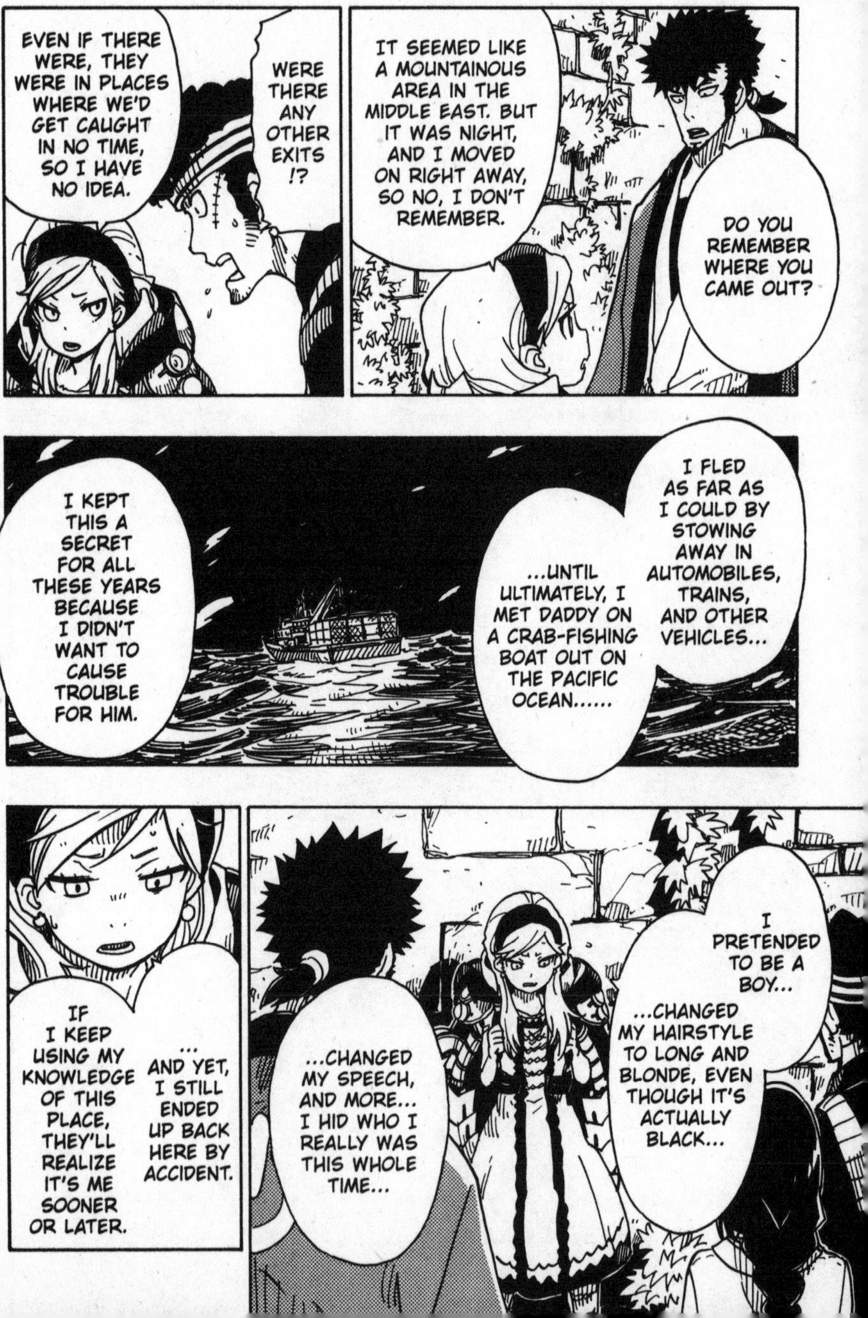
DO YOU REMEMBER WHERE YOU CAME OUT?
IT SEEMED LIKE A MOUNTAINOUS AREA IN THE MIDDLE EAST. BUT IT WAS NIGHT, AND I MOVED ON RIGHT AWAY, SO NO, I DON'T REMEMBER.
WERE THERE ANY OTHER EXITS !?
EVEN IF THERE WERE, THEY WERE IN PLACES WHERE WE'D GET CAUGHT IN NO TIME, SO I HAVE NO IDEA.
I FLED AS FAR AS I COULD BY STOWING AWAY IN AUTOMOBILES, TRAINS, AND OTHER VEHICLES...
...UNTIL ULTIMATELY, I MET DADDY ON A CRAB-FISHING BOAT OUT ON THE PACIFIC OCEAN......
I KEPT THIS A SECRET FOR ALL THESE YEARS BECAUSE I DIDN'T WANT TO CAUSE TROUBLE FOR HIM.
I PRETENDED TO BE A BOY...
...CHANGED MY HAIRSTYLE TO LONG AND BLONDE, EVEN THOUGH IT'S ACTUALLY BLACK...
...CHANGED MY SPEECH, AND MORE... I HID WHO I REALLY WAS THIS WHOLE TIME...
...AND YET, I STILL ENDED UP BACK HERE BY ACCIDENT.
IF I KEEP USING MY KNOWLEDGE OF THIS PLACE, THEY'LL REALIZE IT'S ME SOONER OR LATER.

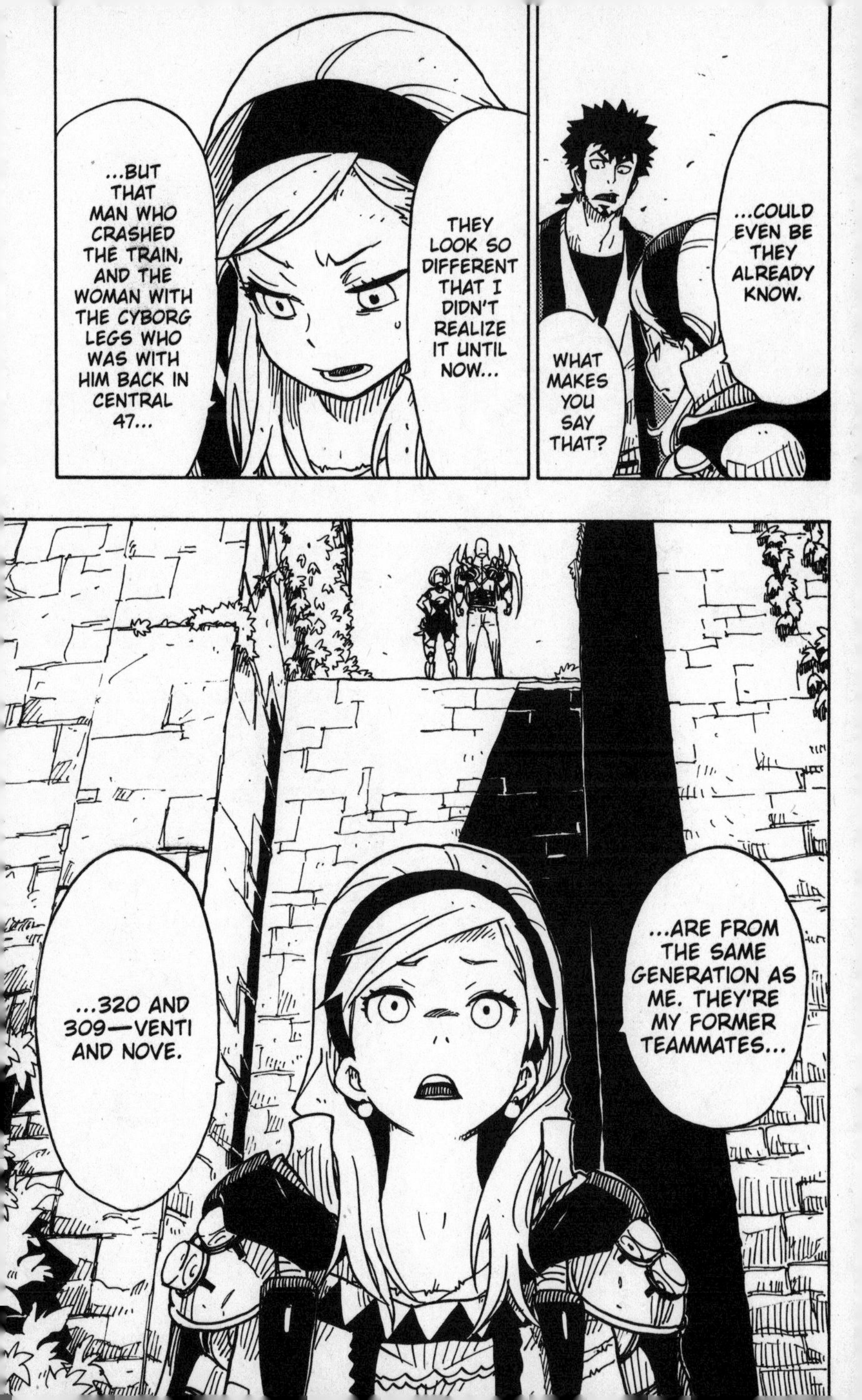
...COULD EVEN BE THEY ALREADY KNOW.
WHAT MAKES YOU SAY THAT?
THEY LOOK SO DIFFERENT THAT I DIDN'T REALIZE IT UNTIL NOW...
...BUT THAT MAN WHO CRASHED THE TRAIN, AND THE WOMAN WITH THE CYBORG LEGS WHO WAS WITH HIM BACK IN CENTRAL 47...
...ARE FROM THE SAME GENERATION AS ME. THEY'RE MY FORMER TEAMMATES...
...320 AND 309—VENTI AND NOVE.

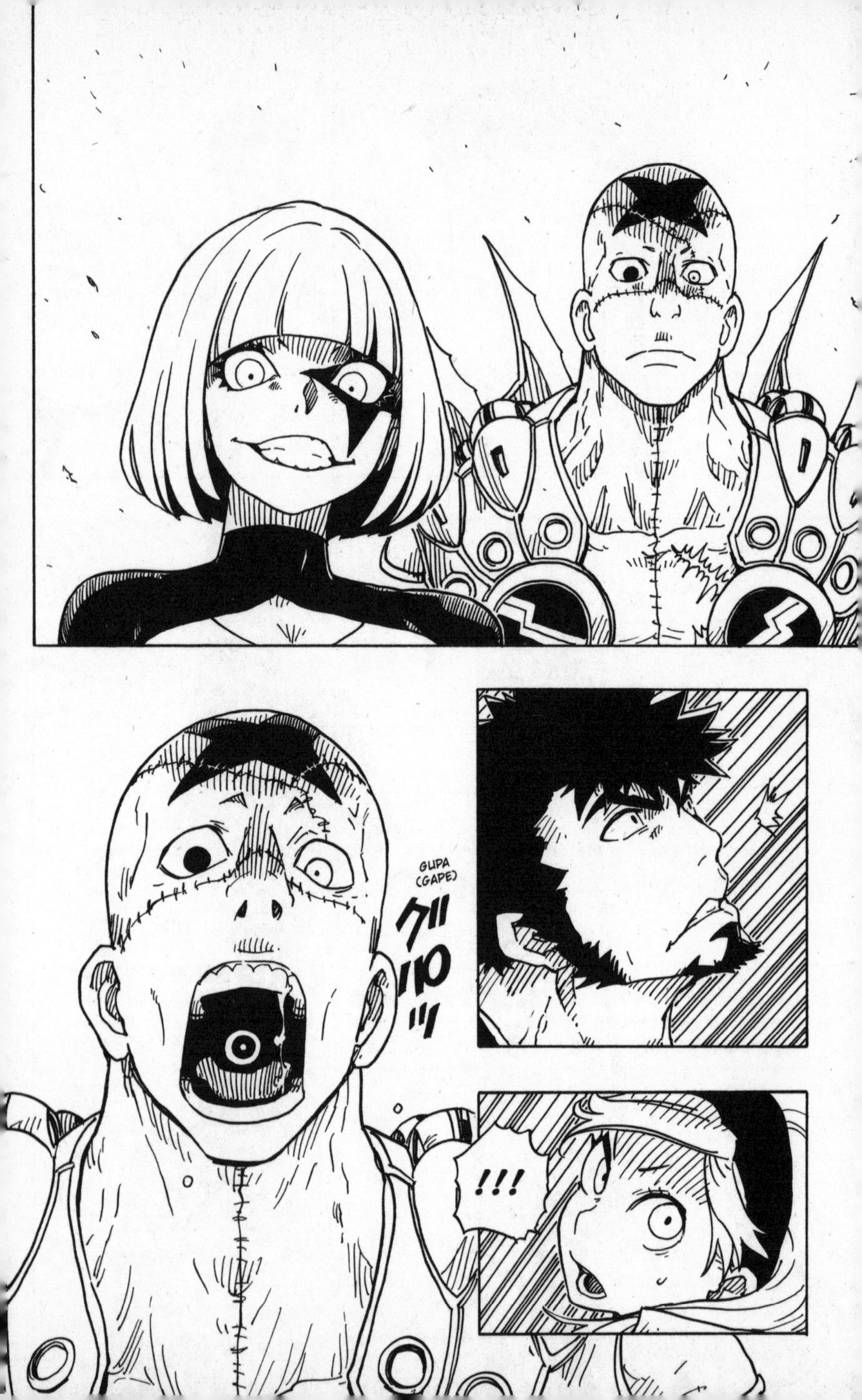
!!!
GUPA
(GAPE)
グパッ

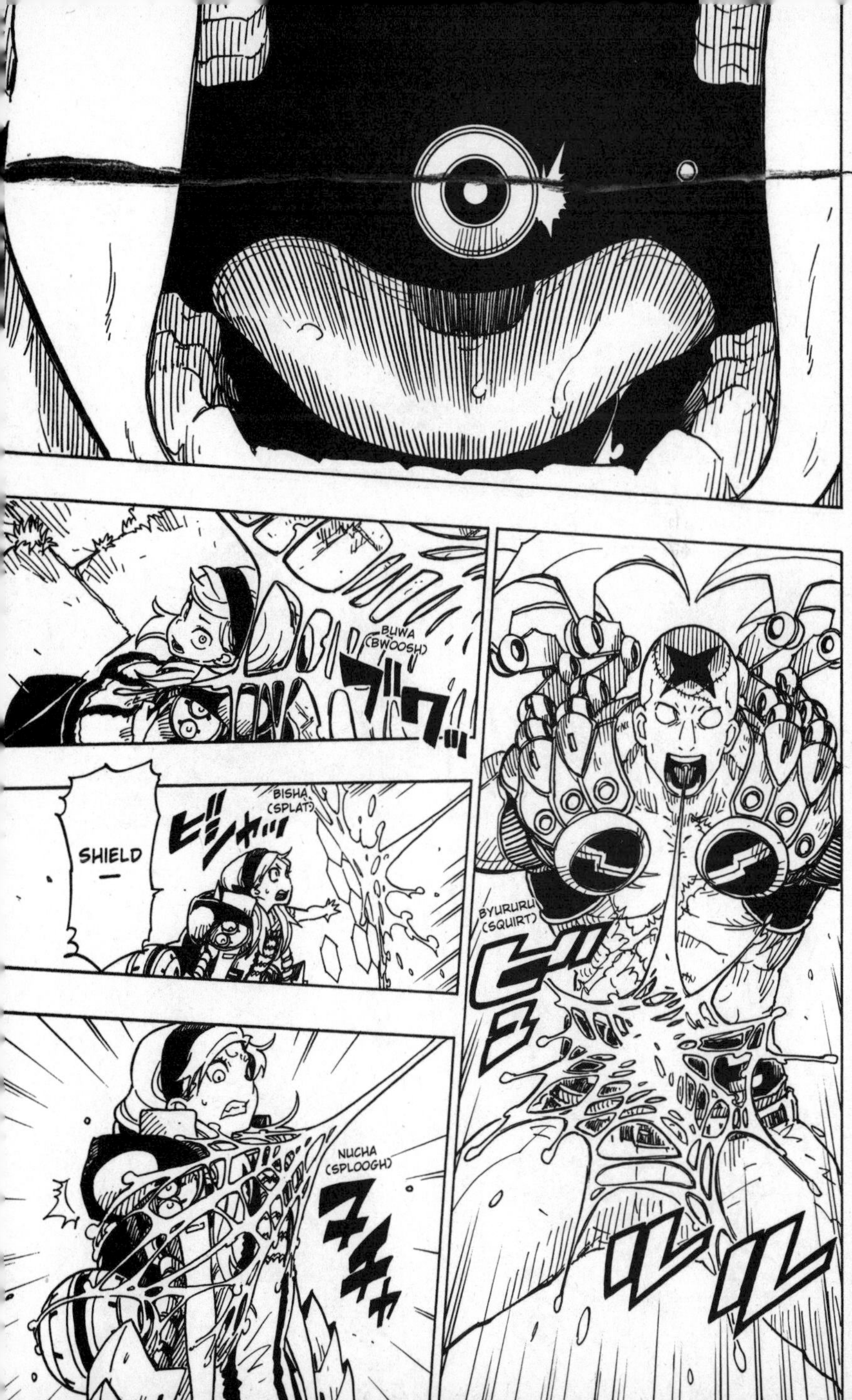
BYURURU
(SQUIRT)
BUWA
(BWOOSH)
BISHA
(SPLAT)
SHIELD
—
NUCHA
(SPLOOGH)

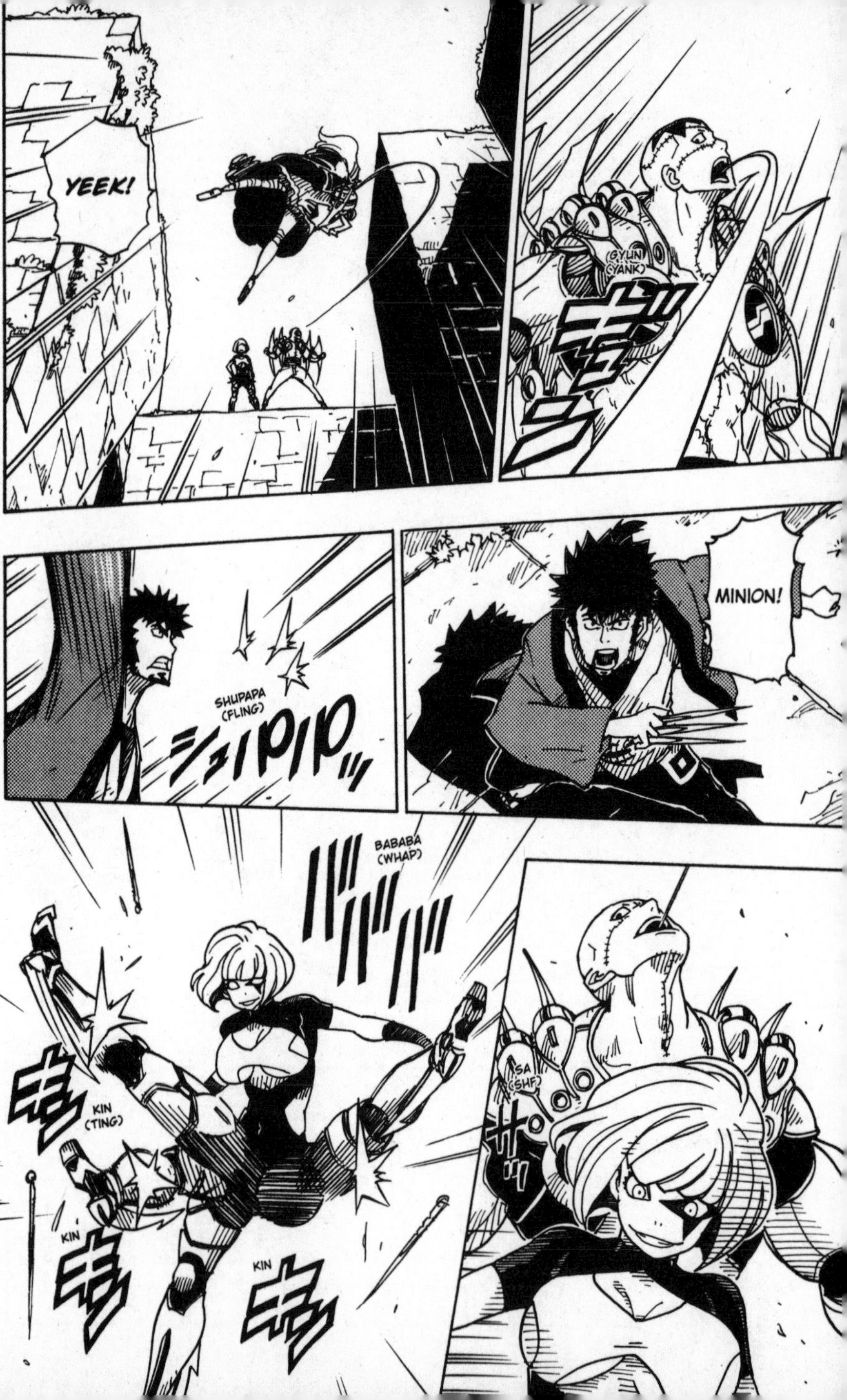
(GYUN
YANK)
YEEK!
MINION!
SHUPAPA
(FLING)
SA
(SHF)
BABABA
(WHAP)
KIN
(TING)
KIN
KIN

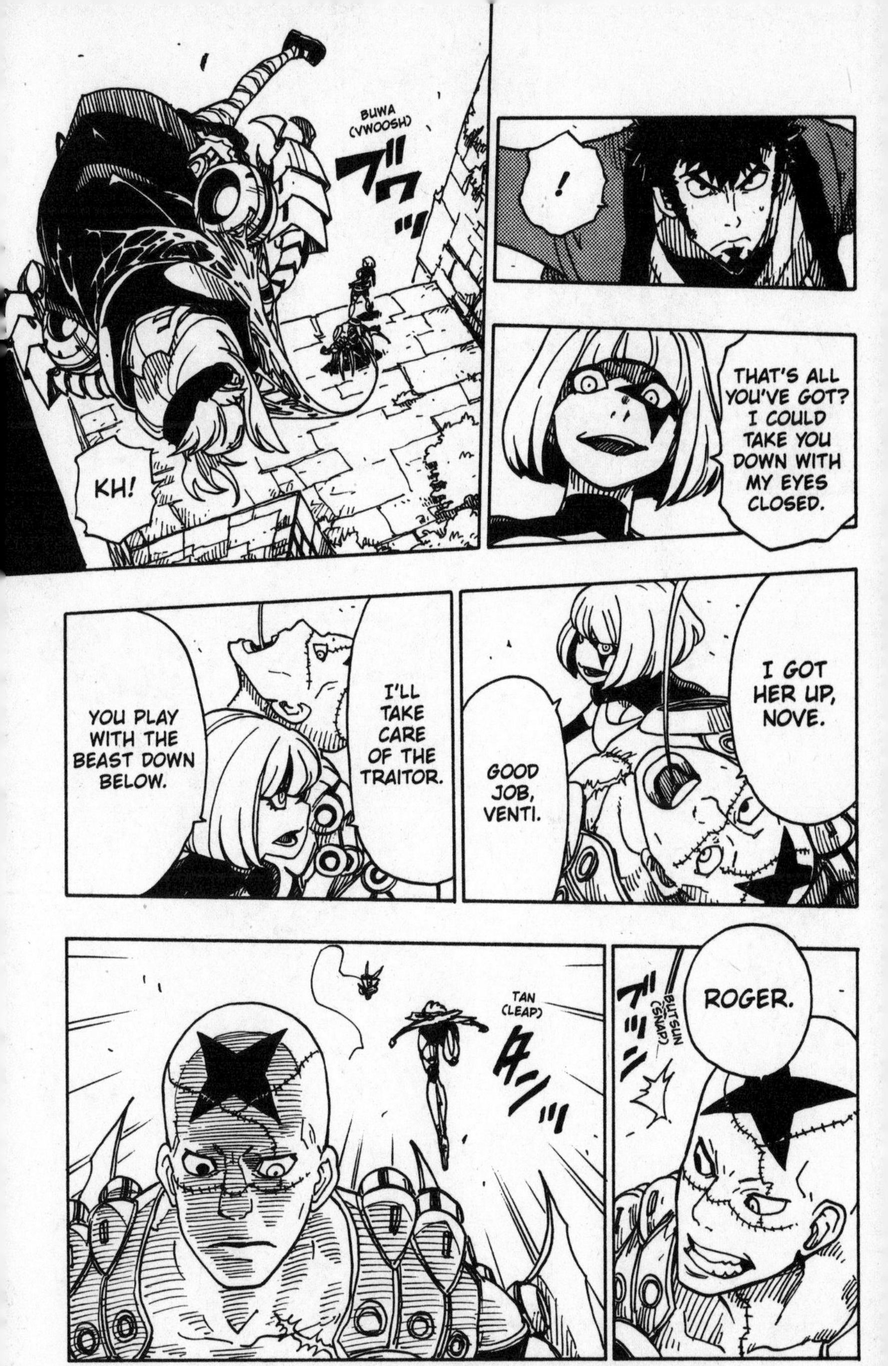
!
THAT'S ALL YOU'VE GOT? I COULD TAKE YOU DOWN WITH MY EYES CLOSED.
BUWA (VWOOSH)
KH!
I GOT HER UP, NOVE.
GOOD JOB, VENTI.
I'LL TAKE CARE OF THE TRAITOR.
YOU PLAY WITH THE BEAST DOWN BELOW.
ROGER.
BUTSUN (SNAP)
TAN (LEAP)

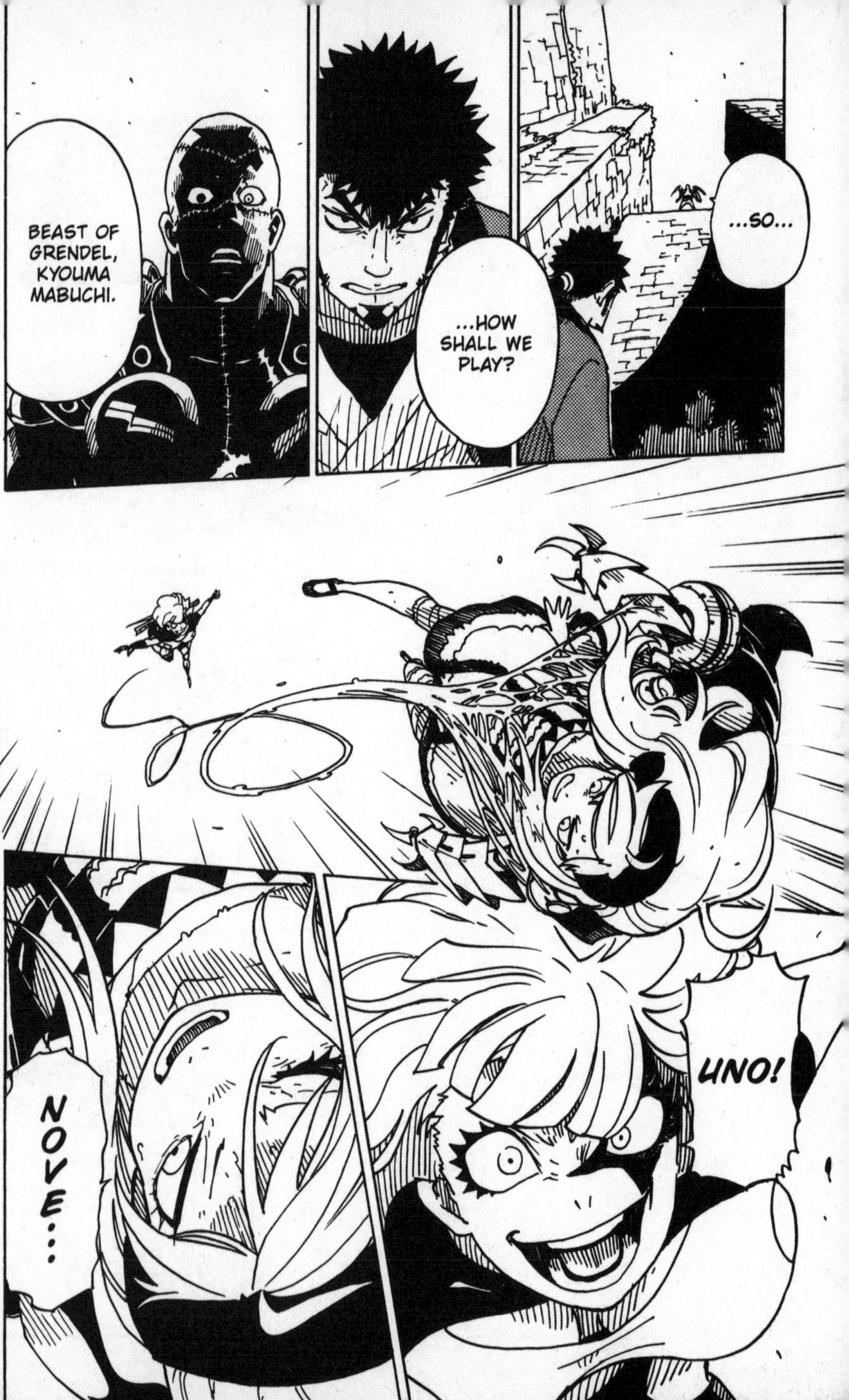
...SO...
...HOW SHALL WE PLAY?
BEAST OF GRENDEL, KYOUMA MABUCHI.
UNO!
NOVE...

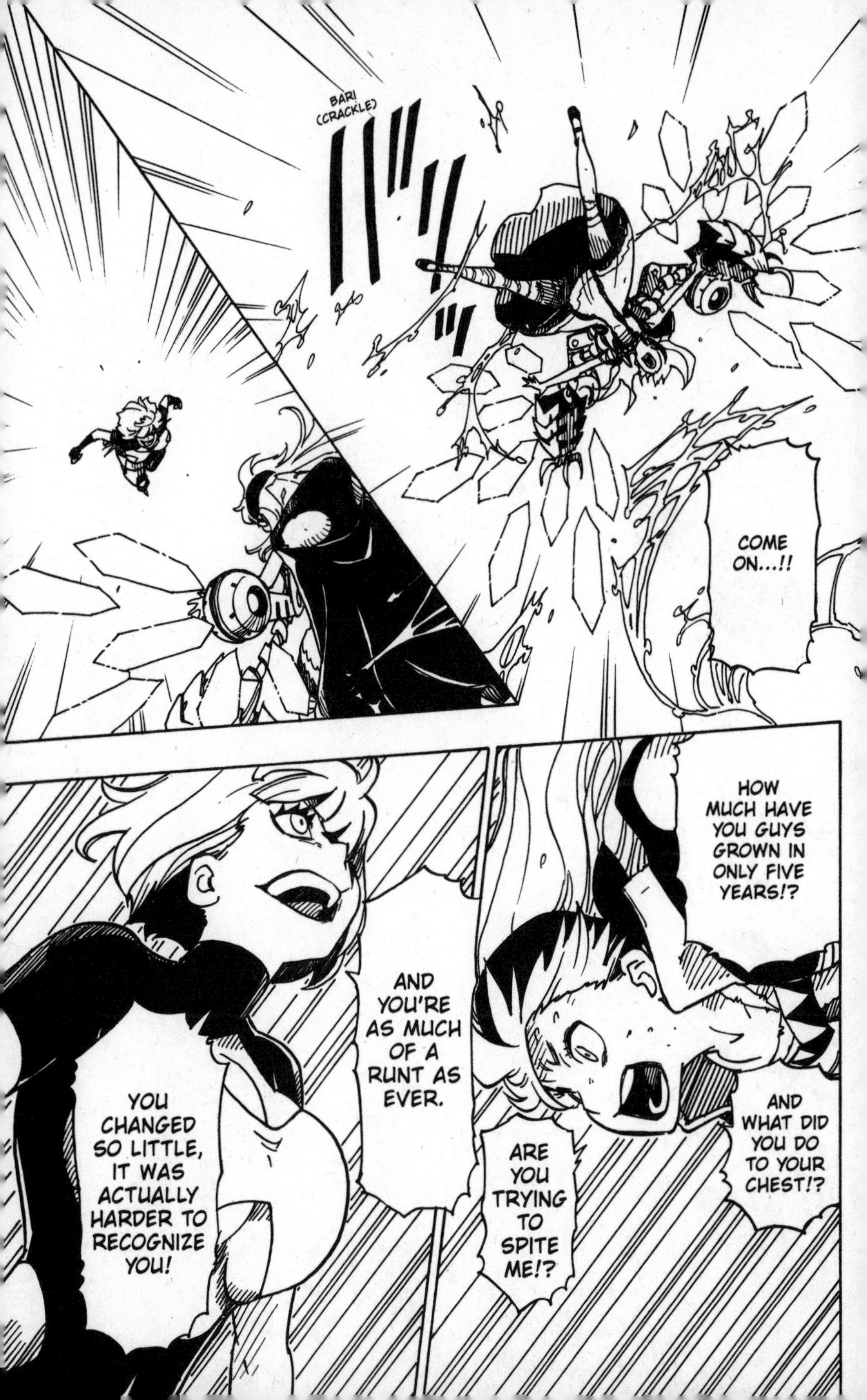
BARI (CRACKLE)
COME ON...!!
HOW MUCH HAVE YOU GUYS GROWN IN ONLY FIVE YEARS!?
AND WHAT DID YOU DO TO YOUR CHEST!?
ARE YOU TRYING TO SPITE ME!?
AND YOU'RE AS MUCH OF A RUNT AS EVER.
YOU CHANGED SO LITTLE, IT WAS ACTUALLY HARDER TO RECOGNIZE YOU!

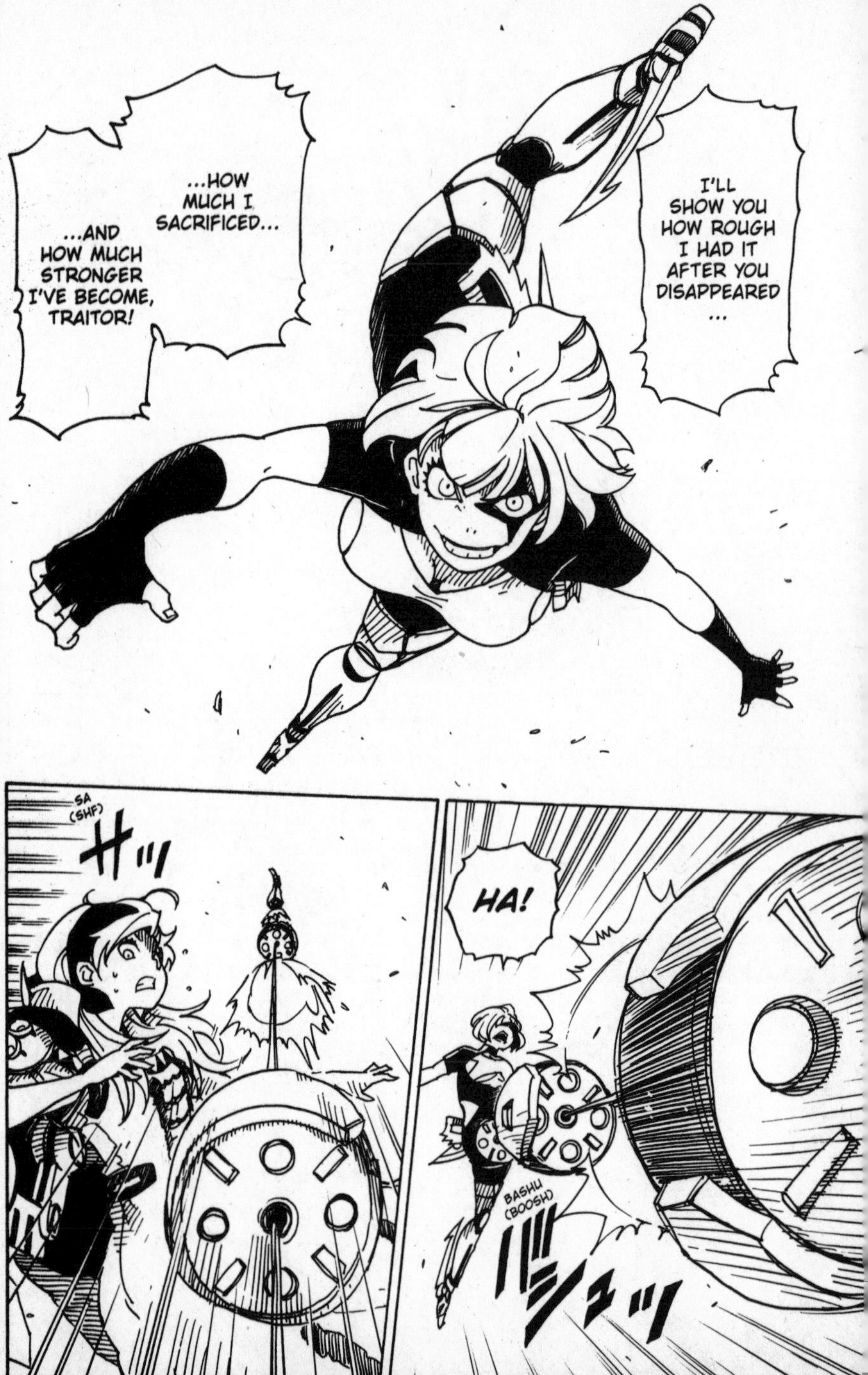
I'LL SHOW YOU HOW ROUGH I HAD IT AFTER YOU DISAPPEARED...
...HOW MUCH I SACRIFICED...
...AND HOW MUCH STRONGER I'VE BECOME, TRAITOR!
HA!
BASHU (BOOSH)
SA (SHF)

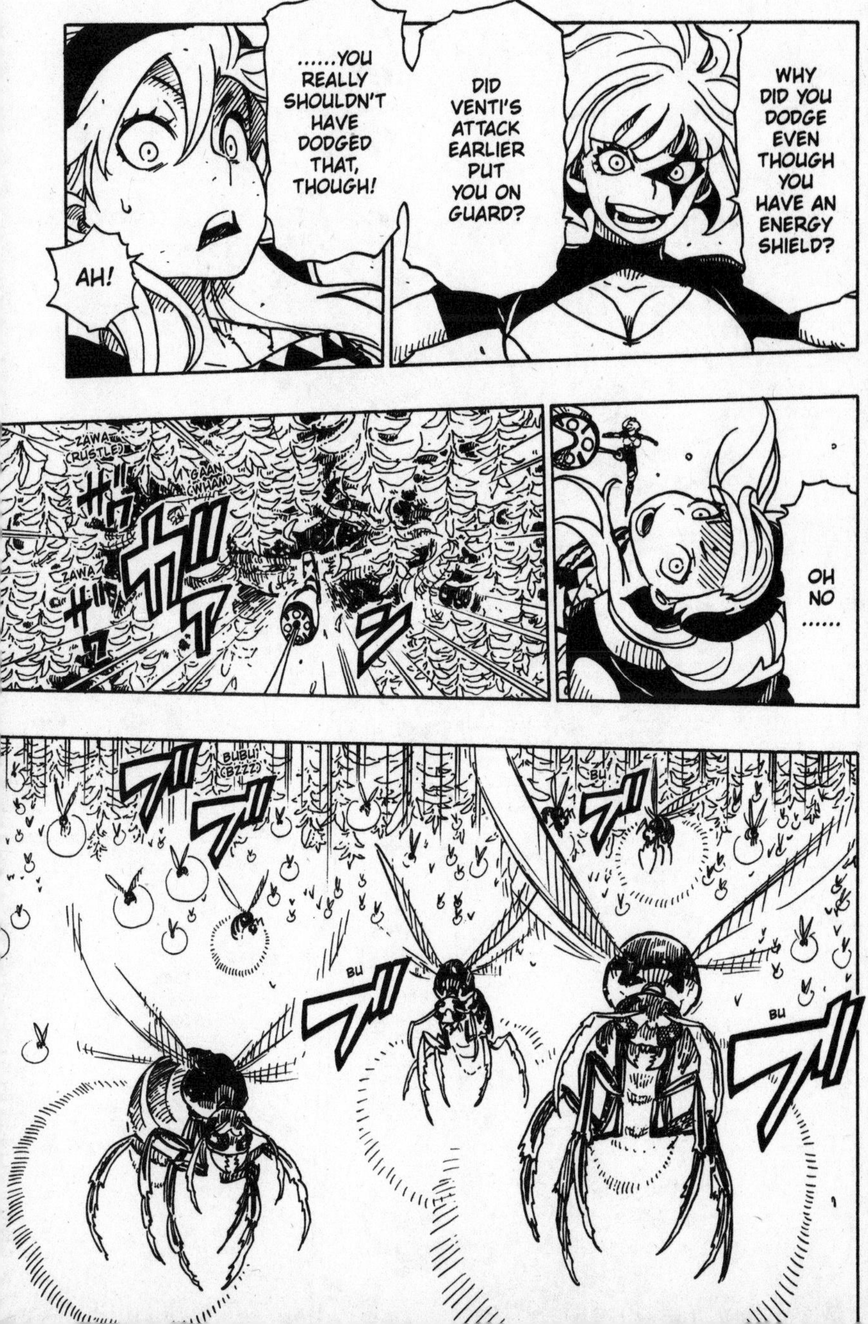
WHY DID YOU DODGE EVEN THOUGH YOU HAVE AN ENERGY SHIELD?
DID VENTI'S ATTACK EARLIER PUT YOU ON GUARD?
......YOU REALLY SHOULDN'T HAVE DODGED THAT, THOUGH!
AH!
OH NO ......
ZAWA (RUSTLE)
GAAN (WHAM)
ZAWA
BUBUI (BZZZ)
BU
BU
BU

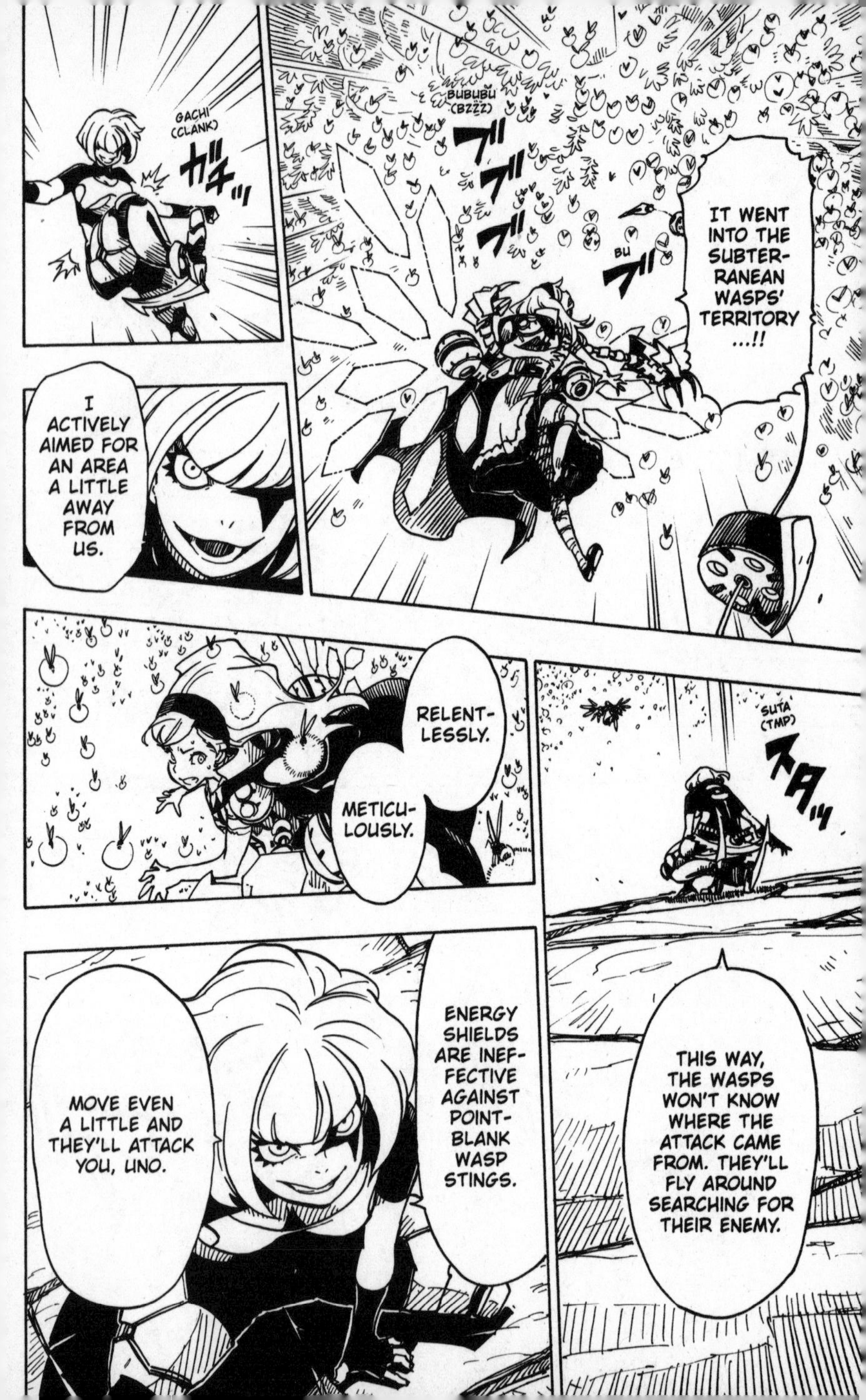
BUBUBU (BZZZ)
BU
IT WENT INTO THE SUBTER-RANEAN WASPS' TERRITORY ...!!
GACHI (CLANK)
I ACTIVELY AIMED FOR AN AREA A LITTLE AWAY FROM US.
SUTA (TMP)
RELENT-LESSLY.
METICU-LOUSLY.
THIS WAY, THE WASPS WON'T KNOW WHERE THE ATTACK CAME FROM. THEY'LL FLY AROUND SEARCHING FOR THEIR ENEMY.
ENERGY SHIELDS ARE INEF-FECTIVE AGAINST POINT-BLANK WASP STINGS.
MOVE EVEN A LITTLE AND THEY'LL ATTACK YOU, UNO.

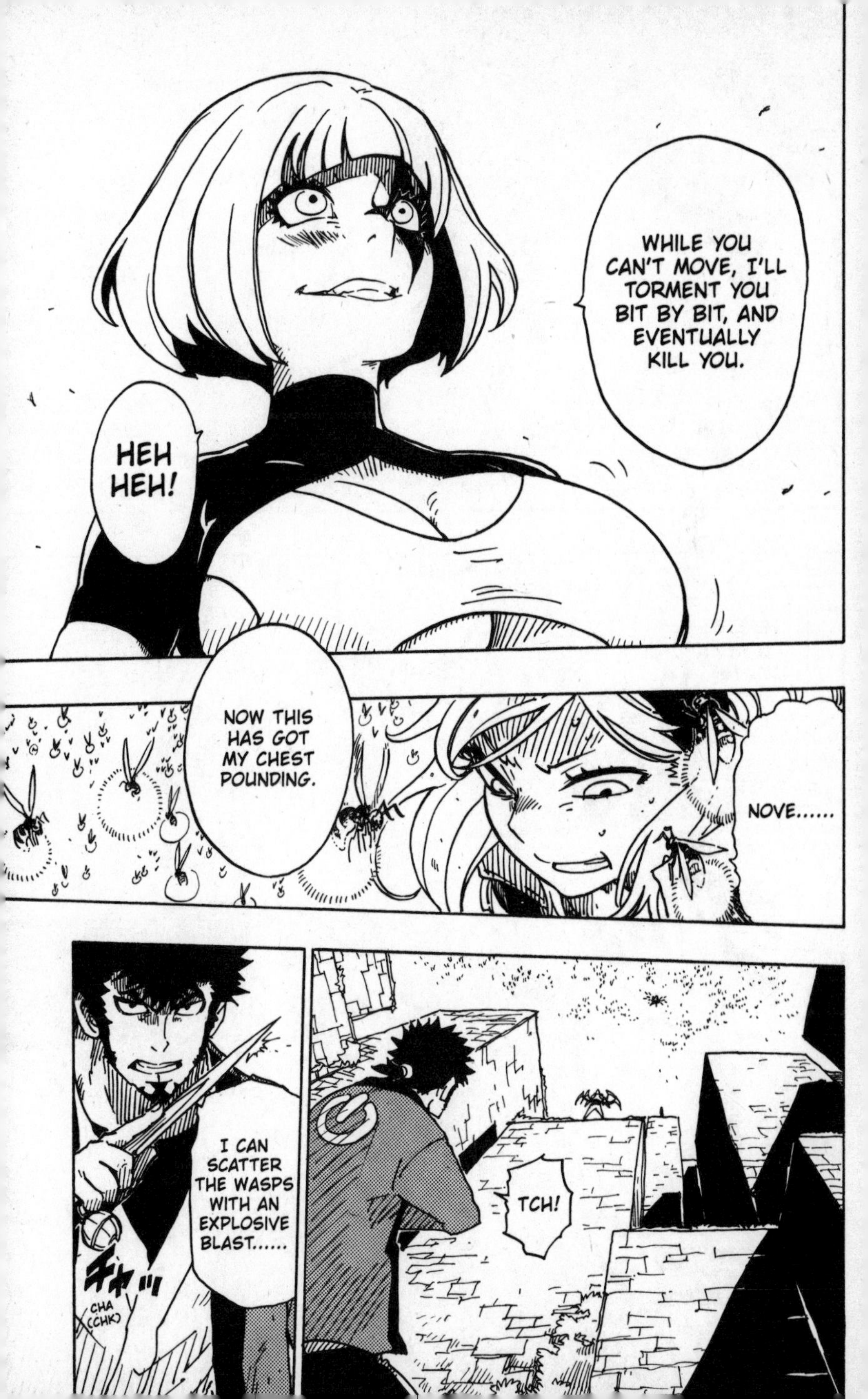
WHILE YOU CAN'T MOVE, I'LL TORMENT YOU BIT BY BIT, AND EVENTUALLY KILL YOU.
HEH HEH!
NOVE......
NOW THIS HAS GOT MY CHEST POUNDING.
TCH!
I CAN SCATTER THE WASPS WITH AN EXPLOSIVE BLAST......
チャッ
CHA (CHK)

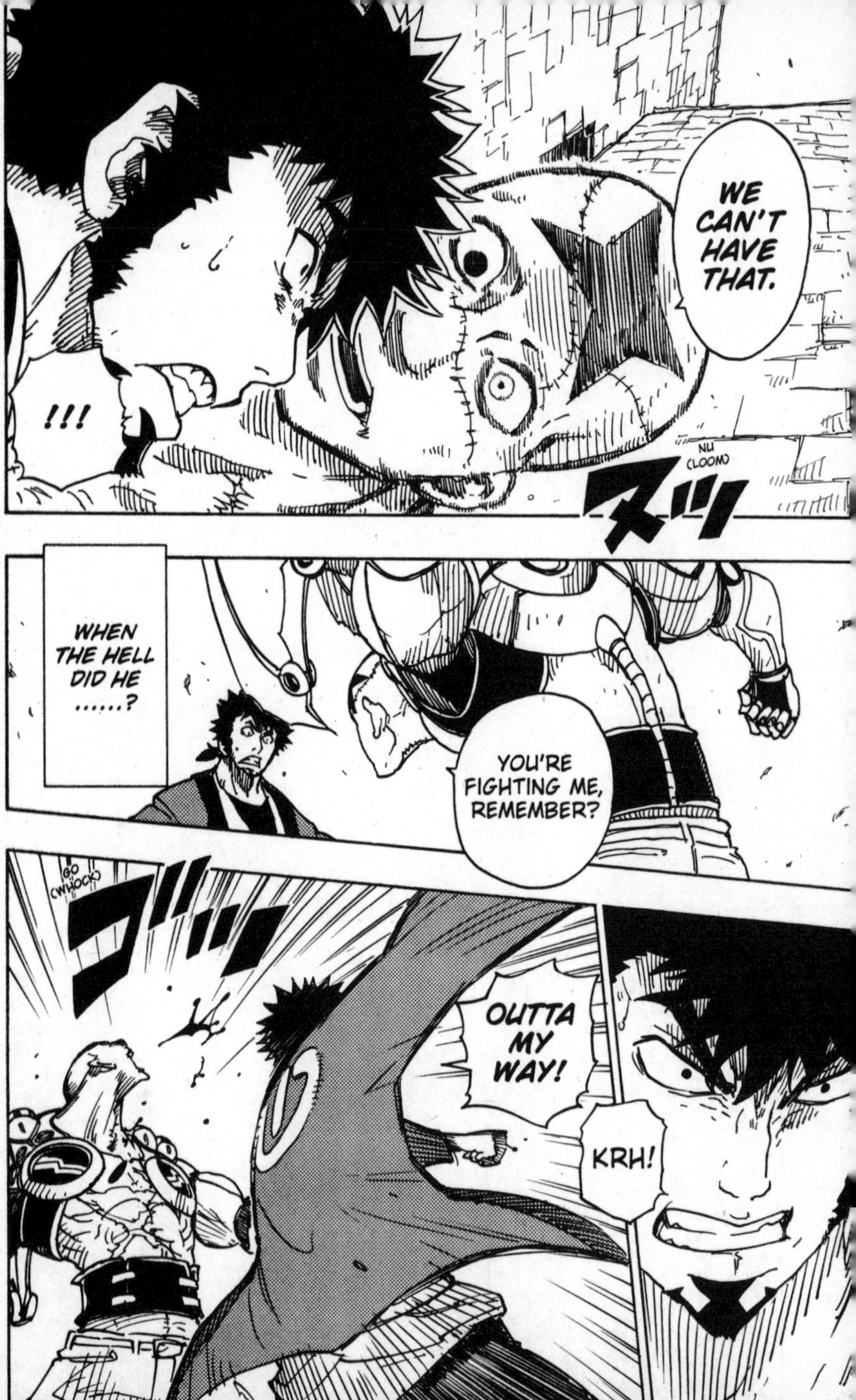
WE CAN'T HAVE THAT.
NU (LOOM)
!!!
YOU'RE FIGHTING ME, REMEMBER?
WHEN THE HELL DID HE ......?
OUTTA MY WAY!
KRH!
GO (WHOCK)

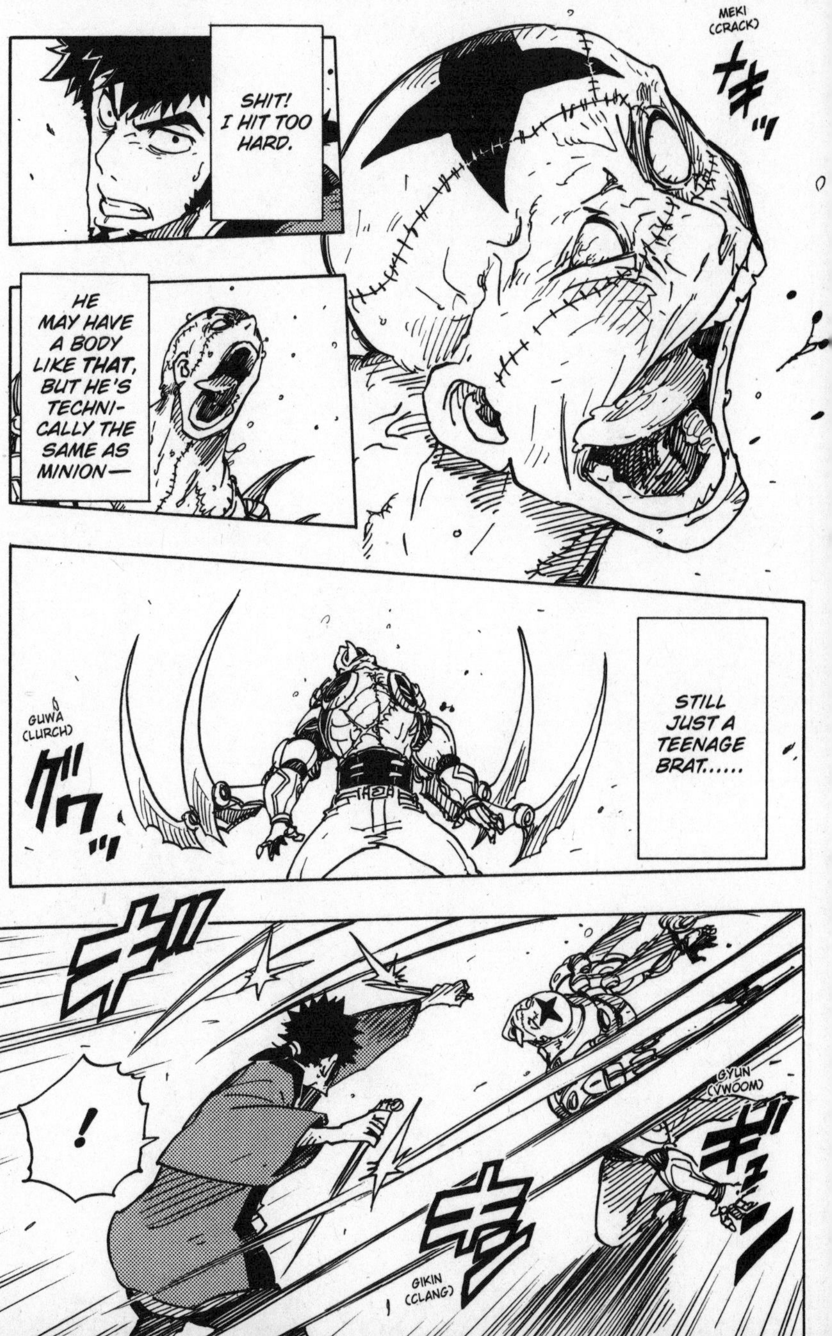
MEKI (CRACK)
SHIT! I HIT TOO HARD.
HE MAY HAVE A BODY LIKE THAT, BUT HE'S TECHNICALLY THE SAME AS MINION—
STILL JUST A TEENAGE BRAT......
GUWA (LURCH)
GYUN (VWOOM)
GIKIN (CLANG)
!

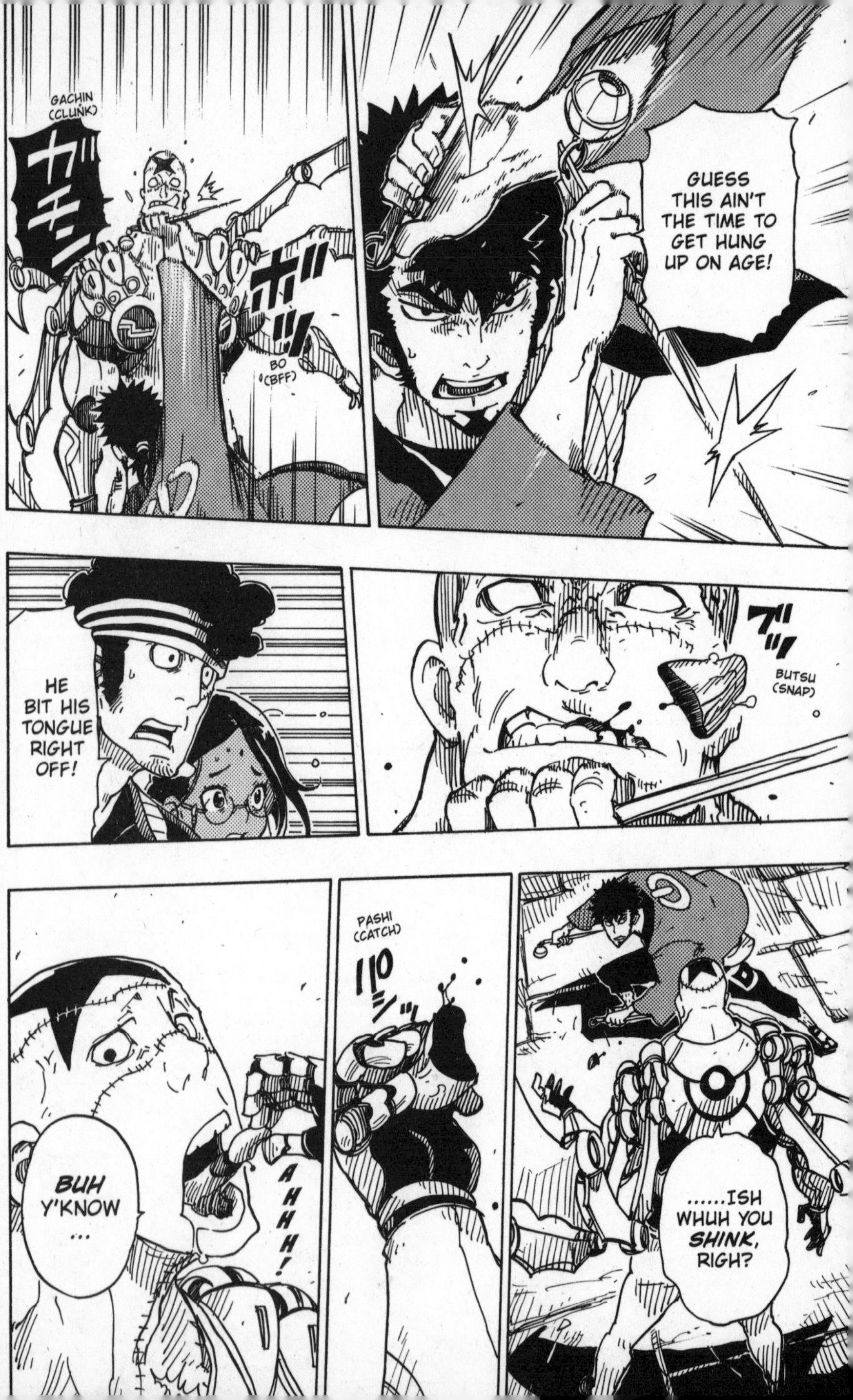
GUESS THIS AIN'T THE TIME TO GET HUNG UP ON AGE!
GACHIN (CLUNK)
BO (BFF)
BUTSU (SNAP)
HE BIT HIS TONGUE RIGHT OFF!
......ISH WHUH YOU SHINK, RIGH?
PASHI (CATCH)
AHHHH!
BUH Y'KNOW ...

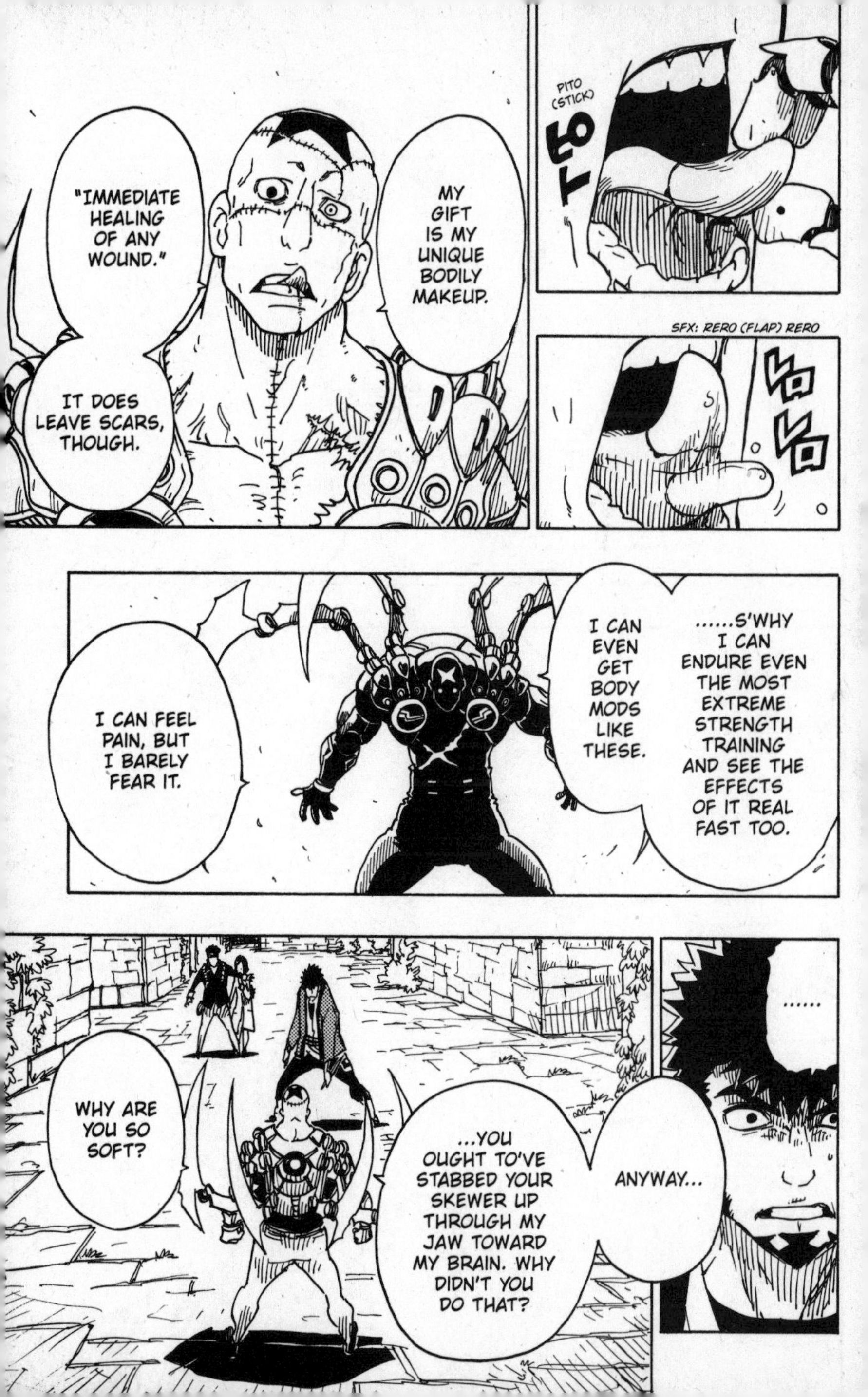
PITO (STICK)
SFX: RERO (FLAP) RERO
MY GIFT IS MY UNIQUE BODILY MAKEUP.
"IMMEDIATE HEALING OF ANY WOUND."
IT DOES LEAVE SCARS, THOUGH.
......S'WHY I CAN ENDURE EVEN THE MOST EXTREME STRENGTH TRAINING AND SEE THE EFFECTS OF IT REAL FAST TOO.
I CAN EVEN GET BODY MODS LIKE THESE.
I CAN FEEL PAIN, BUT I BARELY FEAR IT.
......
ANYWAY...
...YOU OUGHT TO'VE STABBED YOUR SKEWER UP THROUGH MY JAW TOWARD MY BRAIN. WHY DIDN'T YOU DO THAT?
WHY ARE YOU SO SOFT?

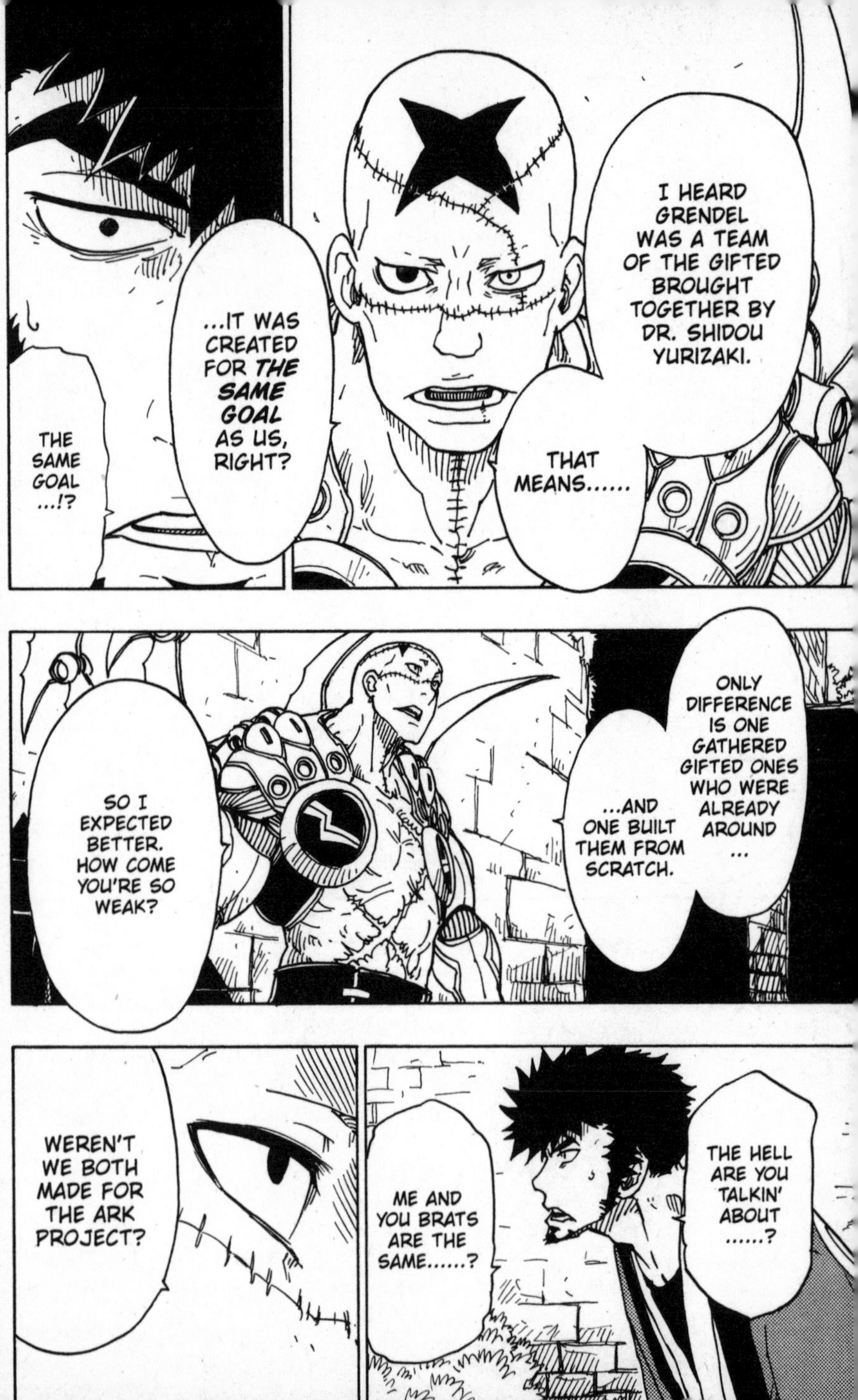
I HEARD GRENDEL WAS A TEAM OF THE GIFTED BROUGHT TOGETHER BY DR. SHIDOU YURIZAKI.
THAT MEANS......
...IT WAS CREATED FOR ***THE SAME GOAL*** AS US, RIGHT?
THE SAME GOAL ...!?
ONLY DIFFERENCE IS ONE GATHERED GIFTED ONES WHO WERE ALREADY AROUND ...
...AND ONE BUILT THEM FROM SCRATCH.
SO I EXPECTED BETTER. HOW COME YOU'RE SO WEAK?
THE HELL ARE YOU TALKIN' ABOUT ......?
ME AND YOU BRATS ARE THE SAME......?
WEREN'T WE BOTH MADE FOR THE ARK PROJECT?

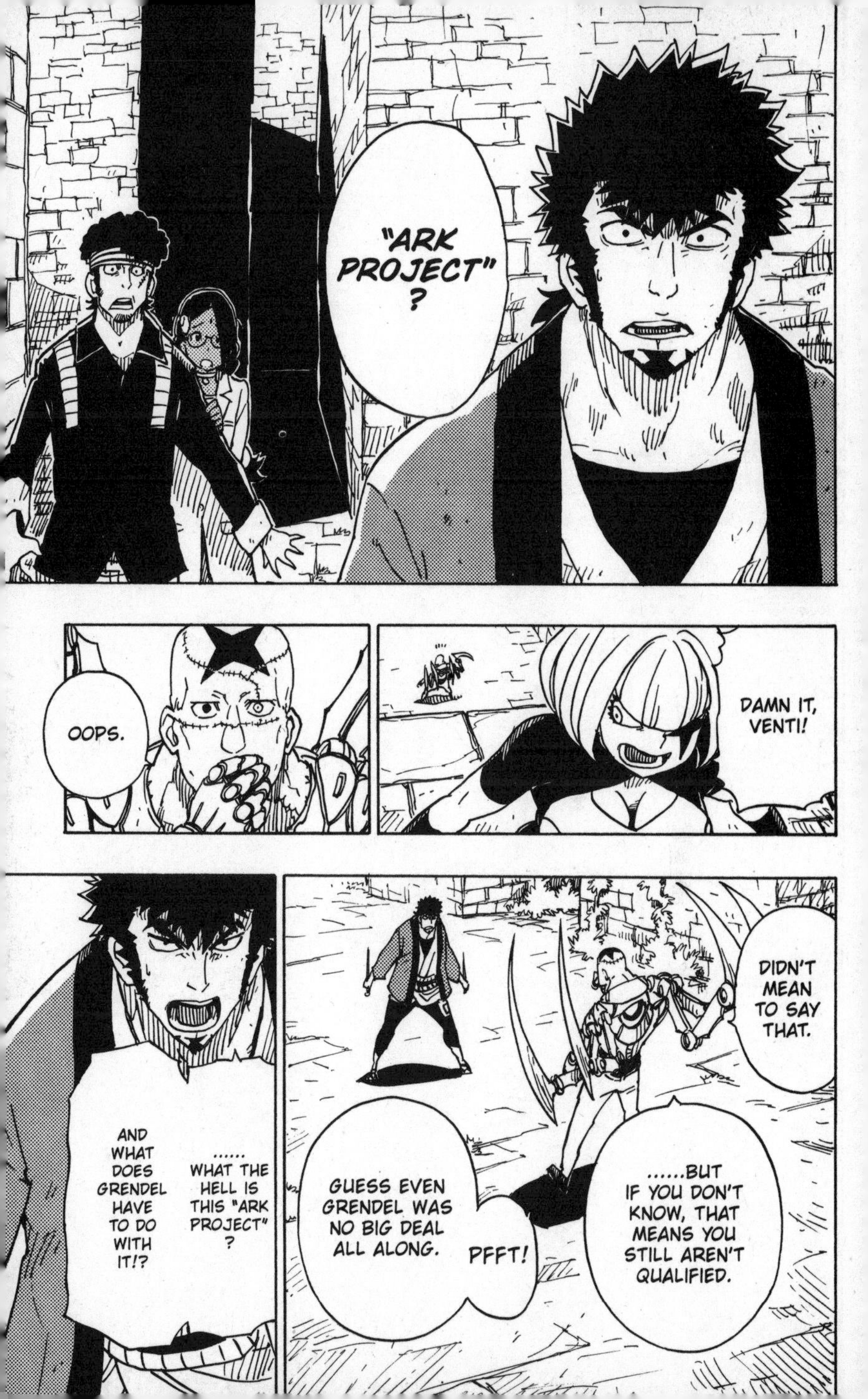
"ARK PROJECT"?
DAMN IT, VENTI!
OOPS.
DIDN'T MEAN TO SAY THAT.
......BUT IF YOU DON'T KNOW, THAT MEANS YOU STILL AREN'T QUALIFIED.
PFFT!
GUESS EVEN GRENDEL WAS NO BIG DEAL ALL ALONG.
......WHAT THE HELL IS THIS "ARK PROJECT"?
AND WHAT DOES GRENDEL HAVE TO DO WITH IT!?

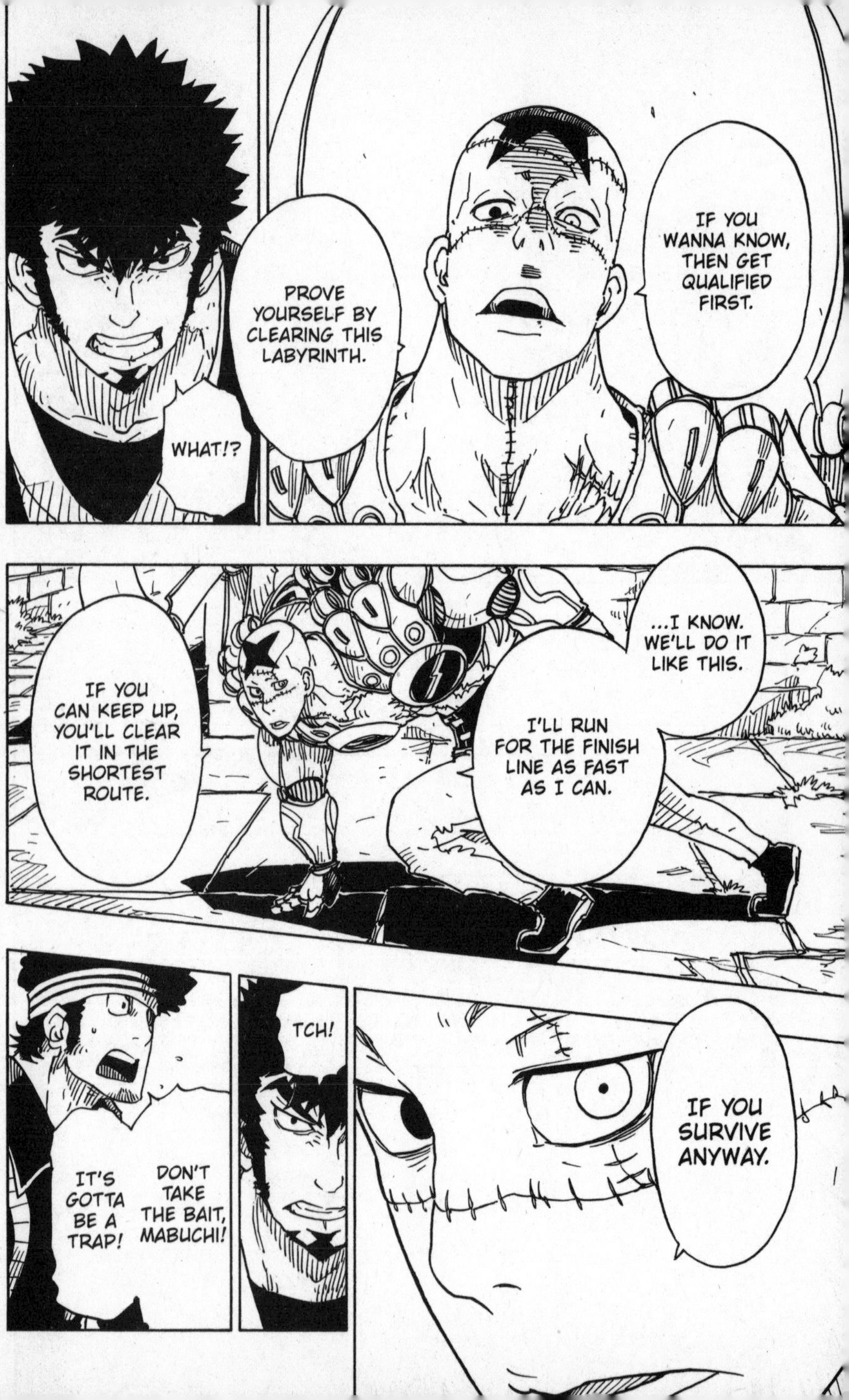
IF YOU WANNA KNOW, THEN GET QUALIFIED FIRST.
PROVE YOURSELF BY CLEARING THIS LABYRINTH.
WHAT!?
...I KNOW. WE'LL DO IT LIKE THIS.
I'LL RUN FOR THE FINISH LINE AS FAST AS I CAN.
IF YOU CAN KEEP UP, YOU'LL CLEAR IT IN THE SHORTEST ROUTE.
IF YOU SURVIVE ANYWAY.
TCH!
DON'T TAKE THE BAIT, MABUCHI!
IT'S GOTTA BE A TRAP!

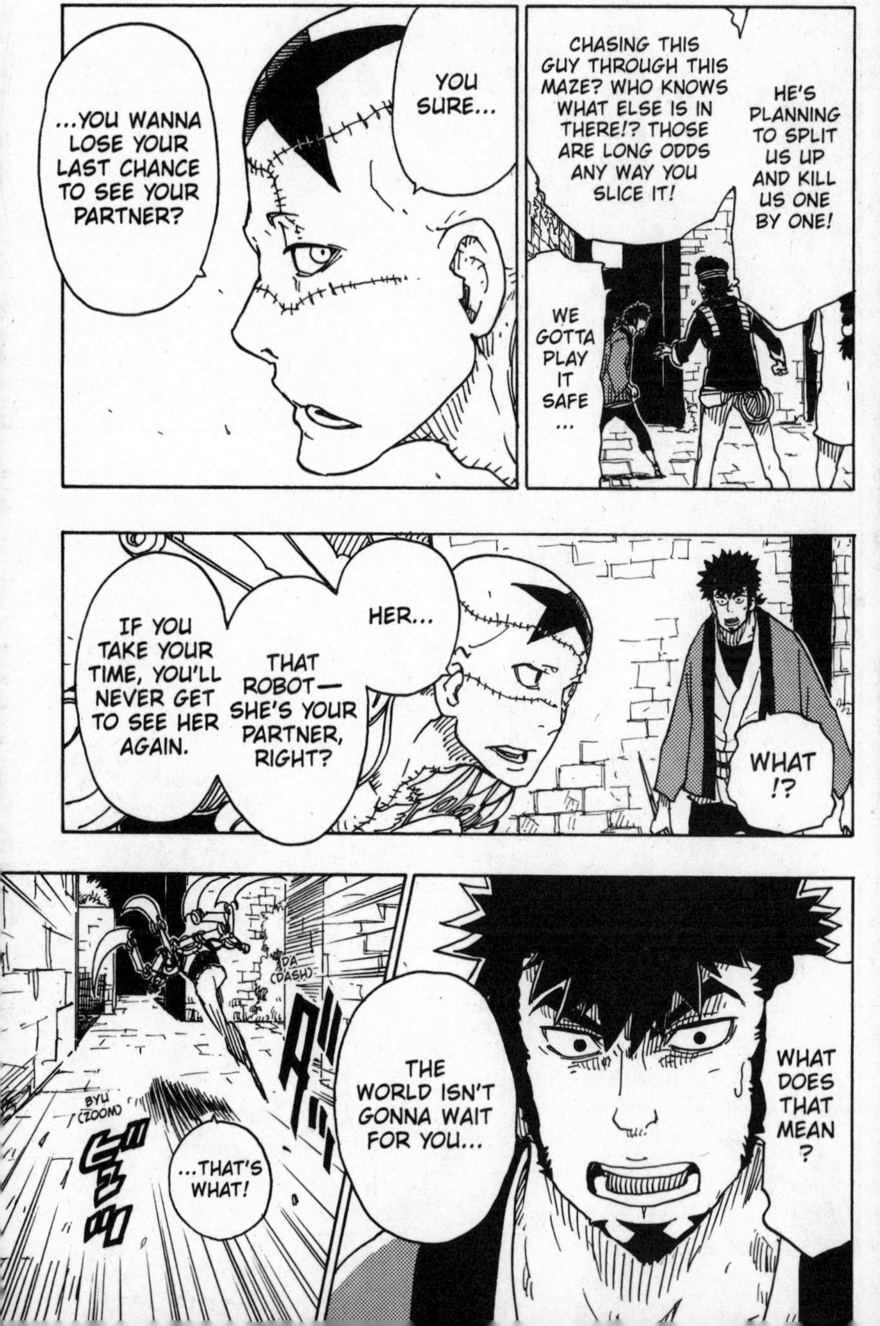
HE'S PLANNING TO SPLIT US UP AND KILL US ONE BY ONE!
CHASING THIS GUY THROUGH THIS MAZE? WHO KNOWS WHAT ELSE IS IN THERE!? THOSE ARE LONG ODDS ANY WAY YOU SLICE IT!
WE GOTTA PLAY IT SAFE...
YOU SURE...
...YOU WANNA LOSE YOUR LAST CHANCE TO SEE YOUR PARTNER?
WHAT!?
HER...
THAT ROBOT—SHE'S YOUR PARTNER, RIGHT?
IF YOU TAKE YOUR TIME, YOU'LL NEVER GET TO SEE HER AGAIN.
WHAT DOES THAT MEAN?
THE WORLD ISN'T GONNA WAIT FOR YOU...
DA (DASH)
...THAT'S WHAT!
BYU (ZOOM)

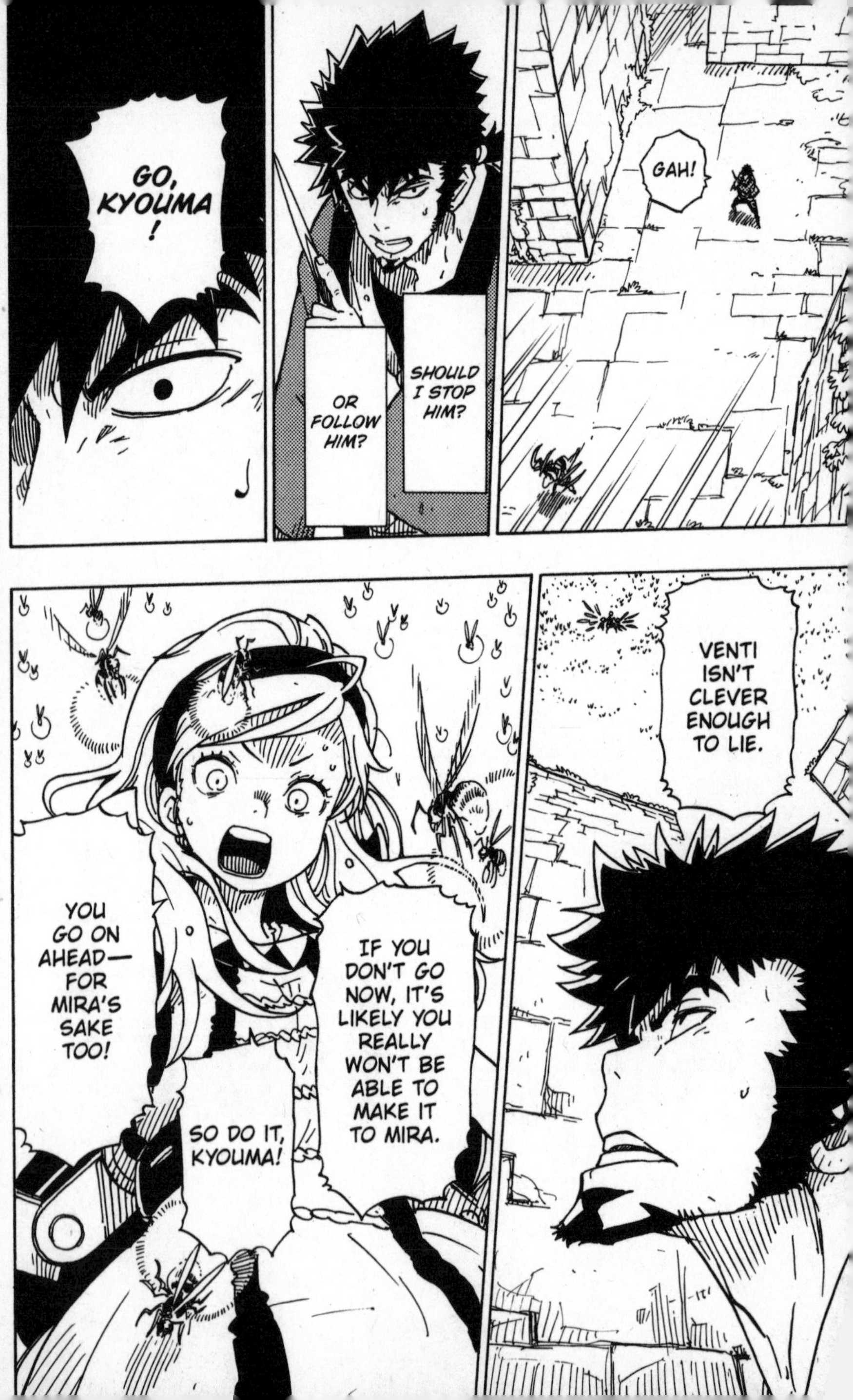
GAH!
SHOULD I STOP HIM?
OR FOLLOW HIM?
GO, KYOUMA!
VENTI ISN'T CLEVER ENOUGH TO LIE.
IF YOU DON'T GO NOW, IT'S LIKELY YOU REALLY WON'T BE ABLE TO MAKE IT TO MIRA.
YOU GO ON AHEAD—FOR MIRA'S SAKE TOO!
SO DO IT, KYOUMA!

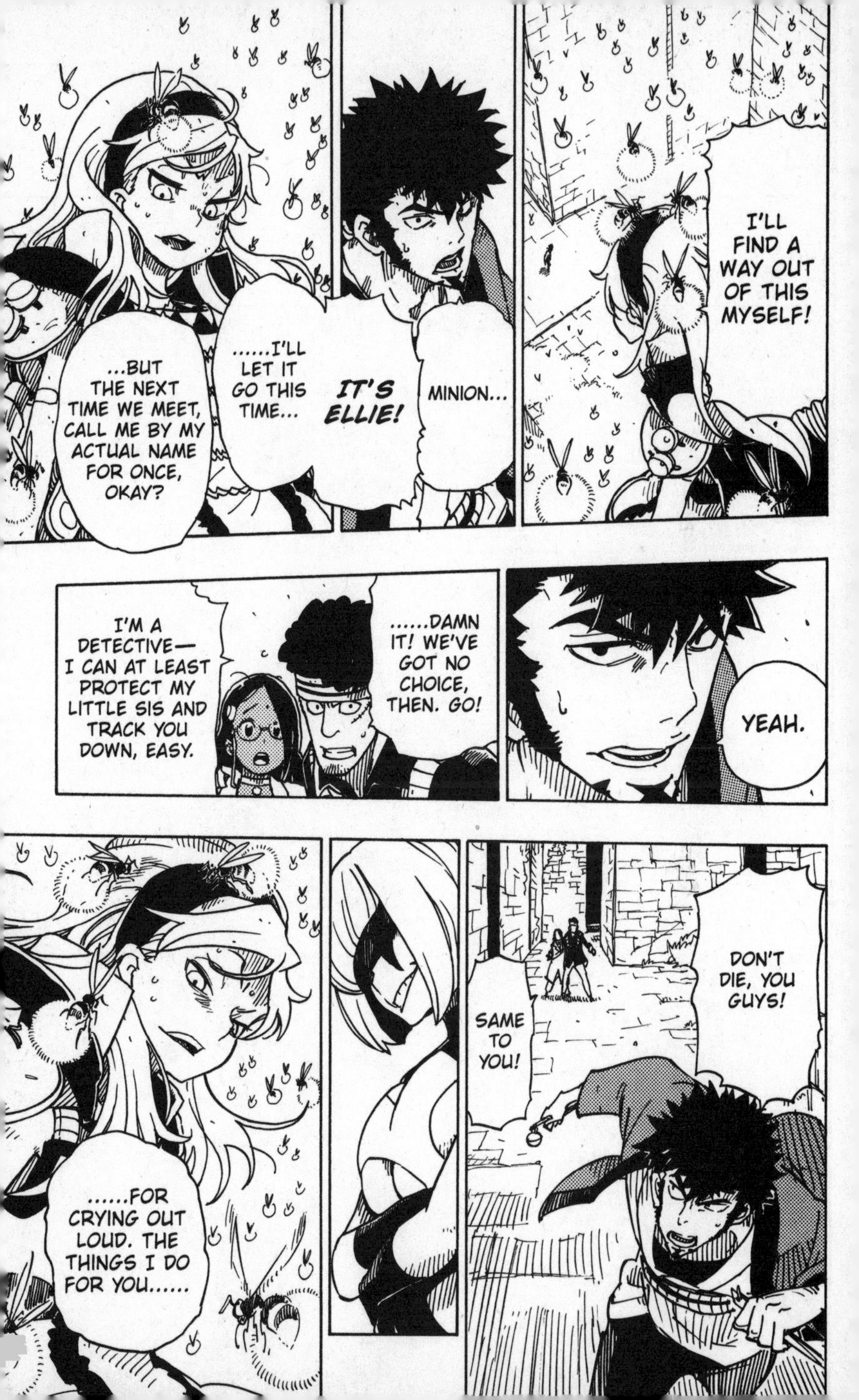
I'LL FIND A WAY OUT OF THIS MYSELF!
MINION...
IT'S ELLIE!
......I'LL LET IT GO THIS TIME...
...BUT THE NEXT TIME WE MEET, CALL ME BY MY ACTUAL NAME FOR ONCE, OKAY?
YEAH.
......DAMN IT! WE'VE GOT NO CHOICE, THEN. GO!
I'M A DETECTIVE— I CAN AT LEAST PROTECT MY LITTLE SIS AND TRACK YOU DOWN, EASY.
DON'T DIE, YOU GUYS!
SAME TO YOU!
......FOR CRYING OUT LOUD. THE THINGS I DO FOR YOU......

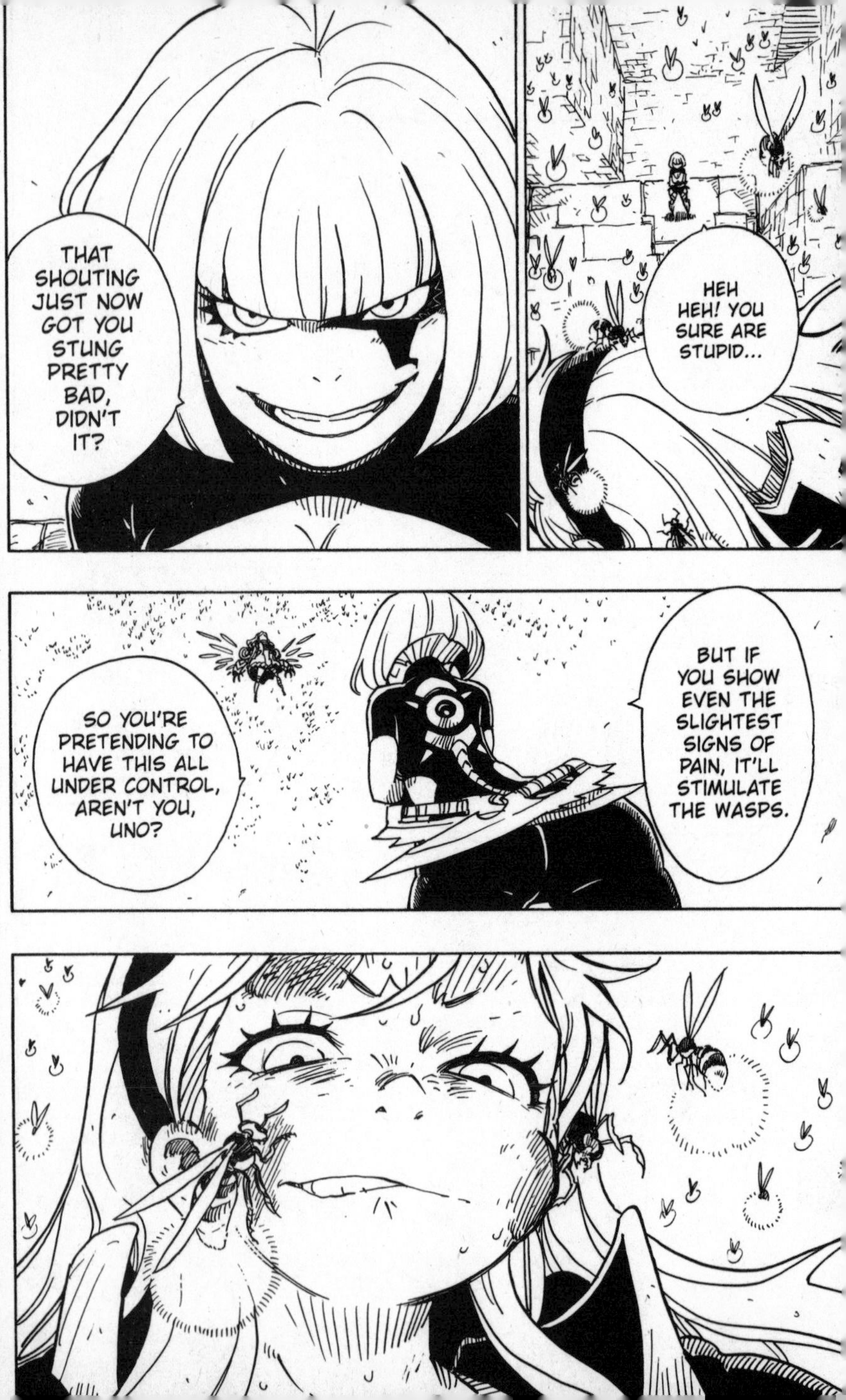
HEH HEH! YOU SURE ARE STUPID...
THAT SHOUTING JUST NOW GOT YOU STUNG PRETTY BAD, DIDN'T IT?
BUT IF YOU SHOW EVEN THE SLIGHTEST SIGNS OF PAIN, IT'LL STIMULATE THE WASPS.
SO YOU'RE PRETENDING TO HAVE THIS ALL UNDER CONTROL, AREN'T YOU, UNO?

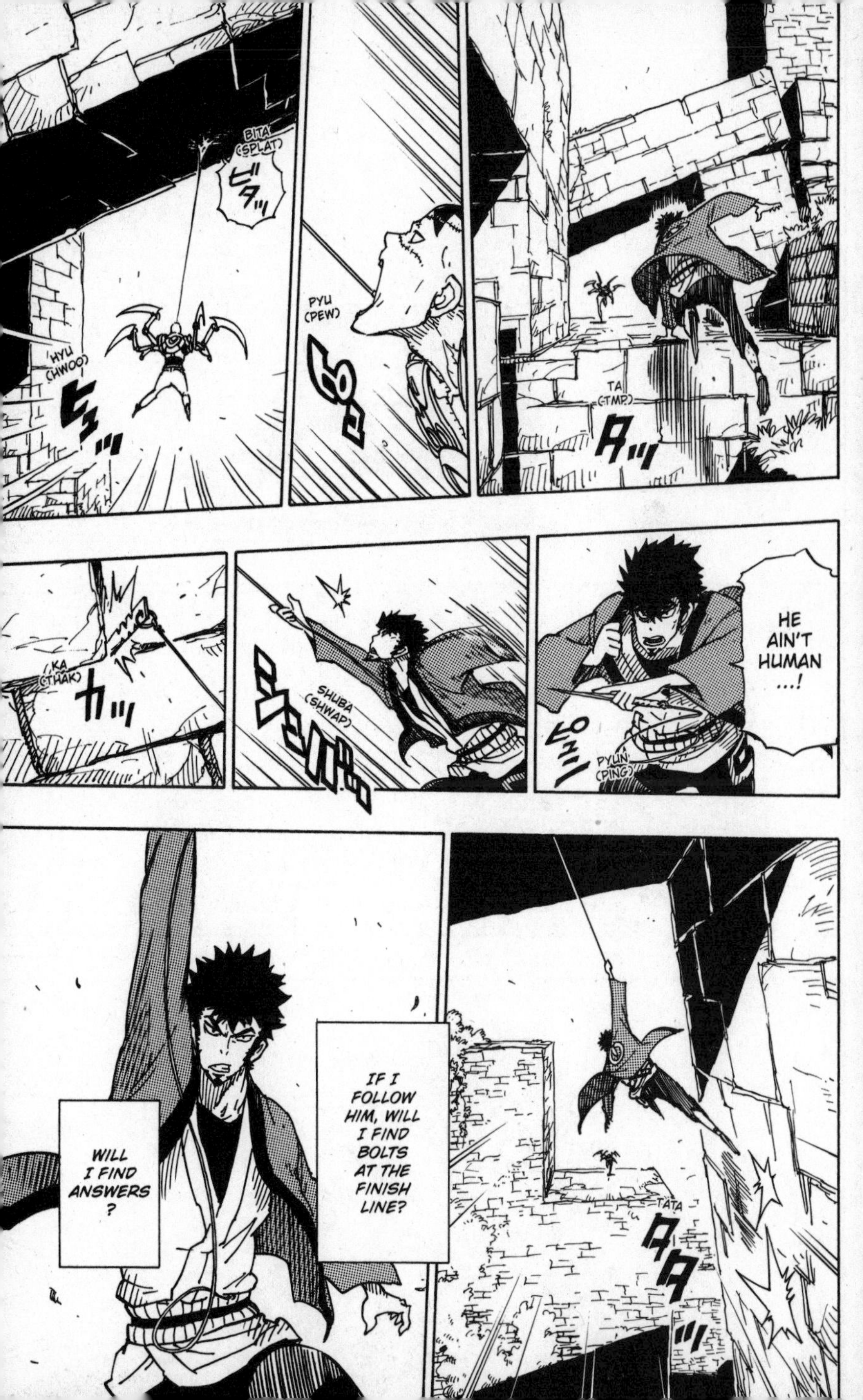
TA (TMP)
PYU (PEW)
BITA (SPLAT)
HYU (HWOO)
HE AIN'T HUMAN ...!
PYUN (PING)
SHUBA (SHWAP)
KA (THAK)
TATA
IF I FOLLOW HIM, WILL I FIND BOLTS AT THE FINISH LINE?
WILL I FIND ANSWERS ?

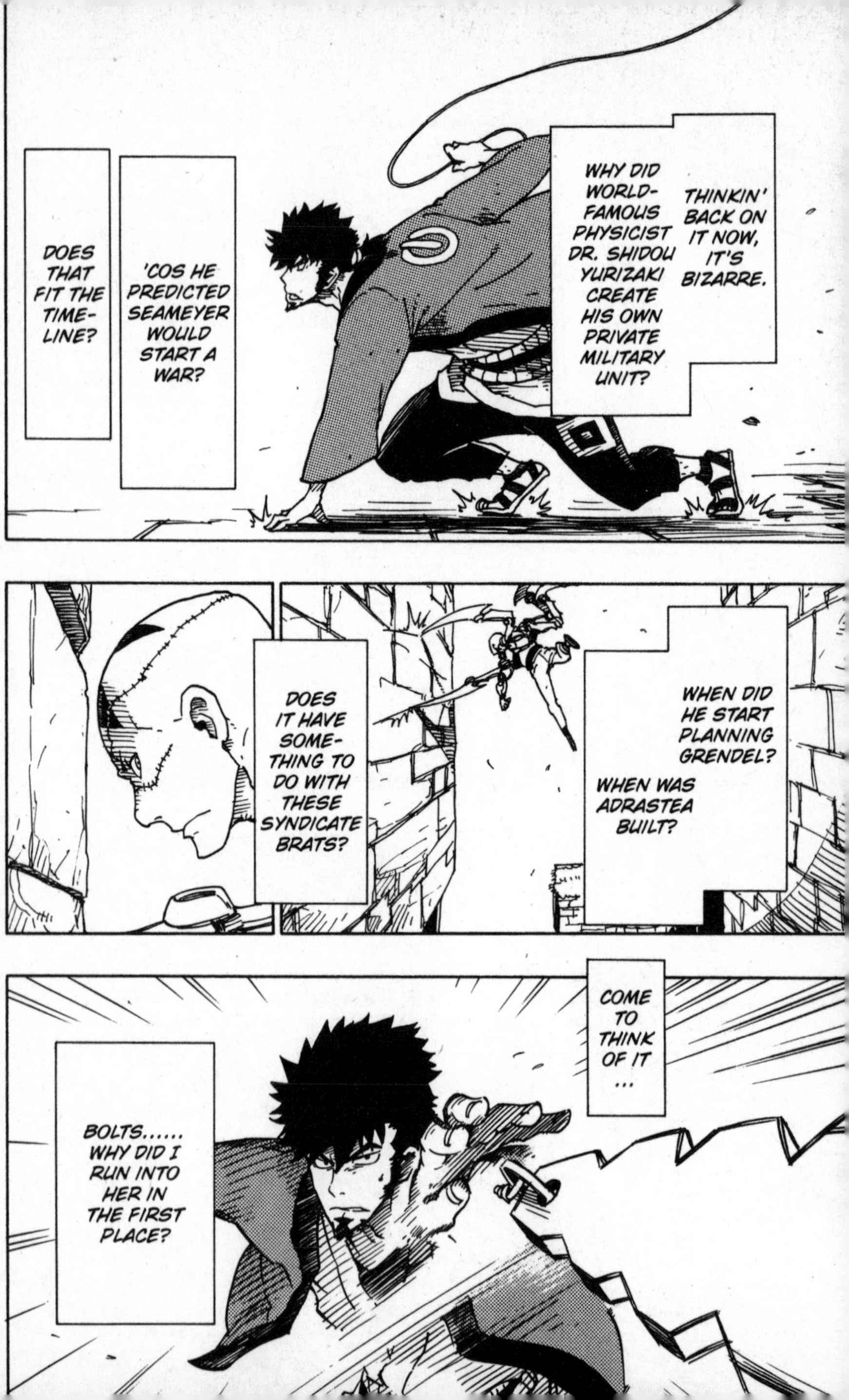
THINKIN' BACK ON IT NOW, IT'S BIZARRE.
WHY DID WORLD-FAMOUS PHYSICIST DR. SHIDOU YURIZAKI CREATE HIS OWN PRIVATE MILITARY UNIT?
'COS HE PREDICTED SEAMEYER WOULD START A WAR?
DOES THAT FIT THE TIME-LINE?
WHEN DID HE START PLANNING GRENDEL?
WHEN WAS ADRASTEA BUILT?
DOES IT HAVE SOME-THING TO DO WITH THESE SYNDICATE BRATS?
COME TO THINK OF IT ...
BOLTS...... WHY DID I RUN INTO HER IN THE FIRST PLACE?

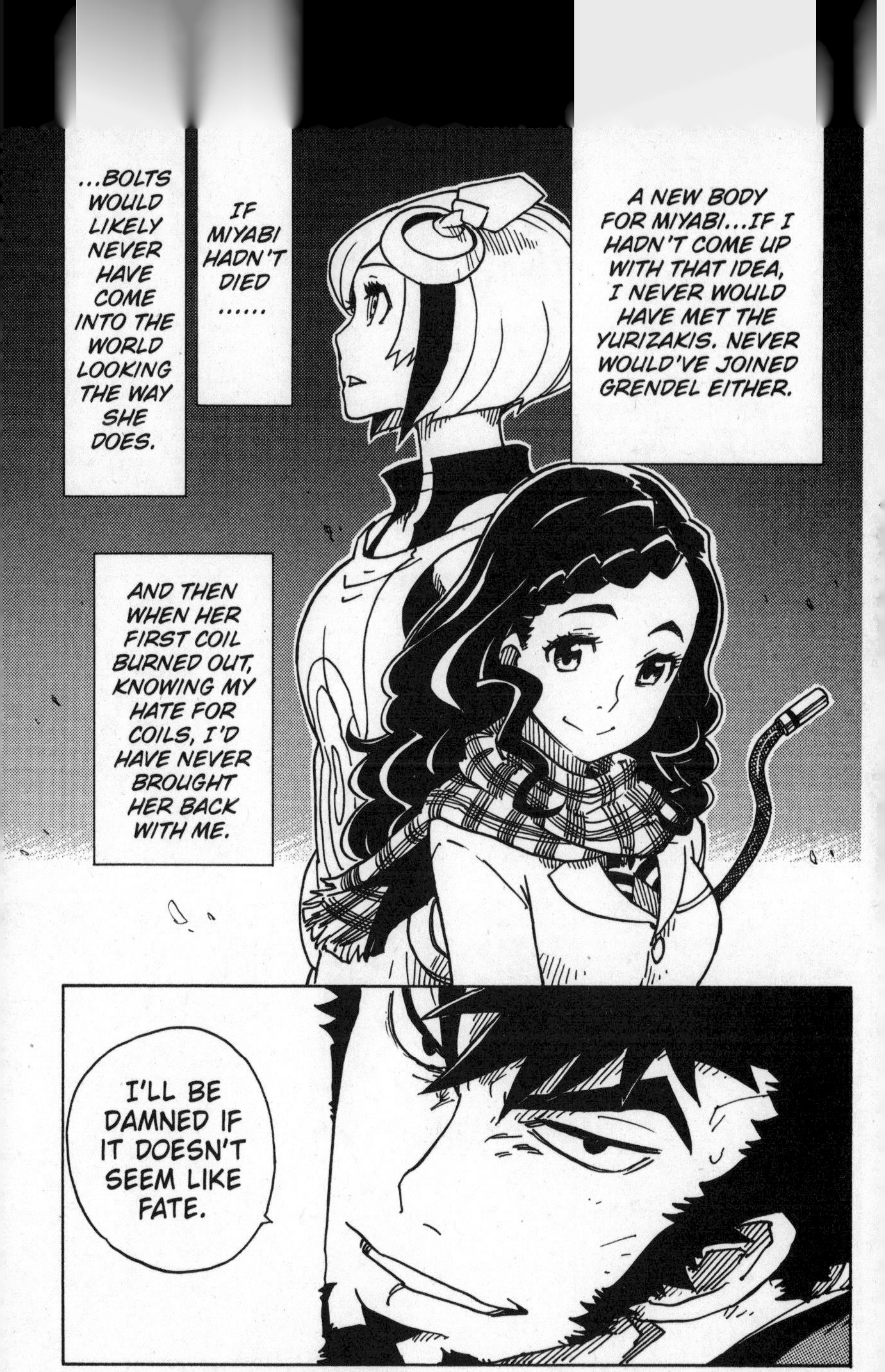
A NEW BODY FOR MIYABI...IF I HADN'T COME UP WITH THAT IDEA, I NEVER WOULD HAVE MET THE YURIZAKIS. NEVER WOULD'VE JOINED GRENDEL EITHER.
IF MIYABI HADN'T DIED ......
...BOLTS WOULD LIKELY NEVER HAVE COME INTO THE WORLD LOOKING THE WAY SHE DOES.
AND THEN WHEN HER FIRST COIL BURNED OUT, KNOWING MY HATE FOR COILS, I'D HAVE NEVER BROUGHT HER BACK WITH ME.
I'LL BE DAMNED IF IT DOESN'T SEEM LIKE FATE.

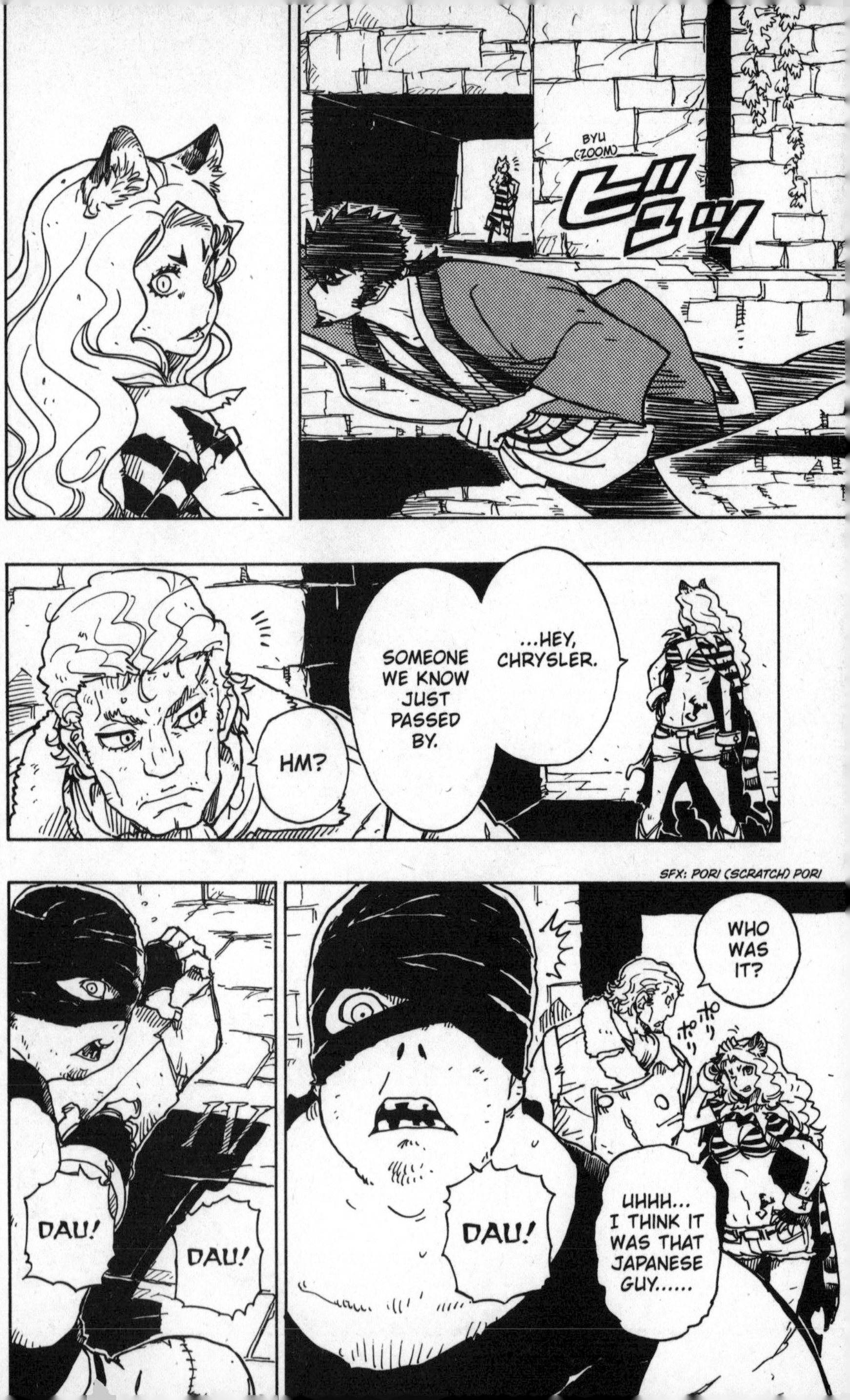
BYU (ZOOM)
...HEY, CHRYSLER.
SOMEONE WE KNOW JUST PASSED BY.
HM?
SFX: PORI (SCRATCH) PORI
WHO WAS IT?
UHHH... I THINK IT WAS THAT JAPANESE GUY......
DAU!
DAU!
DAU!

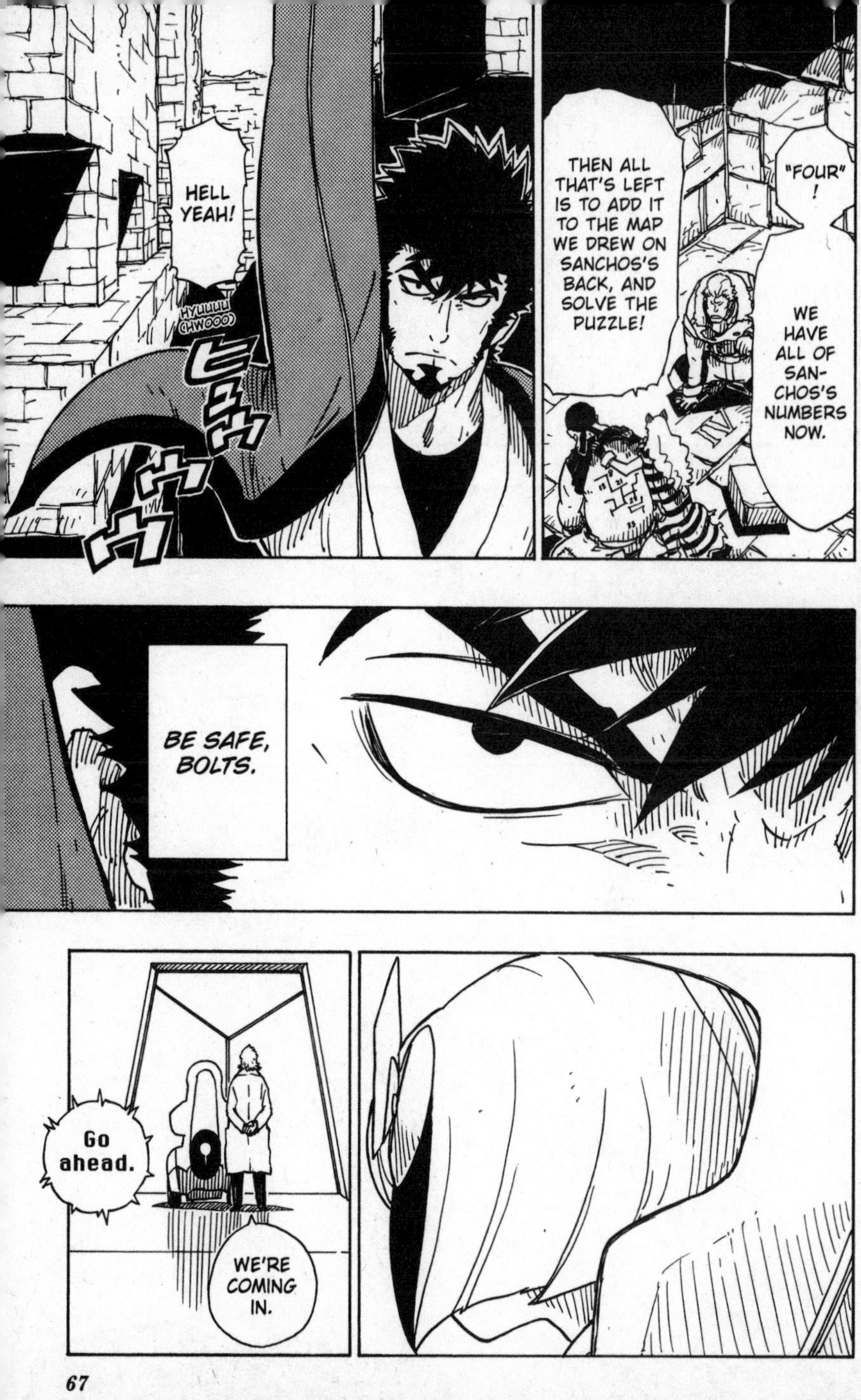
"FOUR"!
WE HAVE ALL OF SAN-CHOS'S NUMBERS NOW.
THEN ALL THAT'S LEFT IS TO ADD IT TO THE MAP WE DREW ON SANCHOS'S BACK, AND SOLVE THE PUZZLE!
HELL YEAH!
HYUUUU (HWOOO)
BE SAFE, BOLTS.
WE'RE COMING IN.
Go ahead.

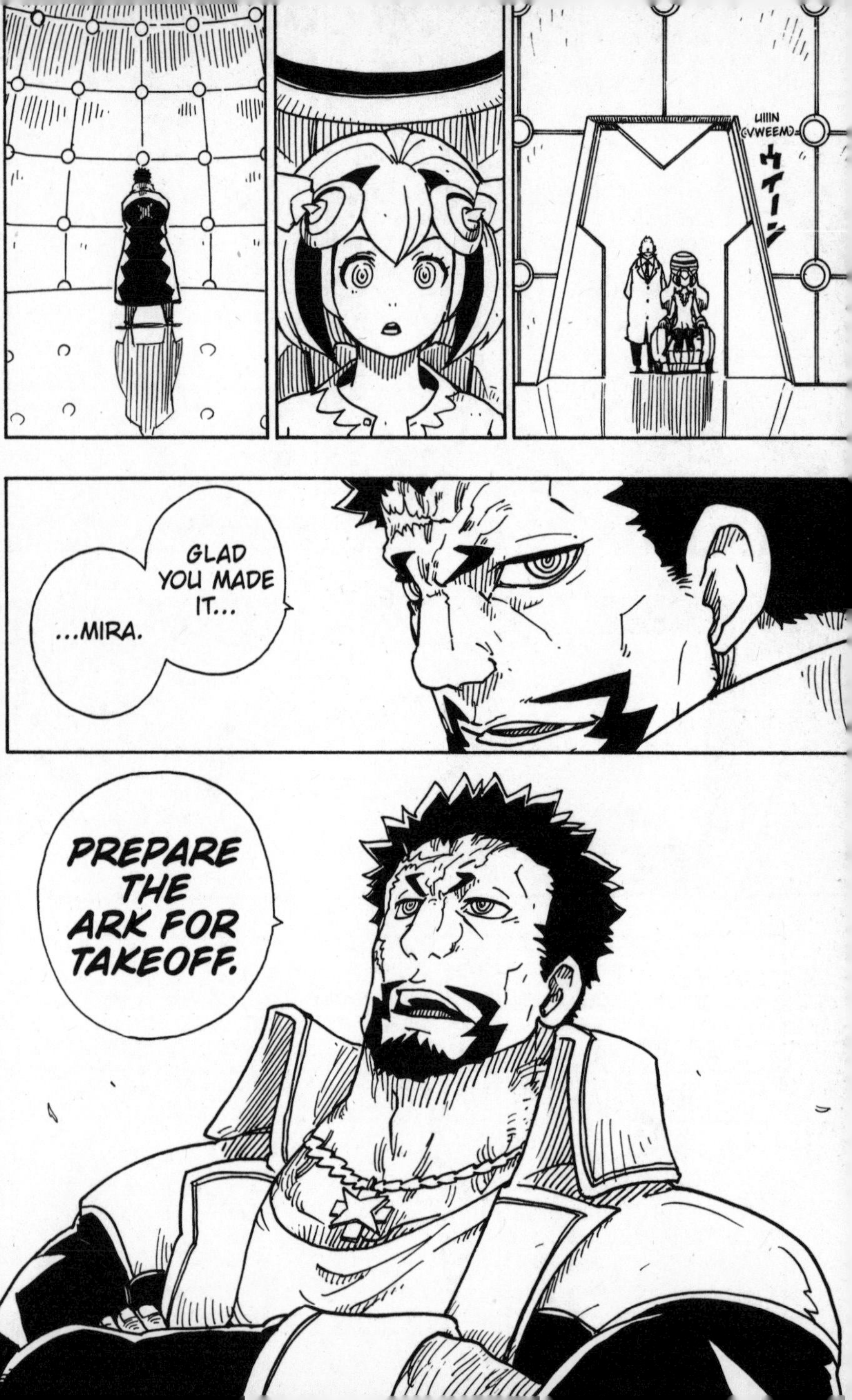
UIIIN (VWEEM)
ウイーン
GLAD YOU MADE IT...
...MIRA.
PREPARE THE ARK FOR TAKEOFF.

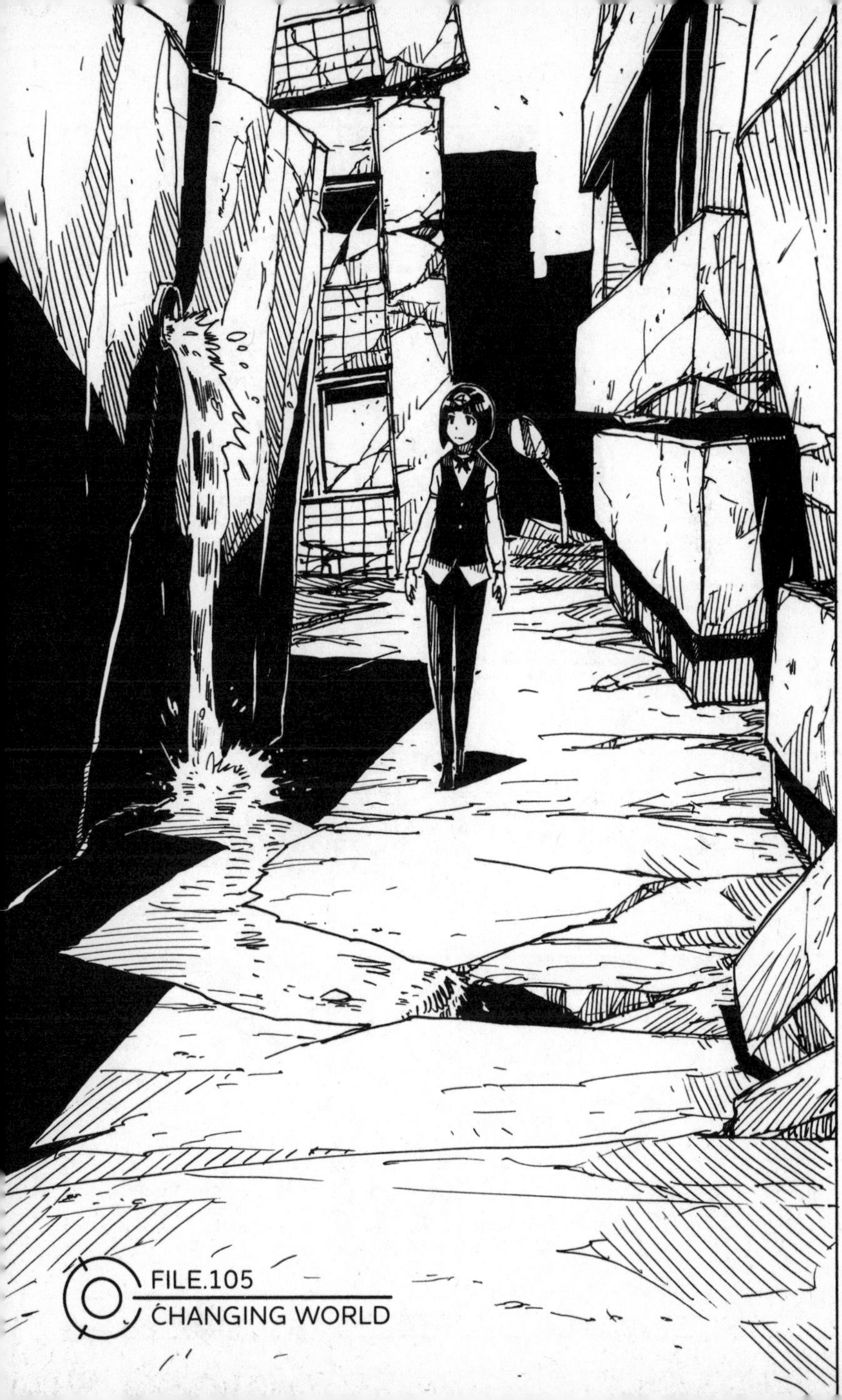
FILE.105
CHANGING WORLD

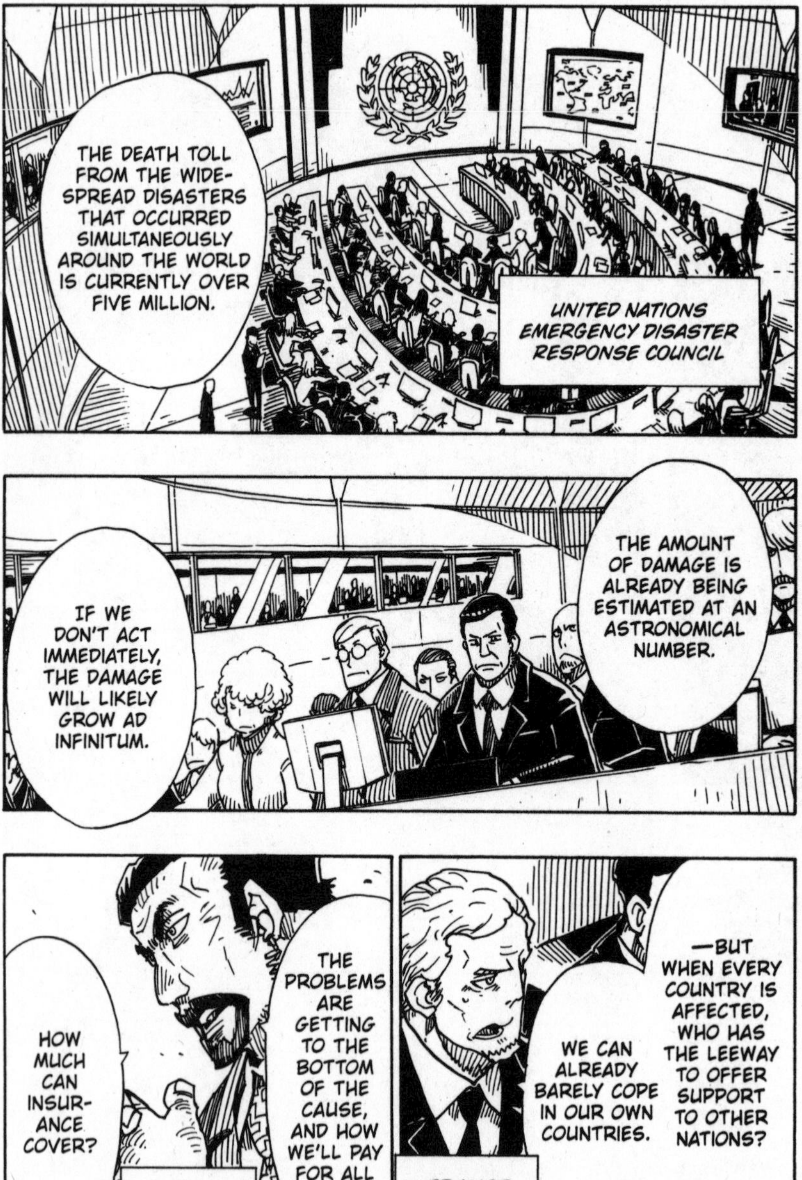
UNITED NATIONS EMERGENCY DISASTER RESPONSE COUNCIL
THE DEATH TOLL FROM THE WIDE-SPREAD DISASTERS THAT OCCURRED SIMULTANEOUSLY AROUND THE WORLD IS CURRENTLY OVER FIVE MILLION.
THE AMOUNT OF DAMAGE IS ALREADY BEING ESTIMATED AT AN ASTRONOMICAL NUMBER.
IF WE DON'T ACT IMMEDIATELY, THE DAMAGE WILL LIKELY GROW AD INFINITUM.
FRANCE
WE CAN ALREADY BARELY COPE IN OUR OWN COUNTRIES.
—BUT WHEN EVERY COUNTRY IS AFFECTED, WHO HAS THE LEEWAY TO OFFER SUPPORT TO OTHER NATIONS?
ITALY
THE PROBLEMS ARE GETTING TO THE BOTTOM OF THE CAUSE, AND HOW WE'LL PAY FOR ALL THIS.
HOW MUCH CAN INSUR-ANCE COVER?

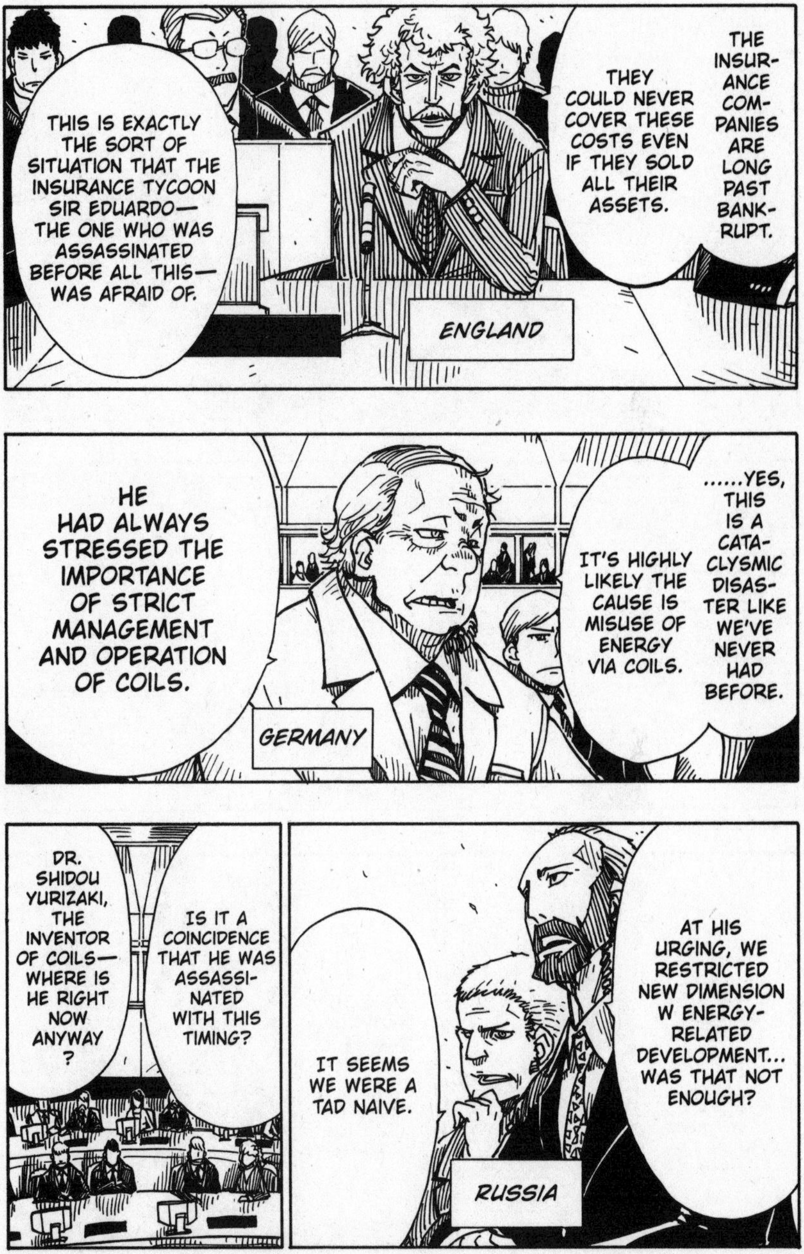
THE INSURANCE COMPANIES ARE LONG PAST BANKRUPT.
THEY COULD NEVER COVER THESE COSTS EVEN IF THEY SOLD ALL THEIR ASSETS.
THIS IS EXACTLY THE SORT OF SITUATION THAT THE INSURANCE TYCOON SIR EDUARDO—THE ONE WHO WAS ASSASSINATED BEFORE ALL THIS—WAS AFRAID OF.
ENGLAND
......YES, THIS IS A CATACLYSMIC DISASTER LIKE WE'VE NEVER HAD BEFORE.
IT'S HIGHLY LIKELY THE CAUSE IS MISUSE OF ENERGY VIA COILS.
HE HAD ALWAYS STRESSED THE IMPORTANCE OF STRICT MANAGEMENT AND OPERATION OF COILS.
GERMANY
AT HIS URGING, WE RESTRICTED NEW DIMENSION W ENERGY-RELATED DEVELOPMENT... WAS THAT NOT ENOUGH?
IT SEEMS WE WERE A TAD NAIVE.
RUSSIA
IS IT A COINCIDENCE THAT HE WAS ASSASSINATED WITH THIS TIMING?
DR. SHIDOU YURIZAKI, THE INVENTOR OF COILS—WHERE IS HE RIGHT NOW ANYWAY?

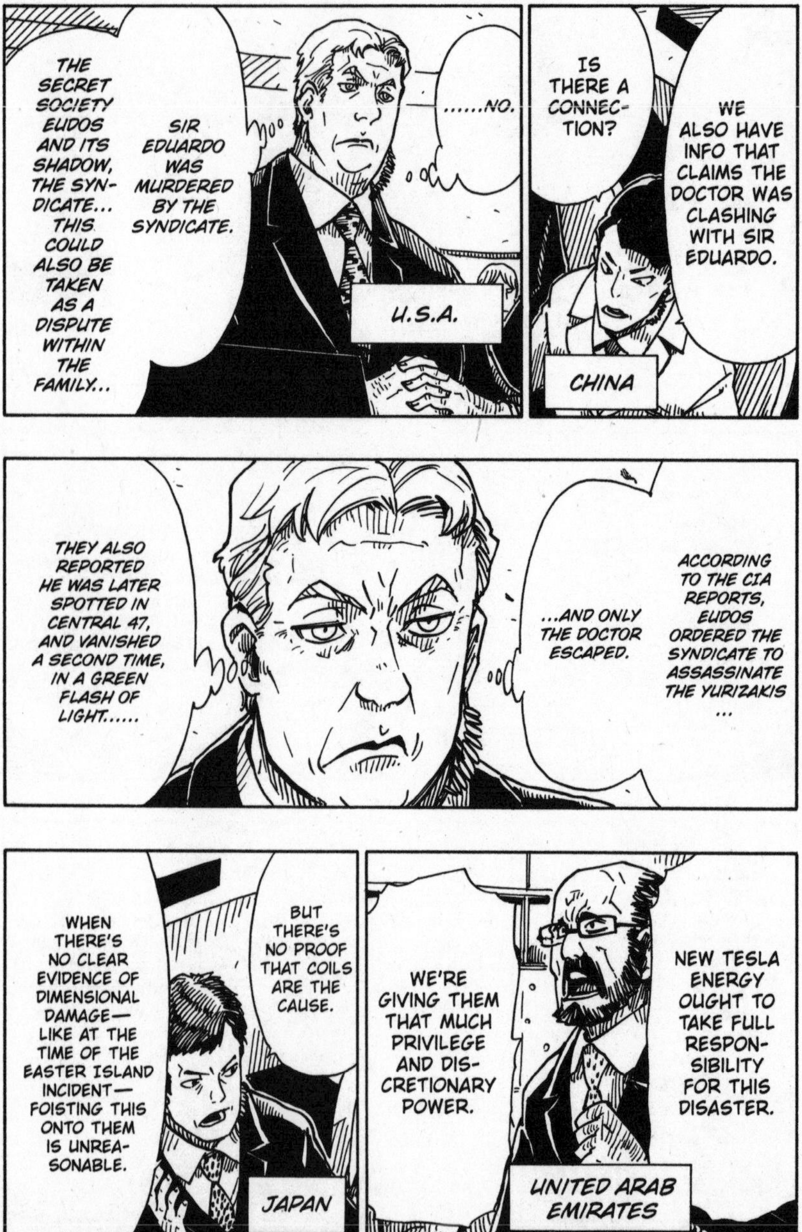
WE ALSO HAVE INFO THAT CLAIMS THE DOCTOR WAS CLASHING WITH SIR EDUARDO.
IS THERE A CONNECTION?
CHINA
......NO.
SIR EDUARDO WAS MURDERED BY THE SYNDICATE.
THE SECRET SOCIETY EUDOS AND ITS SHADOW, THE SYNDICATE... THIS COULD ALSO BE TAKEN AS A DISPUTE WITHIN THE FAMILY...
U.S.A.
ACCORDING TO THE CIA REPORTS, EUDOS ORDERED THE SYNDICATE TO ASSASSINATE THE YURIZAKIS ...
...AND ONLY THE DOCTOR ESCAPED.
THEY ALSO REPORTED HE WAS LATER SPOTTED IN CENTRAL 47, AND VANISHED A SECOND TIME, IN A GREEN FLASH OF LIGHT......
NEW TESLA ENERGY OUGHT TO TAKE FULL RESPONSIBILITY FOR THIS DISASTER.
WE'RE GIVING THEM THAT MUCH PRIVILEGE AND DISCRETIONARY POWER.
UNITED ARAB EMIRATES
BUT THERE'S NO PROOF THAT COILS ARE THE CAUSE.
WHEN THERE'S NO CLEAR EVIDENCE OF DIMENSIONAL DAMAGE—LIKE AT THE TIME OF THE EASTER ISLAND INCIDENT—FOISTING THIS ONTO THEM IS UNREASONABLE.
JAPAN

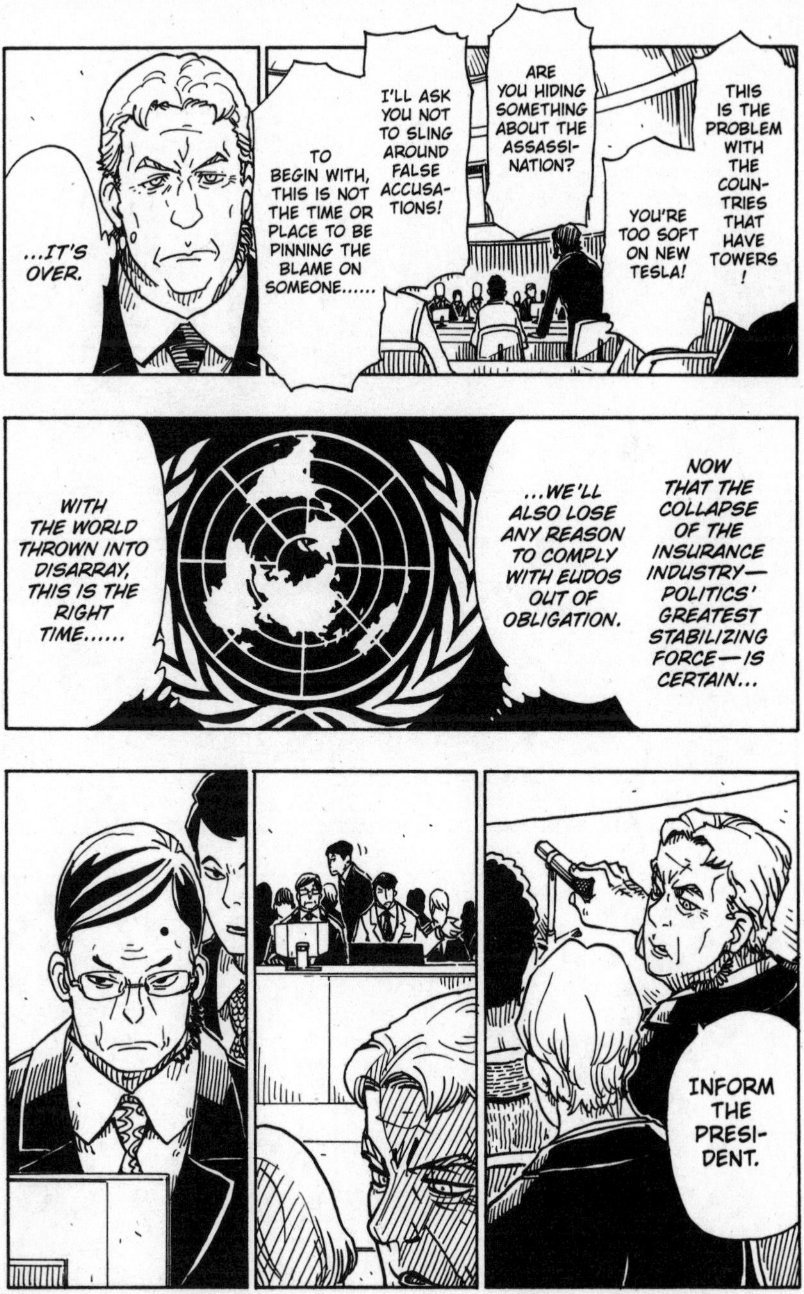
THIS IS THE PROBLEM WITH THE COUNTRIES THAT HAVE TOWERS!
YOU'RE TOO SOFT ON NEW TESLA!
ARE YOU HIDING SOMETHING ABOUT THE ASSASSINATION?
I'LL ASK YOU NOT TO SLING AROUND FALSE ACCUSATIONS!
TO BEGIN WITH, THIS IS NOT THE TIME OR PLACE TO BE PINNING THE BLAME ON SOMEONE......
...IT'S OVER.
NOW THAT THE COLLAPSE OF THE INSURANCE INDUSTRY—POLITICS' GREATEST STABILIZING FORCE—IS CERTAIN...
...WE'LL ALSO LOSE ANY REASON TO COMPLY WITH EUDOS OUT OF OBLIGATION.
WITH THE WORLD THROWN INTO DISARRAY, THIS IS THE RIGHT TIME......
INFORM THE PRESIDENT.

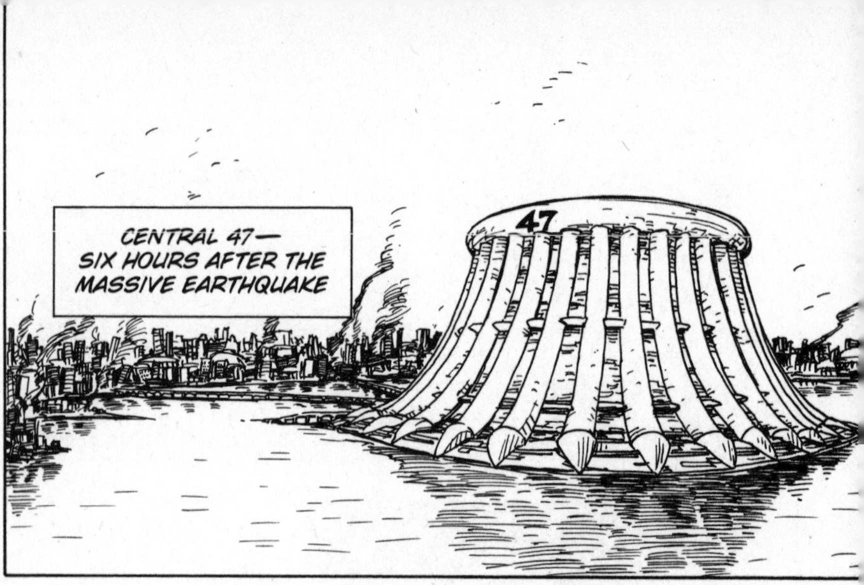
CENTRAL 47—
SIX HOURS AFTER THE
MASSIVE EARTHQUAKE
47

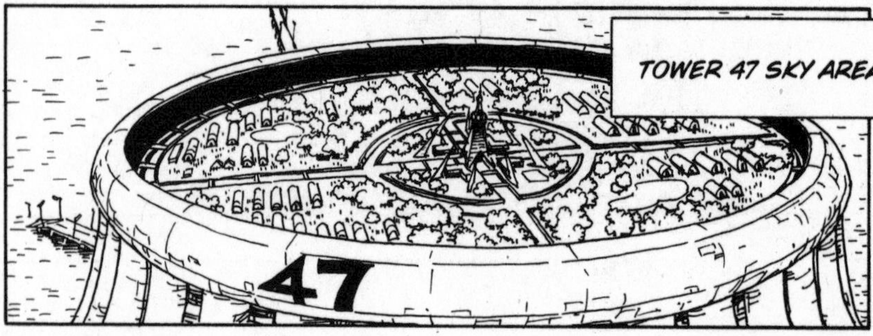
TOWER 47 SKY AREA
47

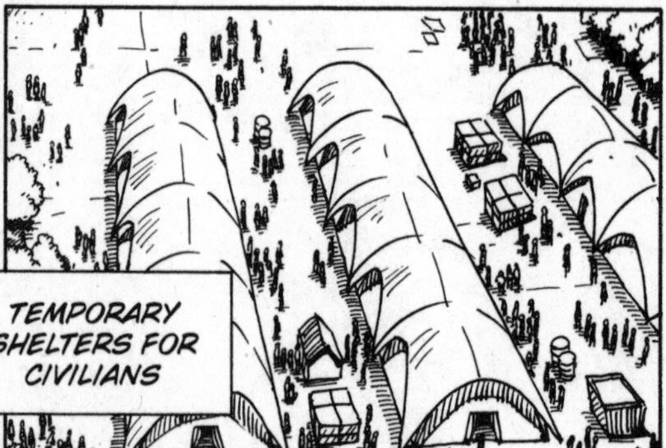
TEMPORARY
SHELTERS FOR
CIVILIANS

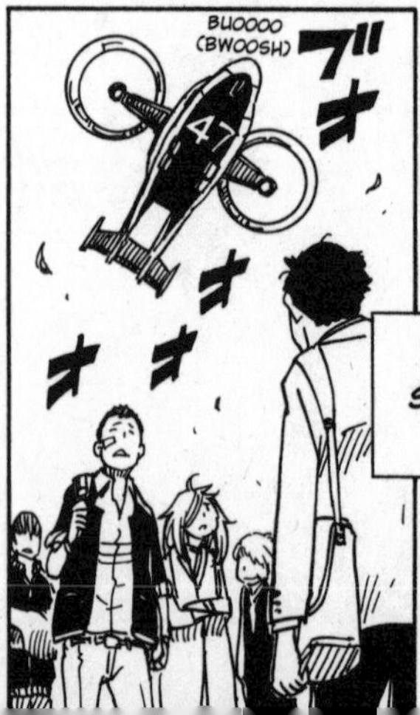
BUOOOO
(BWOOSH)
47

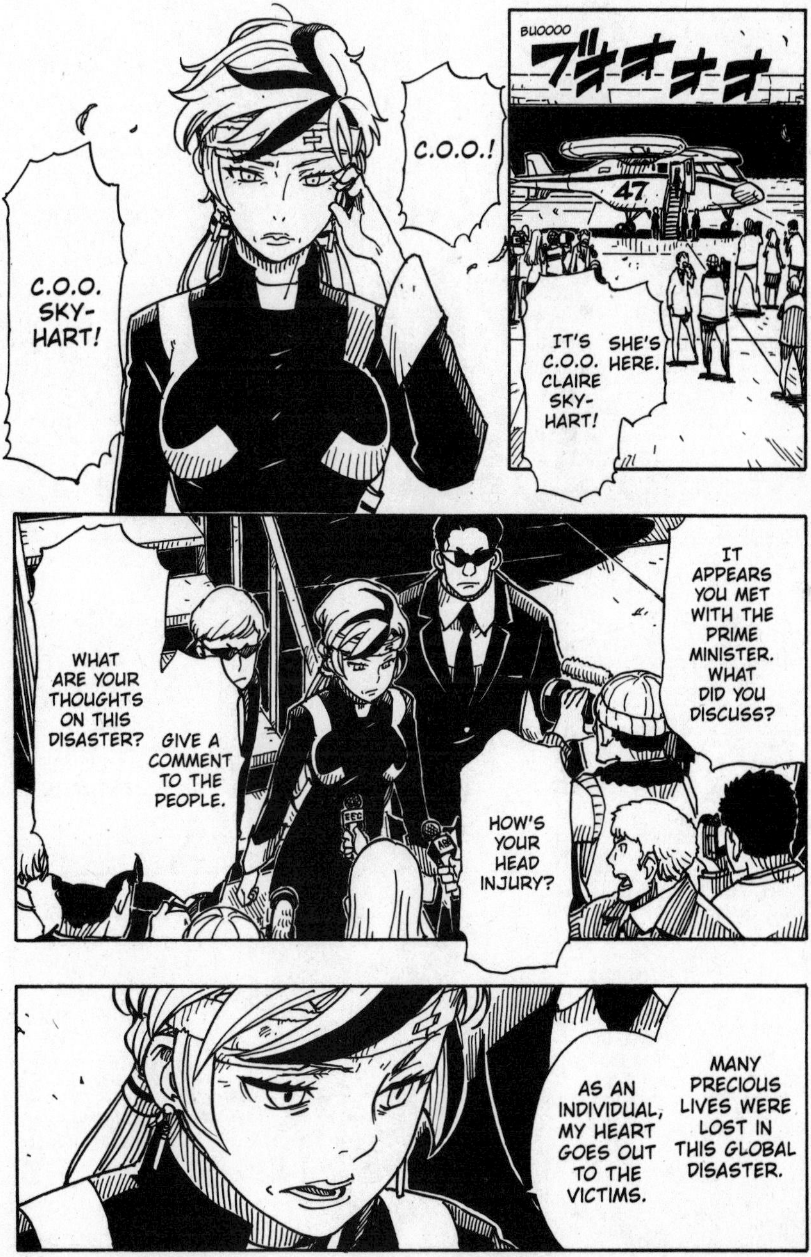
BUOOOO
ブオオオオ
SHE'S HERE.
IT'S C.O.O. CLAIRE SKY-HART!
C.O.O.!
C.O.O. SKY-HART!
IT APPEARS YOU MET WITH THE PRIME MINISTER. WHAT DID YOU DISCUSS?
HOW'S YOUR HEAD INJURY?
GIVE A COMMENT TO THE PEOPLE.
WHAT ARE YOUR THOUGHTS ON THIS DISASTER?
MANY PRECIOUS LIVES WERE LOST IN THIS GLOBAL DISASTER.
AS AN INDIVIDUAL, MY HEART GOES OUT TO THE VICTIMS.

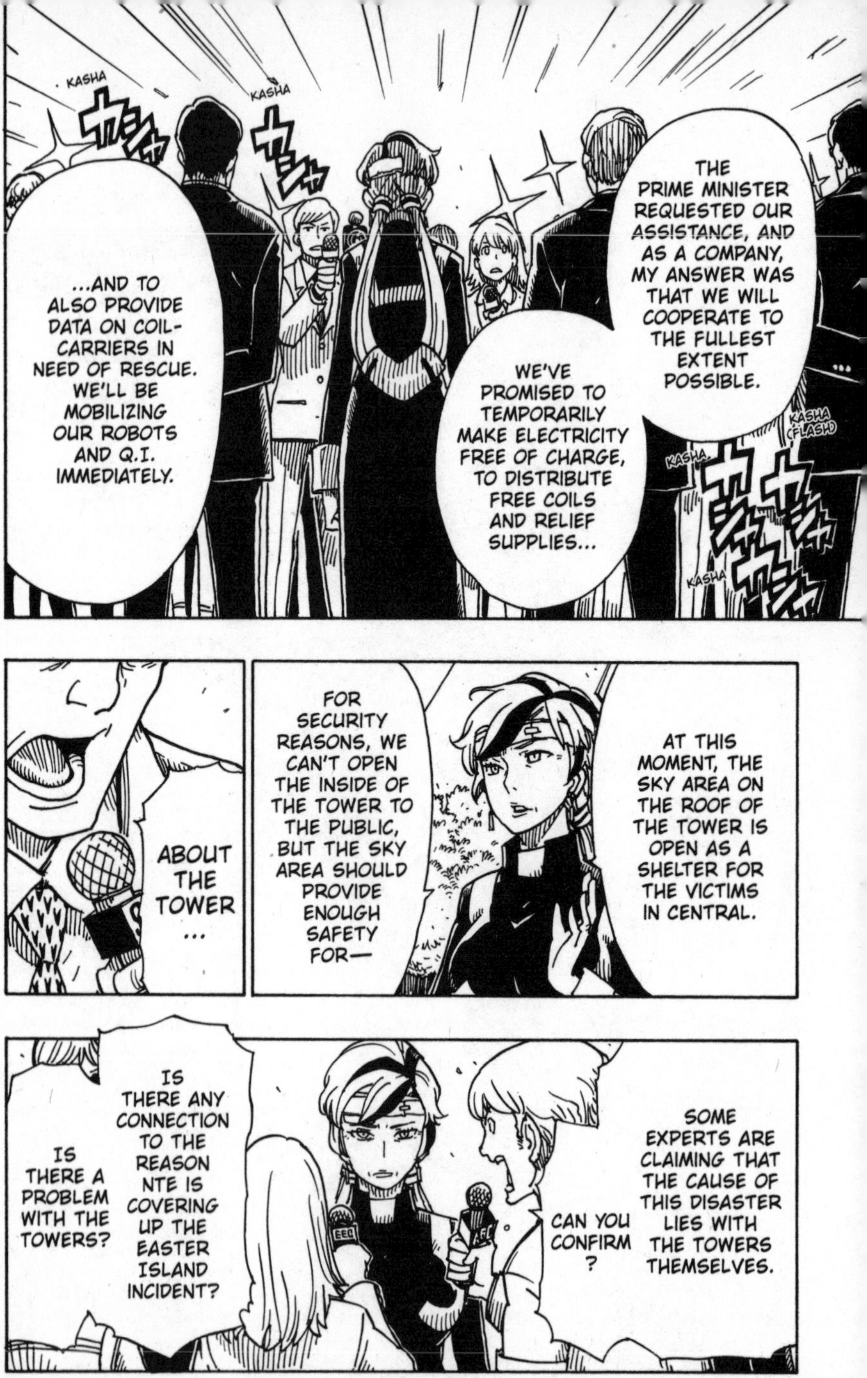
KASHA (FLASH)
KASHA
KASHA
THE PRIME MINISTER REQUESTED OUR ASSISTANCE, AND AS A COMPANY, MY ANSWER WAS THAT WE WILL COOPERATE TO THE FULLEST EXTENT POSSIBLE.
WE'VE PROMISED TO TEMPORARILY MAKE ELECTRICITY FREE OF CHARGE, TO DISTRIBUTE FREE COILS AND RELIEF SUPPLIES...
KASHA
KASHA
...AND TO ALSO PROVIDE DATA ON COIL-CARRIERS IN NEED OF RESCUE. WE'LL BE MOBILIZING OUR ROBOTS AND Q.I. IMMEDIATELY.
AT THIS MOMENT, THE SKY AREA ON THE ROOF OF THE TOWER IS OPEN AS A SHELTER FOR THE VICTIMS IN CENTRAL.
FOR SECURITY REASONS, WE CAN'T OPEN THE INSIDE OF THE TOWER TO THE PUBLIC, BUT THE SKY AREA SHOULD PROVIDE ENOUGH SAFETY FOR—
ABOUT THE TOWER...
SOME EXPERTS ARE CLAIMING THAT THE CAUSE OF THIS DISASTER LIES WITH THE TOWERS THEMSELVES.
CAN YOU CONFIRM?
IS THERE ANY CONNECTION TO THE REASON NTE IS COVERING UP THE EASTER ISLAND INCIDENT?
IS THERE A PROBLEM WITH THE TOWERS?

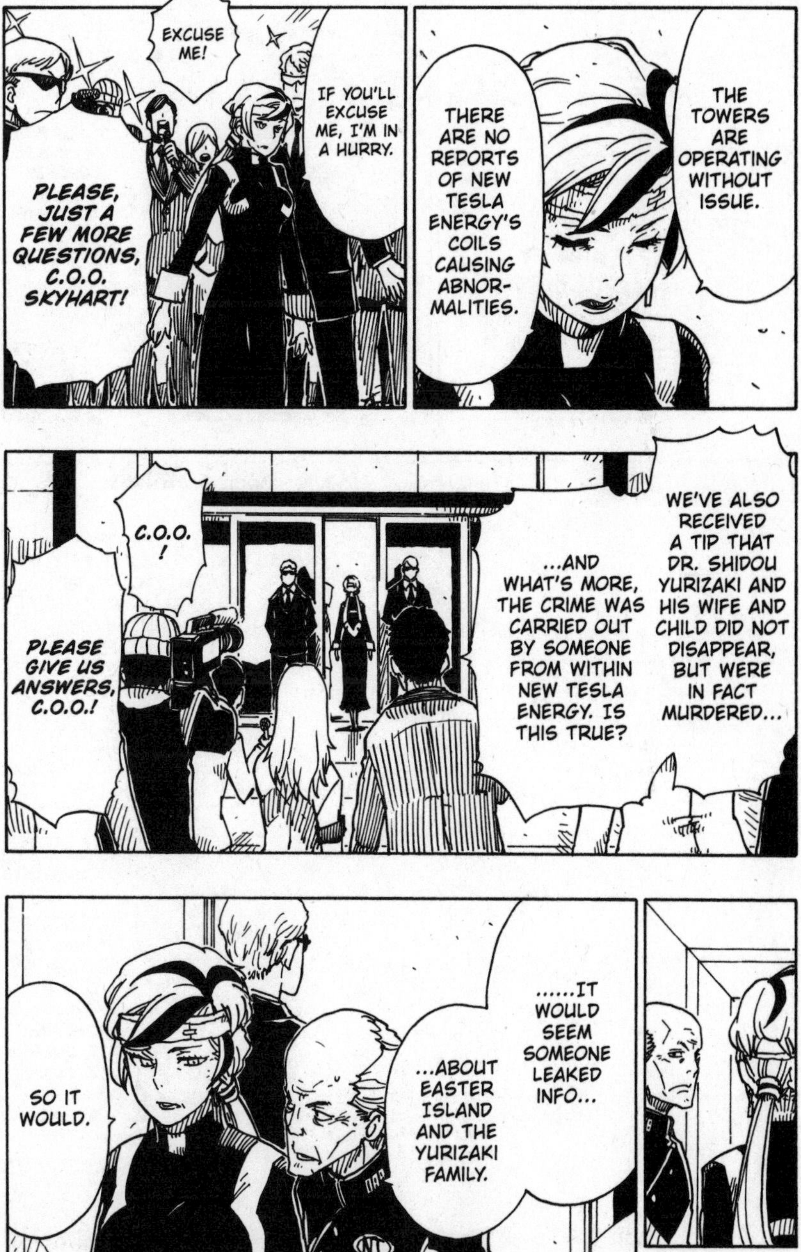
THE TOWERS ARE OPERATING WITHOUT ISSUE.
THERE ARE NO REPORTS OF NEW TESLA ENERGY'S COILS CAUSING ABNOR-MALITIES.
IF YOU'LL EXCUSE ME, I'M IN A HURRY.
EXCUSE ME!
PLEASE, JUST A FEW MORE QUESTIONS, C.O.O. SKYHART!
WE'VE ALSO RECEIVED A TIP THAT DR. SHIDOU YURIZAKI AND HIS WIFE AND CHILD DID NOT DISAPPEAR, BUT WERE IN FACT MURDERED...
...AND WHAT'S MORE, THE CRIME WAS CARRIED OUT BY SOMEONE FROM WITHIN NEW TESLA ENERGY. IS THIS TRUE?
C.O.O. !
PLEASE GIVE US ANSWERS, C.O.O.!
......IT WOULD SEEM SOMEONE LEAKED INFO...
...ABOUT EASTER ISLAND AND THE YURIZAKI FAMILY.
SO IT WOULD.

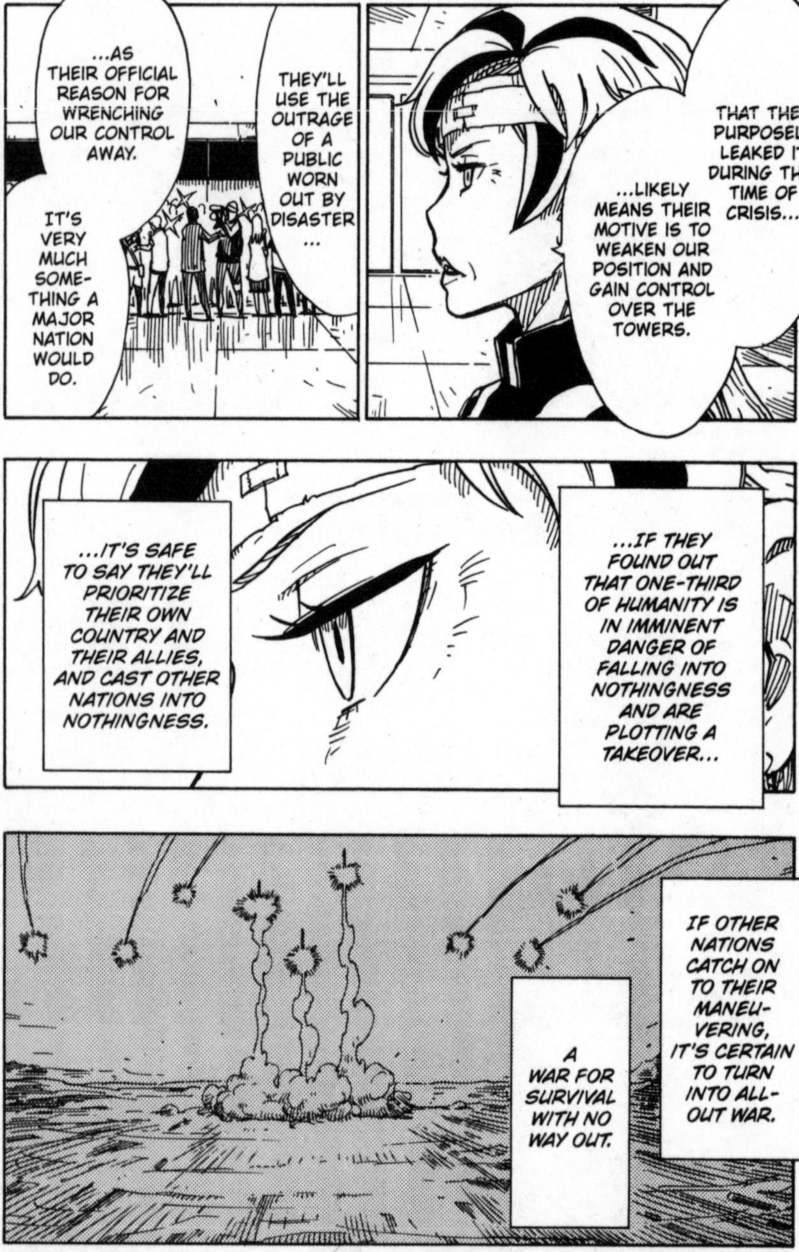
THAT THEY PURPOSELY LEAKED IT DURING THIS TIME OF CRISIS...
...LIKELY MEANS THEIR MOTIVE IS TO WEAKEN OUR POSITION AND GAIN CONTROL OVER THE TOWERS.
THEY'LL USE THE OUTRAGE OF A PUBLIC WORN OUT BY DISASTER...
...AS THEIR OFFICIAL REASON FOR WRENCHING OUR CONTROL AWAY.
IT'S VERY MUCH SOME-THING A MAJOR NATION WOULD DO.
...IF THEY FOUND OUT THAT ONE-THIRD OF HUMANITY IS IN IMMINENT DANGER OF FALLING INTO NOTHINGNESS AND ARE PLOTTING A TAKEOVER...
...IT'S SAFE TO SAY THEY'LL PRIORITIZE THEIR OWN COUNTRY AND THEIR ALLIES, AND CAST OTHER NATIONS INTO NOTHINGNESS.
IF OTHER NATIONS CATCH ON TO THEIR MANEU-VERING, IT'S CERTAIN TO TURN INTO ALL-OUT WAR.
A WAR FOR SURVIVAL WITH NO WAY OUT.

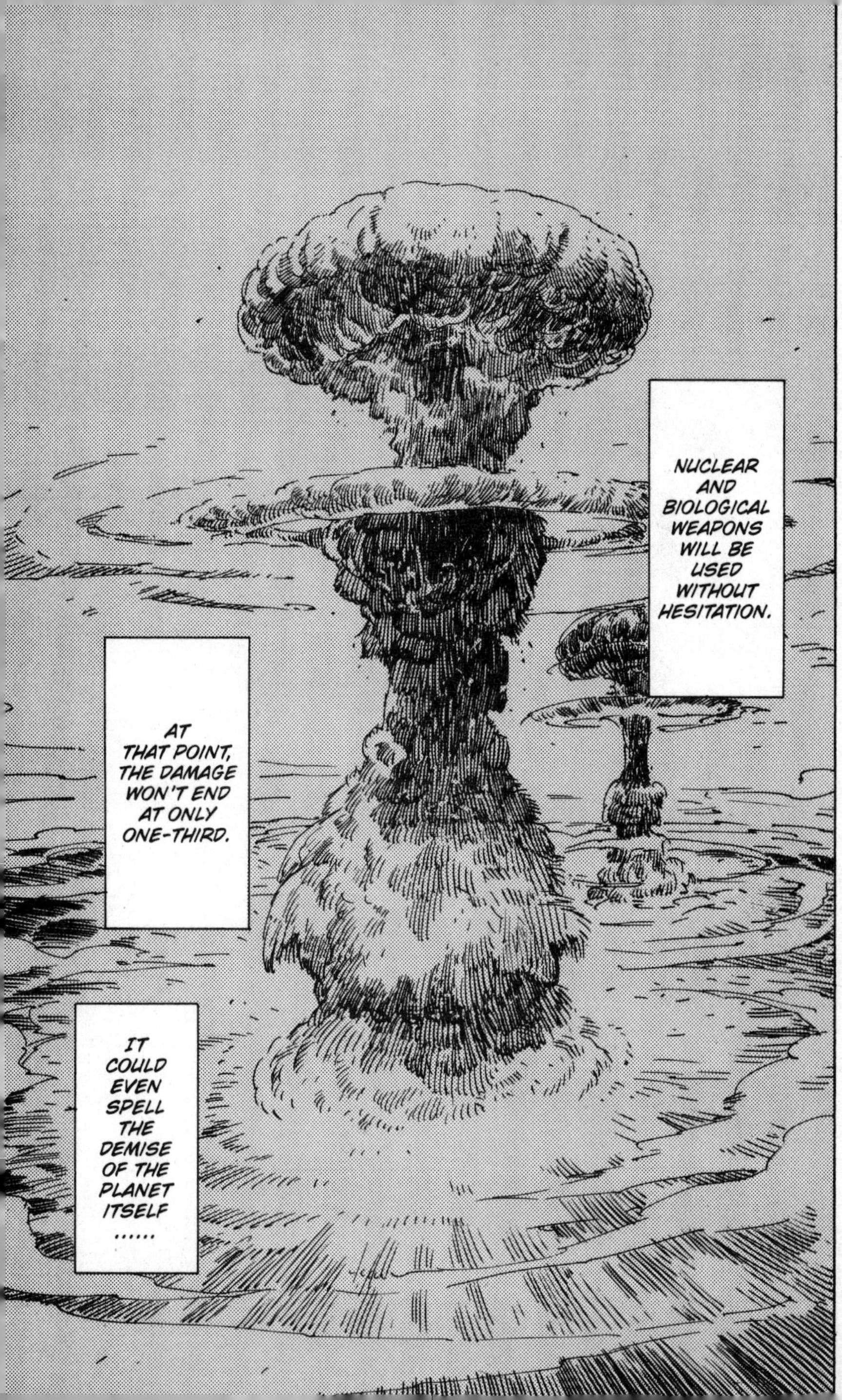
NUCLEAR AND BIOLOGICAL WEAPONS WILL BE USED WITHOUT HESITATION.
AT THAT POINT, THE DAMAGE WON'T END AT ONLY ONE-THIRD.
IT COULD EVEN SPELL THE DEMISE OF THE PLANET ITSELF ......

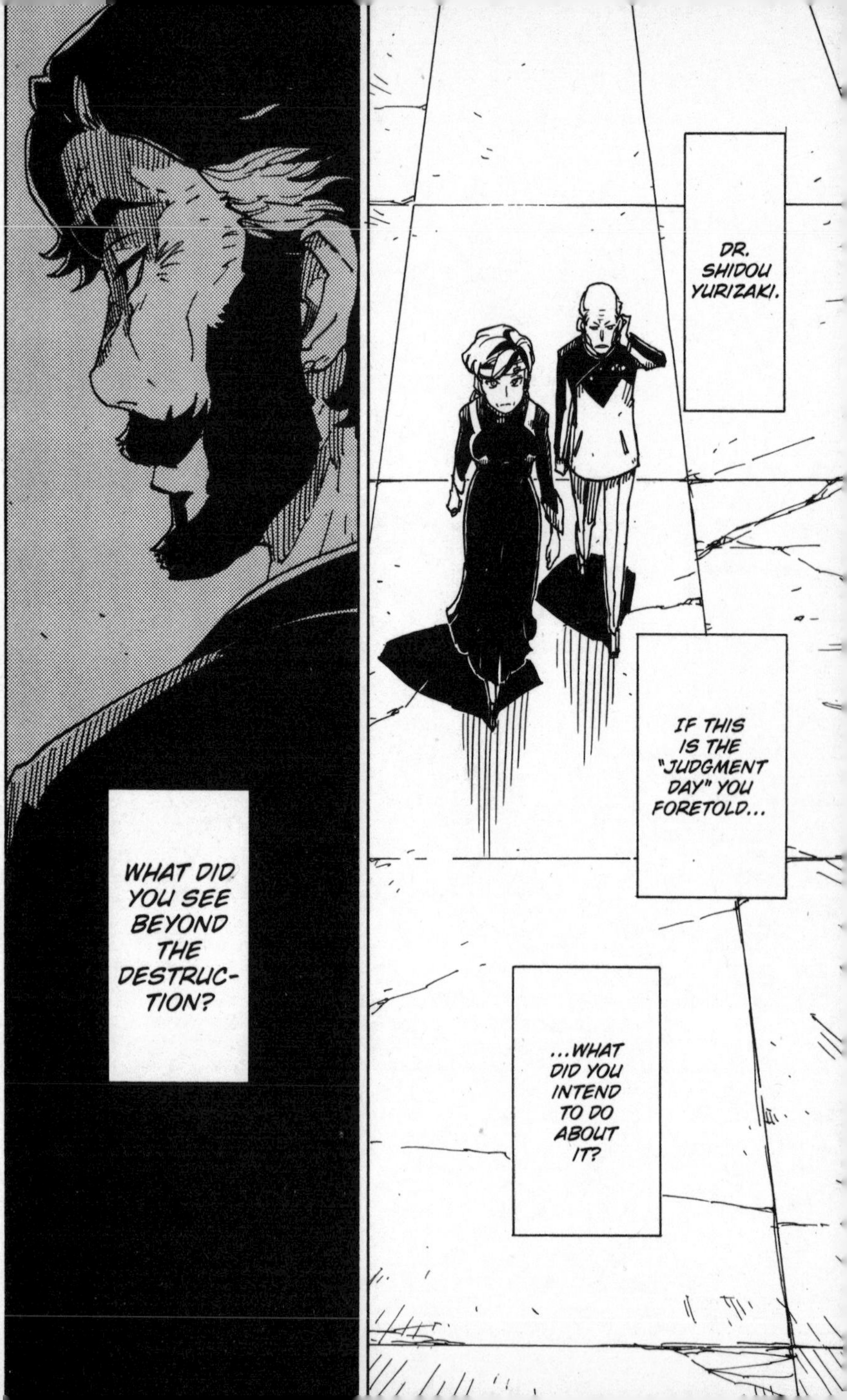
DR. SHIDOU YURIZAKI.
IF THIS IS THE "JUDGMENT DAY" YOU FORETOLD...
...WHAT DID YOU INTEND TO DO ABOUT IT?
WHAT DID YOU SEE BEYOND THE DESTRUCTION?

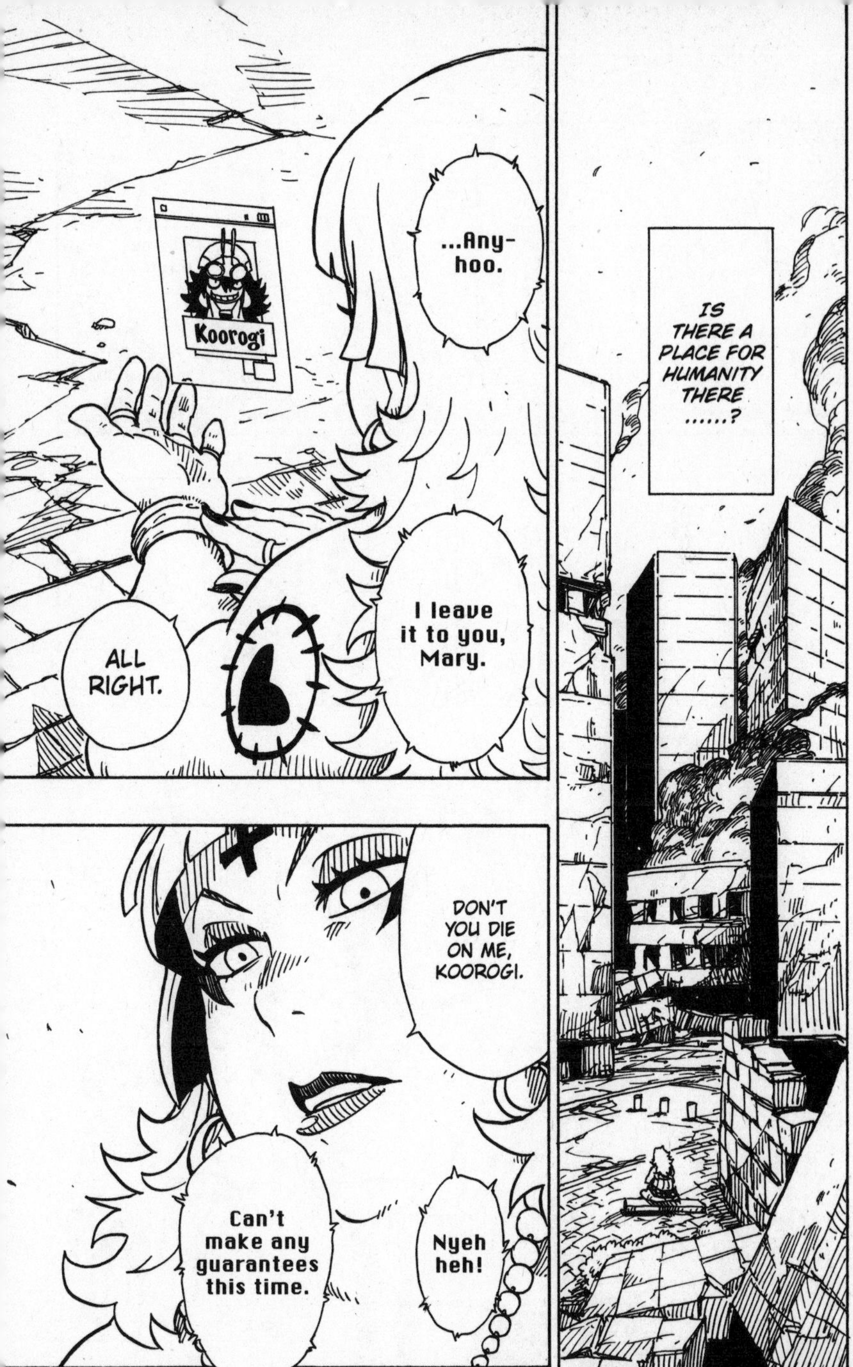
IS THERE A PLACE FOR HUMANITY THERE ......?
...Any-hoo.
I leave it to you, Mary.
Koorogi
ALL RIGHT.
DON'T YOU DIE ON ME, KOOROGI.
Nyeh heh!
Can't make any guarantees this time.

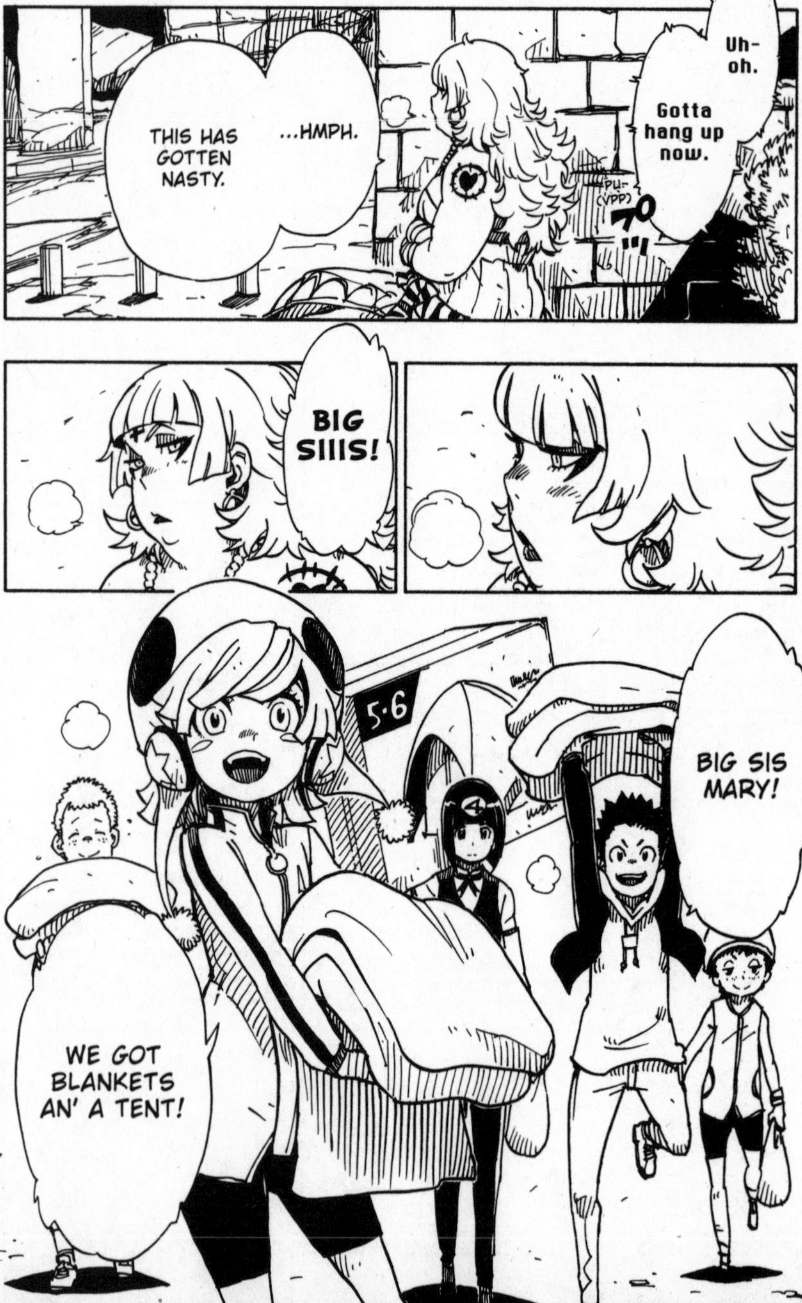
Uh-oh.
Gotta hang up now.
PU-(VPP)
...HMPH.
THIS HAS GOTTEN NASTY.
BIG SIIIS!
BIG SIS MARY!
5·6
WE GOT BLANKETS AN' A TENT!

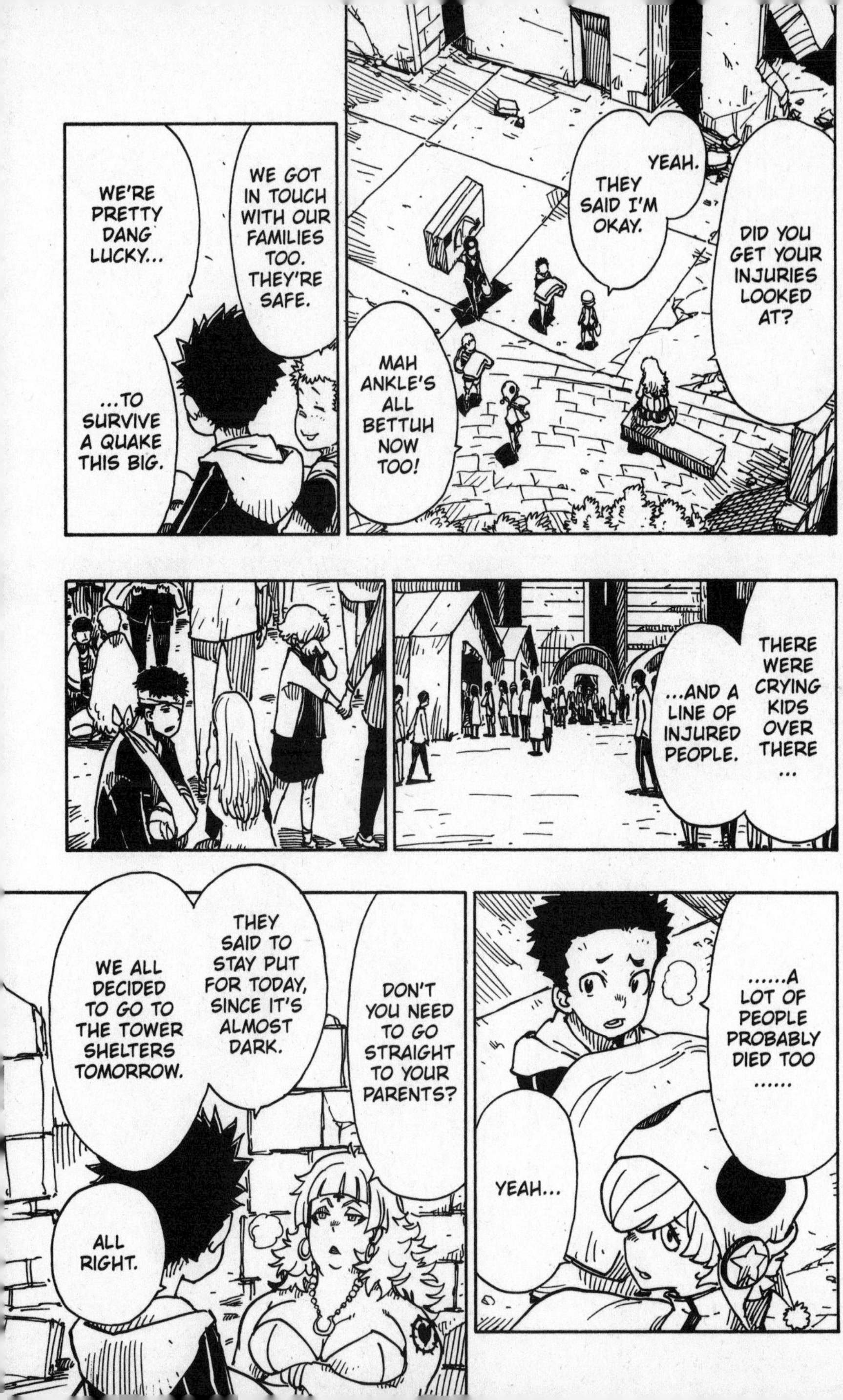
DID YOU GET YOUR INJURIES LOOKED AT?
YEAH. THEY SAID I'M OKAY.
MAH ANKLE'S ALL BETTUH NOW TOO!
WE GOT IN TOUCH WITH OUR FAMILIES TOO. THEY'RE SAFE.
WE'RE PRETTY DANG LUCKY...
...TO SURVIVE A QUAKE THIS BIG.
THERE WERE CRYING KIDS OVER THERE...
...AND A LINE OF INJURED PEOPLE.
......A LOT OF PEOPLE PROBABLY DIED TOO......
YEAH...
DON'T YOU NEED TO GO STRAIGHT TO YOUR PARENTS?
THEY SAID TO STAY PUT FOR TODAY, SINCE IT'S ALMOST DARK.
WE ALL DECIDED TO GO TO THE TOWER SHELTERS TOMORROW.
ALL RIGHT.

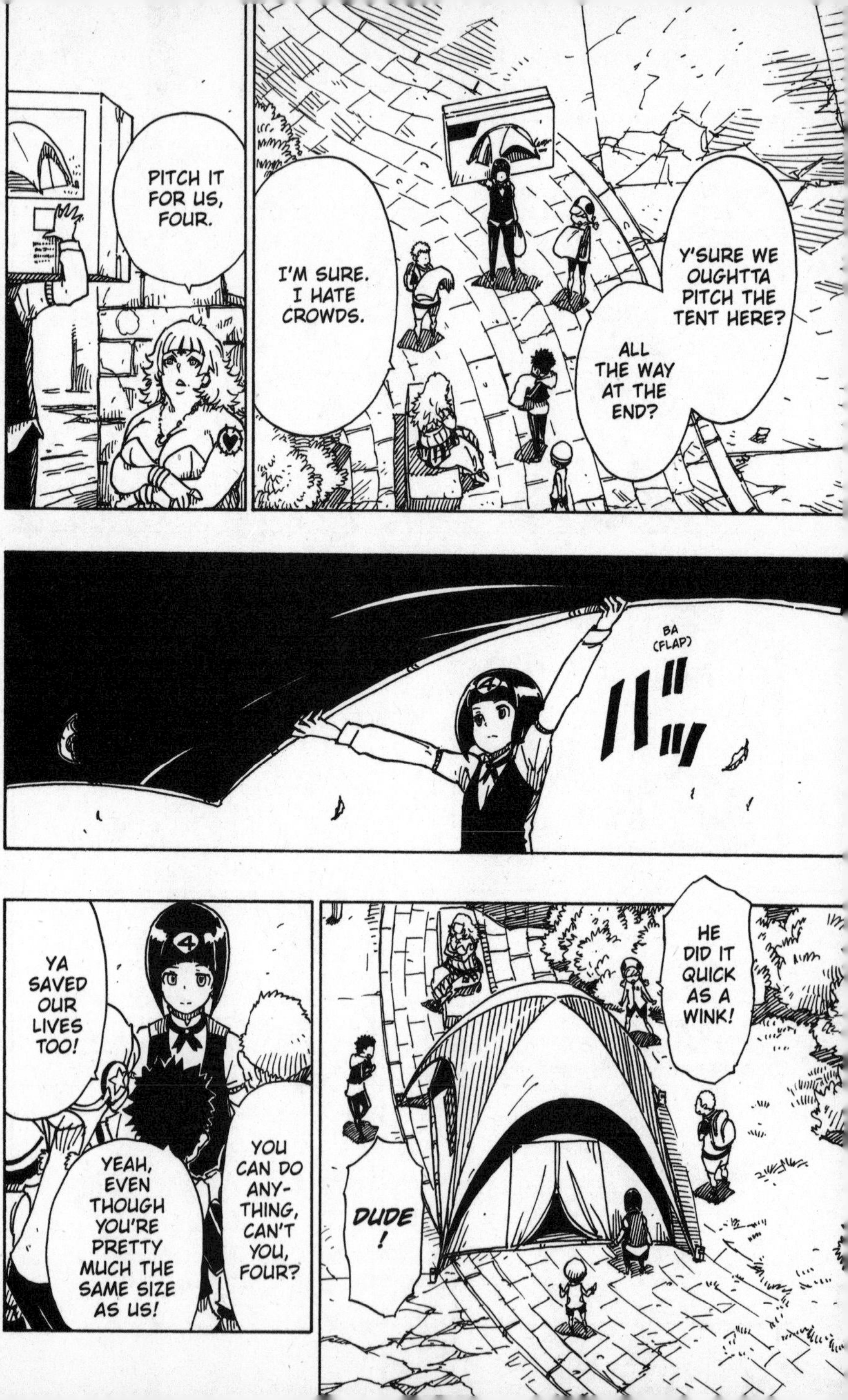
Y'SURE WE OUGHTTA PITCH THE TENT HERE?
ALL THE WAY AT THE END?
I'M SURE. I HATE CROWDS.
PITCH IT FOR US, FOUR.
BA (FLAP)
HE DID IT QUICK AS A WINK!
DUDE!
YA SAVED OUR LIVES TOO!
YOU CAN DO ANY-THING, CAN'T YOU, FOUR?
YEAH, EVEN THOUGH YOU'RE PRETTY MUCH THE SAME SIZE AS US!

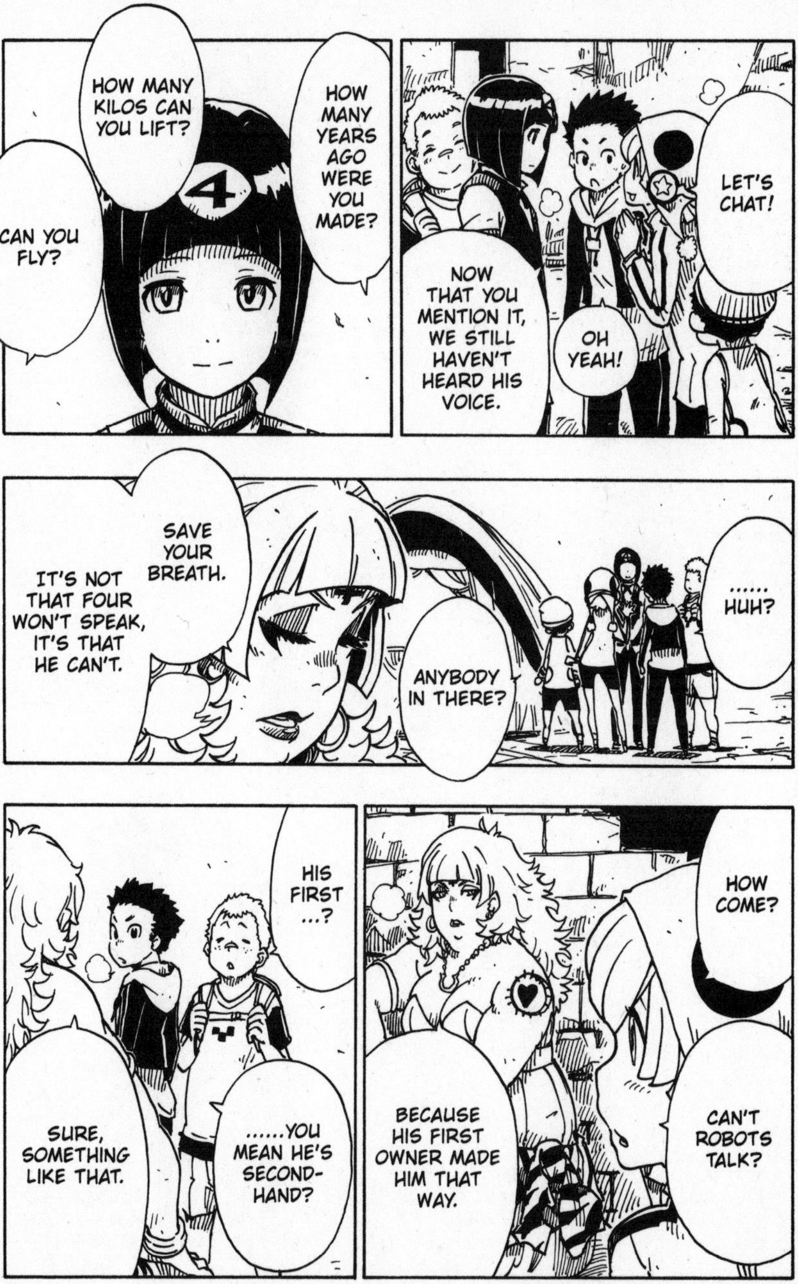
LET'S CHAT!
OH YEAH!
NOW THAT YOU MENTION IT, WE STILL HAVEN'T HEARD HIS VOICE.
HOW MANY YEARS AGO WERE YOU MADE?
HOW MANY KILOS CAN YOU LIFT?
CAN YOU FLY?
...... HUH?
ANYBODY IN THERE?
SAVE YOUR BREATH.
IT'S NOT THAT FOUR WON'T SPEAK, IT'S THAT HE CAN'T.
HOW COME?
CAN'T ROBOTS TALK?
BECAUSE HIS FIRST OWNER MADE HIM THAT WAY.
HIS FIRST ...?
......YOU MEAN HE'S SECOND-HAND?
SURE, SOMETHING LIKE THAT.

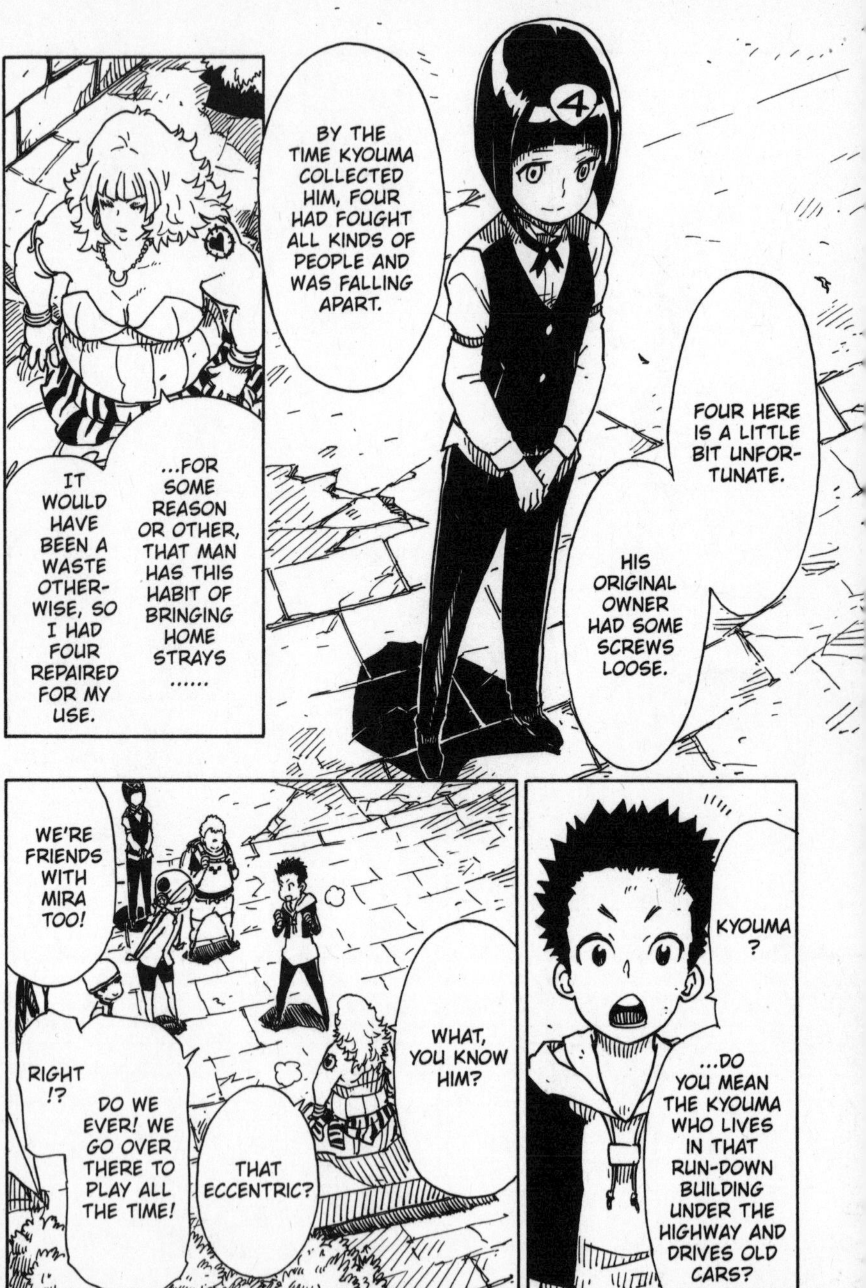
FOUR HERE IS A LITTLE BIT UNFORTUNATE.
HIS ORIGINAL OWNER HAD SOME SCREWS LOOSE.
BY THE TIME KYOUMA COLLECTED HIM, FOUR HAD FOUGHT ALL KINDS OF PEOPLE AND WAS FALLING APART.
...FOR SOME REASON OR OTHER, THAT MAN HAS THIS HABIT OF BRINGING HOME STRAYS......
IT WOULD HAVE BEEN A WASTE OTHERWISE, SO I HAD FOUR REPAIRED FOR MY USE.
KYOUMA?
...DO YOU MEAN THE KYOUMA WHO LIVES IN THAT RUN-DOWN BUILDING UNDER THE HIGHWAY AND DRIVES OLD CARS?
WHAT, YOU KNOW HIM?
THAT ECCENTRIC?
DO WE EVER! WE GO OVER THERE TO PLAY ALL THE TIME!
RIGHT!?
WE'RE FRIENDS WITH MIRA TOO!

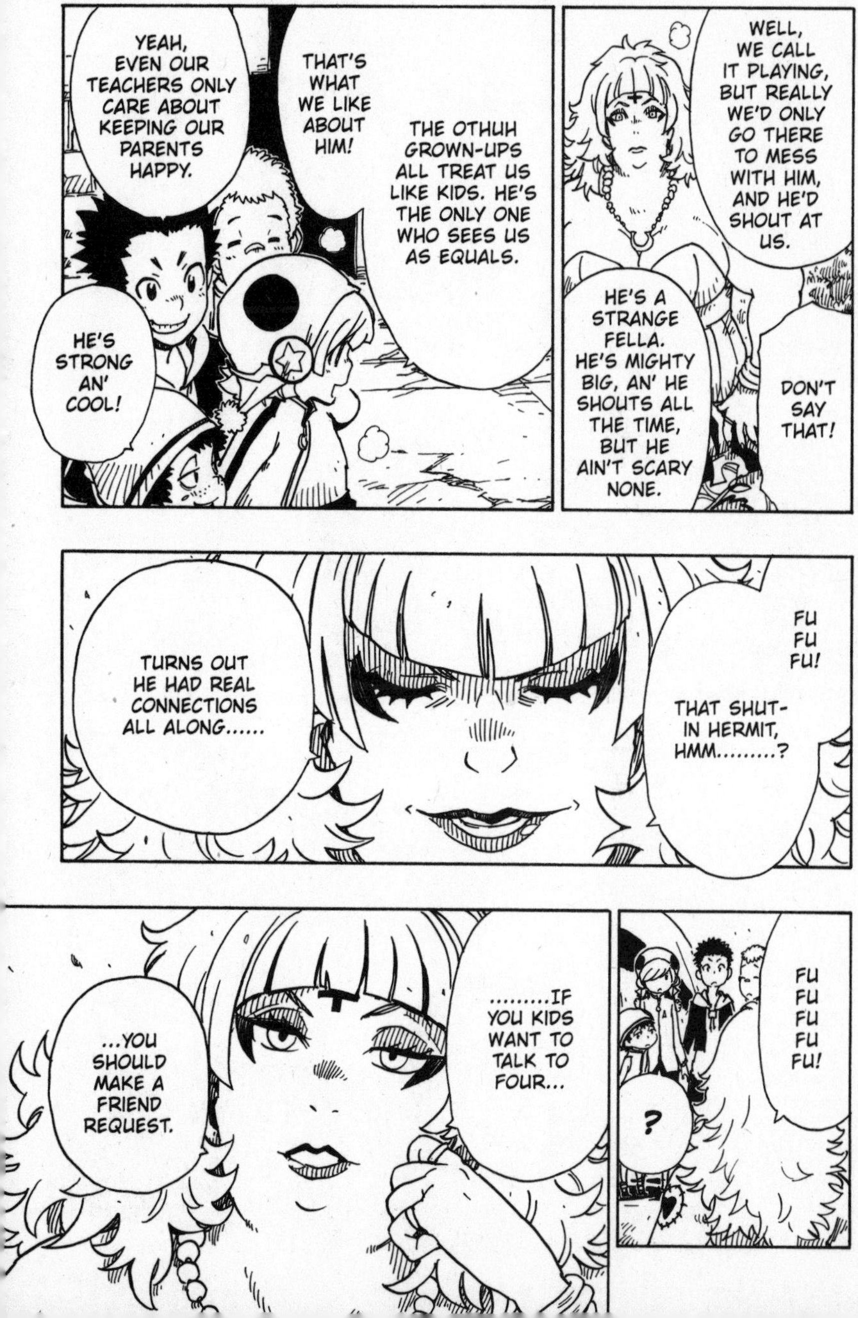
WELL, WE CALL IT PLAYING, BUT REALLY WE'D ONLY GO THERE TO MESS WITH HIM, AND HE'D SHOUT AT US.
HE'S A STRANGE FELLA. HE'S MIGHTY BIG, AN' HE SHOUTS ALL THE TIME, BUT HE AIN'T SCARY NONE.
DON'T SAY THAT!
THE OTHUH GROWN-UPS ALL TREAT US LIKE KIDS. HE'S THE ONLY ONE WHO SEES US AS EQUALS.
THAT'S WHAT WE LIKE ABOUT HIM!
YEAH, EVEN OUR TEACHERS ONLY CARE ABOUT KEEPING OUR PARENTS HAPPY.
HE'S STRONG AN' COOL!
FU FU FU!
THAT SHUT-IN HERMIT, HMM.........?
TURNS OUT HE HAD REAL CONNECTIONS ALL ALONG......
FU FU FU FU FU!
?
.........IF YOU KIDS WANT TO TALK TO FOUR...
...YOU SHOULD MAKE A FRIEND REQUEST.

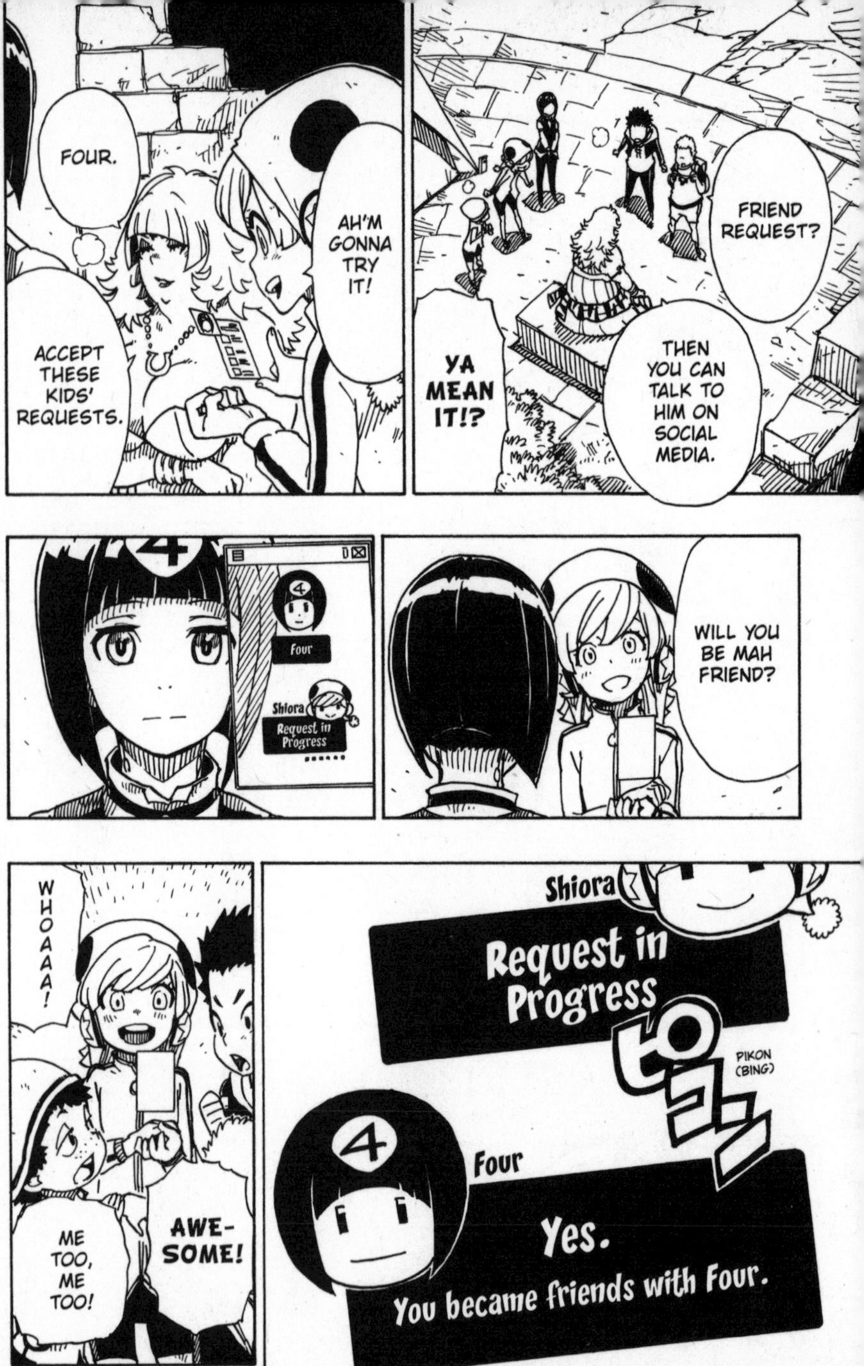
FRIEND REQUEST?
THEN YOU CAN TALK TO HIM ON SOCIAL MEDIA.
YA MEAN IT!?
AH'M GONNA TRY IT!
FOUR.
ACCEPT THESE KIDS' REQUESTS.
WILL YOU BE MAH FRIEND?
Four
Shiora
Request in Progress
Shiora
Request in Progress
PIKON (BING)
Four
Yes.
You became friends with Four.
WHOAAAA!
AWE-SOME!
ME TOO, ME TOO!

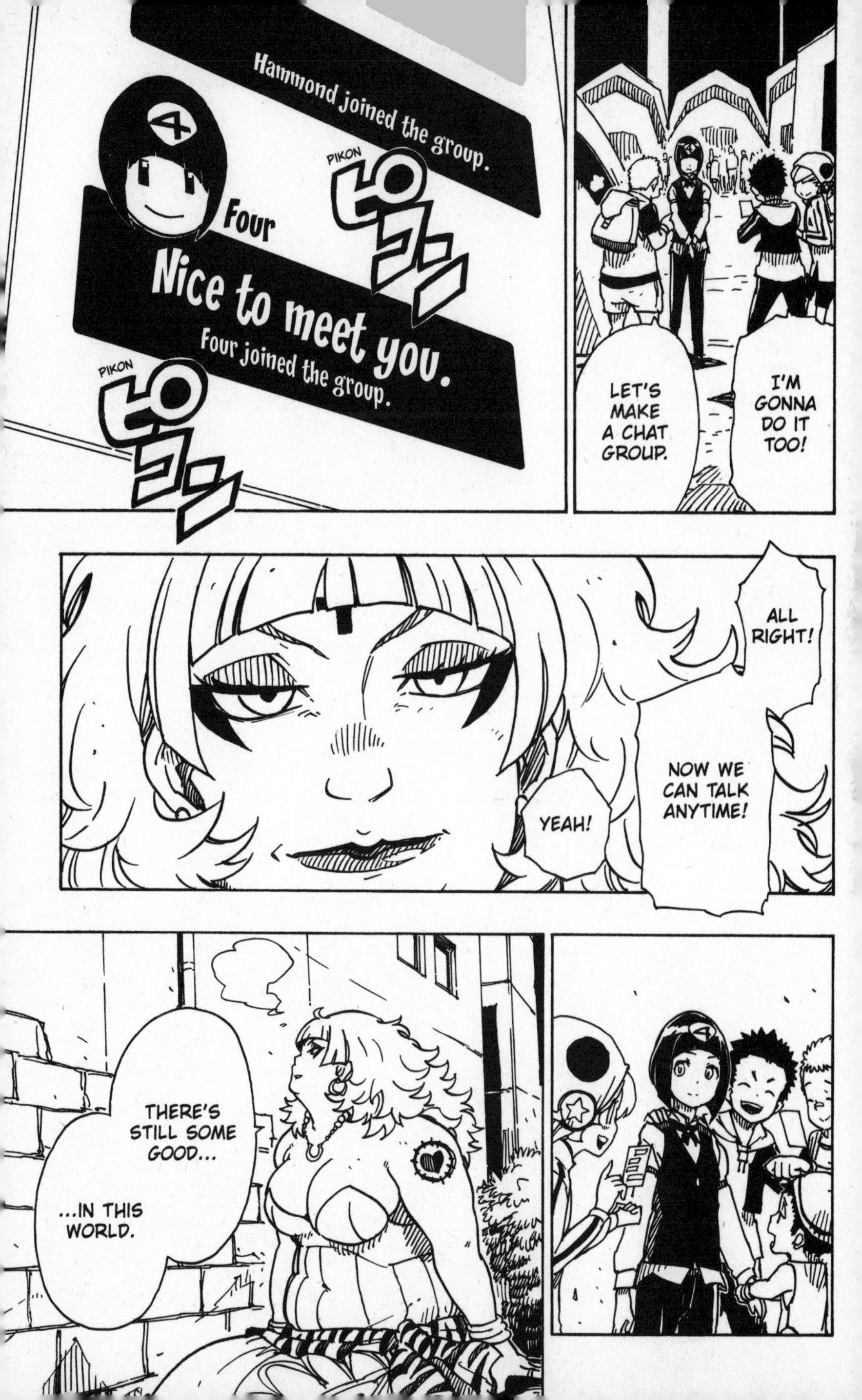
I'M GONNA DO IT TOO!
LET'S MAKE A CHAT GROUP.
Hammond joined the group.
PIKON
Four
Nice to meet you.
Four joined the group.
PIKON
ALL RIGHT!
NOW WE CAN TALK ANYTIME!
YEAH!
THERE'S STILL SOME GOOD...
...IN THIS WORLD.

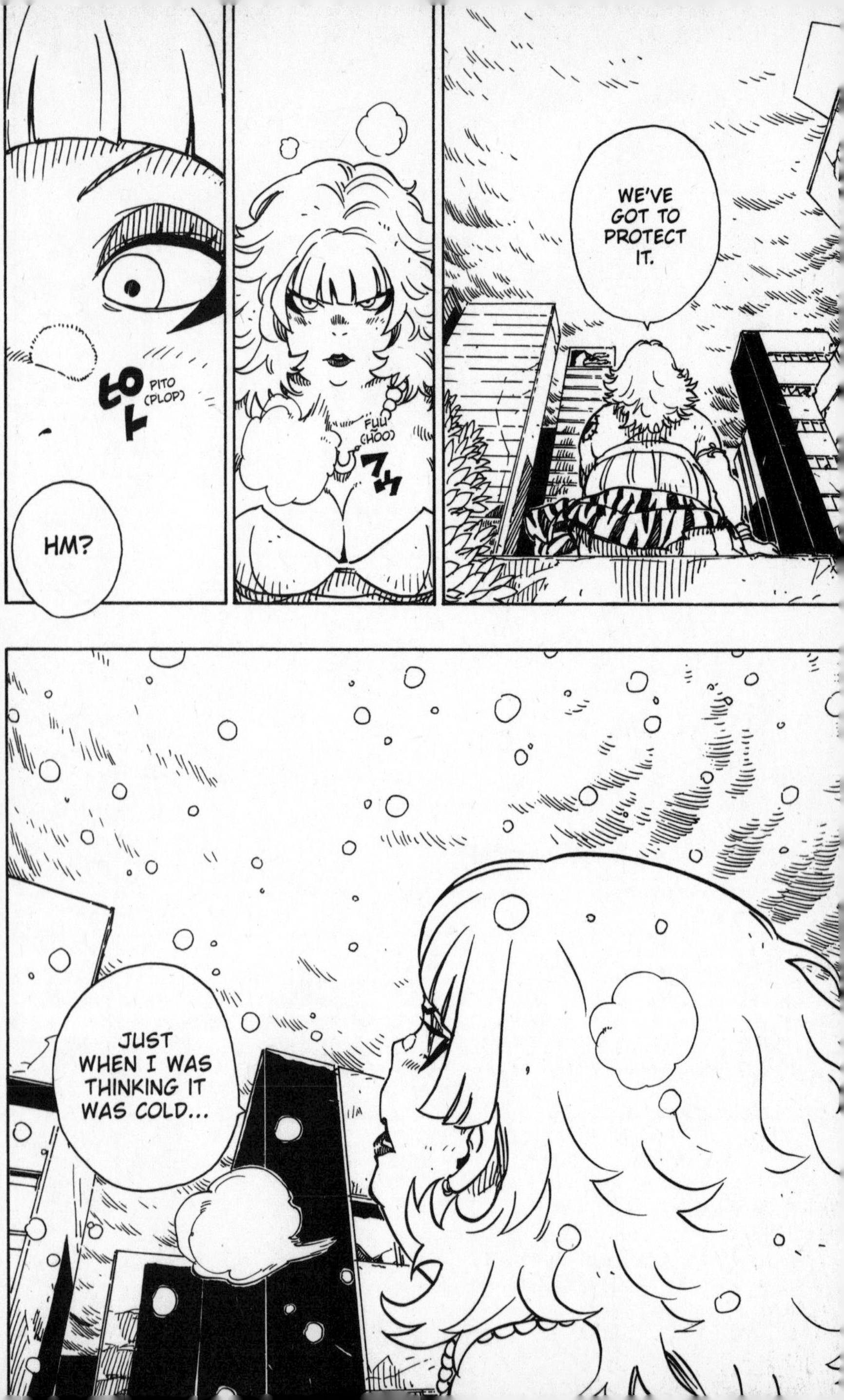
WE'VE GOT TO PROTECT IT.
FUU (HOO)
PITO (PLOP)
HM?
JUST WHEN I WAS THINKING IT WAS COLD...

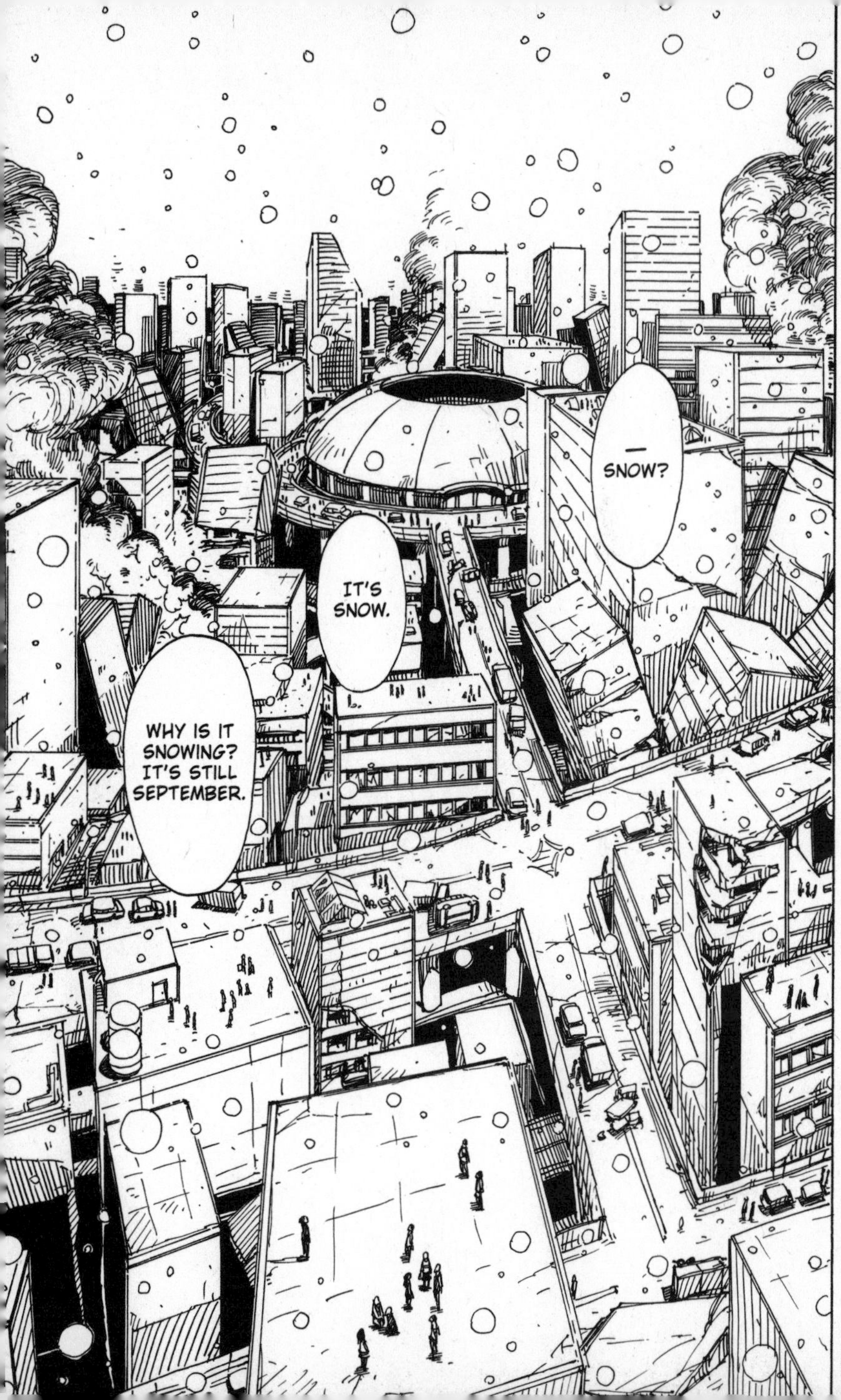
— SNOW?
IT'S SNOW.
WHY IS IT SNOWING? IT'S STILL SEPTEMBER.

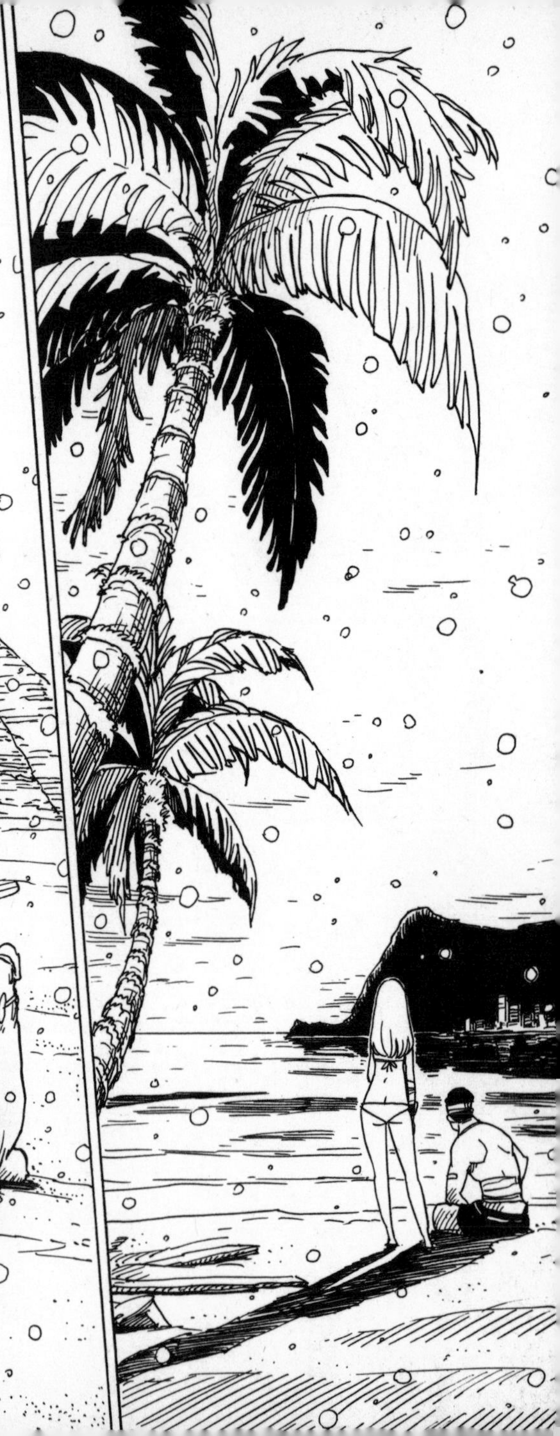
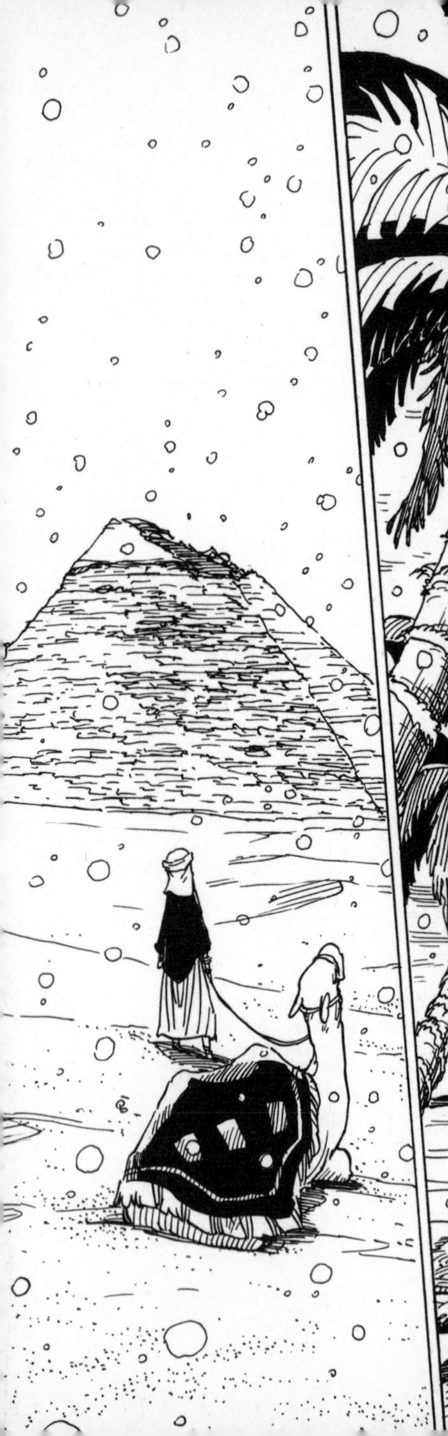

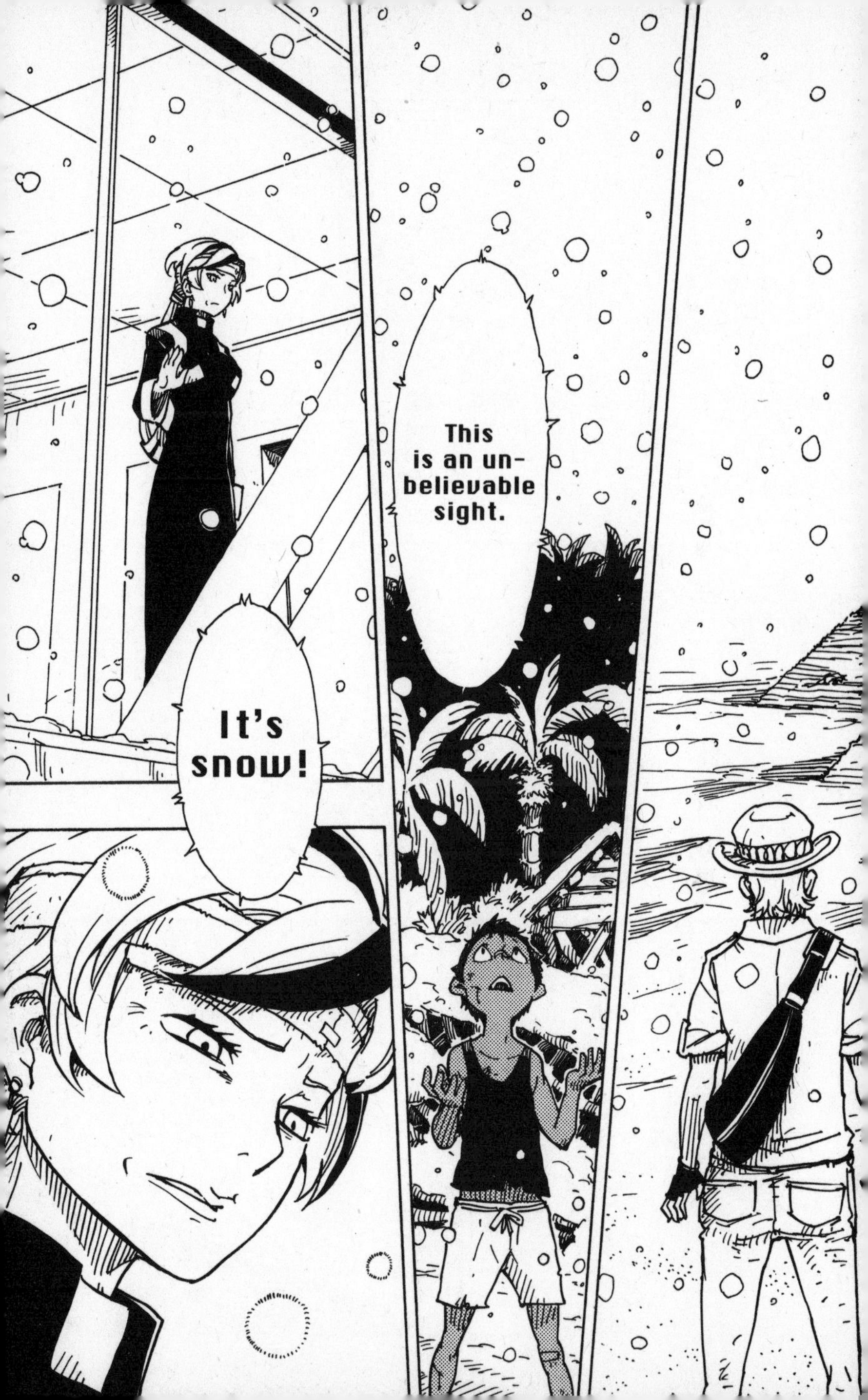
This is an un- believable sight.
It's snow!

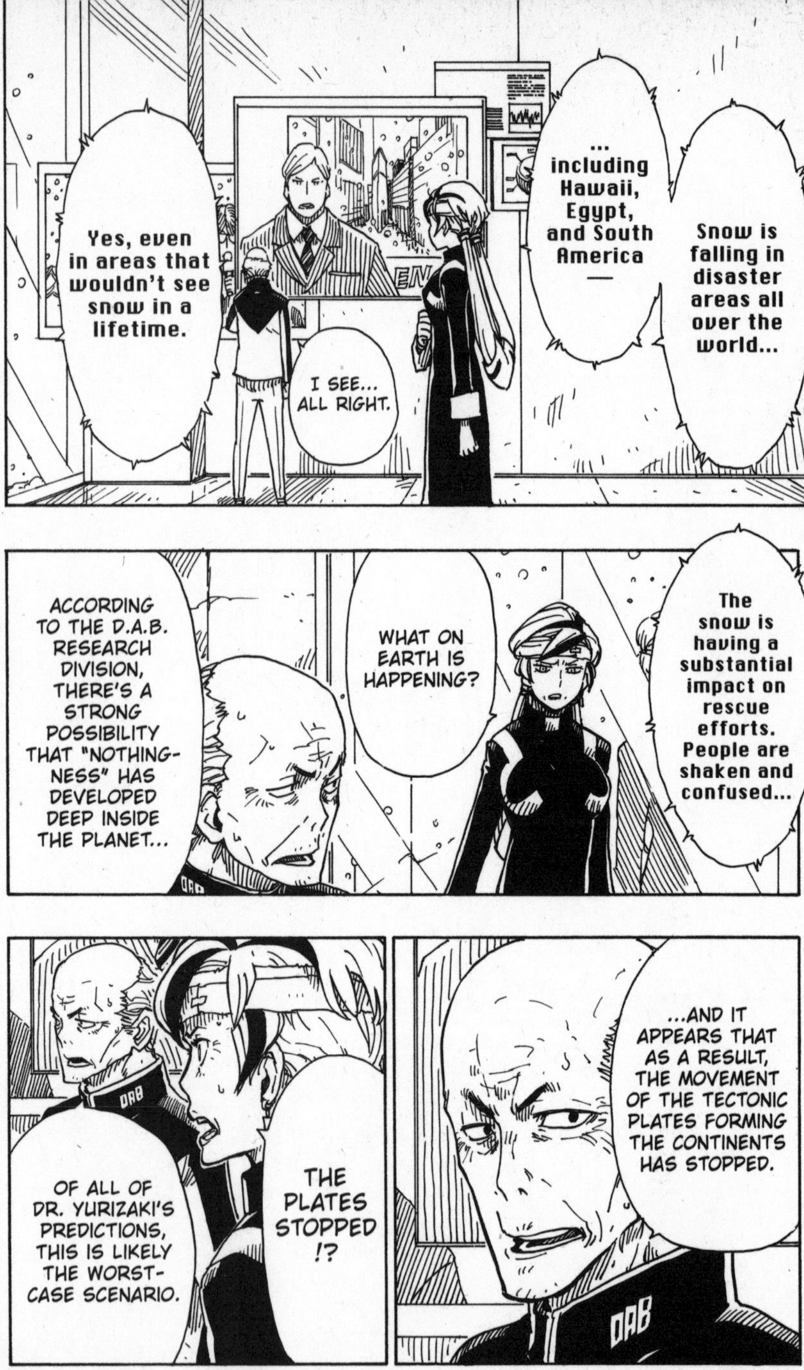
Snow is falling in disaster areas all over the world...
...including Hawaii, Egypt, and South America—
Yes, even in areas that wouldn't see snow in a lifetime.
I SEE... ALL RIGHT.
The snow is having a substantial impact on rescue efforts. People are shaken and confused...
WHAT ON EARTH IS HAPPENING?
ACCORDING TO THE D.A.B. RESEARCH DIVISION, THERE'S A STRONG POSSIBILITY THAT "NOTHINGNESS" HAS DEVELOPED DEEP INSIDE THE PLANET...
...AND IT APPEARS THAT AS A RESULT, THE MOVEMENT OF THE TECTONIC PLATES FORMING THE CONTINENTS HAS STOPPED.
THE PLATES STOPPED!?
OF ALL OF DR. YURIZAKI'S PREDICTIONS, THIS IS LIKELY THE WORST-CASE SCENARIO.

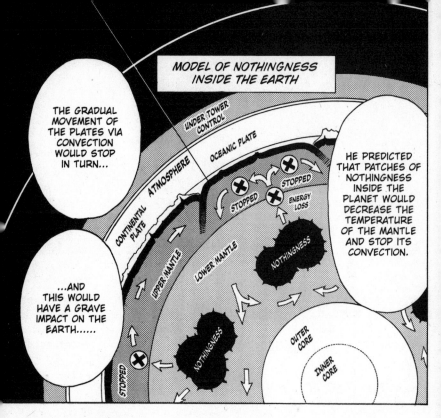

MODEL OF NOTHINGNESS INSIDE THE EARTH
HE PREDICTED THAT PATCHES OF NOTHINGNESS INSIDE THE PLANET WOULD DECREASE THE TEMPERATURE OF THE MANTLE AND STOP ITS CONVECTION.
UNDER TOWER CONTROL
OCEANIC PLATE
ATMOSPHERE
STOPPED
STOPPED
ENERGY LOSS
CONTINENTAL PLATE
UPPER MANTLE
LOWER MANTLE
NOTHINGNESS
NOTHINGNESS
OUTER CORE
INNER CORE
STOPPED
THE GRADUAL MOVEMENT OF THE PLATES VIA CONVECTION WOULD STOP IN TURN...
...AND THIS WOULD HAVE A GRAVE IMPACT ON THE EARTH......
THEN THE SIMULTANEOUS WORLDWIDE CRISES SO FAR WERE ...?
AN EFFECT CAUSED BY THE STRAIN ON THE EARTH FROM THE PLATES STOPPING, MOST LIKELY.
THERE WILL NEVER BE ANOTHER EARTHQUAKE OR VOLCANIC ERUPTION, BUT INSTEAD, THE PLANET'S TEMPERATURE WILL CONTINUE TO PLUMMET.
IF THE DOCTOR'S PREDICTIONS WERE CORRECT, THEN AFTER THIS...
AFTER THIS...

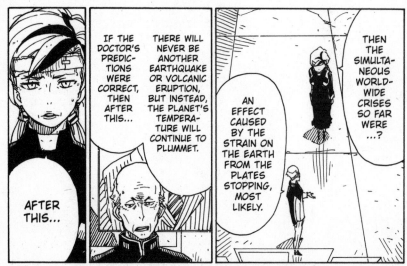

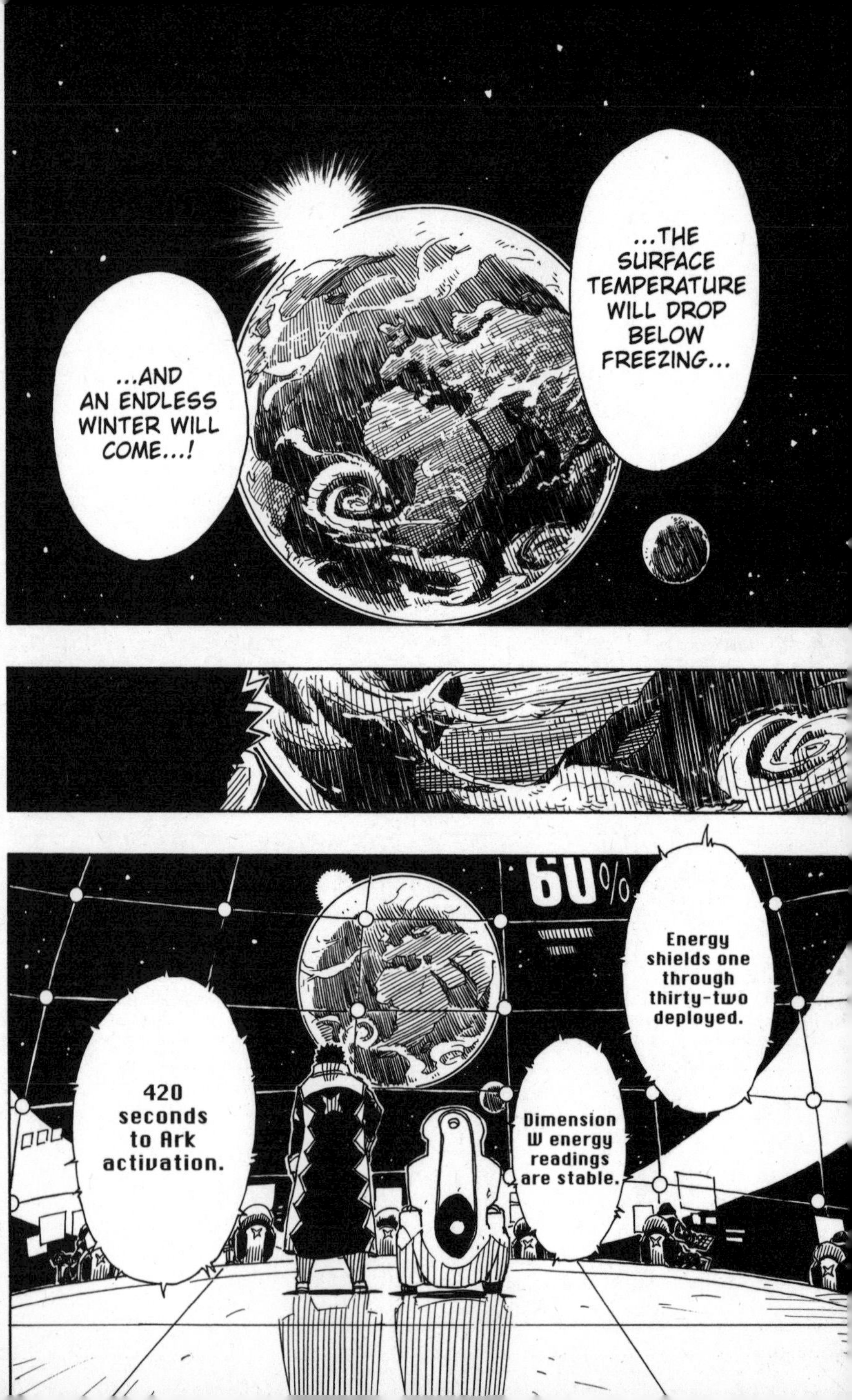
...THE SURFACE TEMPERATURE WILL DROP BELOW FREEZING...
...AND AN ENDLESS WINTER WILL COME...!
60%
Energy shields one through thirty-two deployed.
Dimension W energy readings are stable.
420 seconds to Ark activation.

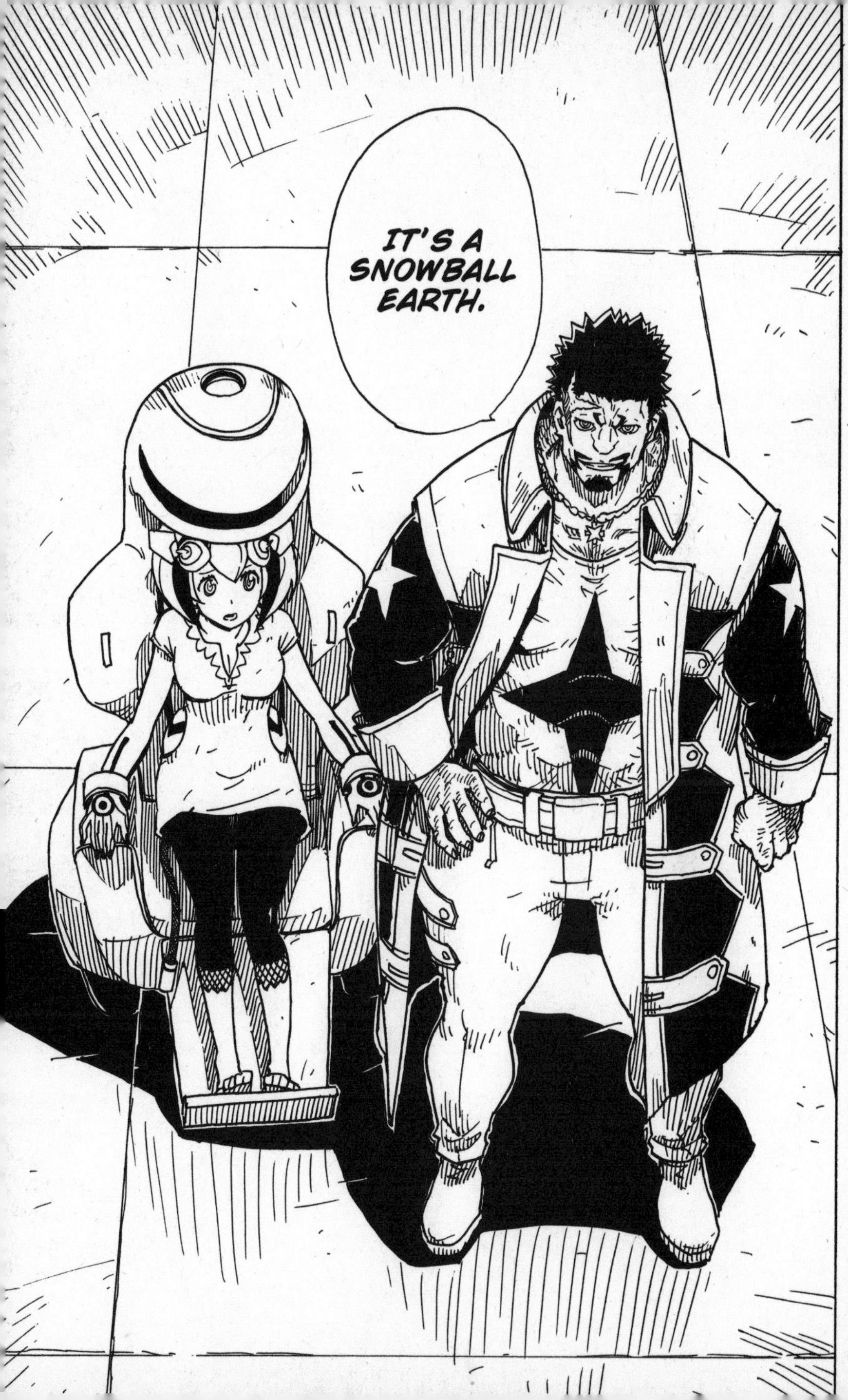
IT'S A SNOWBALL EARTH.

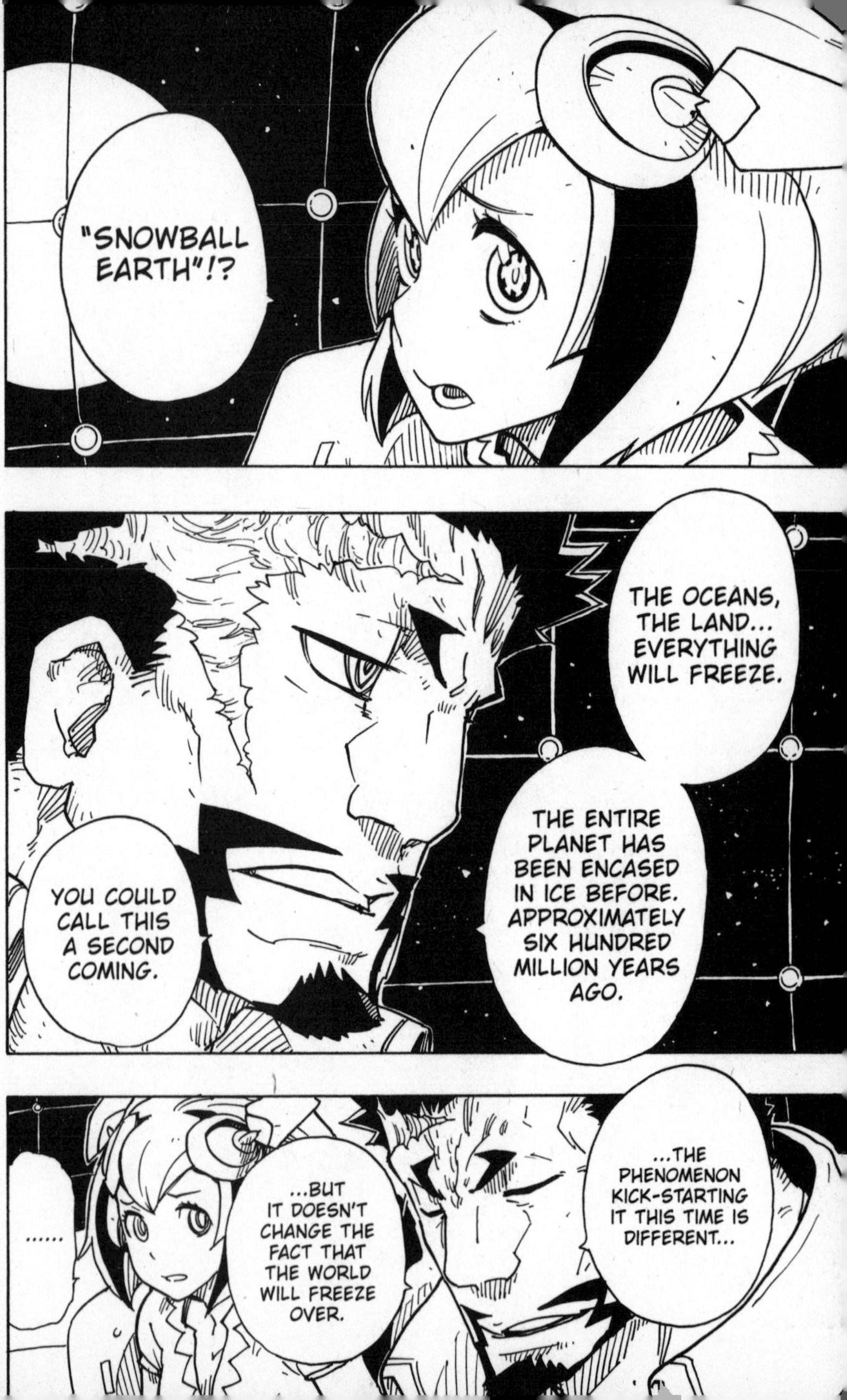
"SNOWBALL EARTH"!?
THE OCEANS, THE LAND... EVERYTHING WILL FREEZE.
THE ENTIRE PLANET HAS BEEN ENCASED IN ICE BEFORE. APPROXIMATELY SIX HUNDRED MILLION YEARS AGO.
YOU COULD CALL THIS A SECOND COMING.
...THE PHENOMENON KICK-STARTING IT THIS TIME IS DIFFERENT...
...BUT IT DOESN'T CHANGE THE FACT THAT THE WORLD WILL FREEZE OVER.
......

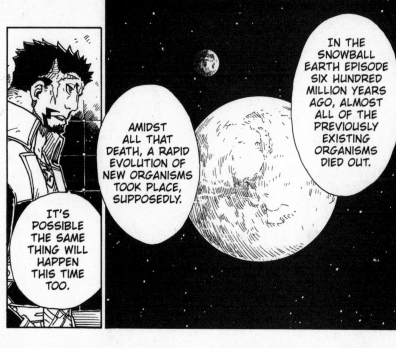

IN THE SNOWBALL EARTH EPISODE SIX HUNDRED MILLION YEARS AGO, ALMOST ALL OF THE PREVIOUSLY EXISTING ORGANISMS DIED OUT.

AMIDST ALL THAT DEATH, A RAPID EVOLUTION OF NEW ORGANISMS TOOK PLACE, SUPPOSEDLY.

IT'S POSSIBLE THE SAME THING WILL HAPPEN THIS TIME TOO.

......IS THAT...

...YOUR SO-CALLED ARK PROJECT?

I'M NOT SAYING THAT...... BUT...

RAPID EVOLUTION FOLLOWING THE RAPID EXTINC- TION OF HUMANITY.

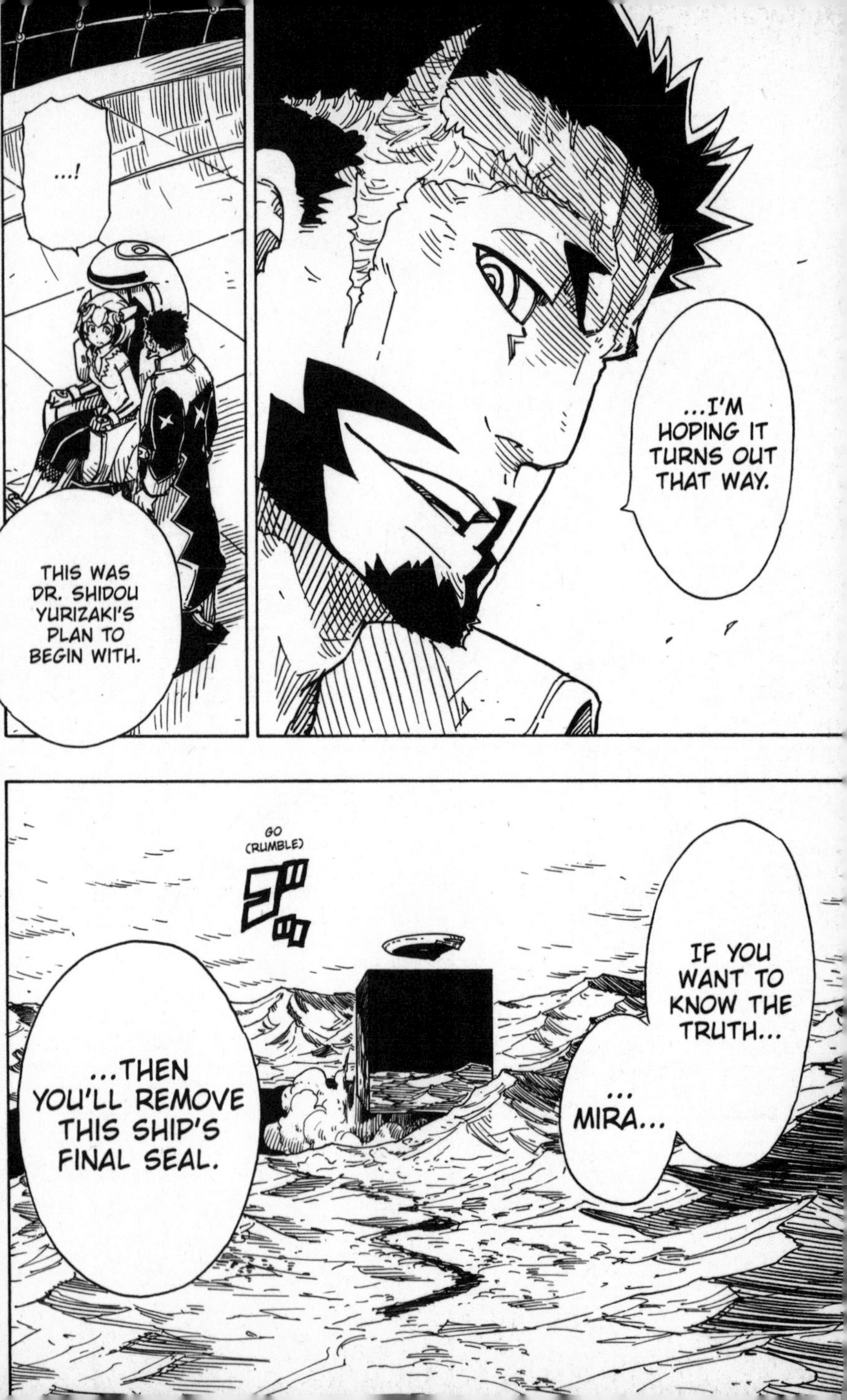
...I'M HOPING IT TURNS OUT THAT WAY.
...!
THIS WAS DR. SHIDOU YURIZAKI'S PLAN TO BEGIN WITH.
IF YOU WANT TO KNOW THE TRUTH...
... MIRA...
GO (RUMBLE)
...THEN YOU'LL REMOVE THIS SHIP'S FINAL SEAL.

Dimension W

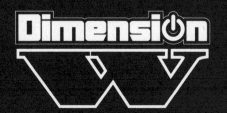

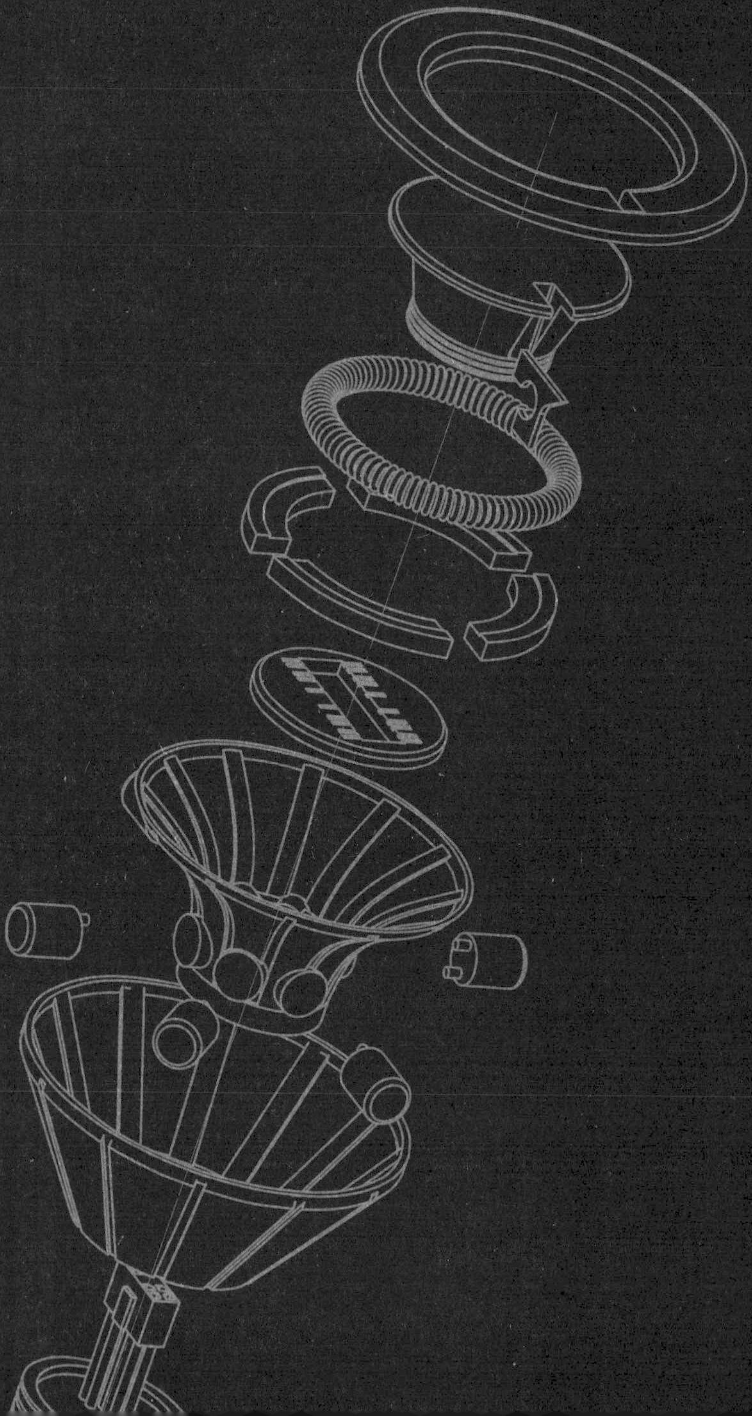

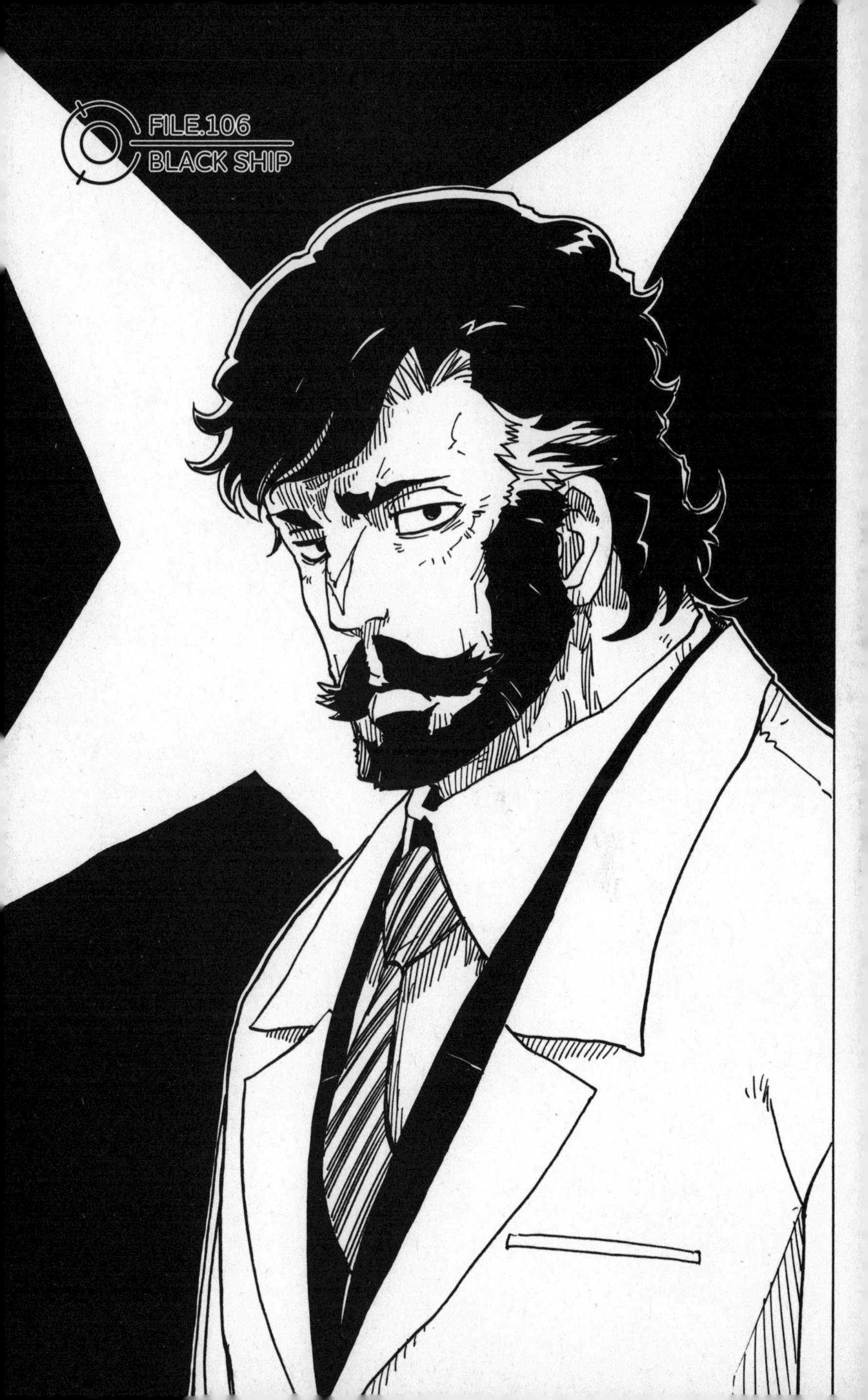
FILE.106
BLACK SHIP

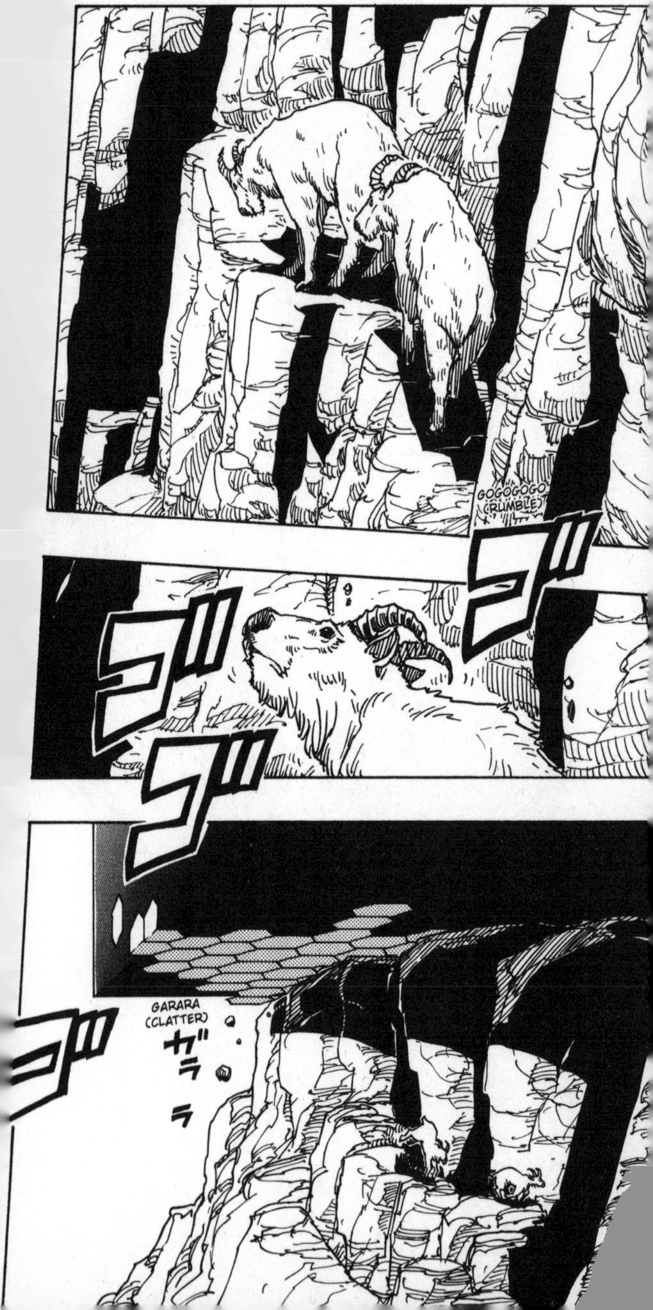
GOGOGOGO
(RUMBLE)
ゴ
ゴ
ゴ
ゴ
GARARA
(CLATTER)
ガララ

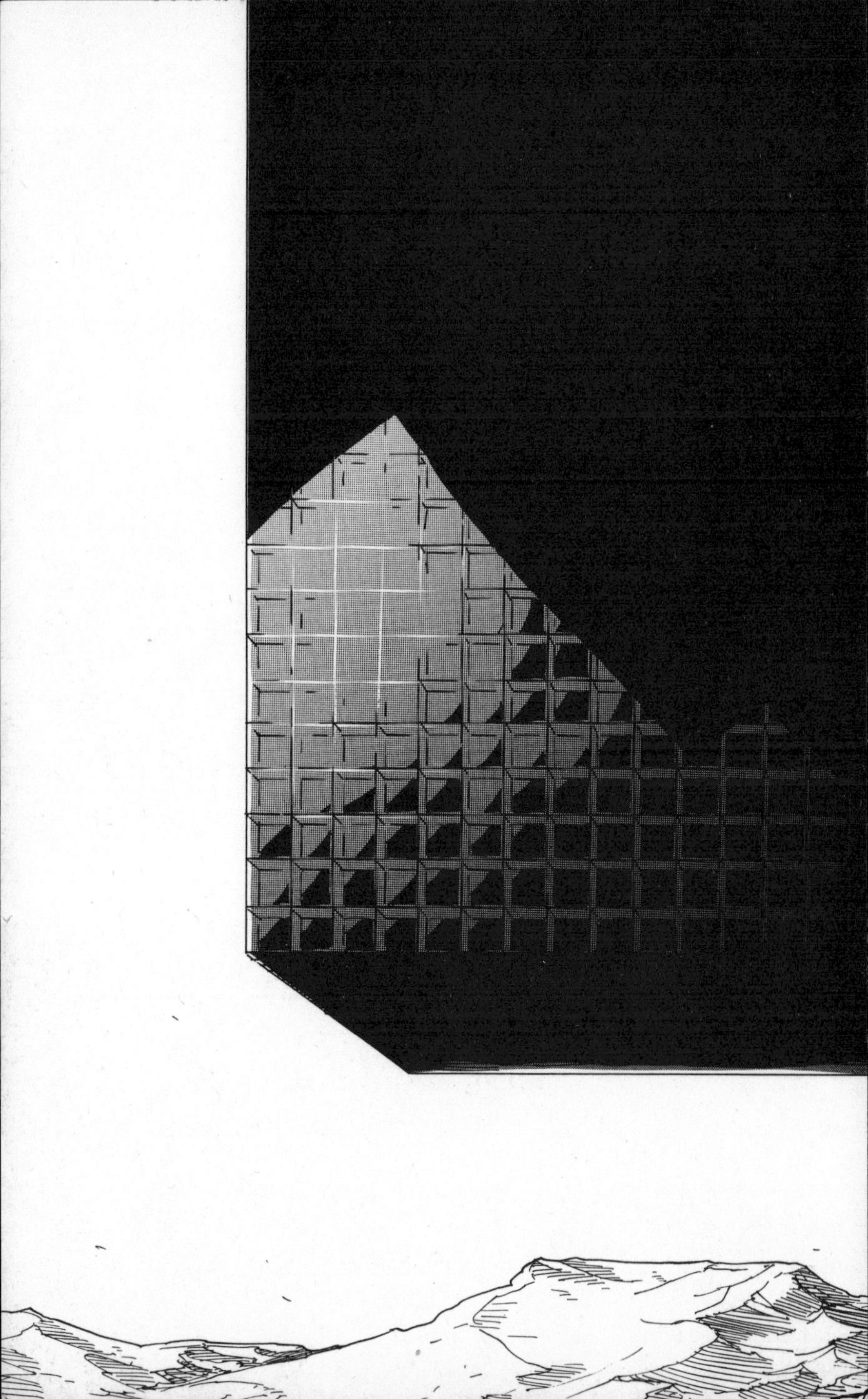

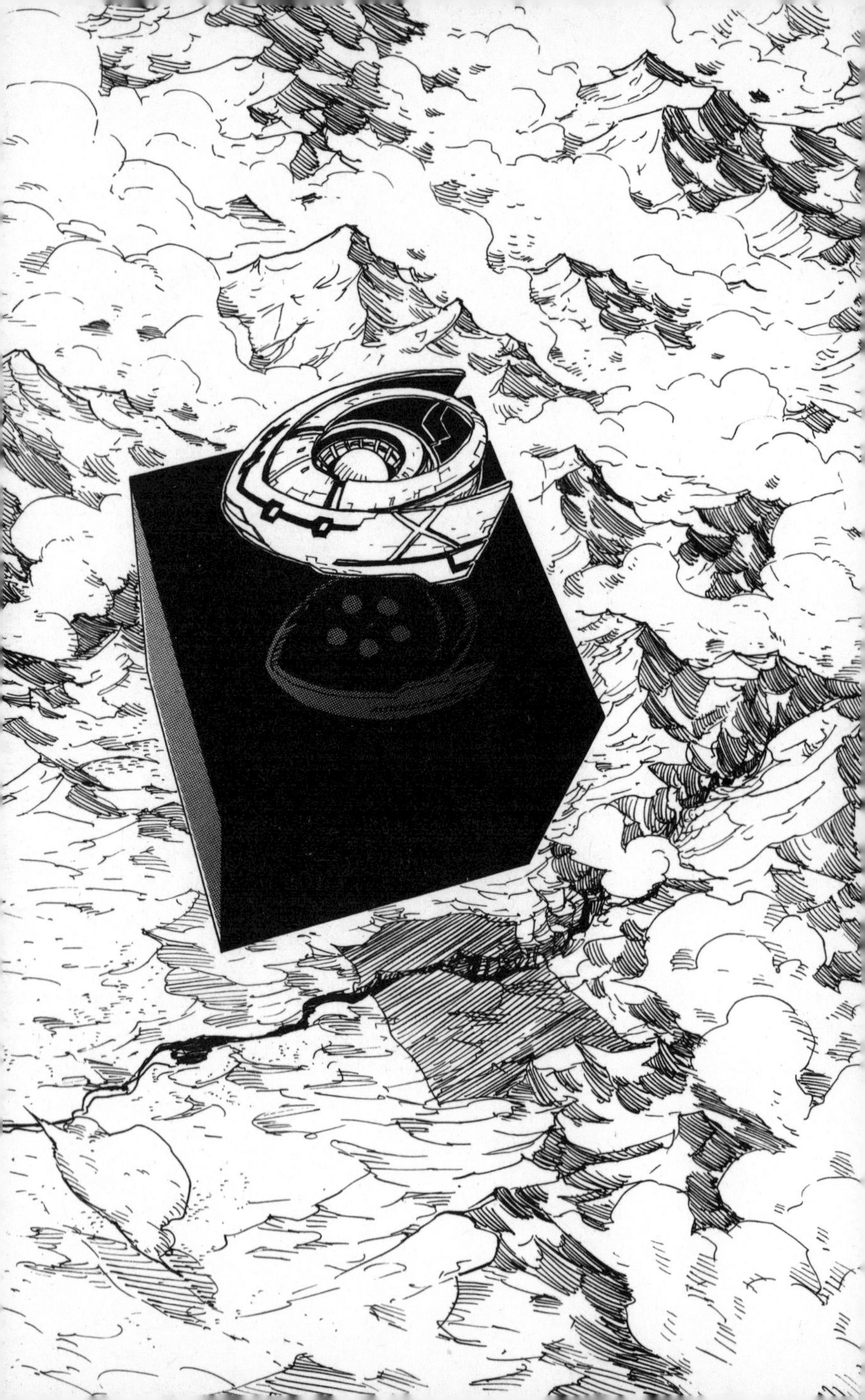

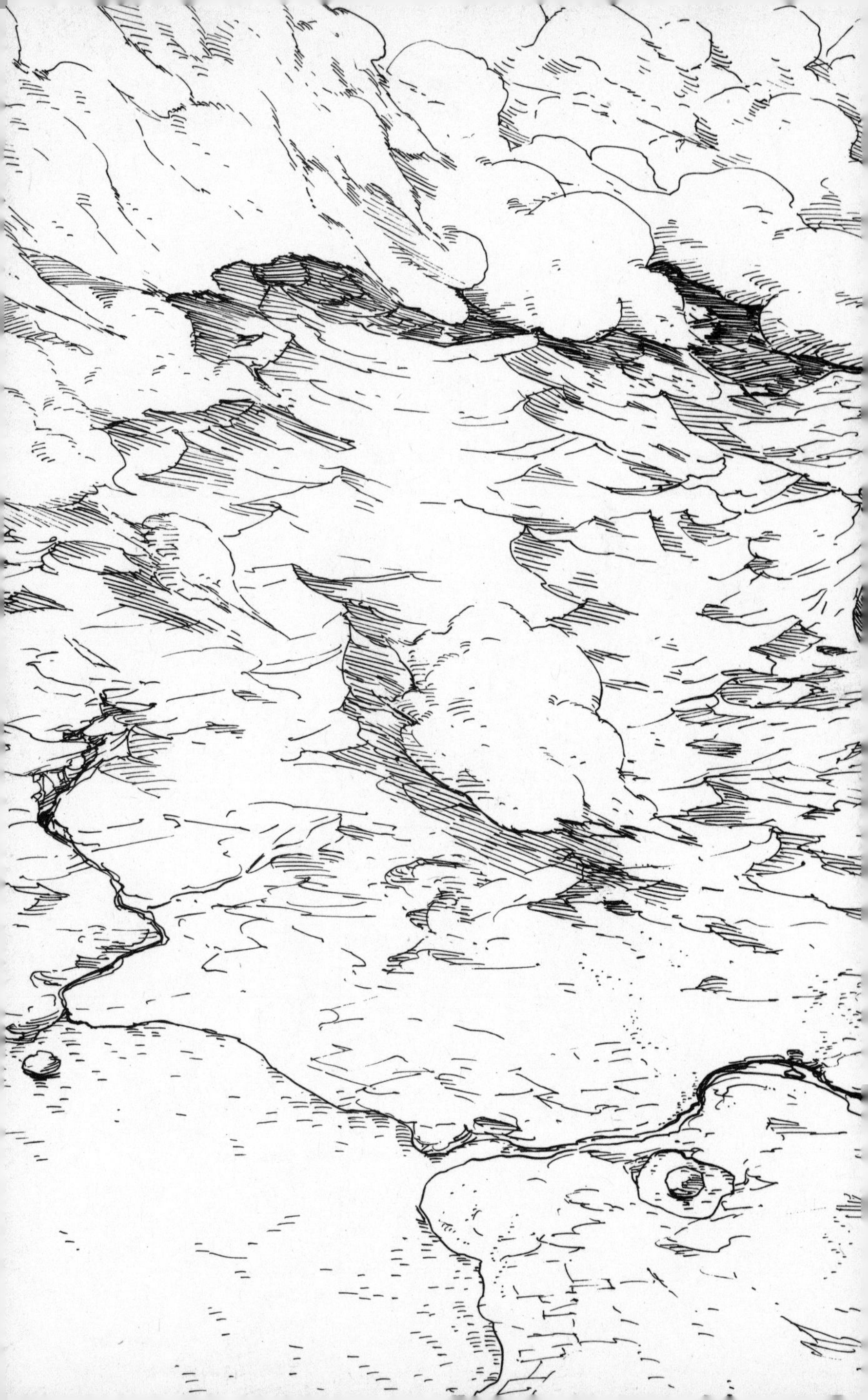

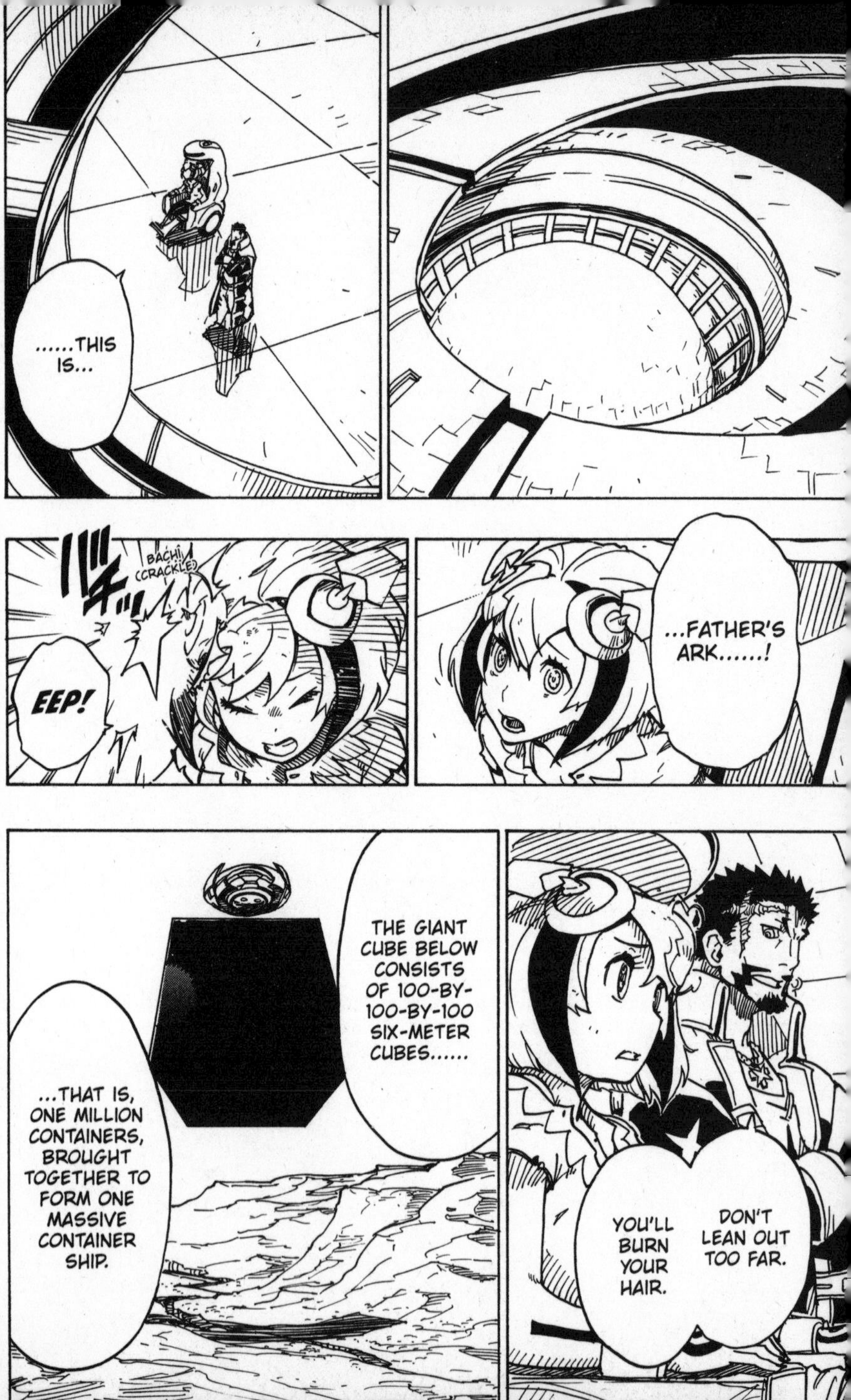
......THIS IS...
...FATHER'S ARK......!
BACHI (CRACKLE)
EEP!
DON'T LEAN OUT TOO FAR.
YOU'LL BURN YOUR HAIR.
THE GIANT CUBE BELOW CONSISTS OF 100-BY-100-BY-100 SIX-METER CUBES......
...THAT IS, ONE MILLION CONTAINERS, BROUGHT TOGETHER TO FORM ONE MASSIVE CONTAINER SHIP.

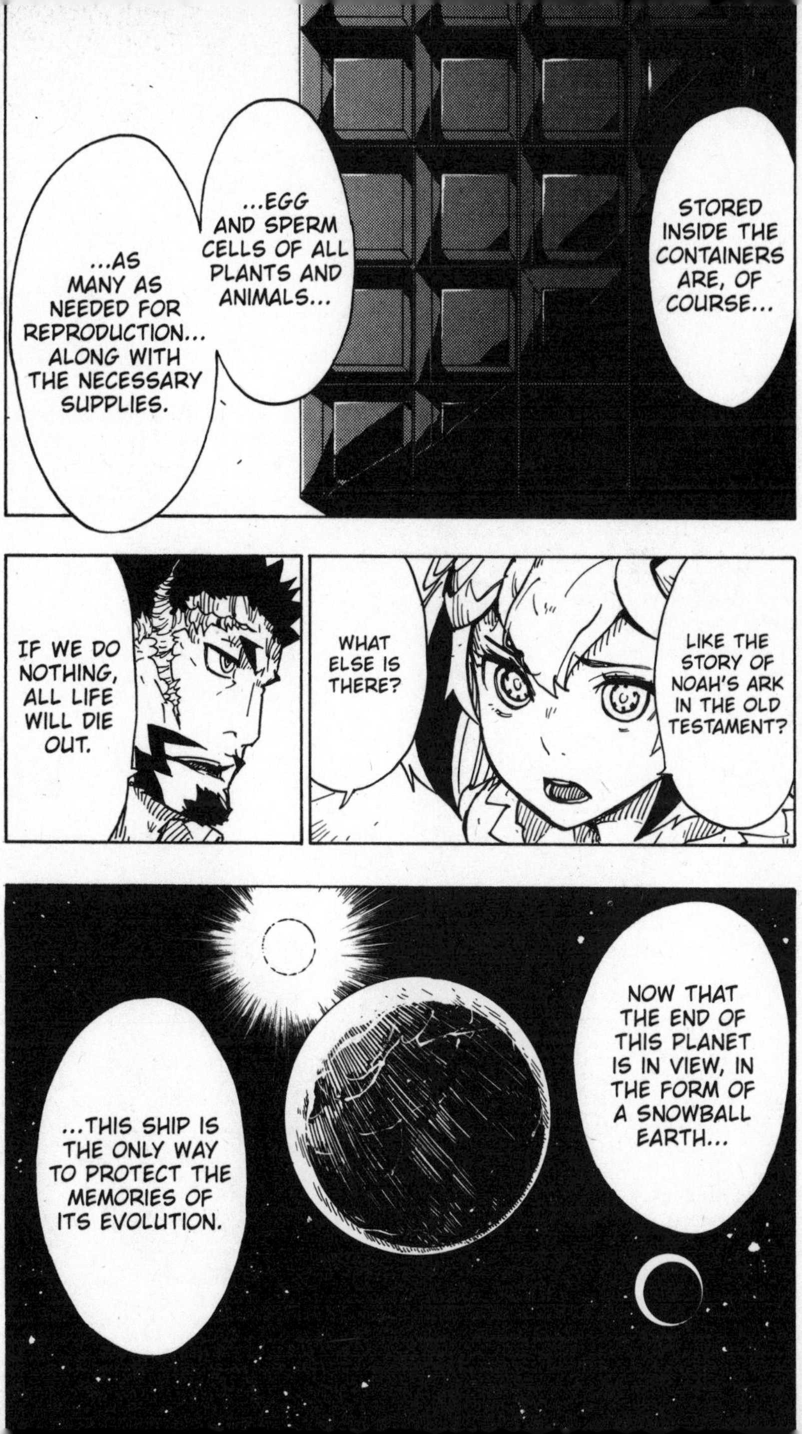
STORED INSIDE THE CONTAINERS ARE, OF COURSE...
...EGG AND SPERM CELLS OF ALL PLANTS AND ANIMALS...
...AS MANY AS NEEDED FOR REPRODUCTION... ALONG WITH THE NECESSARY SUPPLIES.
LIKE THE STORY OF NOAH'S ARK IN THE OLD TESTAMENT?
WHAT ELSE IS THERE?
IF WE DO NOTHING, ALL LIFE WILL DIE OUT.
NOW THAT THE END OF THIS PLANET IS IN VIEW, IN THE FORM OF A SNOWBALL EARTH...
...THIS SHIP IS THE ONLY WAY TO PROTECT THE MEMORIES OF ITS EVOLUTION.

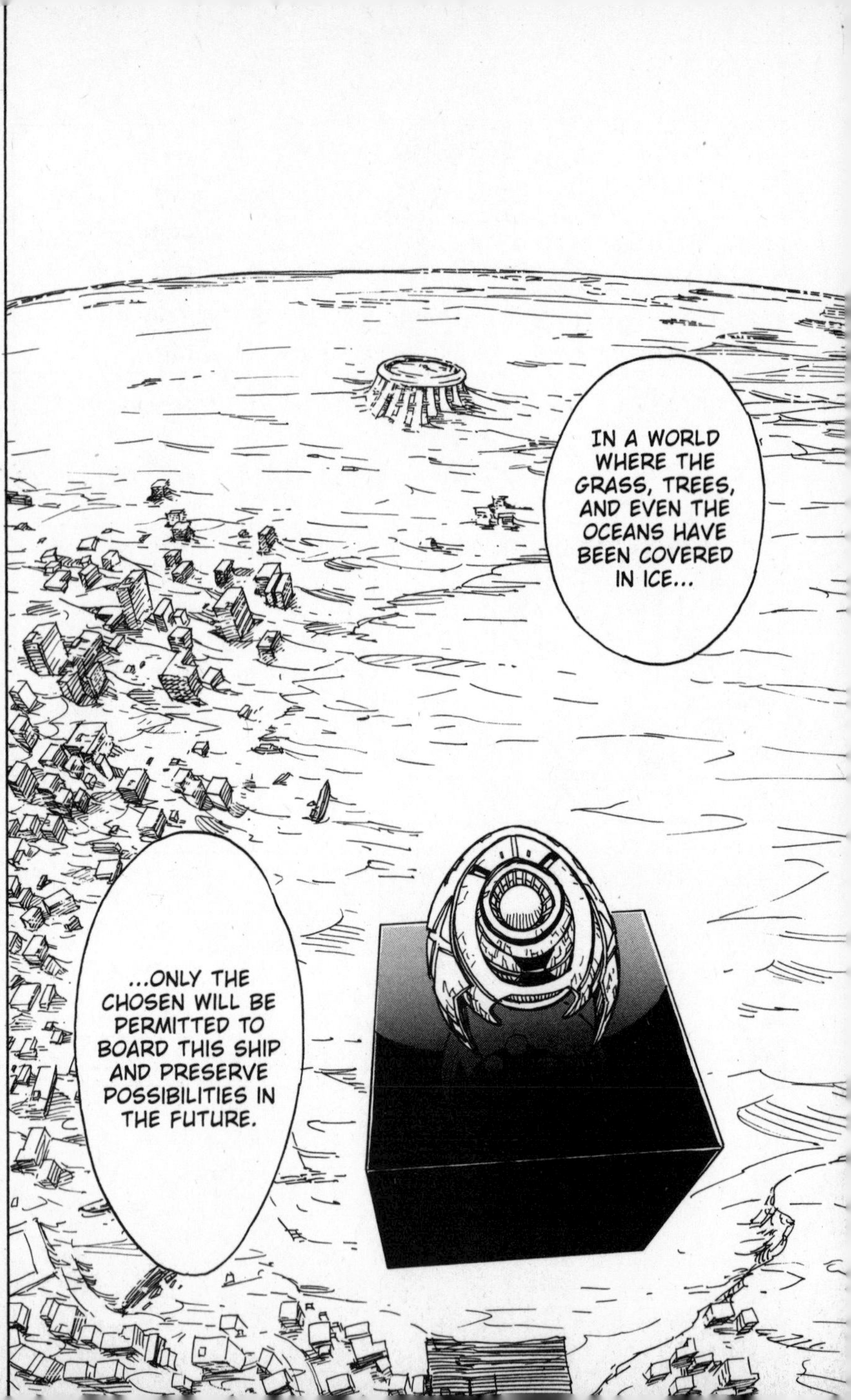
IN A WORLD WHERE THE GRASS, TREES, AND EVEN THE OCEANS HAVE BEEN COVERED IN ICE...
...ONLY THE CHOSEN WILL BE PERMITTED TO BOARD THIS SHIP AND PRESERVE POSSIBILITIES IN THE FUTURE.

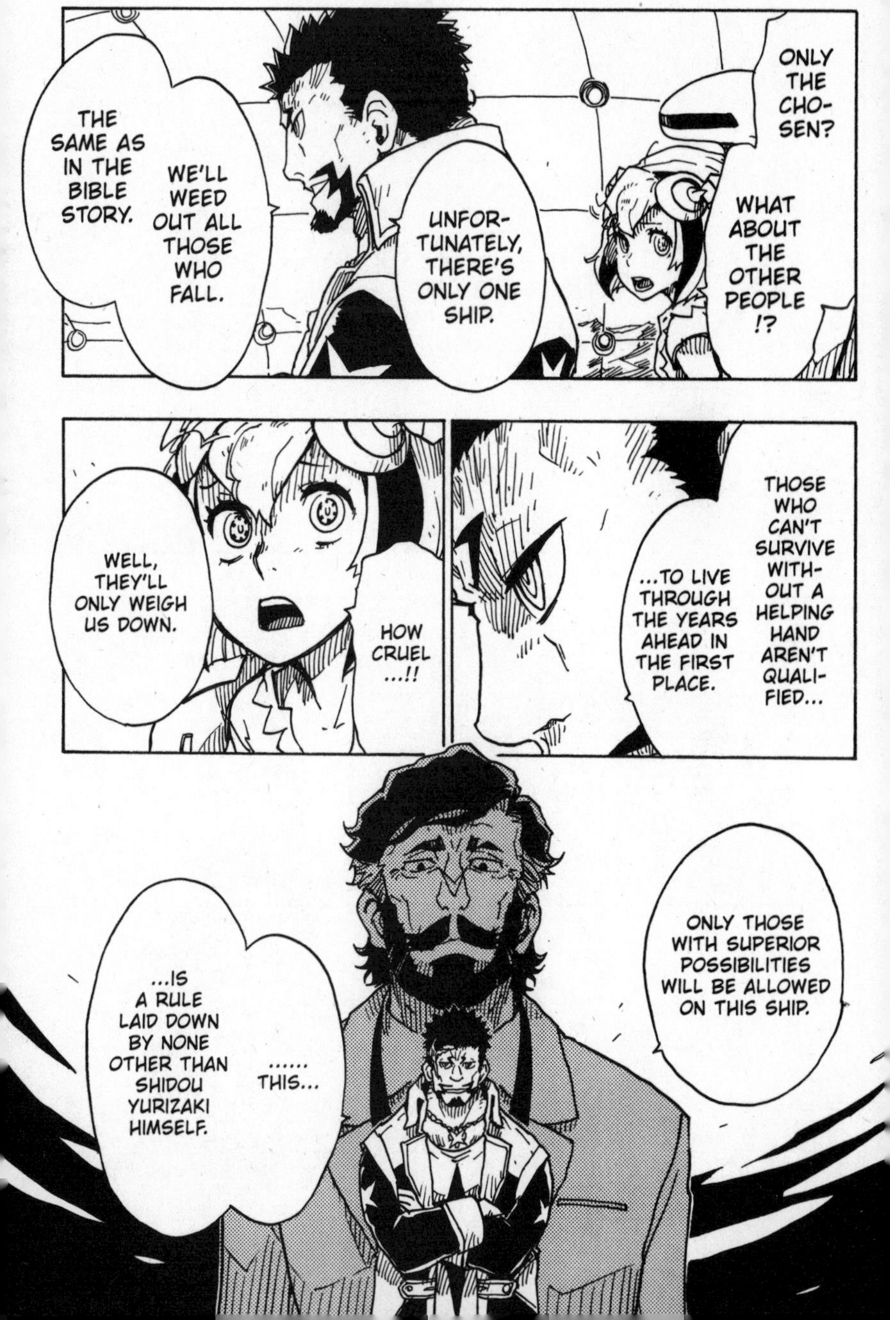
ONLY THE CHO-SEN?
WHAT ABOUT THE OTHER PEOPLE!?
UNFOR-TUNATELY, THERE'S ONLY ONE SHIP.
WE'LL WEED OUT ALL THOSE WHO FALL.
THE SAME AS IN THE BIBLE STORY.
THOSE WHO CAN'T SURVIVE WITH-OUT A HELPING HAND AREN'T QUALI-FIED...
...TO LIVE THROUGH THE YEARS AHEAD IN THE FIRST PLACE.
HOW CRUEL...!!
WELL, THEY'LL ONLY WEIGH US DOWN.
ONLY THOSE WITH SUPERIOR POSSIBILITIES WILL BE ALLOWED ON THIS SHIP.
...... THIS...
...IS A RULE LAID DOWN BY NONE OTHER THAN SHIDOU YURIZAKI HIMSELF.

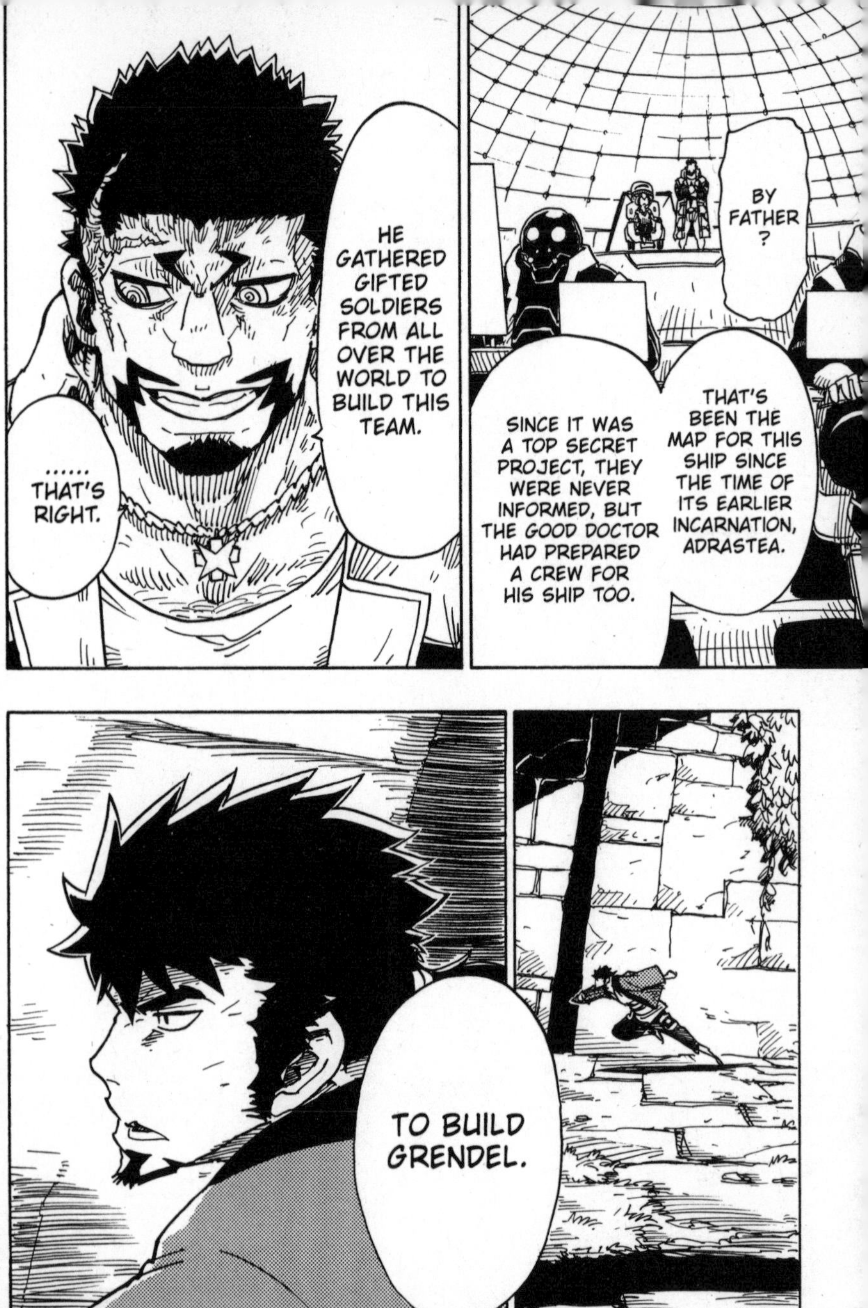
BY FATHER ?
THAT'S BEEN THE MAP FOR THIS SHIP SINCE THE TIME OF ITS EARLIER INCARNATION, ADRASTEA.
SINCE IT WAS A TOP SECRET PROJECT, THEY WERE NEVER INFORMED, BUT THE GOOD DOCTOR HAD PREPARED A CREW FOR HIS SHIP TOO.
HE GATHERED GIFTED SOLDIERS FROM ALL OVER THE WORLD TO BUILD THIS TEAM.
...... THAT'S RIGHT.
TO BUILD GRENDEL.

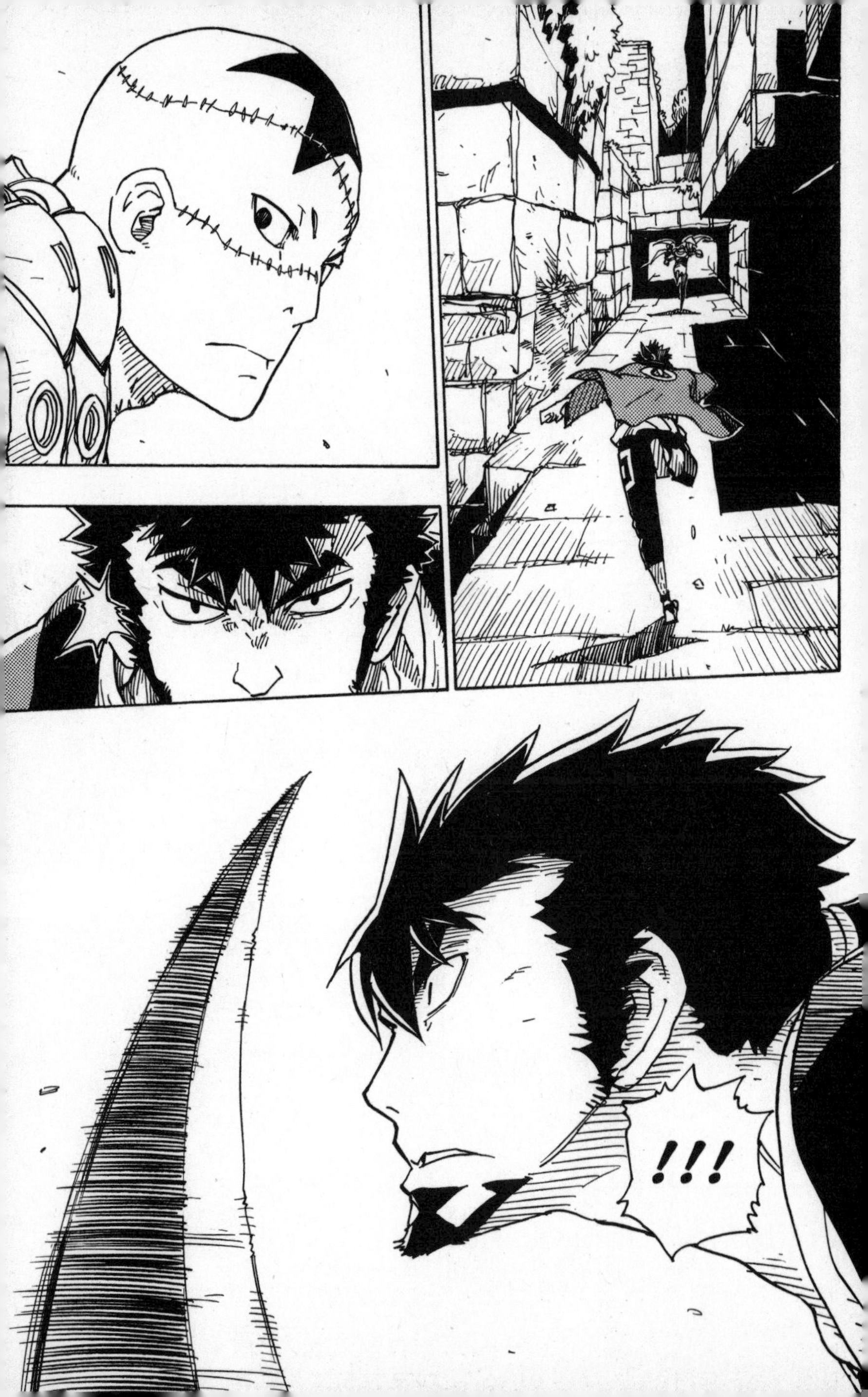
!!!

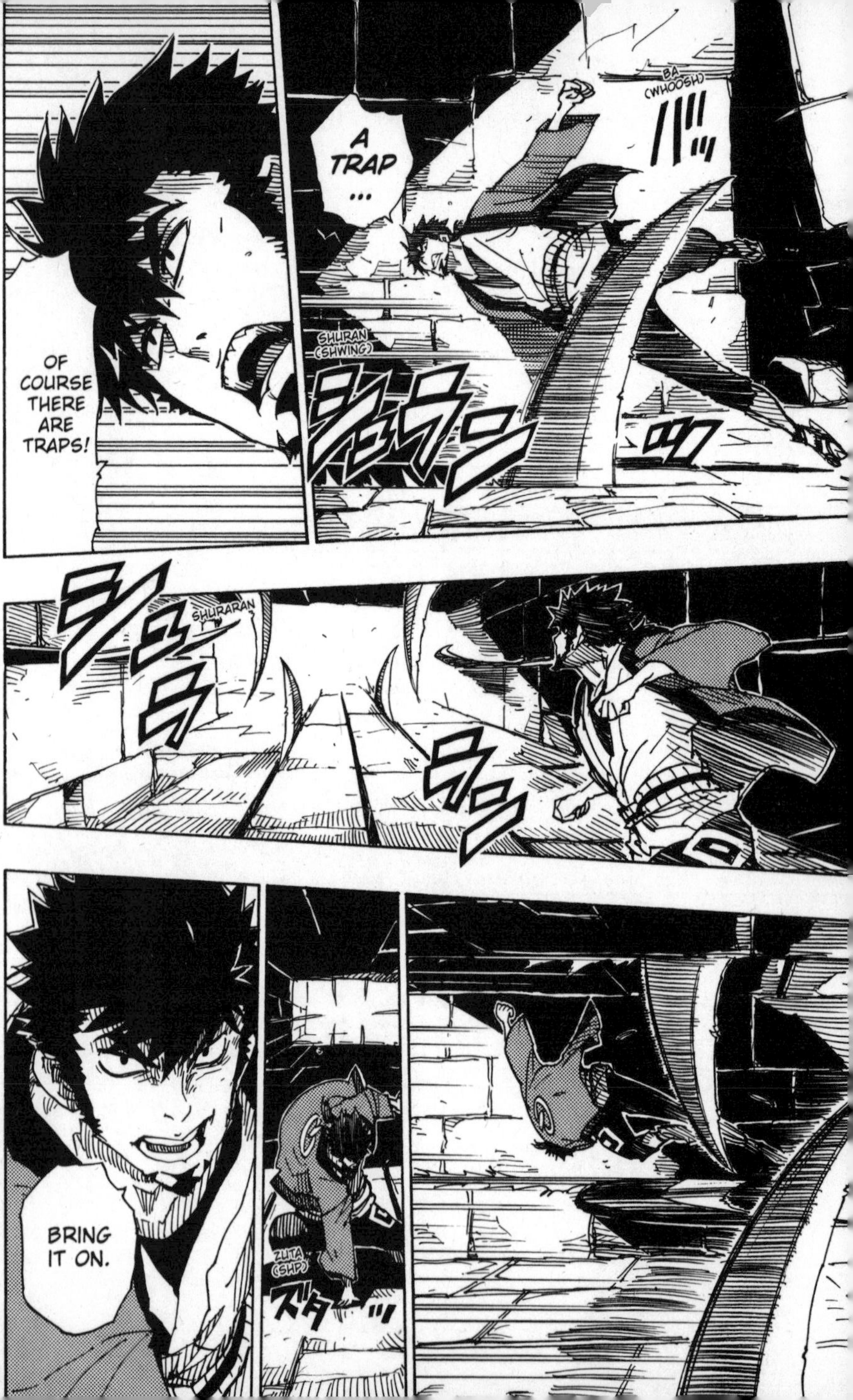
BA (WHOOSH)
A TRAP ...
SHURAN (SHWING)
OF COURSE THERE ARE TRAPS!
SHURARAN
ZUTA (SHP)
BRING IT ON.

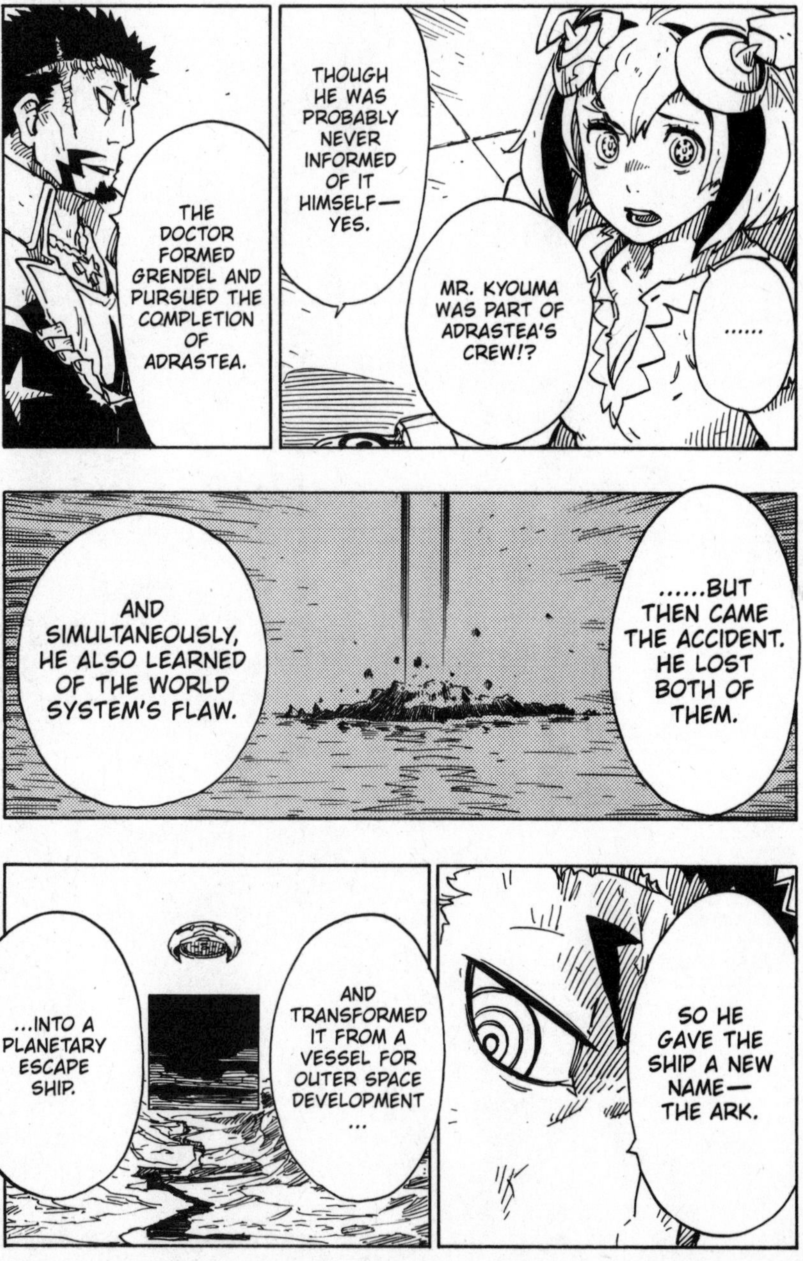
MR. KYOUMA WAS PART OF ADRASTEA'S CREW!?
THOUGH HE WAS PROBABLY NEVER INFORMED OF IT HIMSELF— YES.
......
THE DOCTOR FORMED GRENDEL AND PURSUED THE COMPLETION OF ADRASTEA.
......BUT THEN CAME THE ACCIDENT. HE LOST BOTH OF THEM.
AND SIMULTANEOUSLY, HE ALSO LEARNED OF THE WORLD SYSTEM'S FLAW.
SO HE GAVE THE SHIP A NEW NAME— THE ARK.
AND TRANSFORMED IT FROM A VESSEL FOR OUTER SPACE DEVELOPMENT ...
...INTO A PLANETARY ESCAPE SHIP.

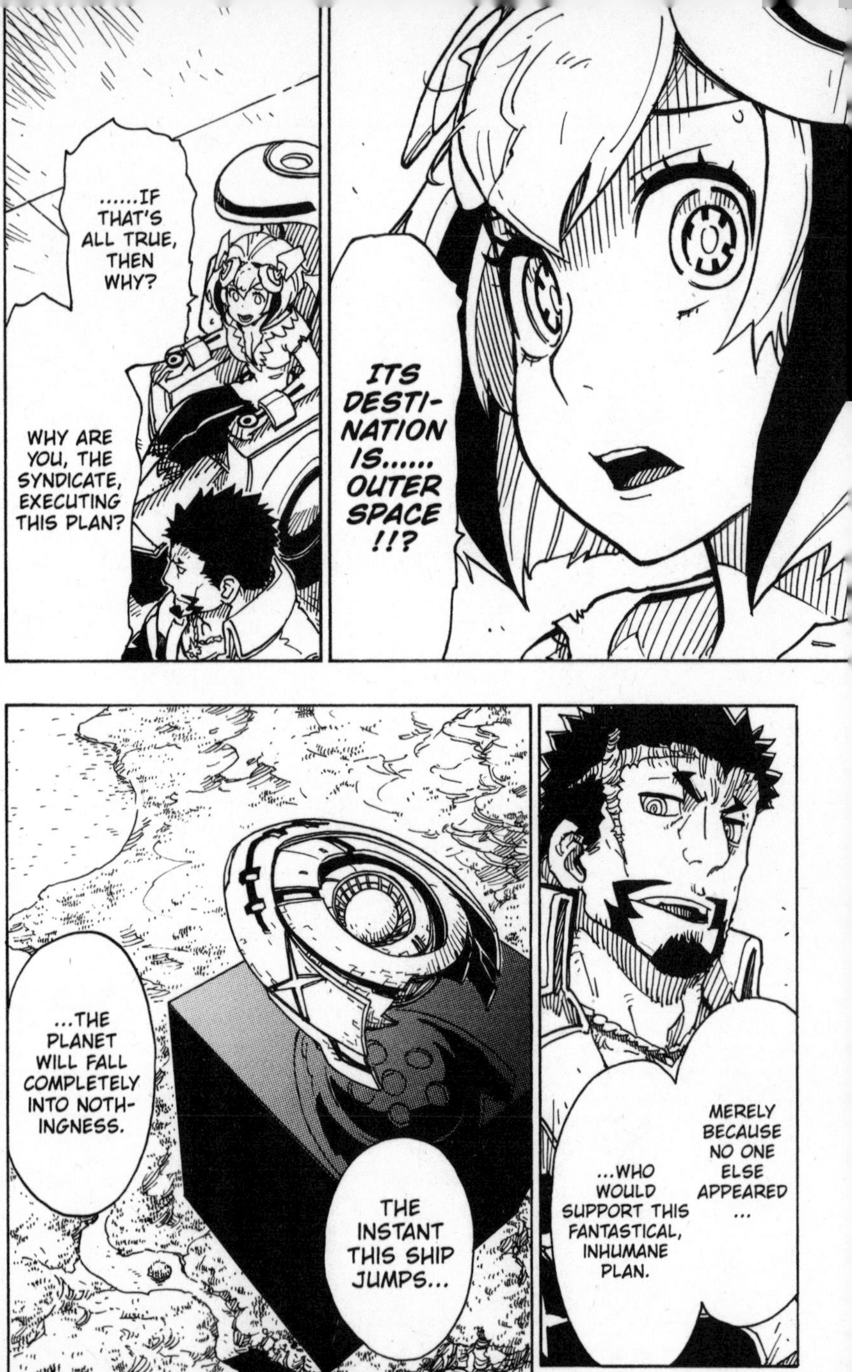
ITS DESTI-NATION IS...... OUTER SPACE!!?
......IF THAT'S ALL TRUE, THEN WHY?
WHY ARE YOU, THE SYNDICATE, EXECUTING THIS PLAN?
MERELY BECAUSE NO ONE ELSE APPEARED ...
...WHO WOULD SUPPORT THIS FANTASTICAL, INHUMANE PLAN.
THE INSTANT THIS SHIP JUMPS...
...THE PLANET WILL FALL COMPLETELY INTO NOTH-INGNESS.

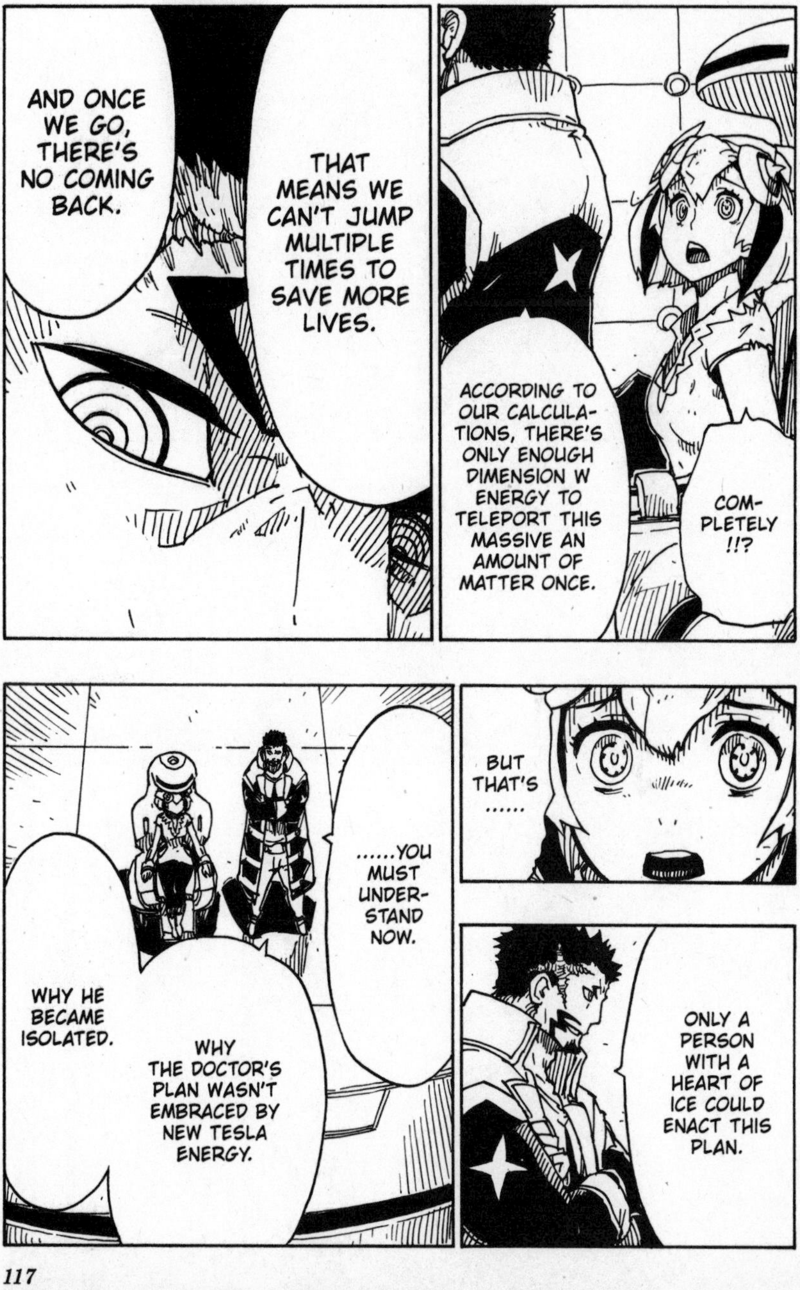
COM-PLETELY!!?
ACCORDING TO OUR CALCULA-TIONS, THERE'S ONLY ENOUGH DIMENSION W ENERGY TO TELEPORT THIS MASSIVE AN AMOUNT OF MATTER ONCE.
THAT MEANS WE CAN'T JUMP MULTIPLE TIMES TO SAVE MORE LIVES.
AND ONCE WE GO, THERE'S NO COMING BACK.
BUT THAT'S ......
ONLY A PERSON WITH A HEART OF ICE COULD ENACT THIS PLAN.
......YOU MUST UNDER-STAND NOW.
WHY THE DOCTOR'S PLAN WASN'T EMBRACED BY NEW TESLA ENERGY.
WHY HE BECAME ISOLATED.

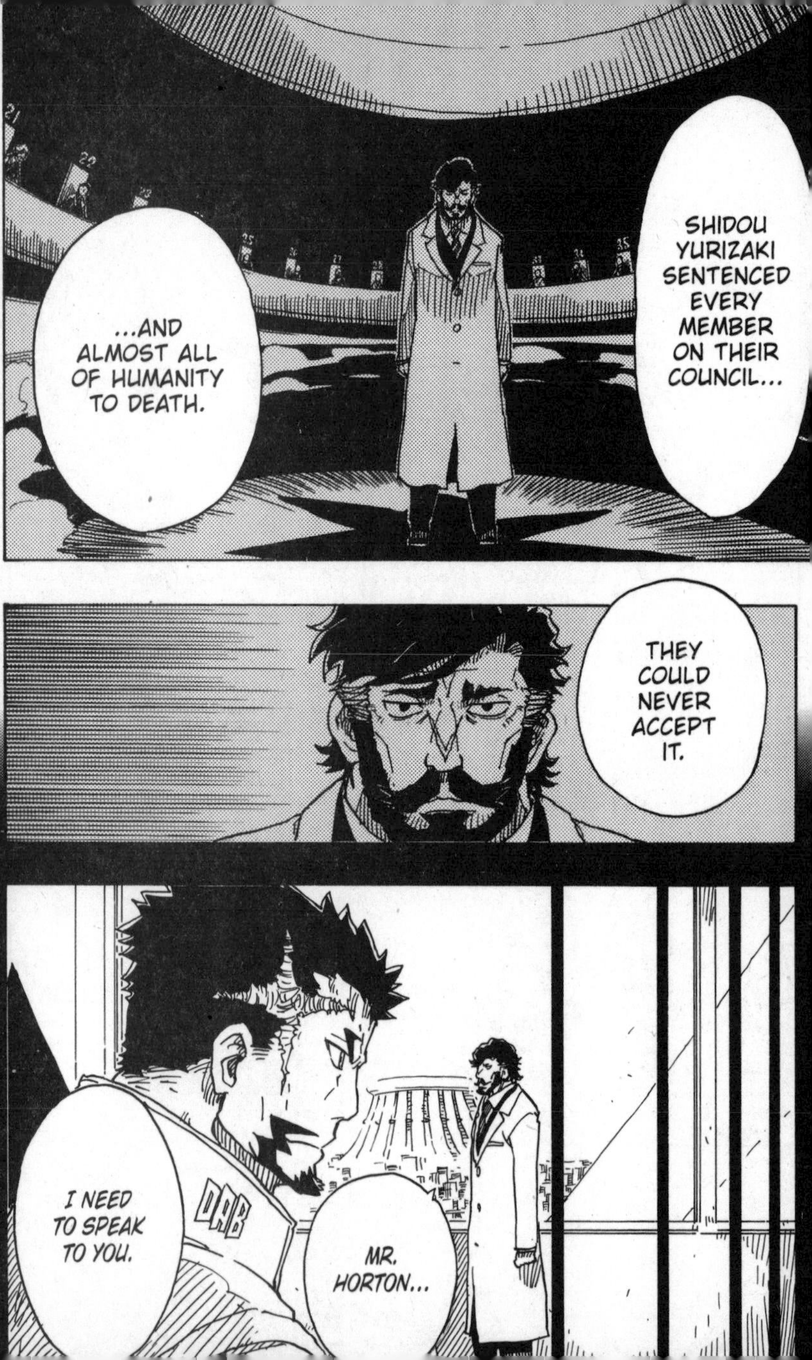
SHIDOU YURIZAKI SENTENCED EVERY MEMBER ON THEIR COUNCIL...
...AND ALMOST ALL OF HUMANITY TO DEATH.
THEY COULD NEVER ACCEPT IT.
MR. HORTON...
I NEED TO SPEAK TO YOU.

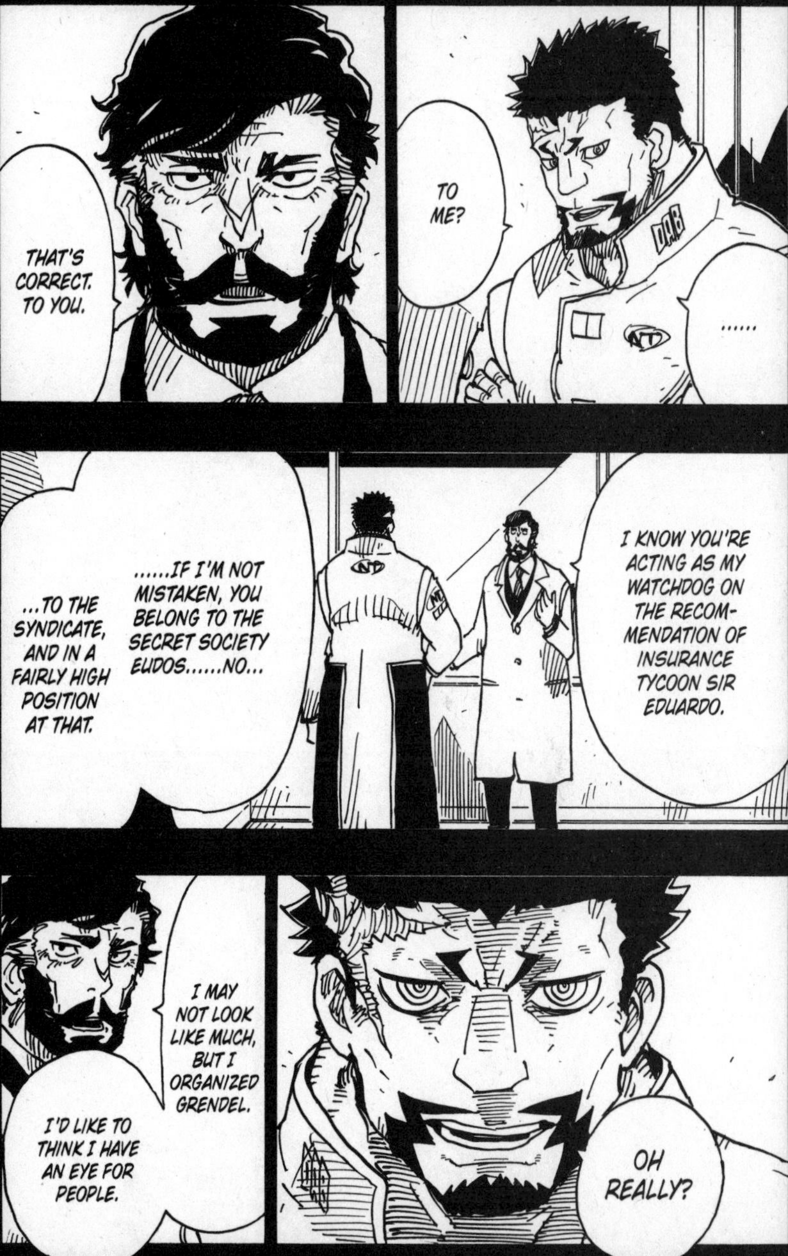
TO ME?
......
THAT'S CORRECT. TO YOU.
I KNOW YOU'RE ACTING AS MY WATCHDOG ON THE RECOMMENDATION OF INSURANCE TYCOON SIR EDUARDO.
......IF I'M NOT MISTAKEN, YOU BELONG TO THE SECRET SOCIETY EUDOS......NO...
...TO THE SYNDICATE, AND IN A FAIRLY HIGH POSITION AT THAT.
OH REALLY?
I MAY NOT LOOK LIKE MUCH, BUT I ORGANIZED GRENDEL.
I'D LIKE TO THINK I HAVE AN EYE FOR PEOPLE.

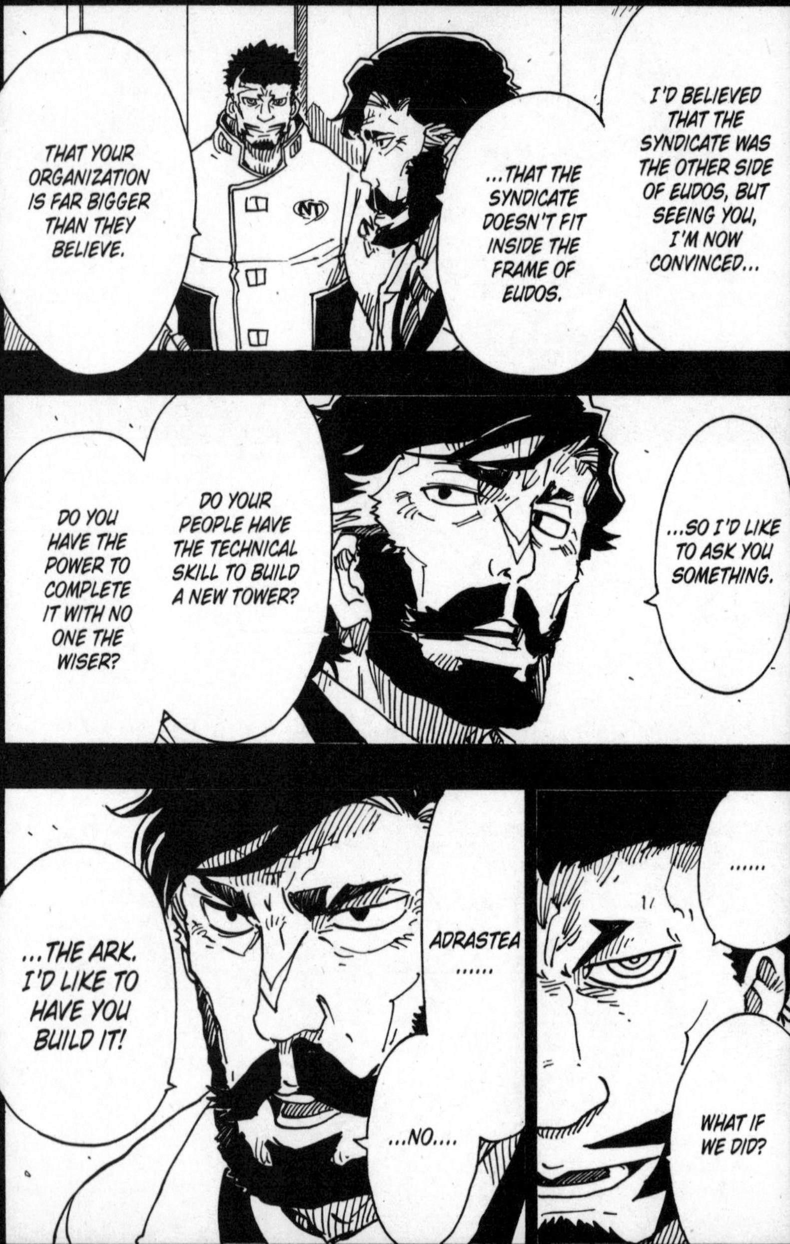
I'D BELIEVED THAT THE SYNDICATE WAS THE OTHER SIDE OF EUDOS, BUT SEEING YOU, I'M NOW CONVINCED...
...THAT THE SYNDICATE DOESN'T FIT INSIDE THE FRAME OF EUDOS.
THAT YOUR ORGANIZATION IS FAR BIGGER THAN THEY BELIEVE.
...SO I'D LIKE TO ASK YOU SOMETHING.
DO YOUR PEOPLE HAVE THE TECHNICAL SKILL TO BUILD A NEW TOWER?
DO YOU HAVE THE POWER TO COMPLETE IT WITH NO ONE THE WISER?
......
WHAT IF WE DID?
ADRASTEA ......
...NO....
...THE ARK. I'D LIKE TO HAVE YOU BUILD IT!

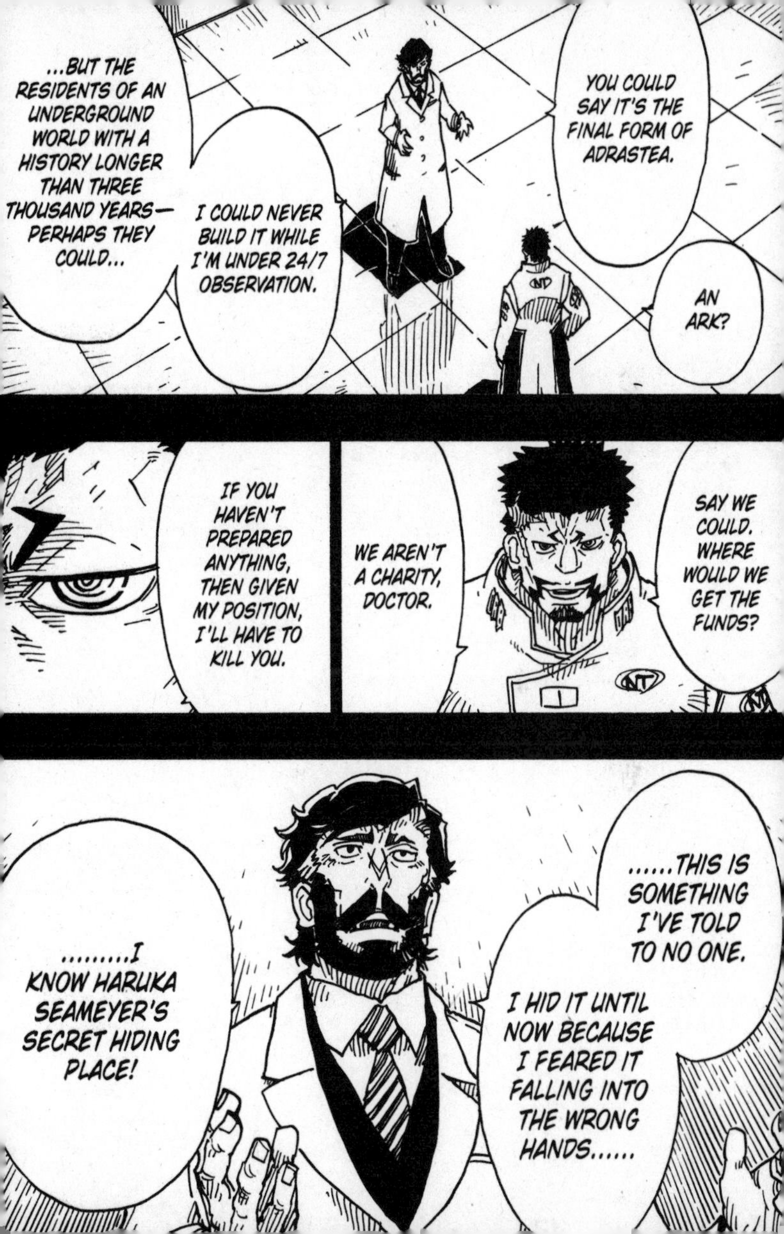
YOU COULD SAY IT'S THE FINAL FORM OF ADRASTEA.
AN ARK?
I COULD NEVER BUILD IT WHILE I'M UNDER 24/7 OBSERVATION.
...BUT THE RESIDENTS OF AN UNDERGROUND WORLD WITH A HISTORY LONGER THAN THREE THOUSAND YEARS—PERHAPS THEY COULD...
SAY WE COULD. WHERE WOULD WE GET THE FUNDS?
WE AREN'T A CHARITY, DOCTOR.
IF YOU HAVEN'T PREPARED ANYTHING, THEN GIVEN MY POSITION, I'LL HAVE TO KILL YOU.
......THIS IS SOMETHING I'VE TOLD TO NO ONE.
I HID IT UNTIL NOW BECAUSE I FEARED IT FALLING INTO THE WRONG HANDS......
.........I KNOW HARUKA SEAMEYER'S SECRET HIDING PLACE!

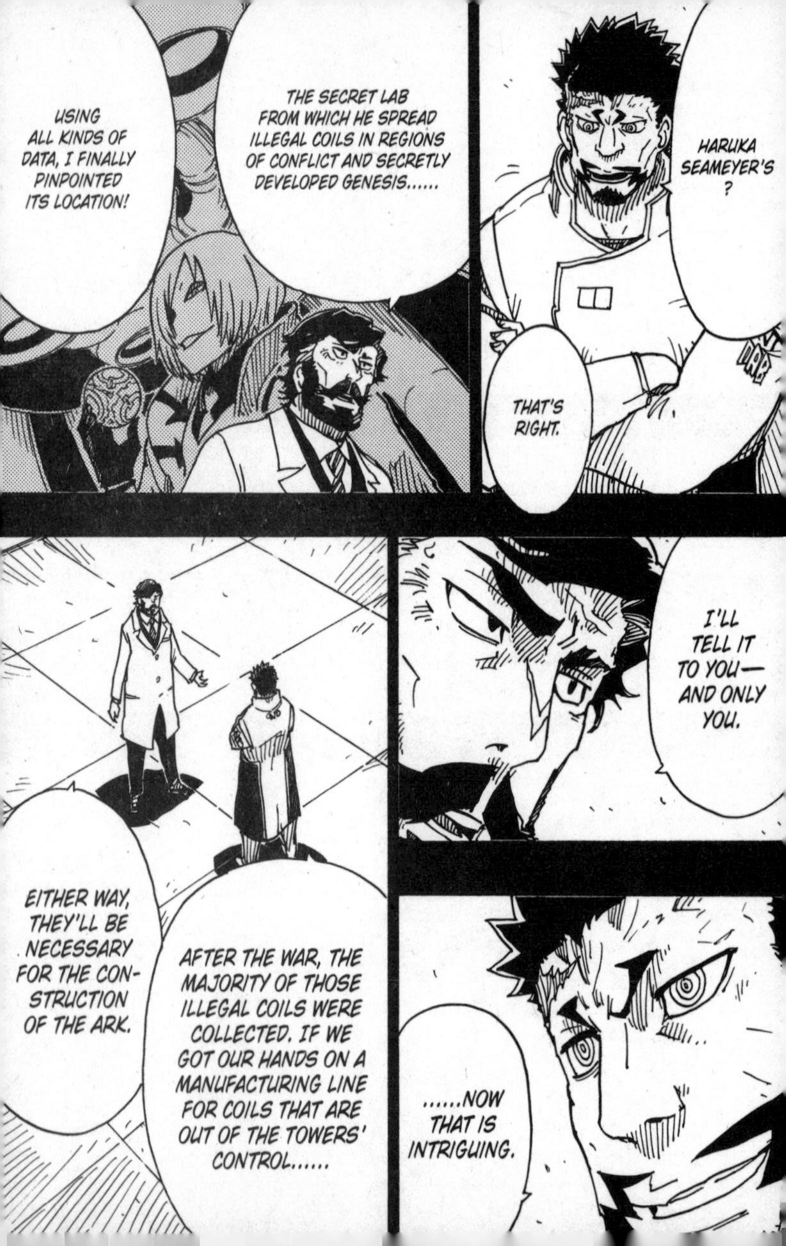
HARUKA SEAMEYER'S?
THAT'S RIGHT.
THE SECRET LAB FROM WHICH HE SPREAD ILLEGAL COILS IN REGIONS OF CONFLICT AND SECRETLY DEVELOPED GENESIS......
USING ALL KINDS OF DATA, I FINALLY PINPOINTED ITS LOCATION!
I'LL TELL IT TO YOU— AND ONLY YOU.
......NOW THAT IS INTRIGUING.
AFTER THE WAR, THE MAJORITY OF THOSE ILLEGAL COILS WERE COLLECTED. IF WE GOT OUR HANDS ON A MANUFACTURING LINE FOR COILS THAT ARE OUT OF THE TOWERS' CONTROL......
EITHER WAY, THEY'LL BE NECESSARY FOR THE CON-STRUCTION OF THE ARK.

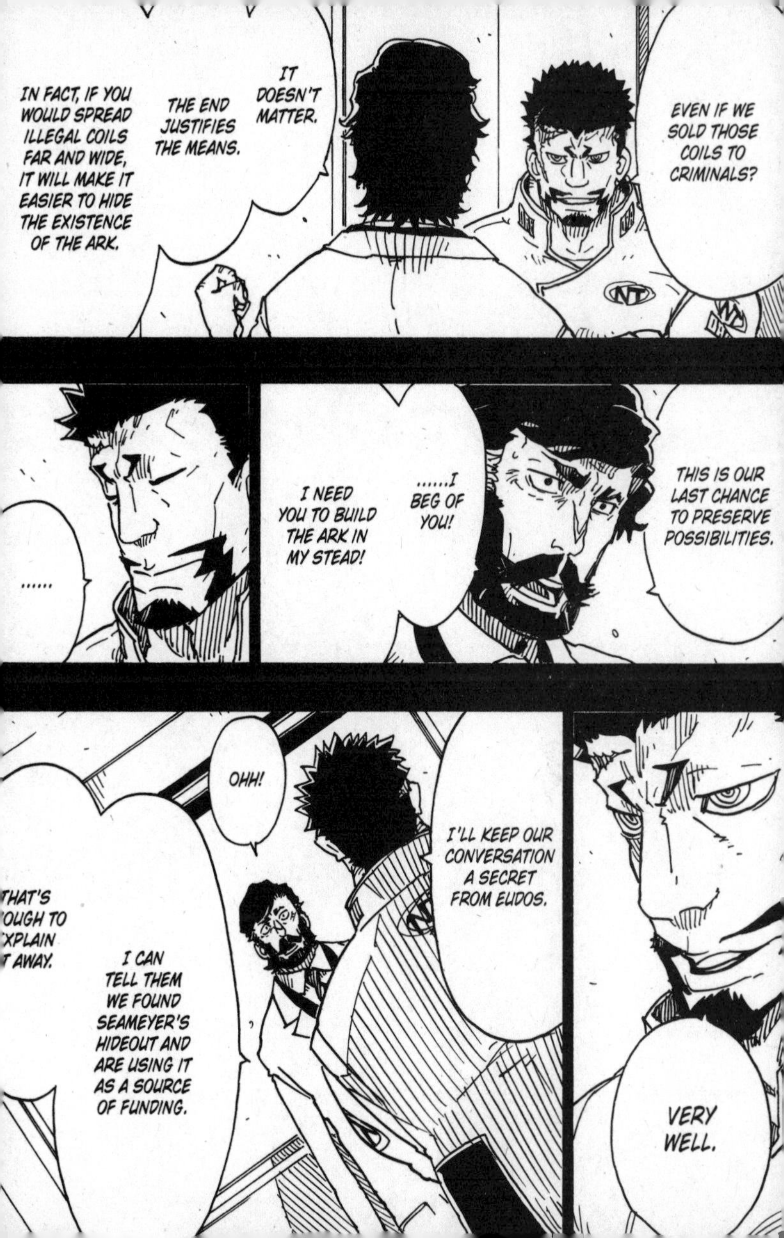
EVEN IF WE SOLD THOSE COILS TO CRIMINALS?
IT DOESN'T MATTER.
THE END JUSTIFIES THE MEANS.
IN FACT, IF YOU WOULD SPREAD ILLEGAL COILS FAR AND WIDE, IT WILL MAKE IT EASIER TO HIDE THE EXISTENCE OF THE ARK.
THIS IS OUR LAST CHANCE TO PRESERVE POSSIBILITIES.
......I BEG OF YOU!
I NEED YOU TO BUILD THE ARK IN MY STEAD!
......
VERY WELL.
I'LL KEEP OUR CONVERSATION A SECRET FROM EUDOS.
OHH!
I CAN TELL THEM WE FOUND SEAMEYER'S HIDEOUT AND ARE USING IT AS A SOURCE OF FUNDING.
THAT'S OUGH TO XPLAIN T AWAY.

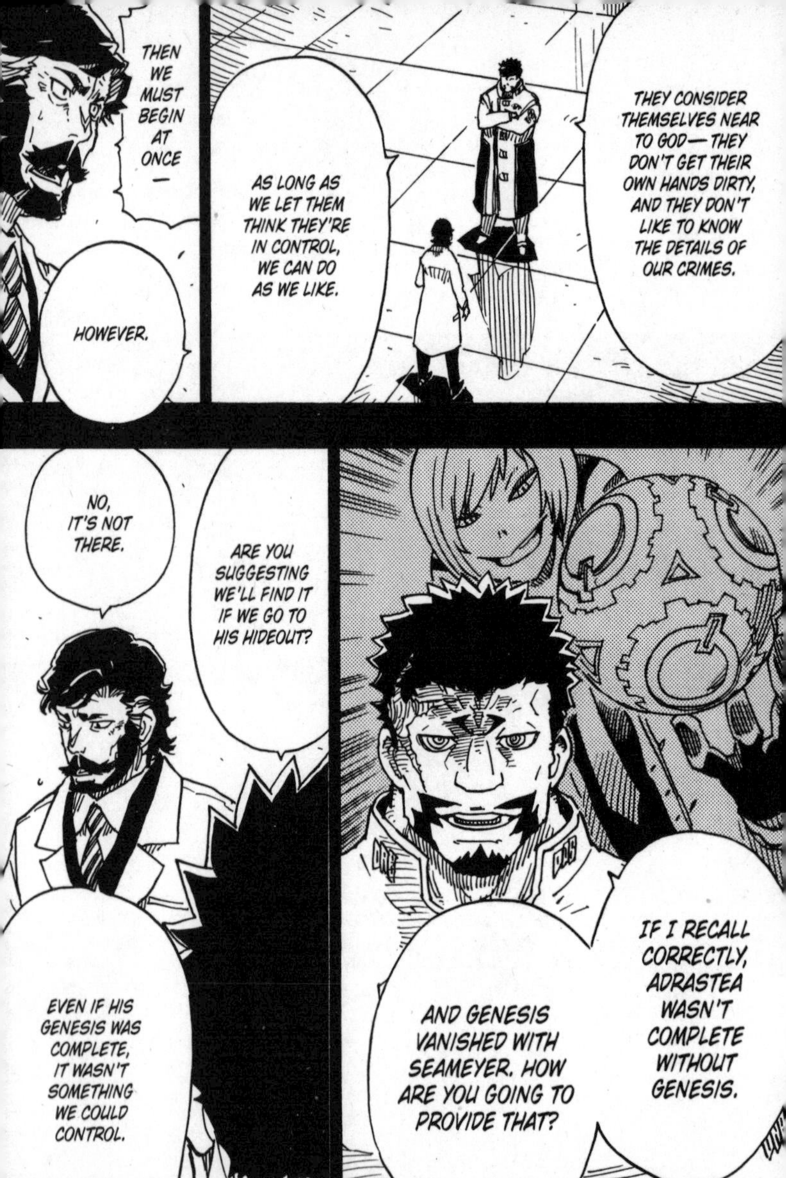
THEY CONSIDER THEMSELVES NEAR TO GOD—THEY DON'T GET THEIR OWN HANDS DIRTY, AND THEY DON'T LIKE TO KNOW THE DETAILS OF OUR CRIMES.
AS LONG AS WE LET THEM THINK THEY'RE IN CONTROL, WE CAN DO AS WE LIKE.
THEN WE MUST BEGIN AT ONCE—
HOWEVER.
IF I RECALL CORRECTLY, ADRASTEA WASN'T COMPLETE WITHOUT GENESIS.
AND GENESIS VANISHED WITH SEAMEYER. HOW ARE YOU GOING TO PROVIDE THAT?
ARE YOU SUGGESTING WE'LL FIND IT IF WE GO TO HIS HIDEOUT?
NO, IT'S NOT THERE.
EVEN IF HIS GENESIS WAS COMPLETE, IT WASN'T SOMETHING WE COULD CONTROL.

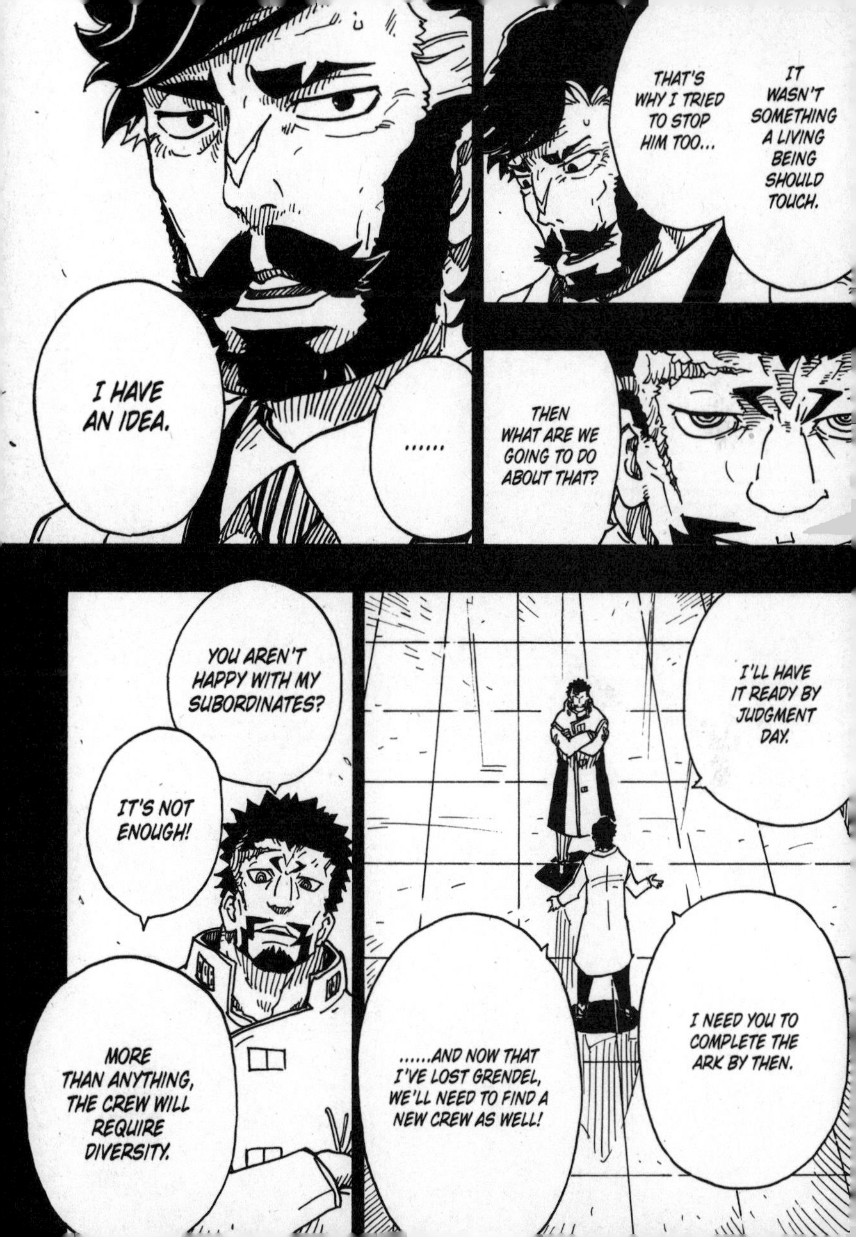
IT WASN'T SOMETHING A LIVING BEING SHOULD TOUCH.
THAT'S WHY I TRIED TO STOP HIM TOO...
THEN WHAT ARE WE GOING TO DO ABOUT THAT?
......
I HAVE AN IDEA.
I'LL HAVE IT READY BY JUDGMENT DAY.
I NEED YOU TO COMPLETE THE ARK BY THEN.
......AND NOW THAT I'VE LOST GRENDEL, WE'LL NEED TO FIND A NEW CREW AS WELL!
YOU AREN'T HAPPY WITH MY SUBORDINATES?
IT'S NOT ENOUGH!
MORE THAN ANYTHING, THE CREW WILL REQUIRE DIVERSITY.

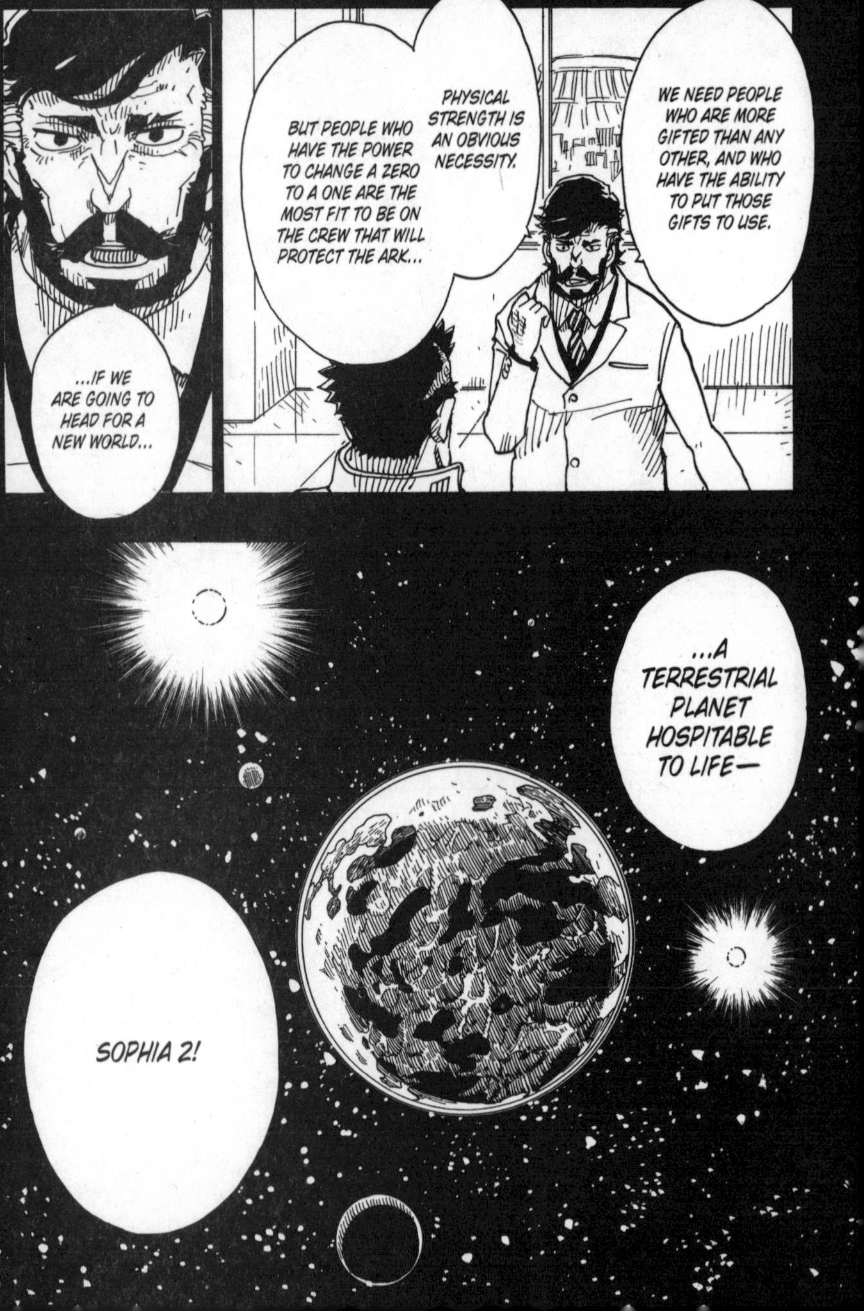
WE NEED PEOPLE WHO ARE MORE GIFTED THAN ANY OTHER, AND WHO HAVE THE ABILITY TO PUT THOSE GIFTS TO USE.
PHYSICAL STRENGTH IS AN OBVIOUS NECESSITY.
BUT PEOPLE WHO HAVE THE POWER TO CHANGE A ZERO TO A ONE ARE THE MOST FIT TO BE ON THE CREW THAT WILL PROTECT THE ARK...
...IF WE ARE GOING TO HEAD FOR A NEW WORLD...
...A TERRESTRIAL PLANET HOSPITABLE TO LIFE—
SOPHIA 2!

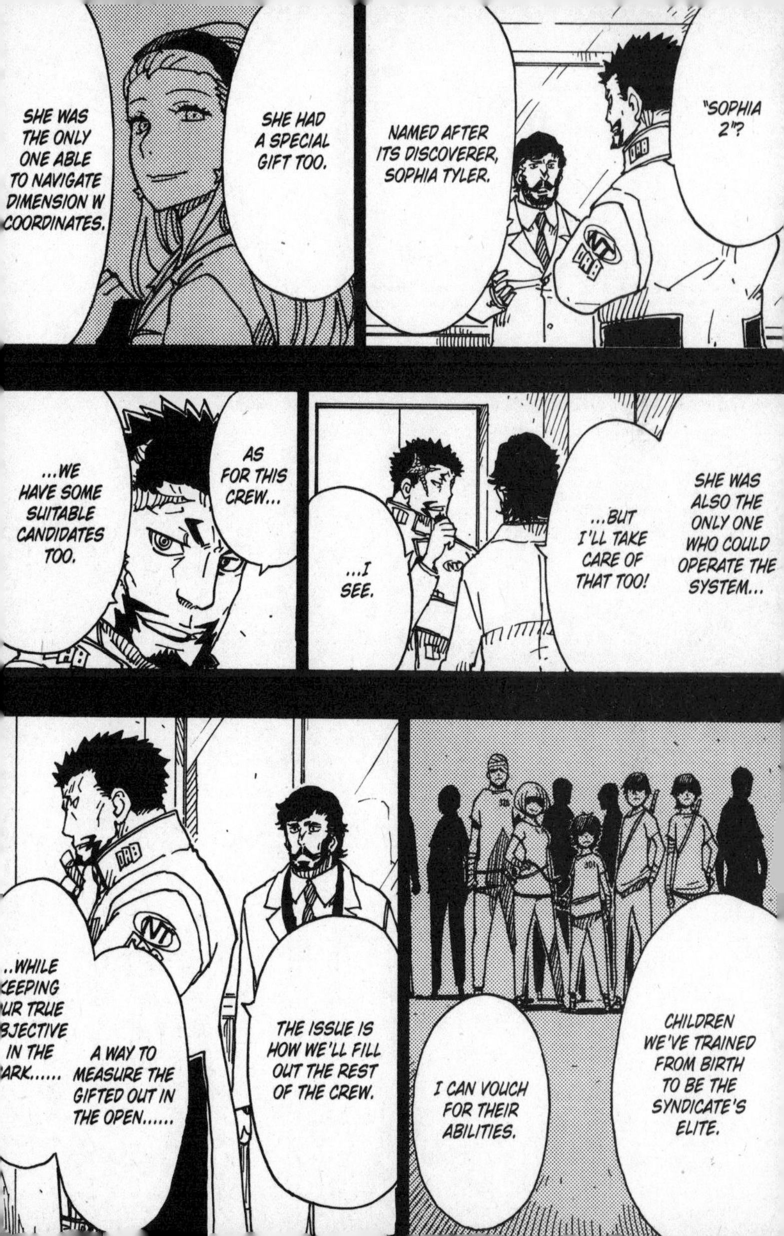
"SOPHIA 2"?
NAMED AFTER ITS DISCOVERER, SOPHIA TYLER.
SHE HAD A SPECIAL GIFT TOO.
SHE WAS THE ONLY ONE ABLE TO NAVIGATE DIMENSION W COORDINATES.
SHE WAS ALSO THE ONLY ONE WHO COULD OPERATE THE SYSTEM...
...BUT I'LL TAKE CARE OF THAT TOO!
...I SEE.
AS FOR THIS CREW...
...WE HAVE SOME SUITABLE CANDIDATES TOO.
CHILDREN WE'VE TRAINED FROM BIRTH TO BE THE SYNDICATE'S ELITE.
I CAN VOUCH FOR THEIR ABILITIES.
THE ISSUE IS HOW WE'LL FILL OUT THE REST OF THE CREW.
A WAY TO MEASURE THE GIFTED OUT IN THE OPEN......
..WHILE KEEPING UR TRUE BJECTIVE IN THE ARK......

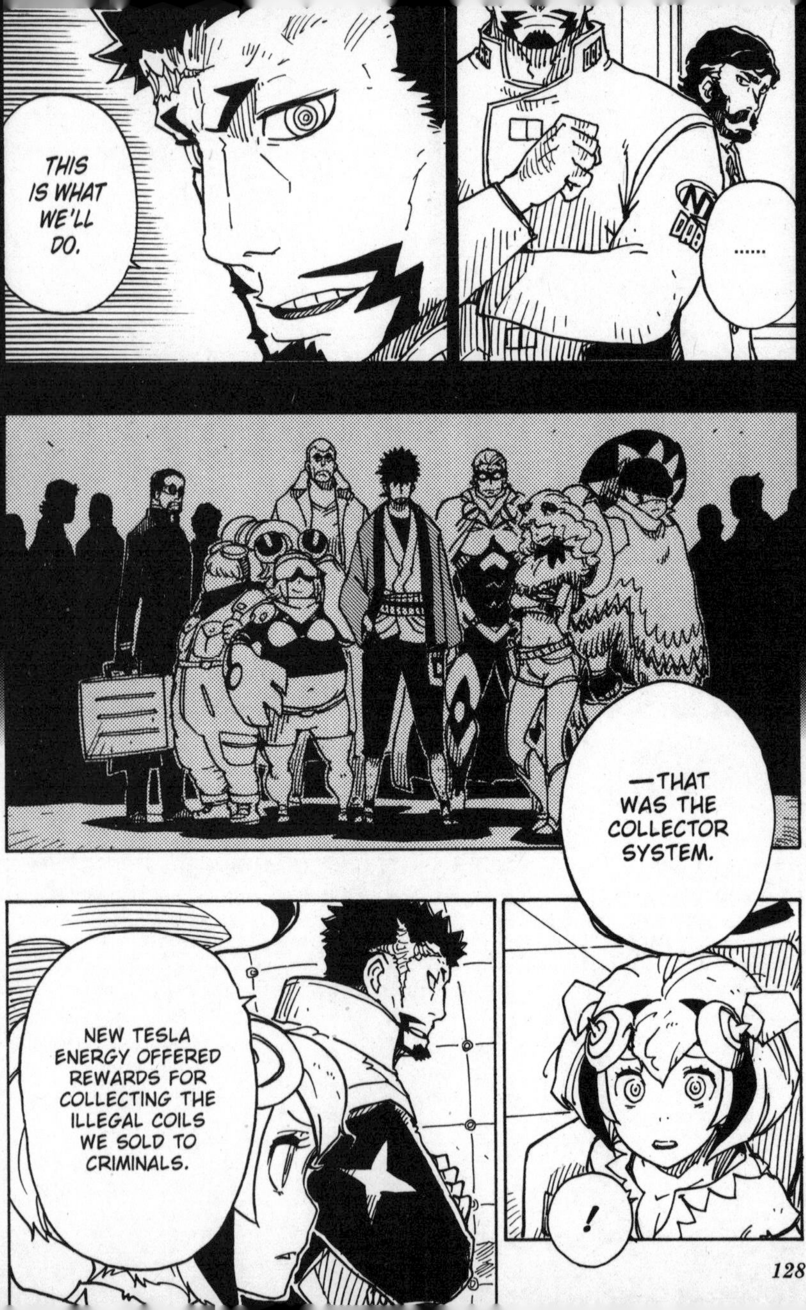
......
THIS IS WHAT WE'LL DO.
—THAT WAS THE COLLECTOR SYSTEM.
!
NEW TESLA ENERGY OFFERED REWARDS FOR COLLECTING THE ILLEGAL COILS WE SOLD TO CRIMINALS.

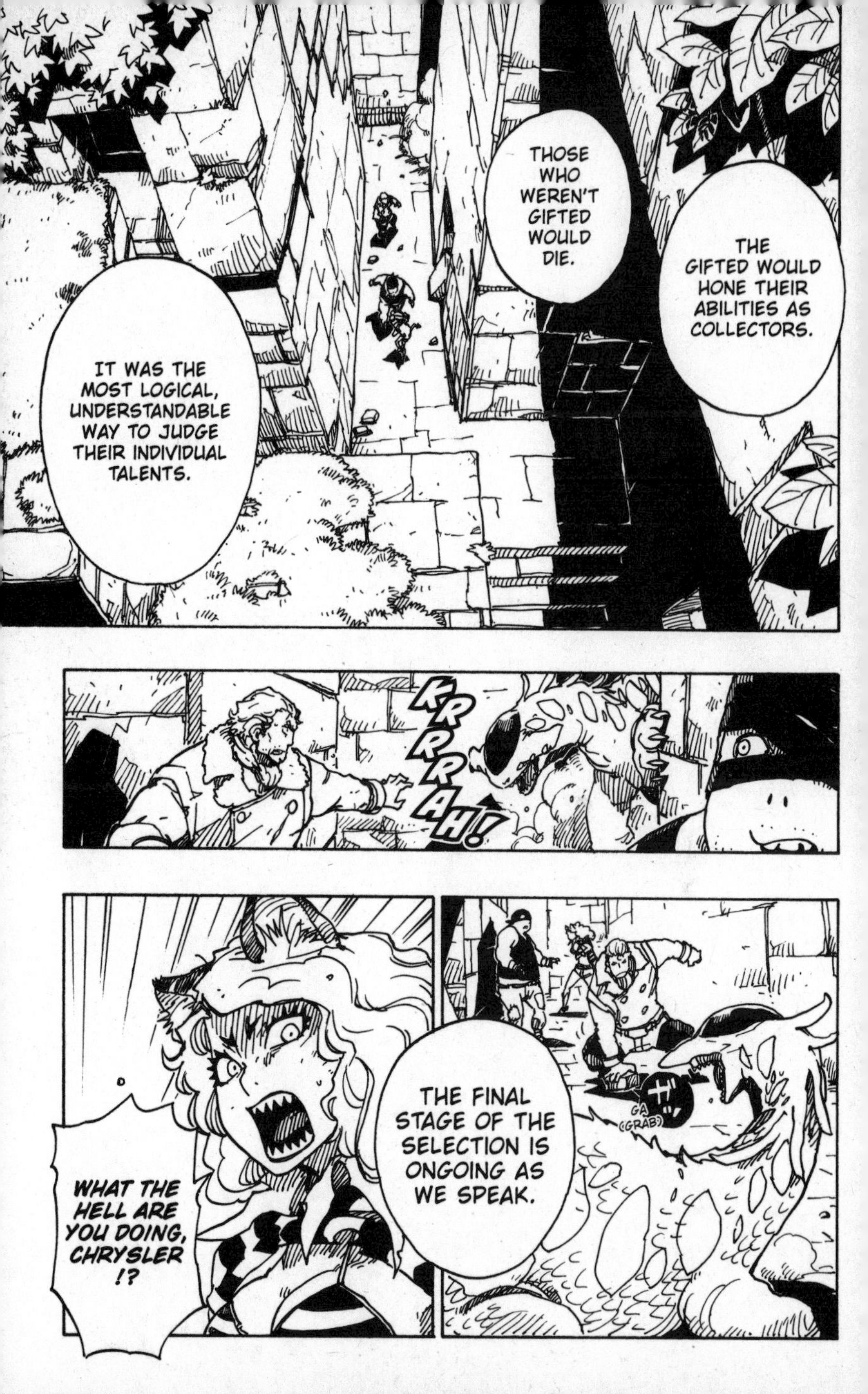
THE GIFTED WOULD HONE THEIR ABILITIES AS COLLECTORS.
THOSE WHO WEREN'T GIFTED WOULD DIE.
IT WAS THE MOST LOGICAL, UNDERSTANDABLE WAY TO JUDGE THEIR INDIVIDUAL TALENTS.
KRRRAH!
GA (GRAB)
THE FINAL STAGE OF THE SELECTION IS ONGOING AS WE SPEAK.
WHAT THE HELL ARE YOU DOING, CHRYSLER!?

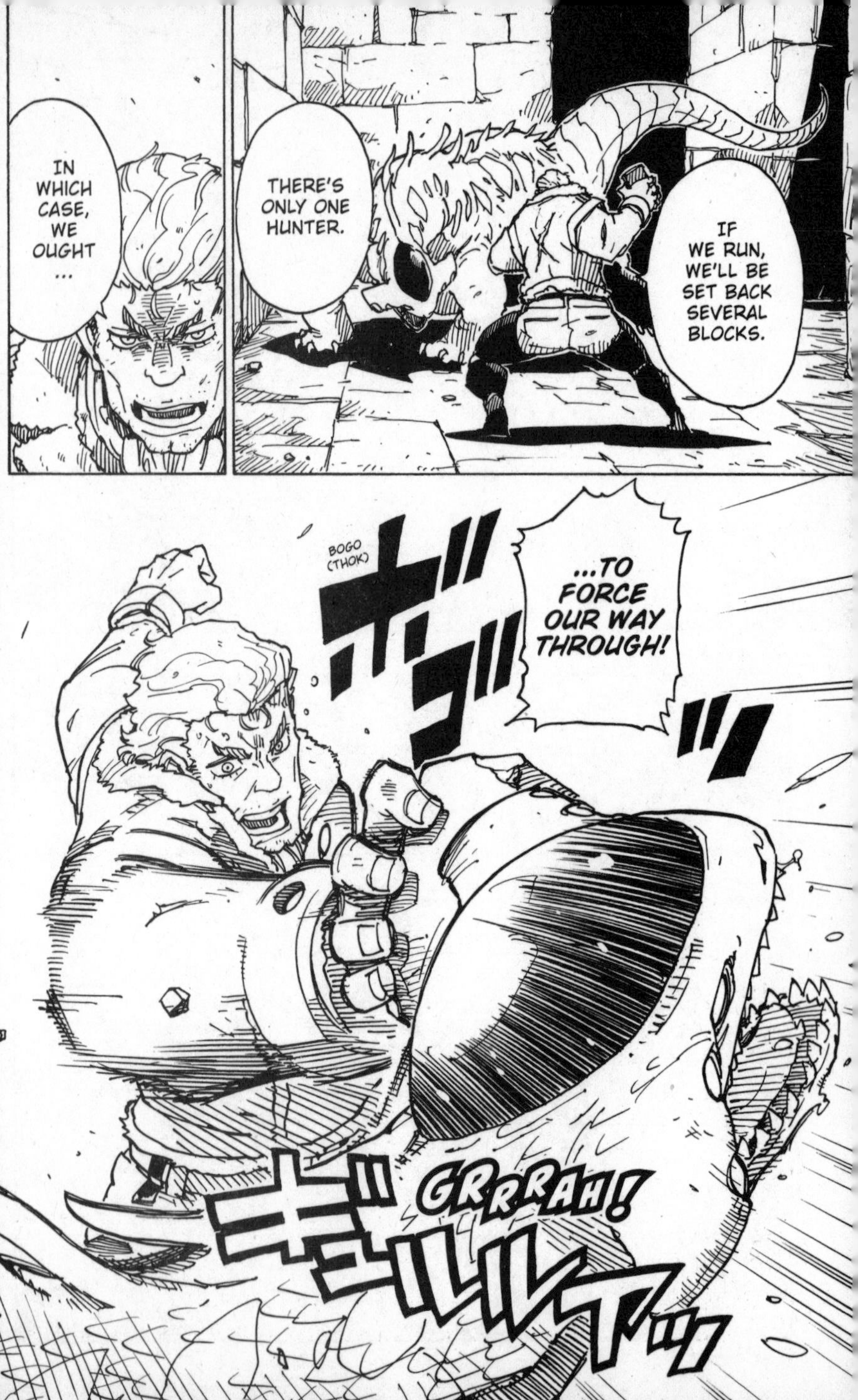
IF WE RUN, WE'LL BE SET BACK SEVERAL BLOCKS.
THERE'S ONLY ONE HUNTER.
IN WHICH CASE, WE OUGHT ...
...TO FORCE OUR WAY THROUGH!
BOGO (THOK)
GRRRAH!

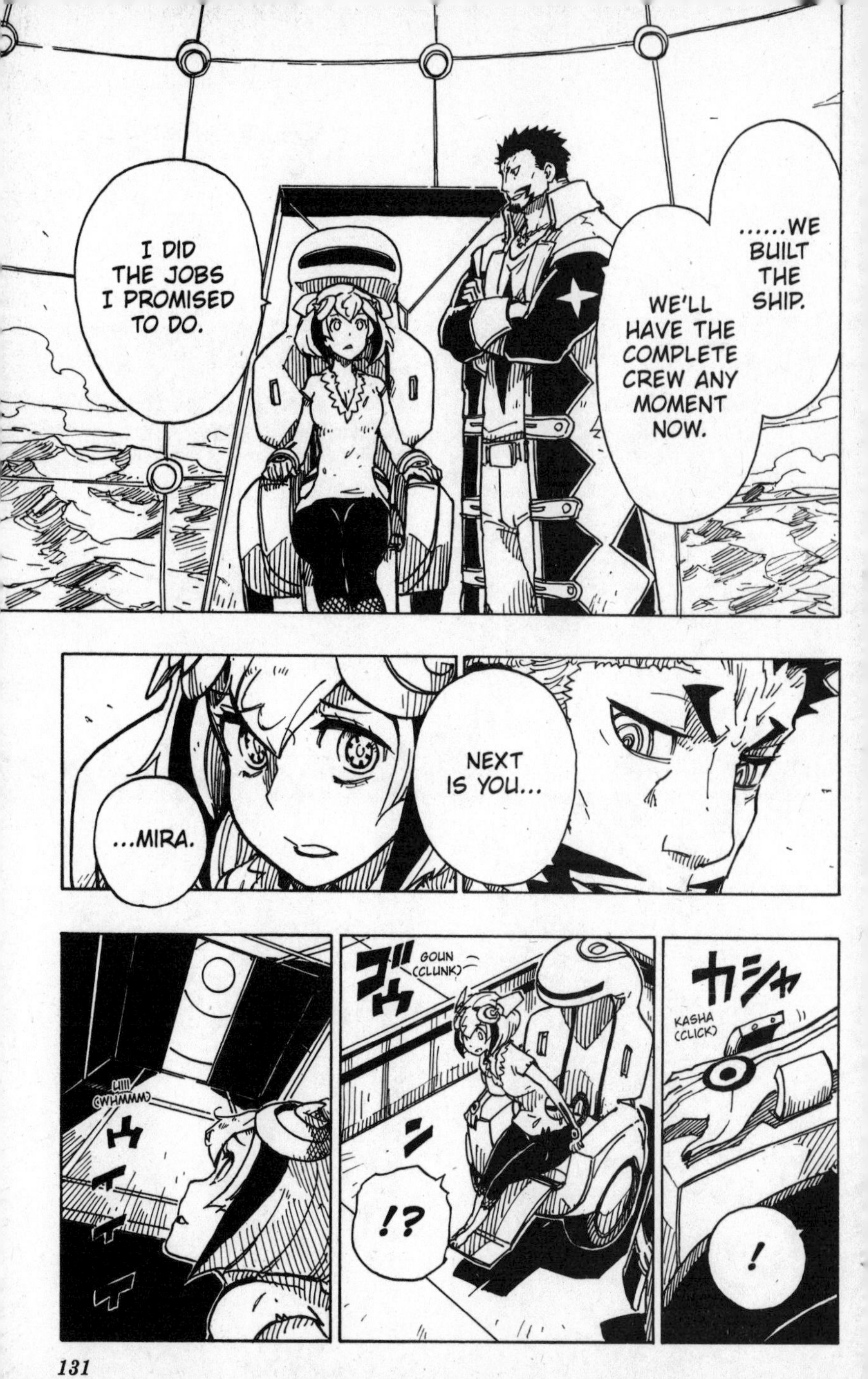
......WE BUILT THE SHIP.
WE'LL HAVE THE COMPLETE CREW ANY MOMENT NOW.
I DID THE JOBS I PROMISED TO DO.
NEXT IS YOU...
...MIRA.
カシャ
KASHA (CLICK)
!
ゴウン
GOUN (CLUNK)
!?
UIII (WHMMM)

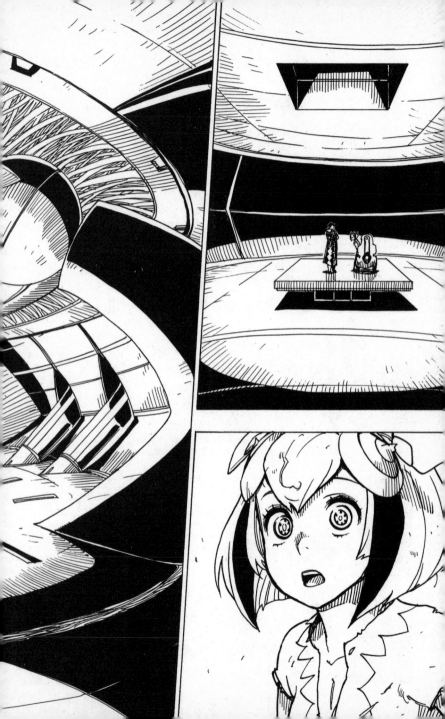

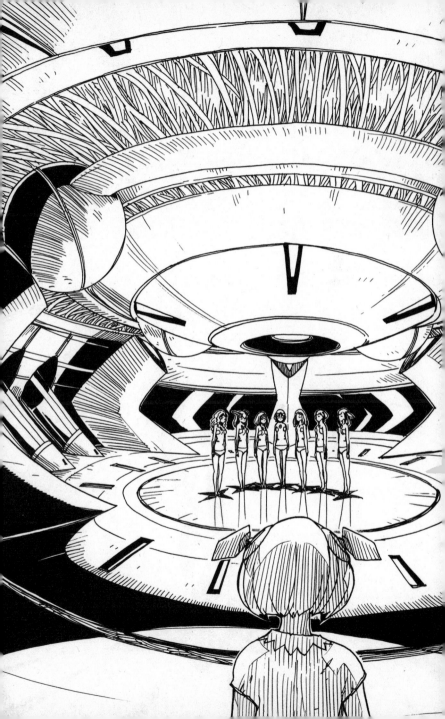

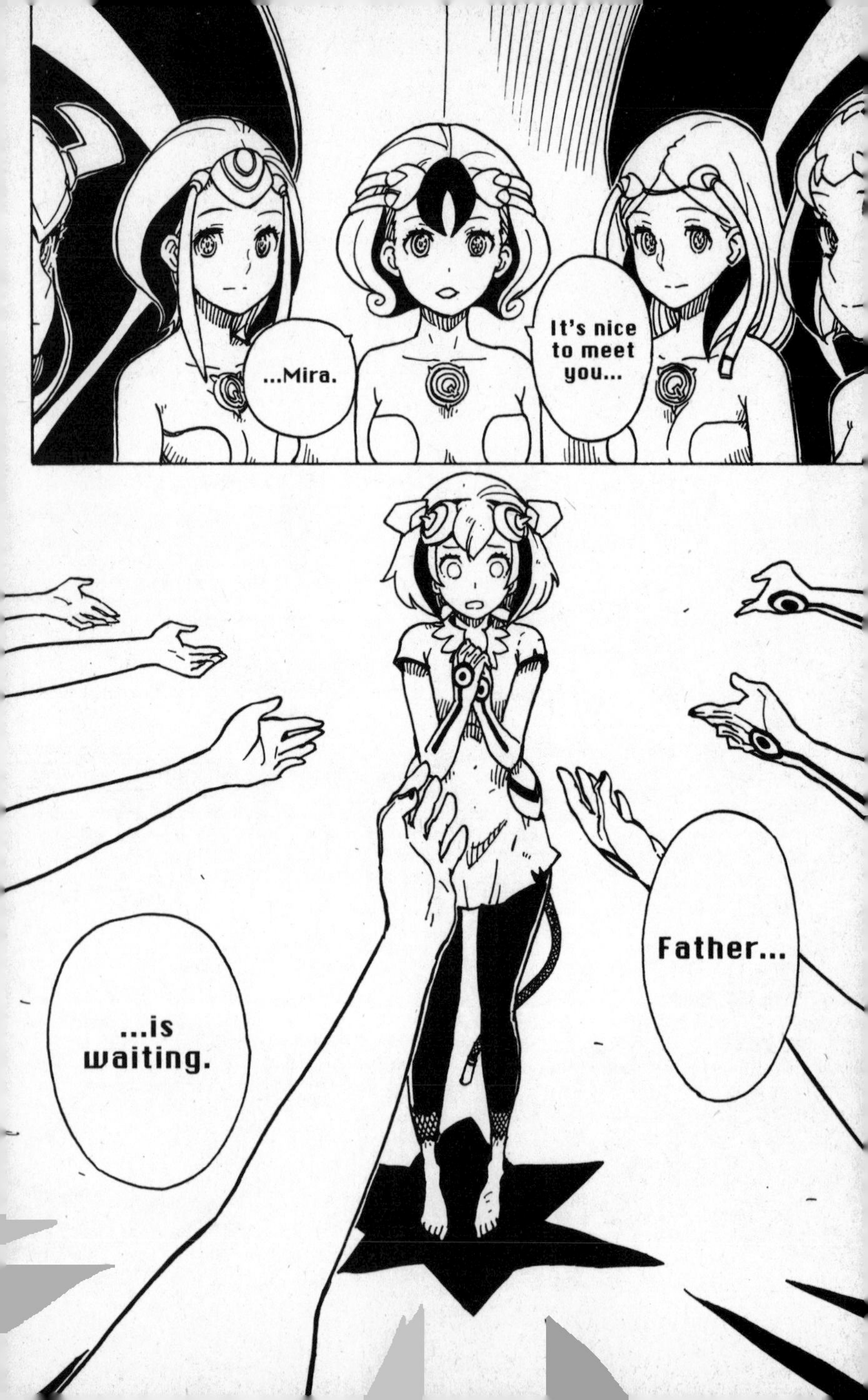
It's nice to meet you...
...Mira.
Father...
...is waiting.

FILE.107
POISON STINGER

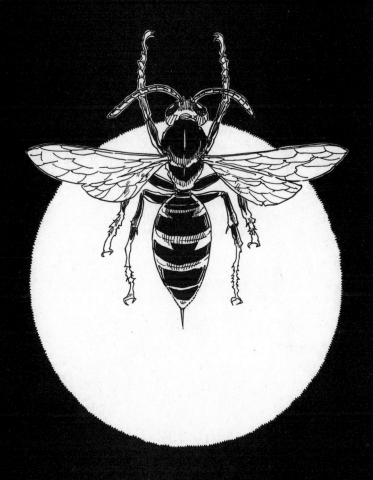

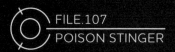

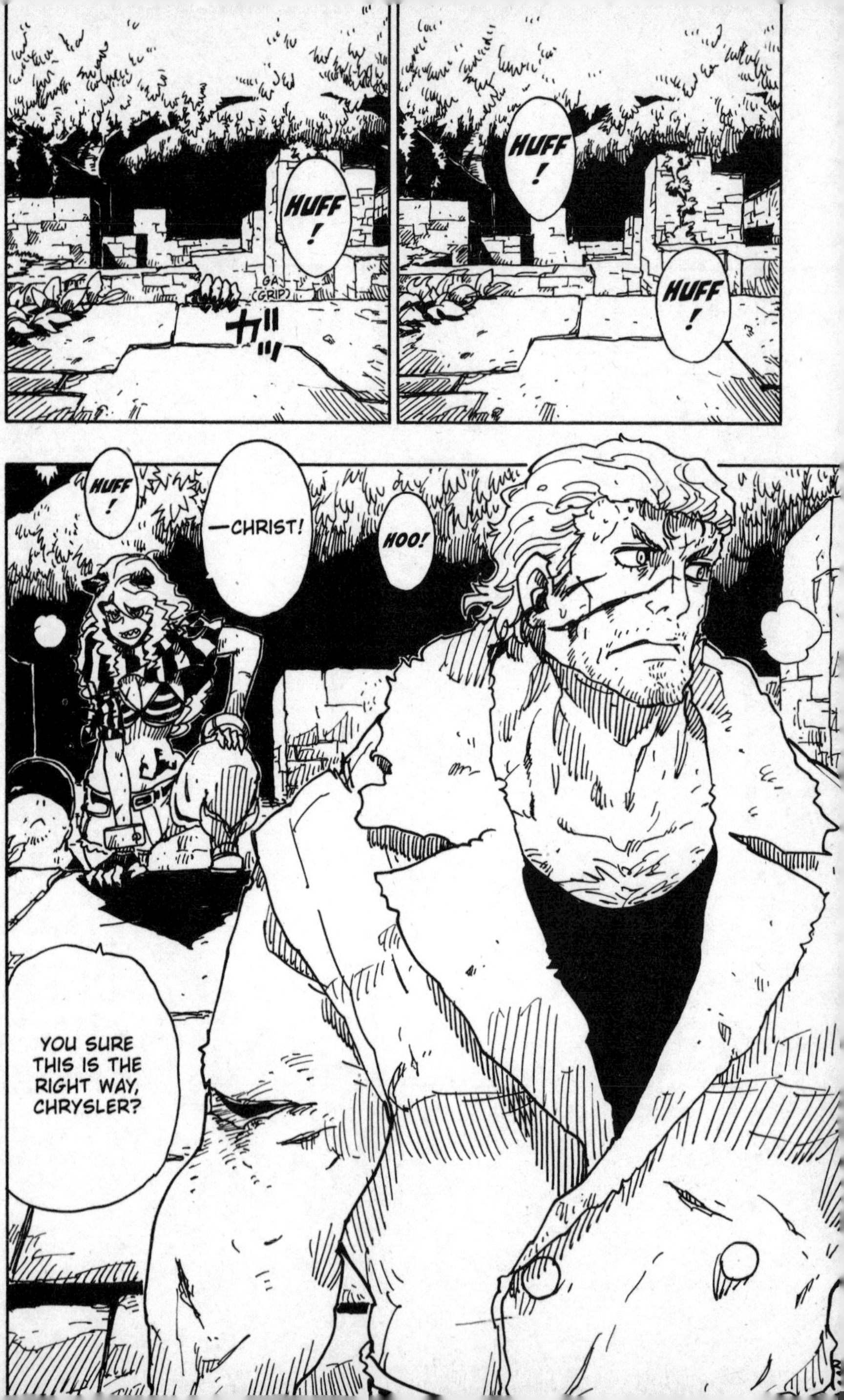
HUFF!
HUFF!
HUFF!
GA (GRIP)
ガッ
HOO!
—CHRIST!
HUFF!
YOU SURE THIS IS THE RIGHT WAY, CHRYSLER?

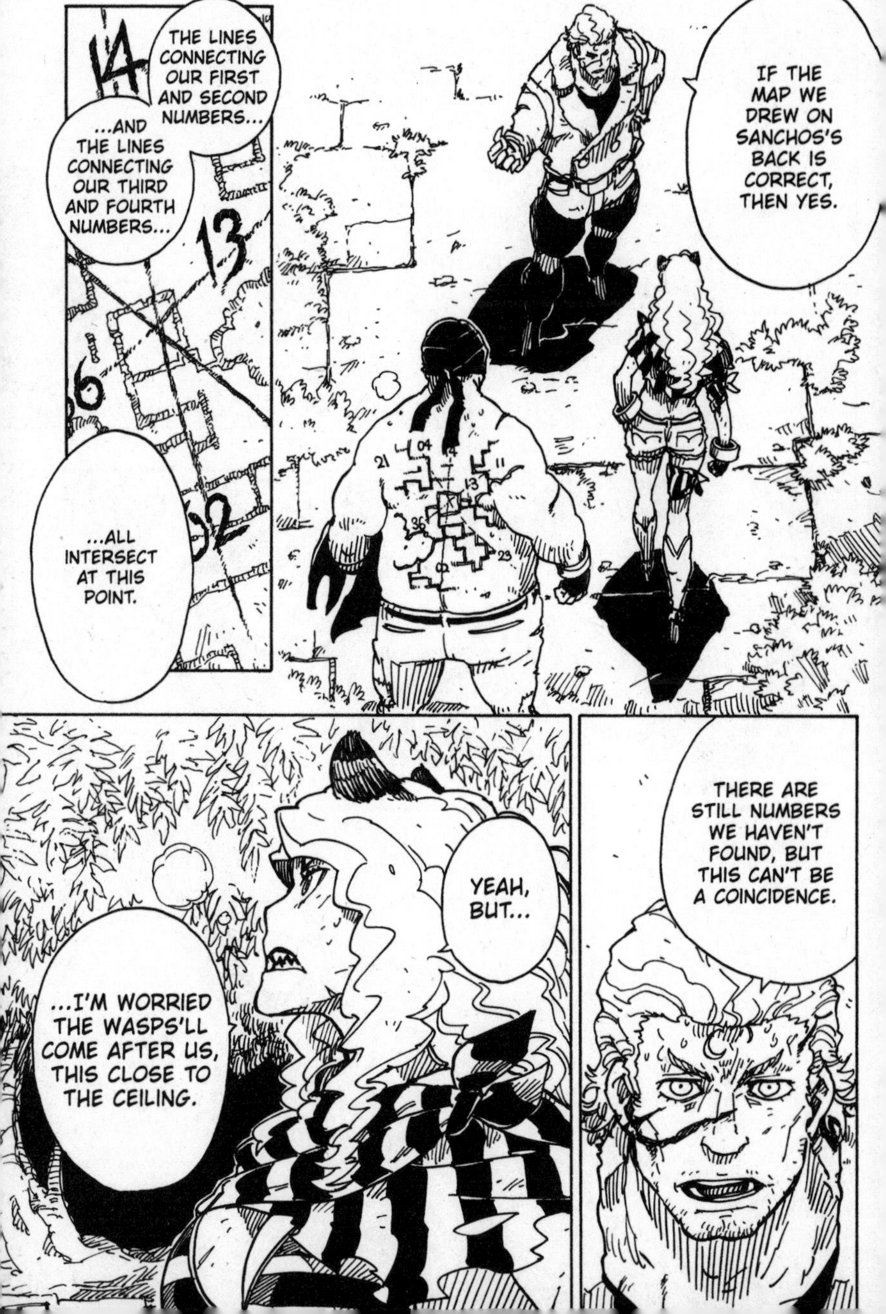
IF THE MAP WE DREW ON SANCHOS'S BACK IS CORRECT, THEN YES.
THE LINES CONNECTING OUR FIRST AND SECOND NUMBERS...
...AND THE LINES CONNECTING OUR THIRD AND FOURTH NUMBERS...
14
13
...ALL INTERSECT AT THIS POINT.
THERE ARE STILL NUMBERS WE HAVEN'T FOUND, BUT THIS CAN'T BE A COINCIDENCE.
YEAH, BUT...
...I'M WORRIED THE WASPS'LL COME AFTER US, THIS CLOSE TO THE CEILING.

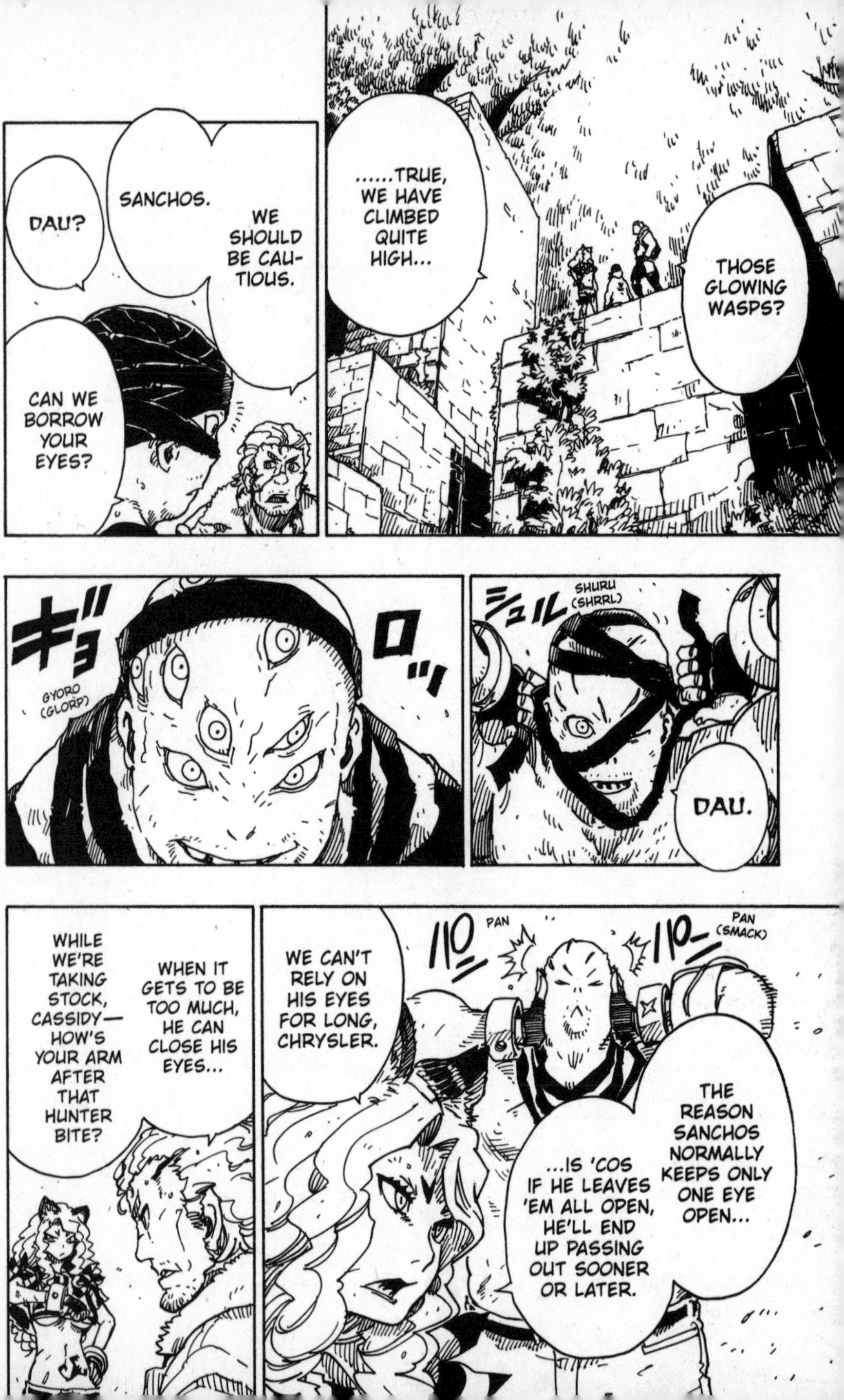
THOSE GLOWING WASPS?
......TRUE, WE HAVE CLIMBED QUITE HIGH...
SANCHOS.
WE SHOULD BE CAU-TIOUS.
DAU?
CAN WE BORROW YOUR EYES?
シュル
SHURU (SHRRL)
DAU.
ギョロ
GYORO (GLORP)
パン
PAN (SMACK)
パン
PAN
THE REASON SANCHOS NORMALLY KEEPS ONLY ONE EYE OPEN...
...IS 'COS IF HE LEAVES 'EM ALL OPEN, HE'LL END UP PASSING OUT SOONER OR LATER.
WE CAN'T RELY ON HIS EYES FOR LONG, CHRYSLER.
WHEN IT GETS TO BE TOO MUCH, HE CAN CLOSE HIS EYES...
WHILE WE'RE TAKING STOCK, CASSIDY— HOW'S YOUR ARM AFTER THAT HUNTER BITE?

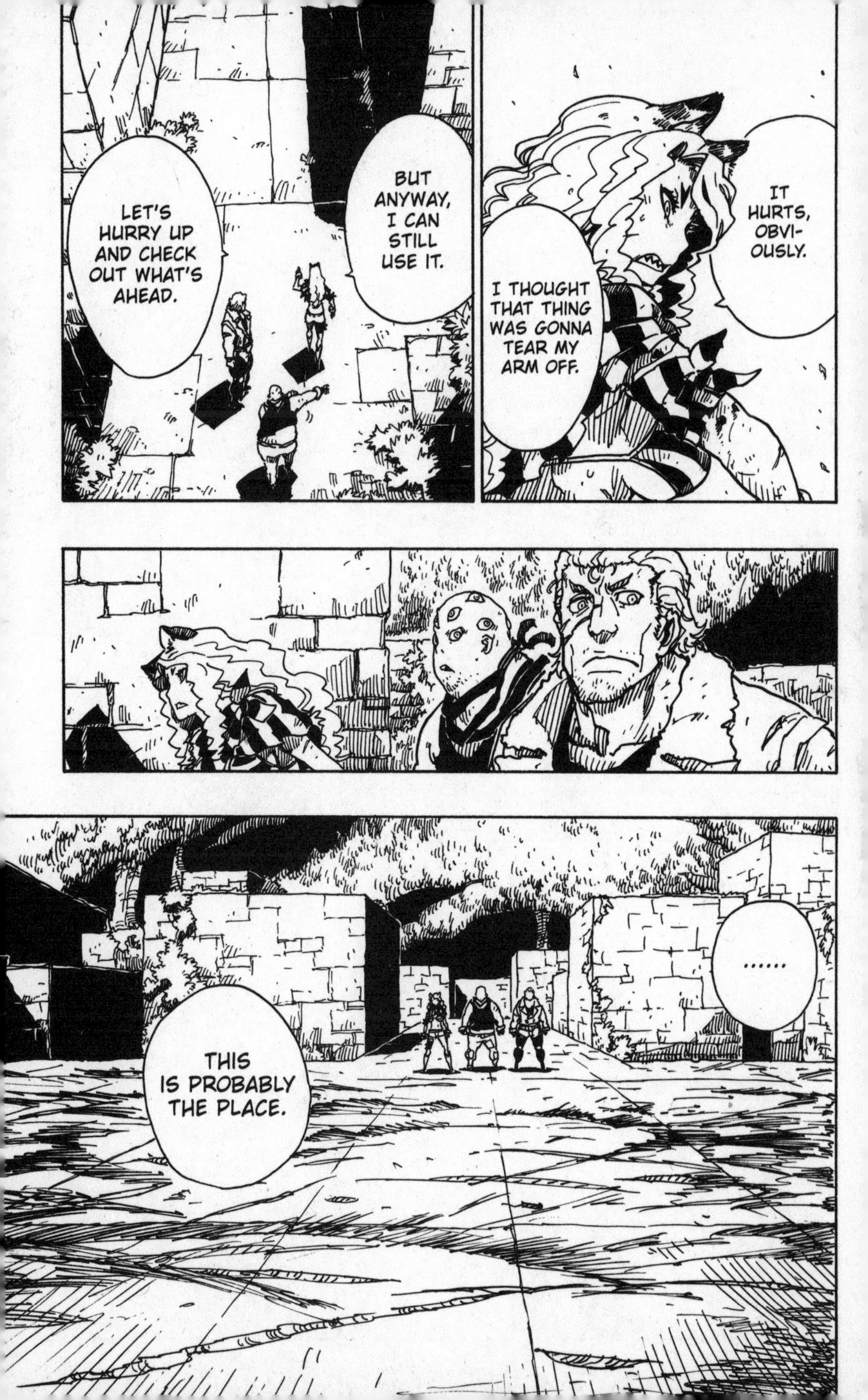
IT HURTS, OBVI-OUSLY.
I THOUGHT THAT THING WAS GONNA TEAR MY ARM OFF.
BUT ANYWAY, I CAN STILL USE IT.
LET'S HURRY UP AND CHECK OUT WHAT'S AHEAD.
......
THIS IS PROBABLY THE PLACE.

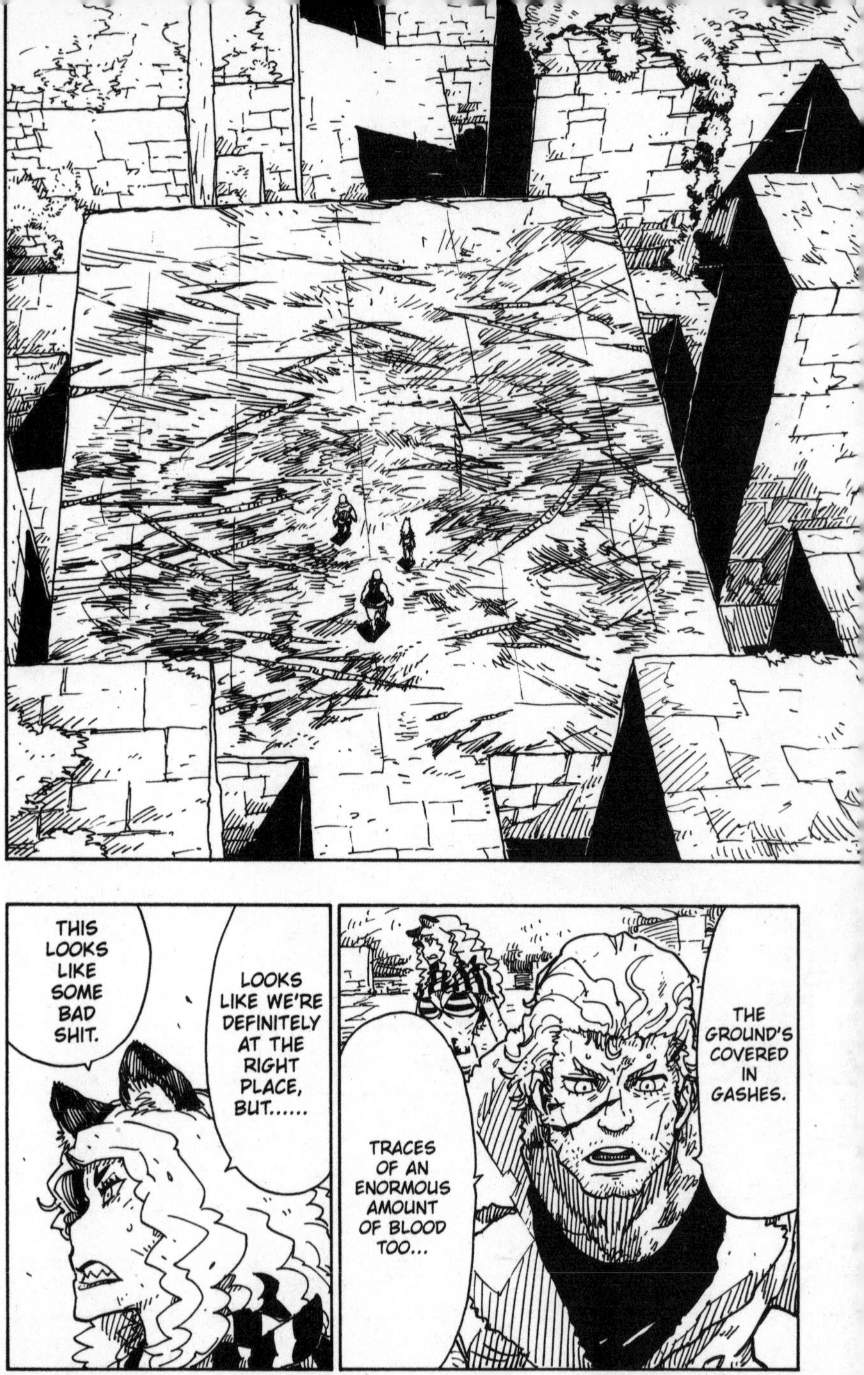
THE GROUND'S COVERED IN GASHES.
TRACES OF AN ENORMOUS AMOUNT OF BLOOD TOO...
LOOKS LIKE WE'RE DEFINITELY AT THE RIGHT PLACE, BUT......
THIS LOOKS LIKE SOME BAD SHIT.

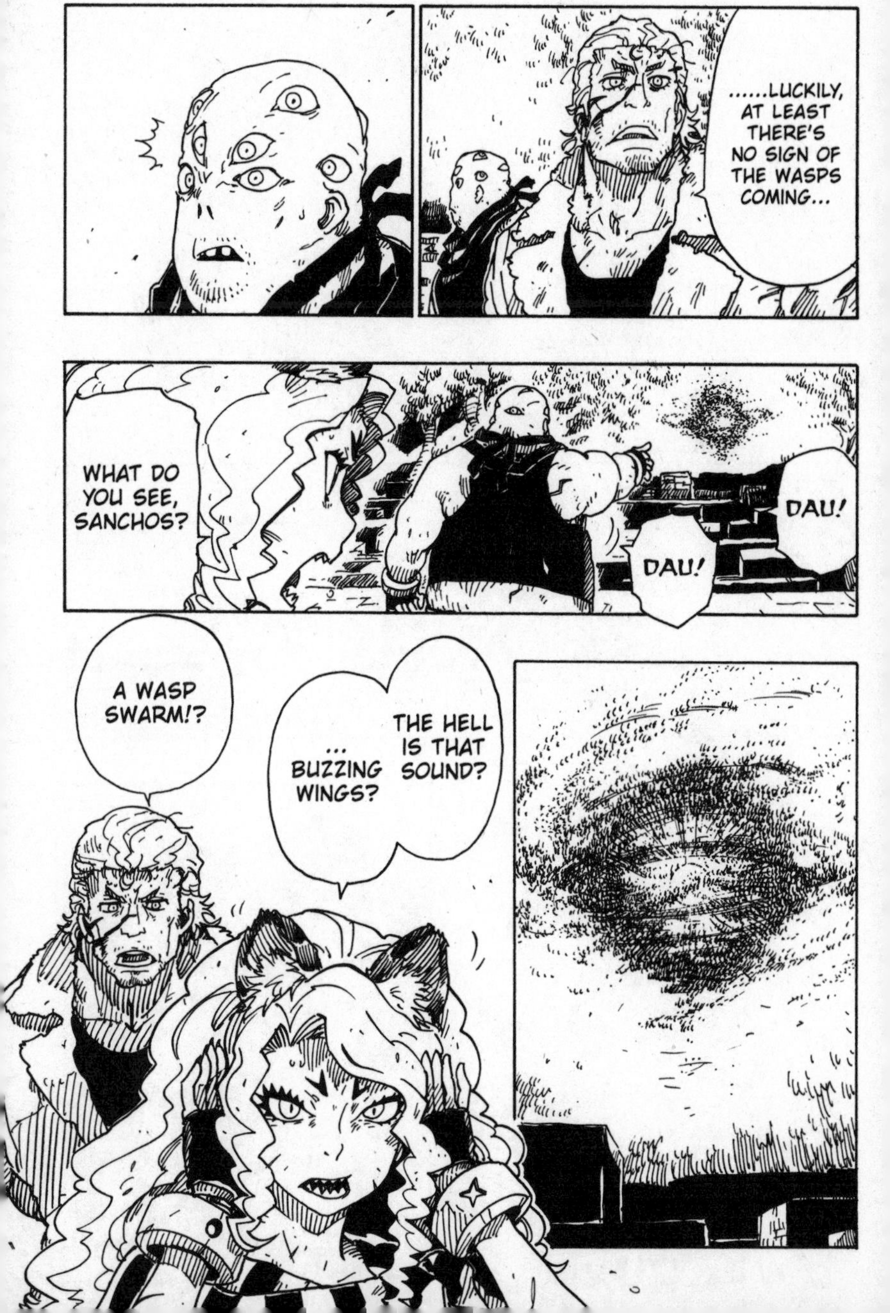
......LUCKILY, AT LEAST THERE'S NO SIGN OF THE WASPS COMING...
DAU!
DAU!
WHAT DO YOU SEE, SANCHOS?
THE HELL IS THAT SOUND?
... BUZZING WINGS?
A WASP SWARM!?

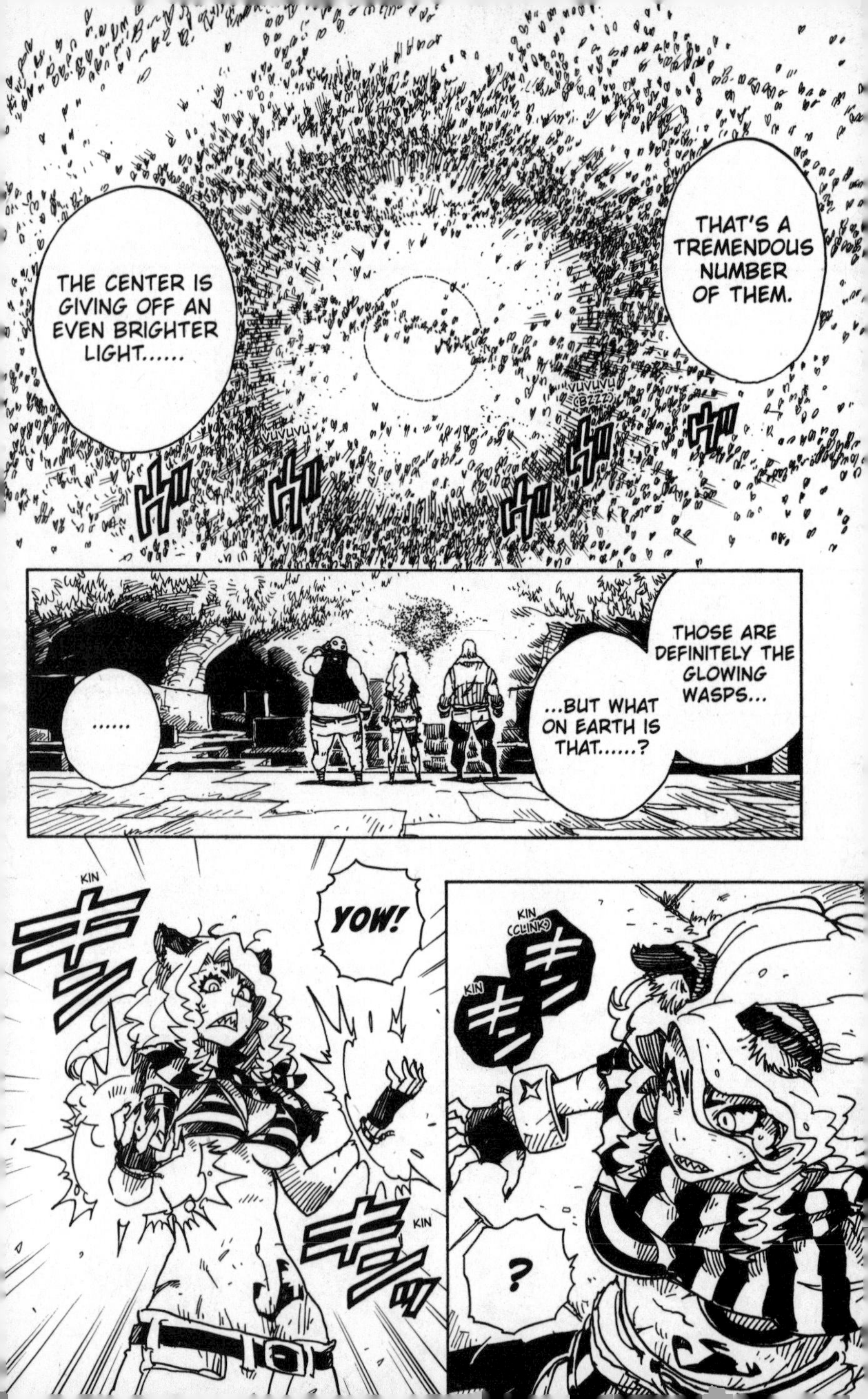
THAT'S A TREMENDOUS NUMBER OF THEM.
VUVUVU (BZZZ)
THE CENTER IS GIVING OFF AN EVEN BRIGHTER LIGHT......
VUVUVU
THOSE ARE DEFINITELY THE GLOWING WASPS...
...BUT WHAT ON EARTH IS THAT......?
......
KIN (CLINK)
KIN
?
KIN
YOW!
KIN

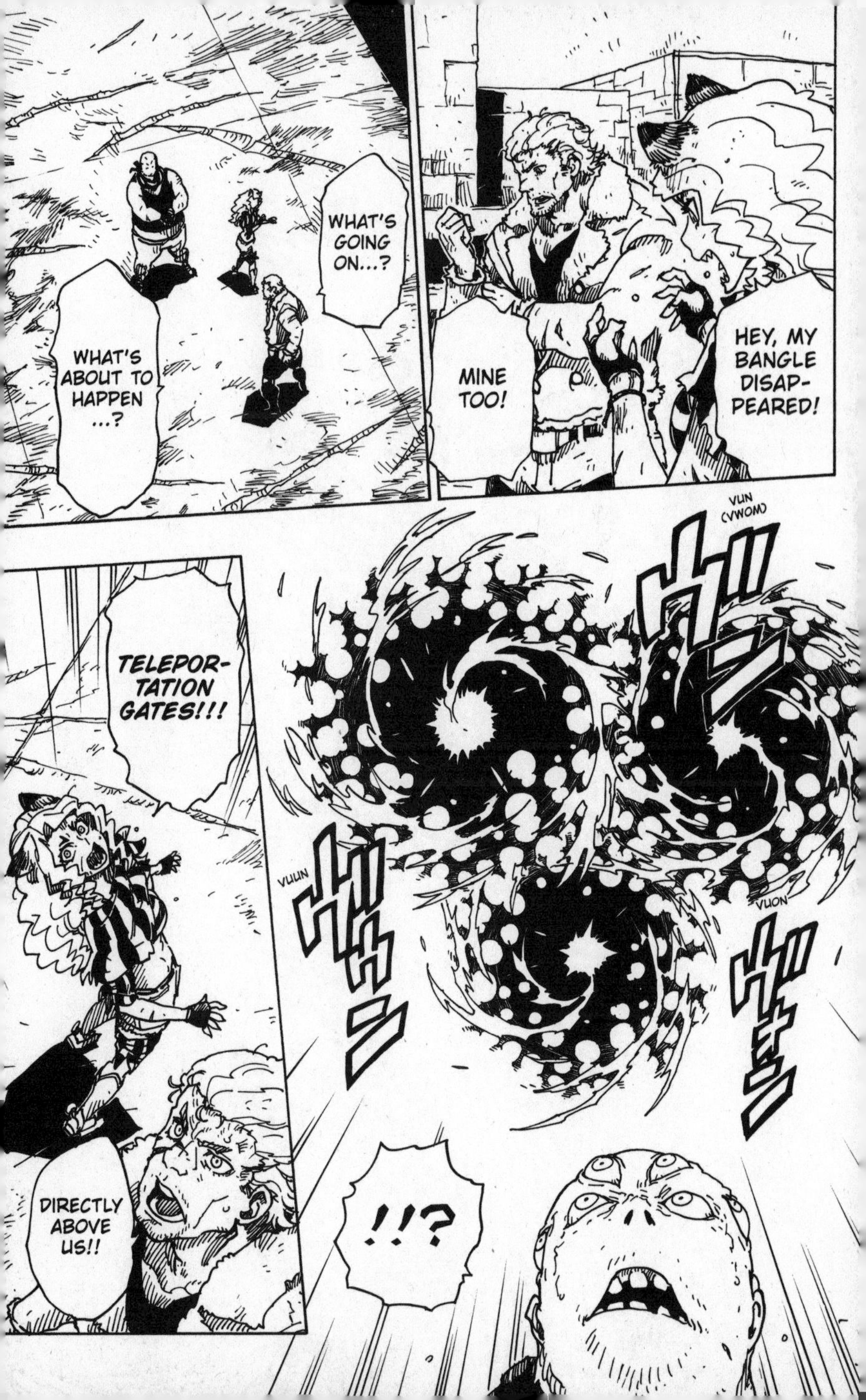
HEY, MY BANGLE DISAPPEARED!
MINE TOO!
WHAT'S GOING ON...?
WHAT'S ABOUT TO HAPPEN...?
VUN (VWOM)
VUON
VUUN
!!?
TELEPORTATION GATES!!!
DIRECTLY ABOVE US!!

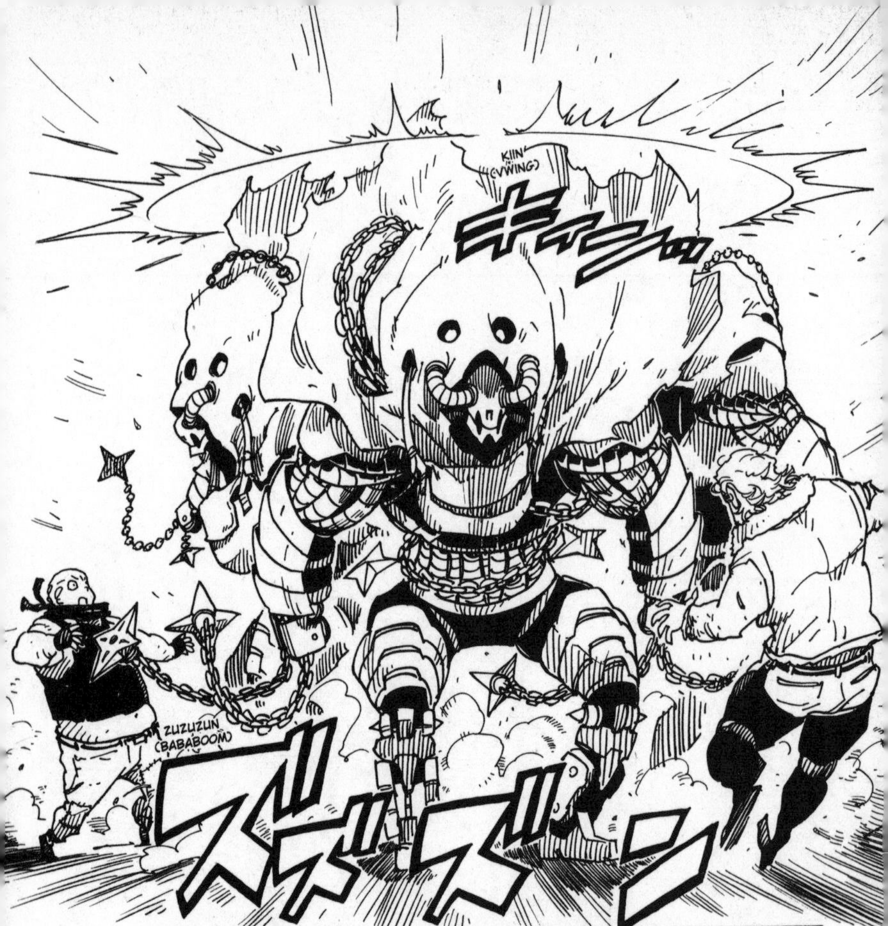
KIIN (VWING)
ZUZUZUN (BABABOOM)
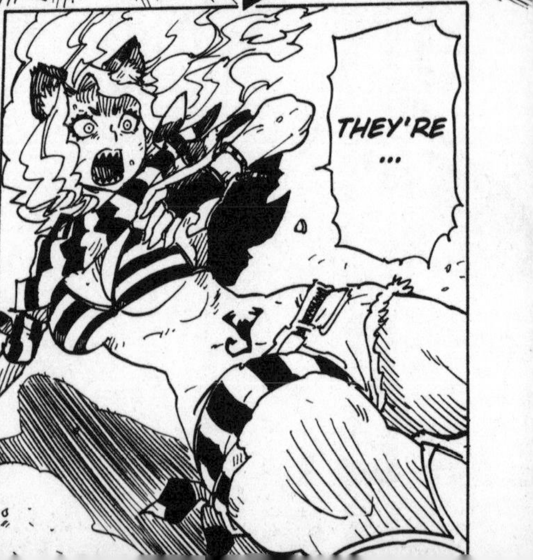
THEY'RE ...
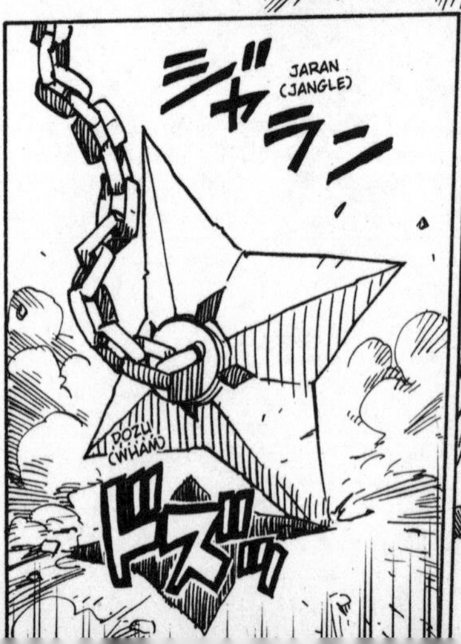
JARAN (JANGLE)
DOZU (WHAM)

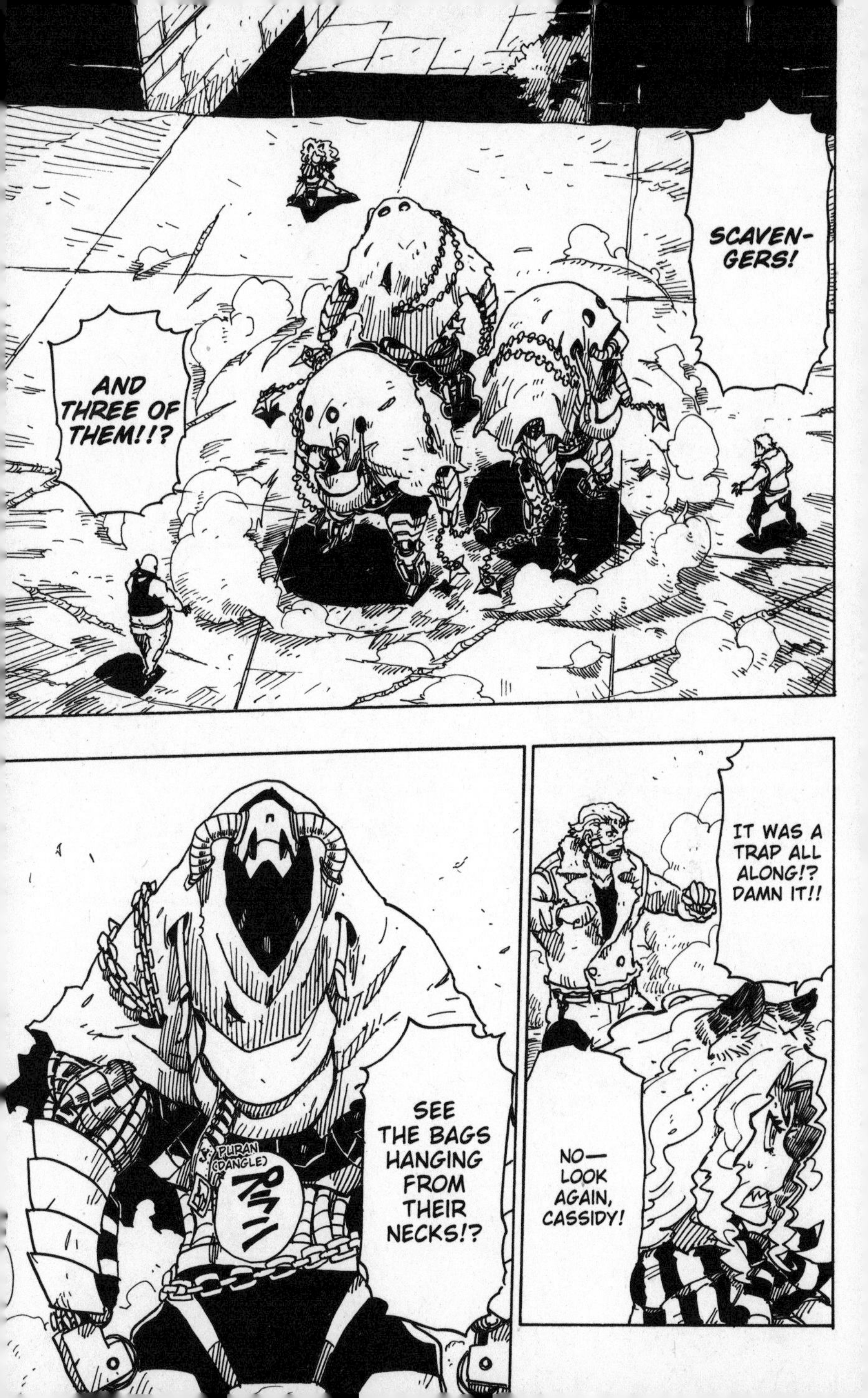
SCAVEN-GERS!
AND THREE OF THEM!!?
IT WAS A TRAP ALL ALONG!? DAMN IT!!
NO— LOOK AGAIN, CASSIDY!
SEE THE BAGS HANGING FROM THEIR NECKS!?
PURAN (DANGLE)

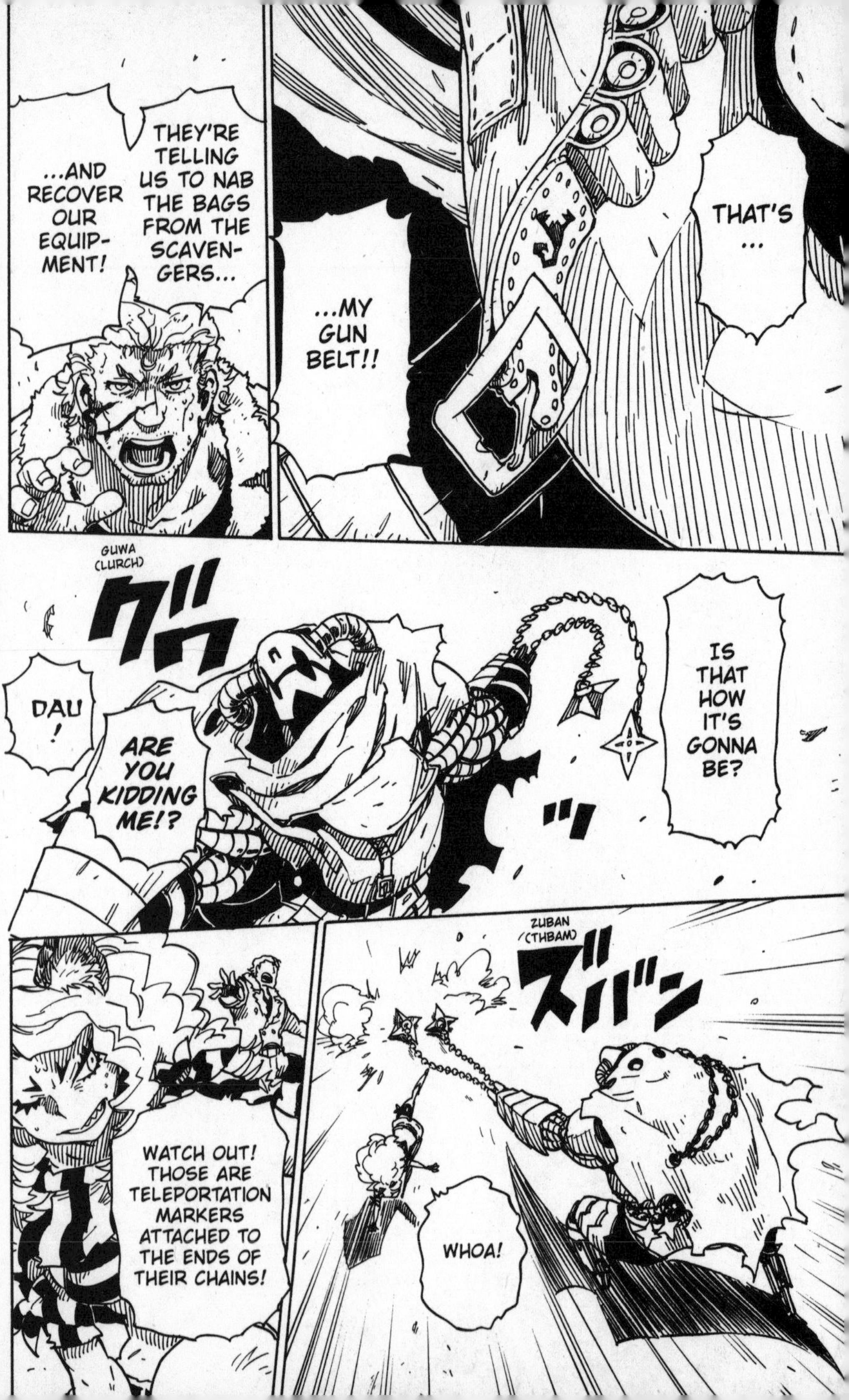
THAT'S ...
...MY GUN BELT!!
THEY'RE TELLING US TO NAB THE BAGS FROM THE SCAVENGERS...
...AND RECOVER OUR EQUIPMENT!
IS THAT HOW IT'S GONNA BE?
GUWA (LURCH)
ARE YOU KIDDING ME!?
DAU!
ZUBAN (THBAM)
WHOA!
WATCH OUT! THOSE ARE TELEPORTATION MARKERS ATTACHED TO THE ENDS OF THEIR CHAINS!

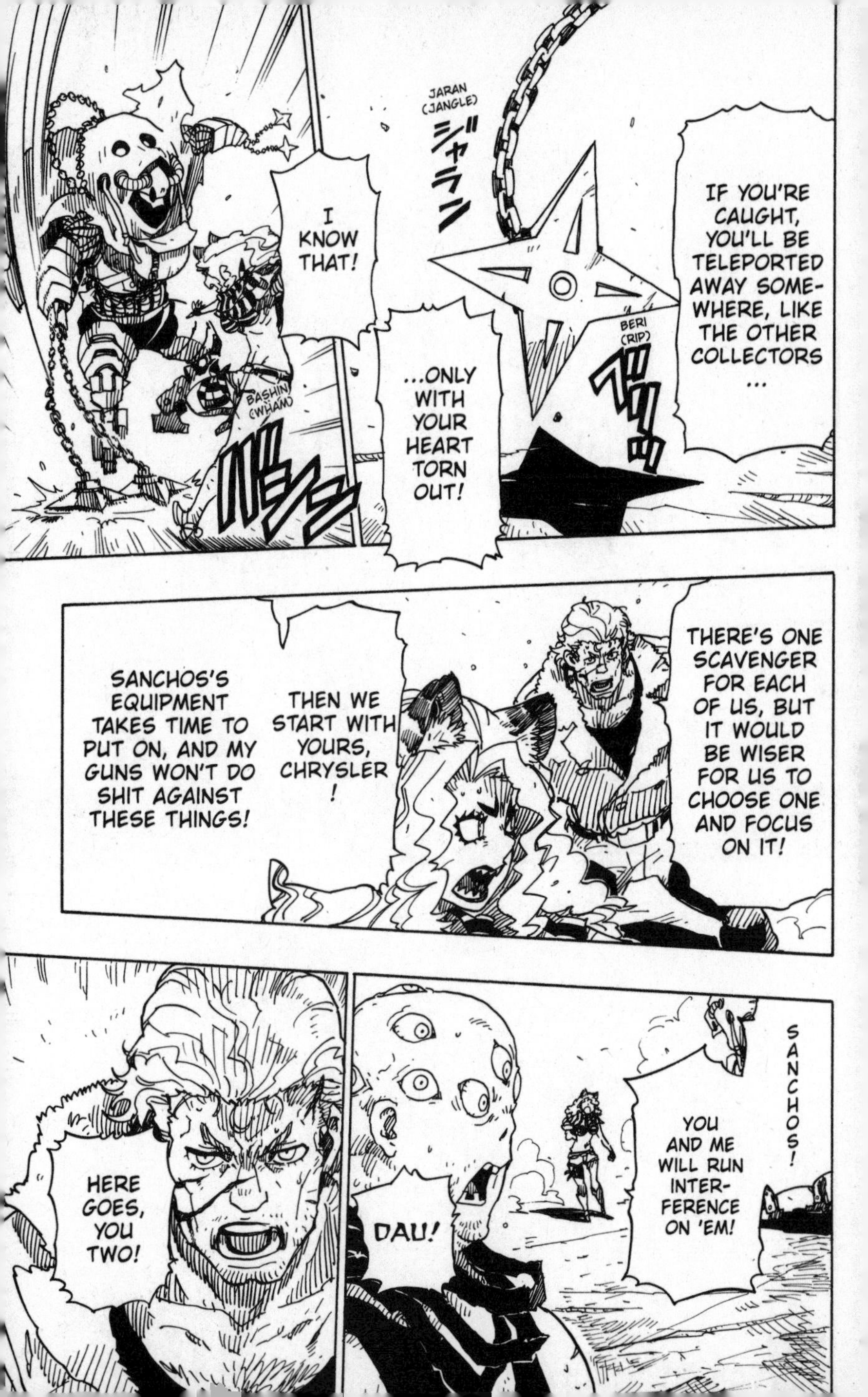
IF YOU'RE CAUGHT, YOU'LL BE TELEPORTED AWAY SOME-WHERE, LIKE THE OTHER COLLECTORS ...
JARAN (JANGLE)
ジャラン
BERI (RIP)
I KNOW THAT!
...ONLY WITH YOUR HEART TORN OUT!
BASHIN (WHAM)
THERE'S ONE SCAVENGER FOR EACH OF US, BUT IT WOULD BE WISER FOR US TO CHOOSE ONE AND FOCUS ON IT!
THEN WE START WITH YOURS, CHRYSLER!
SANCHOS'S EQUIPMENT TAKES TIME TO PUT ON, AND MY GUNS WON'T DO SHIT AGAINST THESE THINGS!
SANCHOS!
YOU AND ME WILL RUN INTER-FERENCE ON 'EM!
DAU!
HERE GOES, YOU TWO!

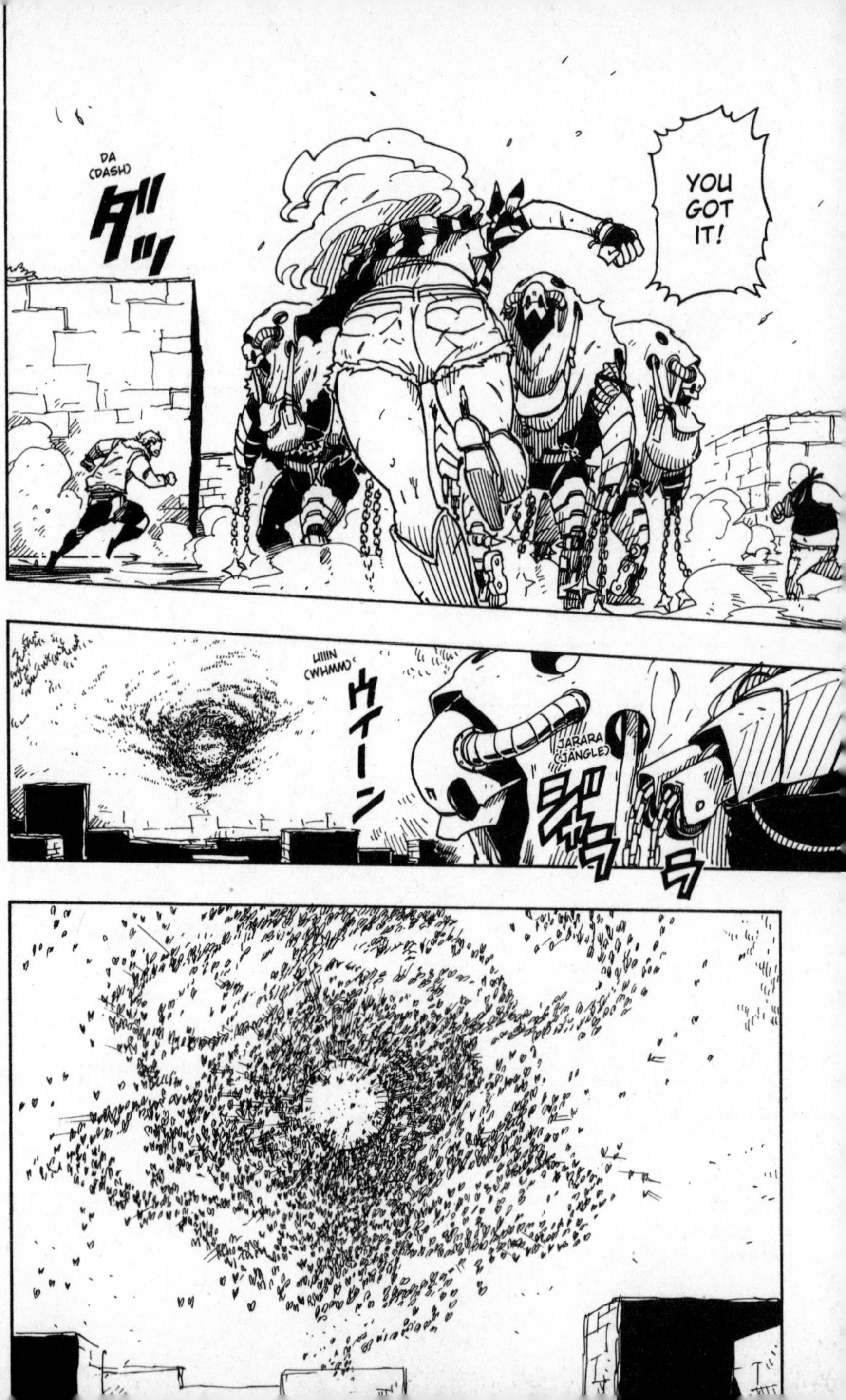
YOU GOT IT!
DA (DASH)
ダッ
JARARA (JANGLE)
ジャラ ラ
UIIIN (WHMM)
ウイーン

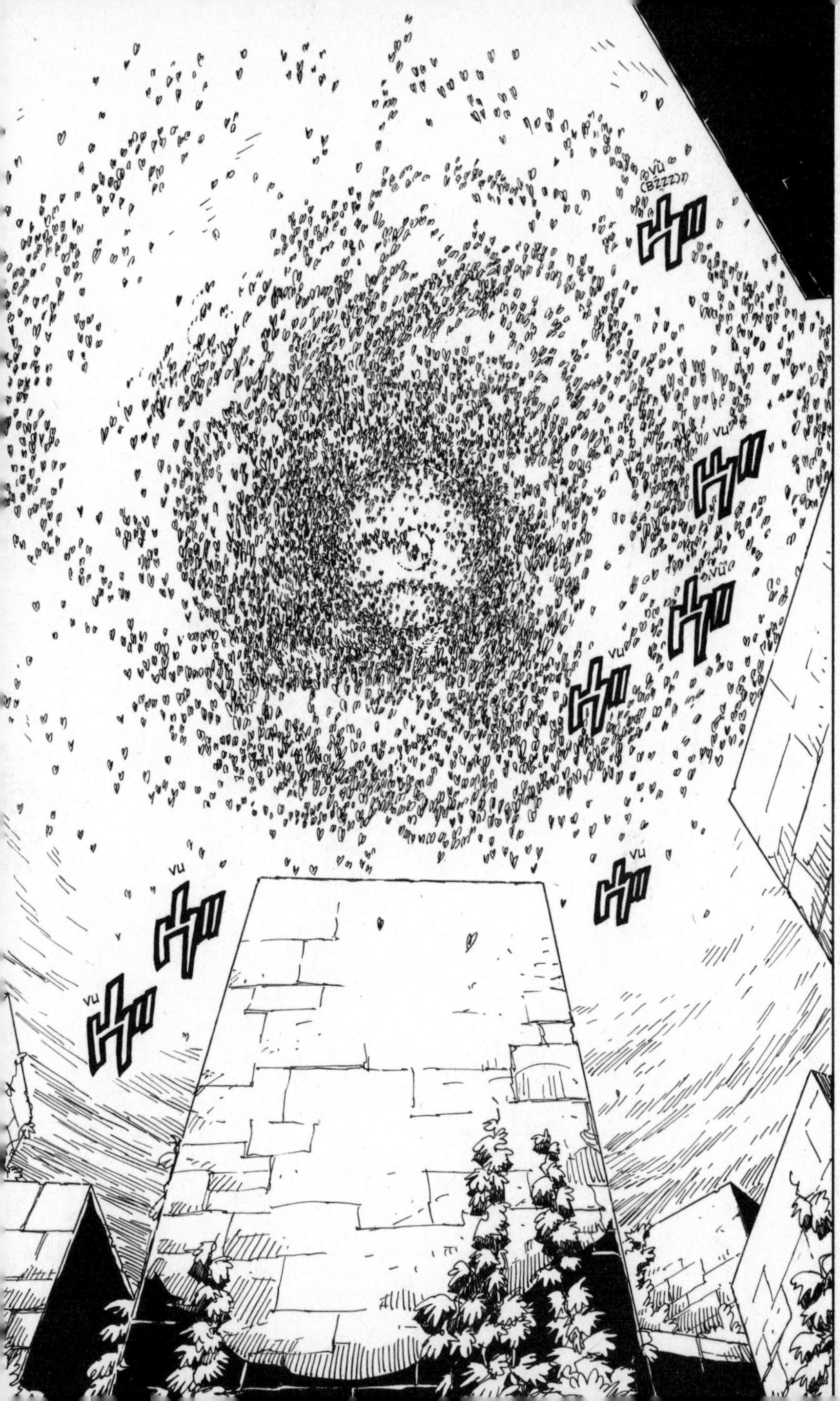
VU (BZZZ)
ヴ
VU
ヴ
VU
ヴ
VU
ヴ
VU
ヴ
VU
ヴ
VU
ヴ

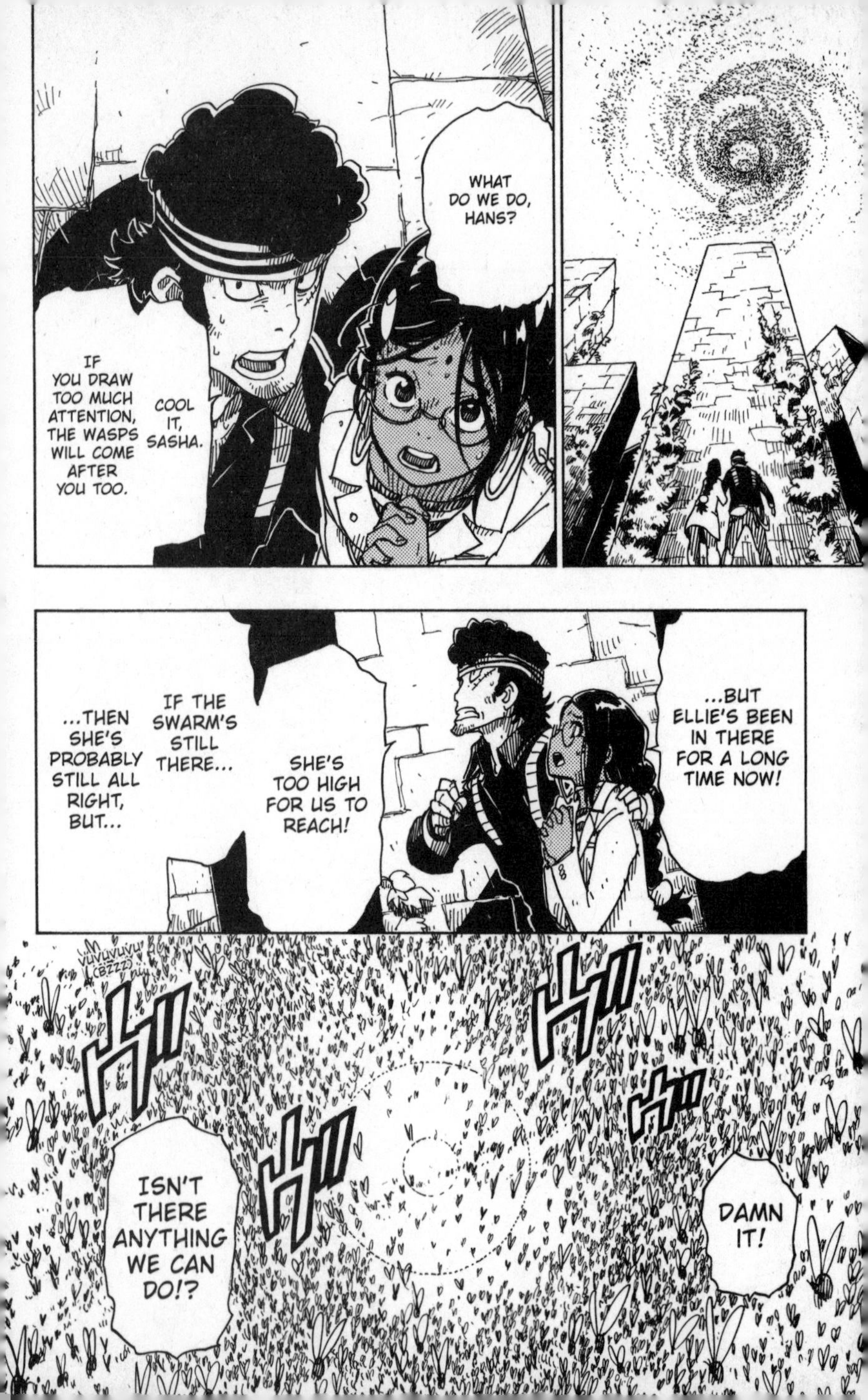
WHAT DO WE DO, HANS?
COOL IT, SASHA.
IF YOU DRAW TOO MUCH ATTENTION, THE WASPS WILL COME AFTER YOU TOO.
...BUT ELLIE'S BEEN IN THERE FOR A LONG TIME NOW!
SHE'S TOO HIGH FOR US TO REACH!
IF THE SWARM'S STILL THERE...
...THEN SHE'S PROBABLY STILL ALL RIGHT, BUT...
VUVUVUVU (BZZZ)
DAMN IT!
ISN'T THERE ANYTHING WE CAN DO!?

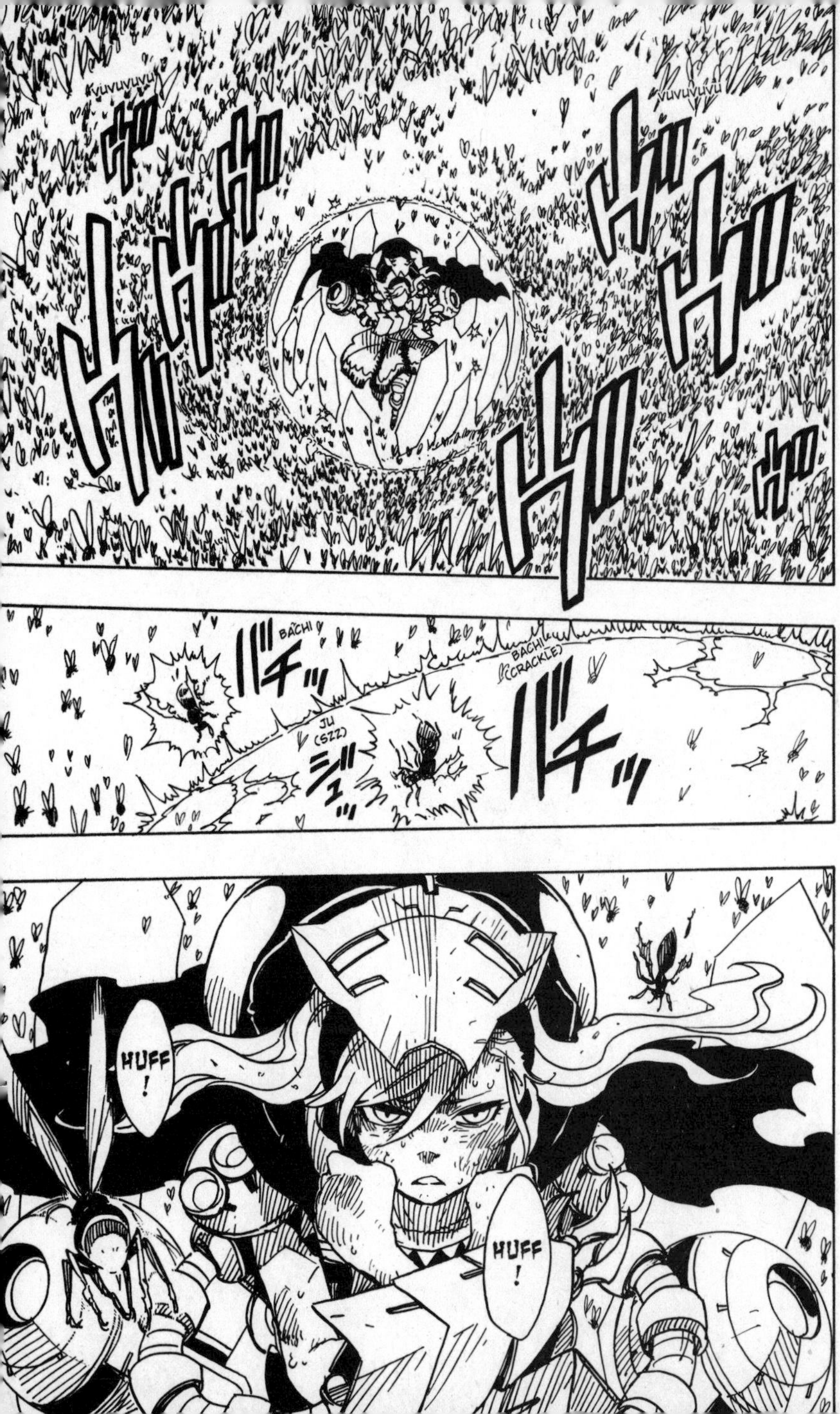
VUVUVUVU
ヴヴヴヴ
VUVUVUVU
ヴヴヴヴ
BACHI (CRACKLE)
バチッ
JU (SZZ)
ジュッ
BACHI
バチッ
HUFF!
HUFF!

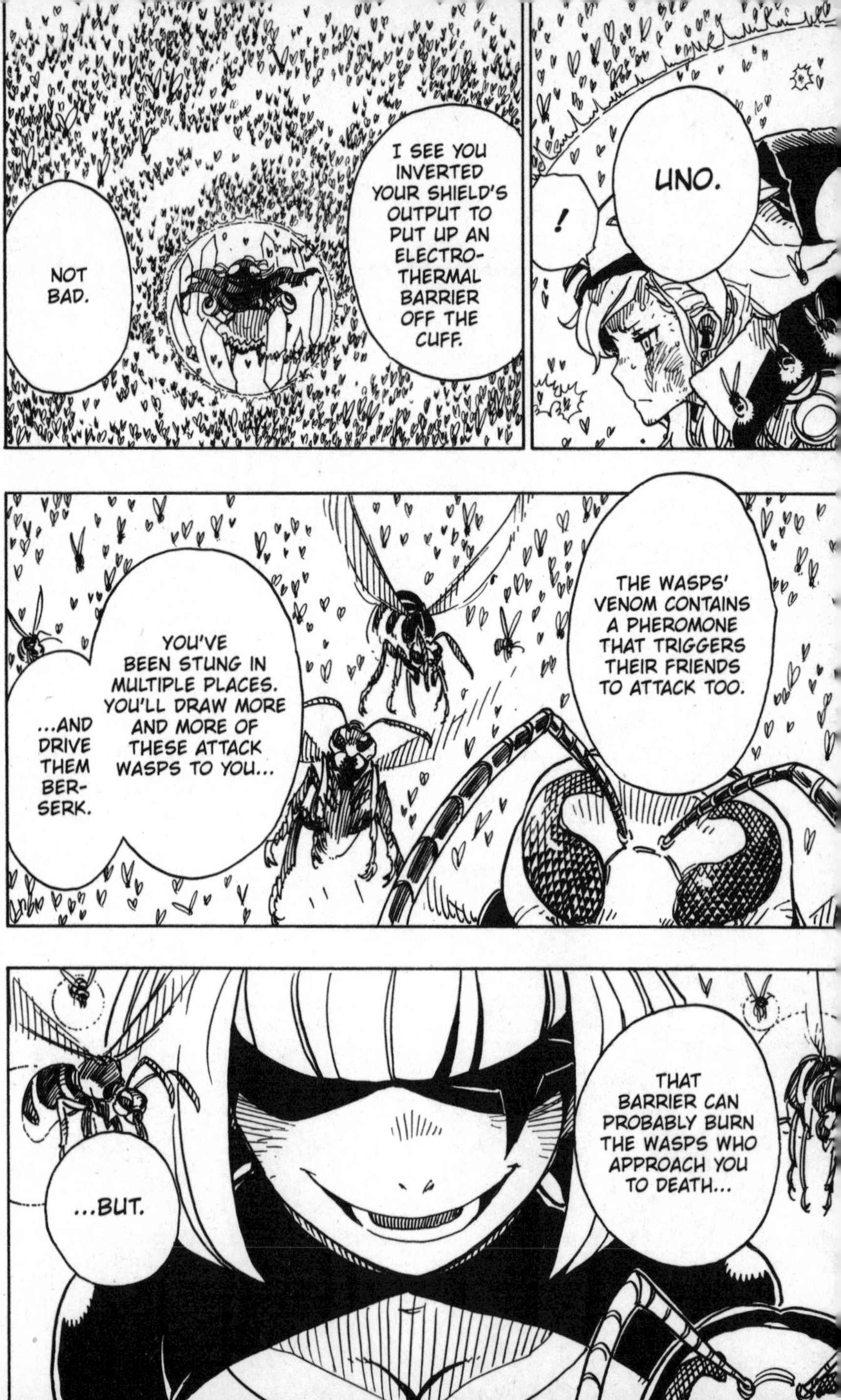
UNO.
!
I SEE YOU INVERTED YOUR SHIELD'S OUTPUT TO PUT UP AN ELECTRO-THERMAL BARRIER OFF THE CUFF.
NOT BAD.
THE WASPS' VENOM CONTAINS A PHEROMONE THAT TRIGGERS THEIR FRIENDS TO ATTACK TOO.
YOU'VE BEEN STUNG IN MULTIPLE PLACES. YOU'LL DRAW MORE AND MORE OF THESE ATTACK WASPS TO YOU...
...AND DRIVE THEM BER-SERK.
THAT BARRIER CAN PROBABLY BURN THE WASPS WHO APPROACH YOU TO DEATH...
...BUT.

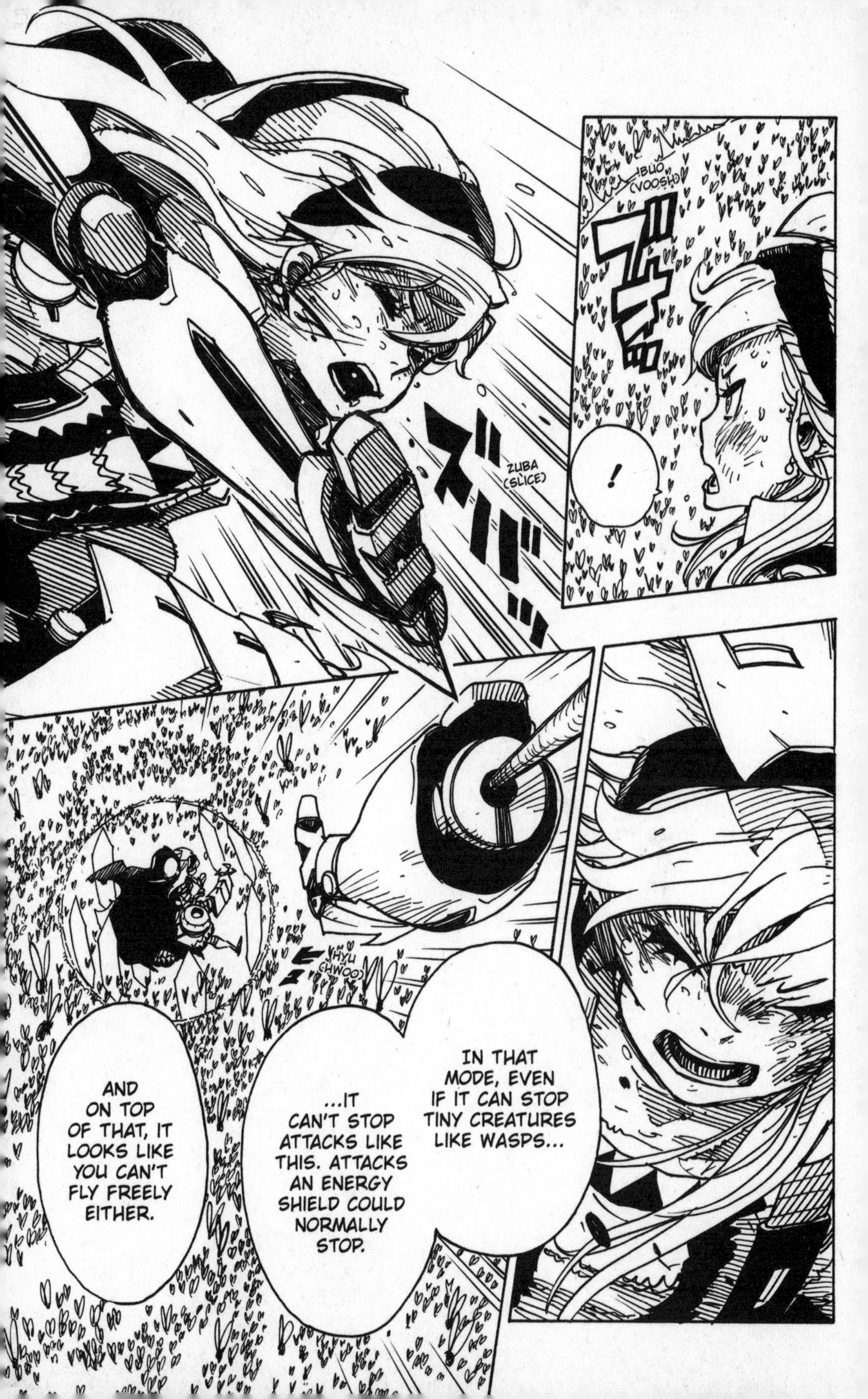
BUO (VOOSH)
!
ZUBA (SLICE)
IN THAT MODE, EVEN IF IT CAN STOP TINY CREATURES LIKE WASPS...
...IT CAN'T STOP ATTACKS LIKE THIS. ATTACKS AN ENERGY SHIELD COULD NORMALLY STOP.
HYU (HWOO)
AND ON TOP OF THAT, IT LOOKS LIKE YOU CAN'T FLY FREELY EITHER.

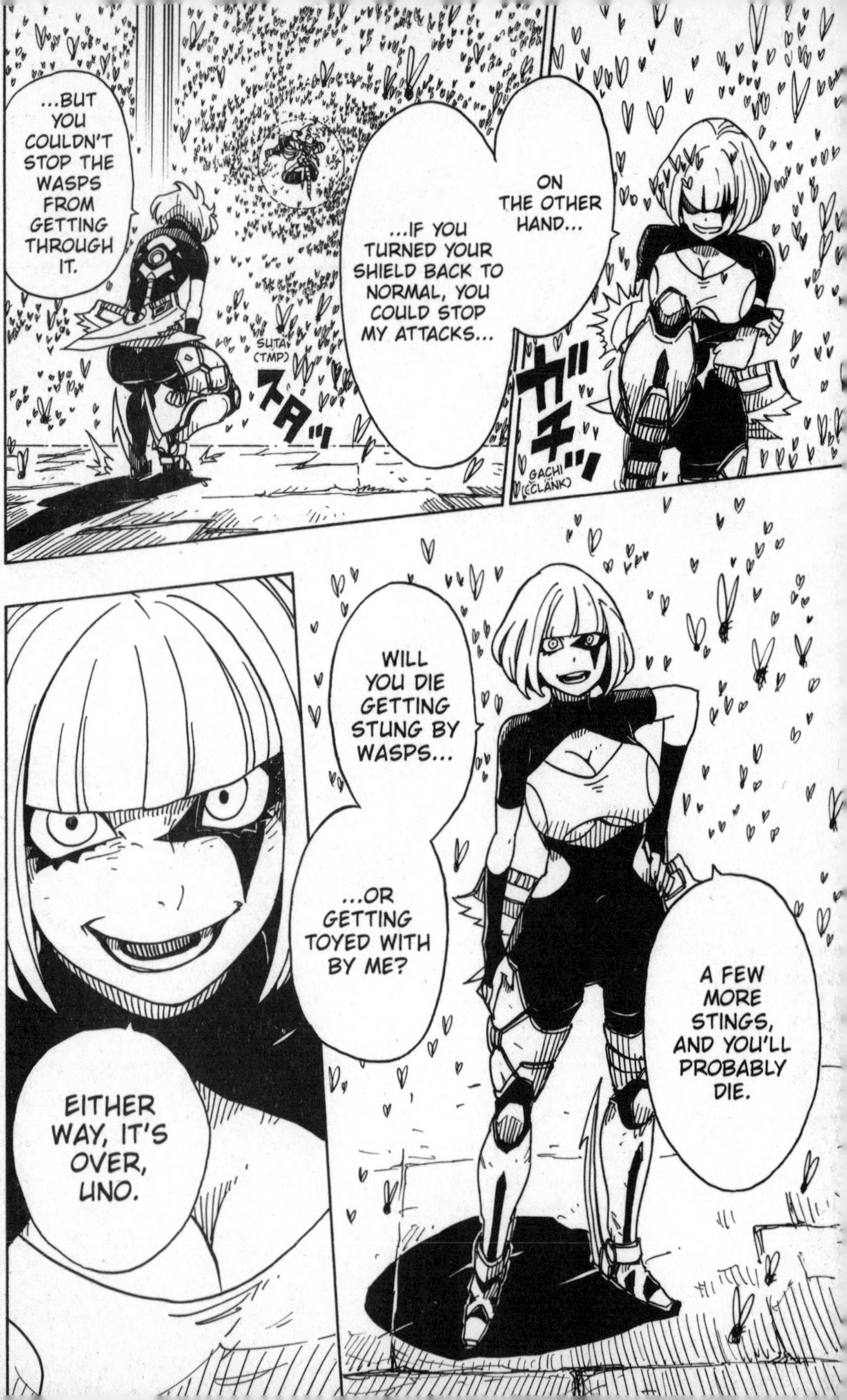
ON THE OTHER HAND...
GACHI (CLANK)
...IF YOU TURNED YOUR SHIELD BACK TO NORMAL, YOU COULD STOP MY ATTACKS...
SUTA (TMP)
...BUT YOU COULDN'T STOP THE WASPS FROM GETTING THROUGH IT.
A FEW MORE STINGS, AND YOU'LL PROBABLY DIE.
WILL YOU DIE GETTING STUNG BY WASPS...
...OR GETTING TOYED WITH BY ME?
EITHER WAY, IT'S OVER, UNO.

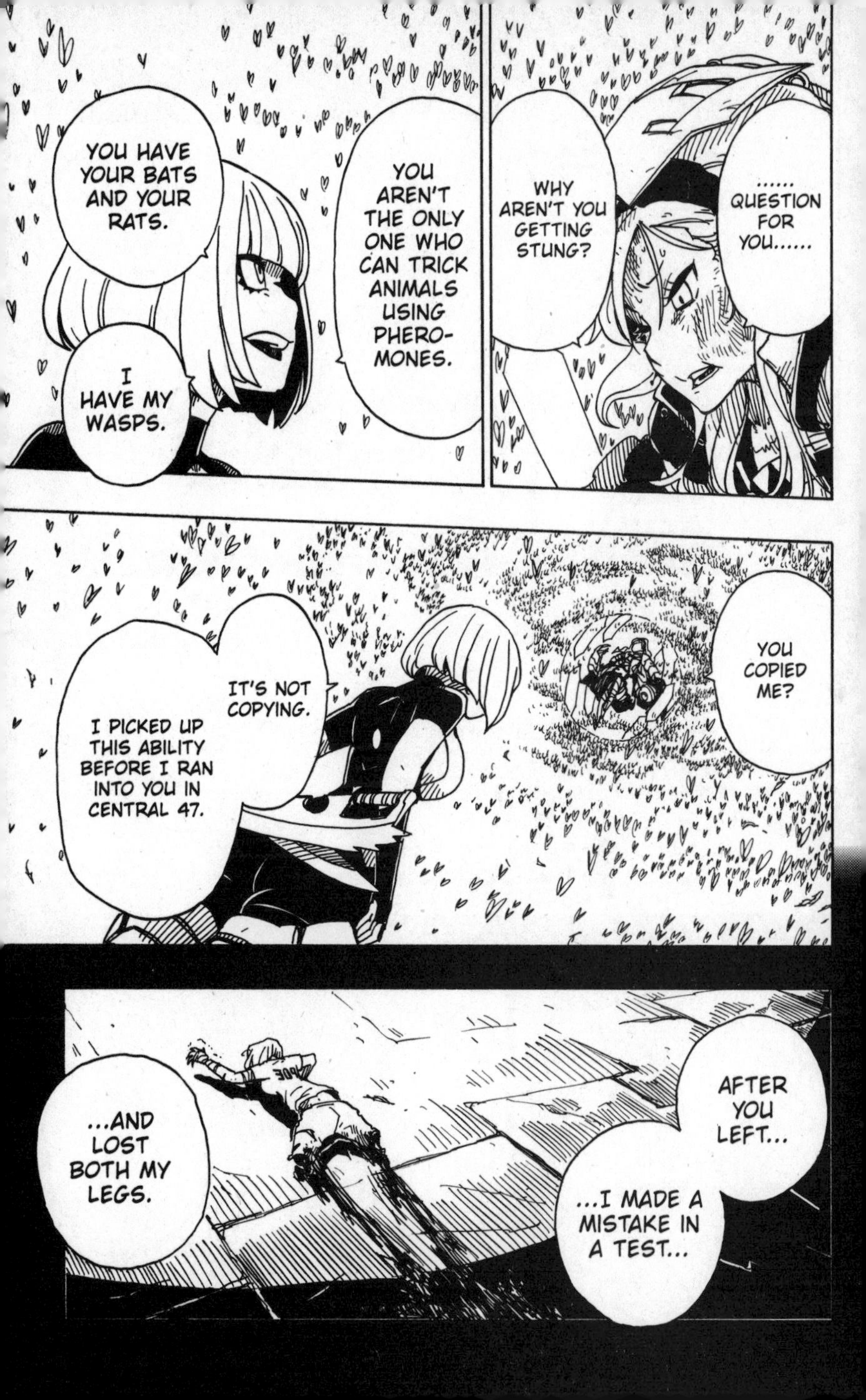
......QUESTION FOR YOU......
WHY AREN'T YOU GETTING STUNG?
YOU AREN'T THE ONLY ONE WHO CAN TRICK ANIMALS USING PHERO-MONES.
YOU HAVE YOUR BATS AND YOUR RATS.
I HAVE MY WASPS.
YOU COPIED ME?
IT'S NOT COPYING.
I PICKED UP THIS ABILITY BEFORE I RAN INTO YOU IN CENTRAL 47.
AFTER YOU LEFT...
...I MADE A MISTAKE IN A TEST...
...AND LOST BOTH MY LEGS.

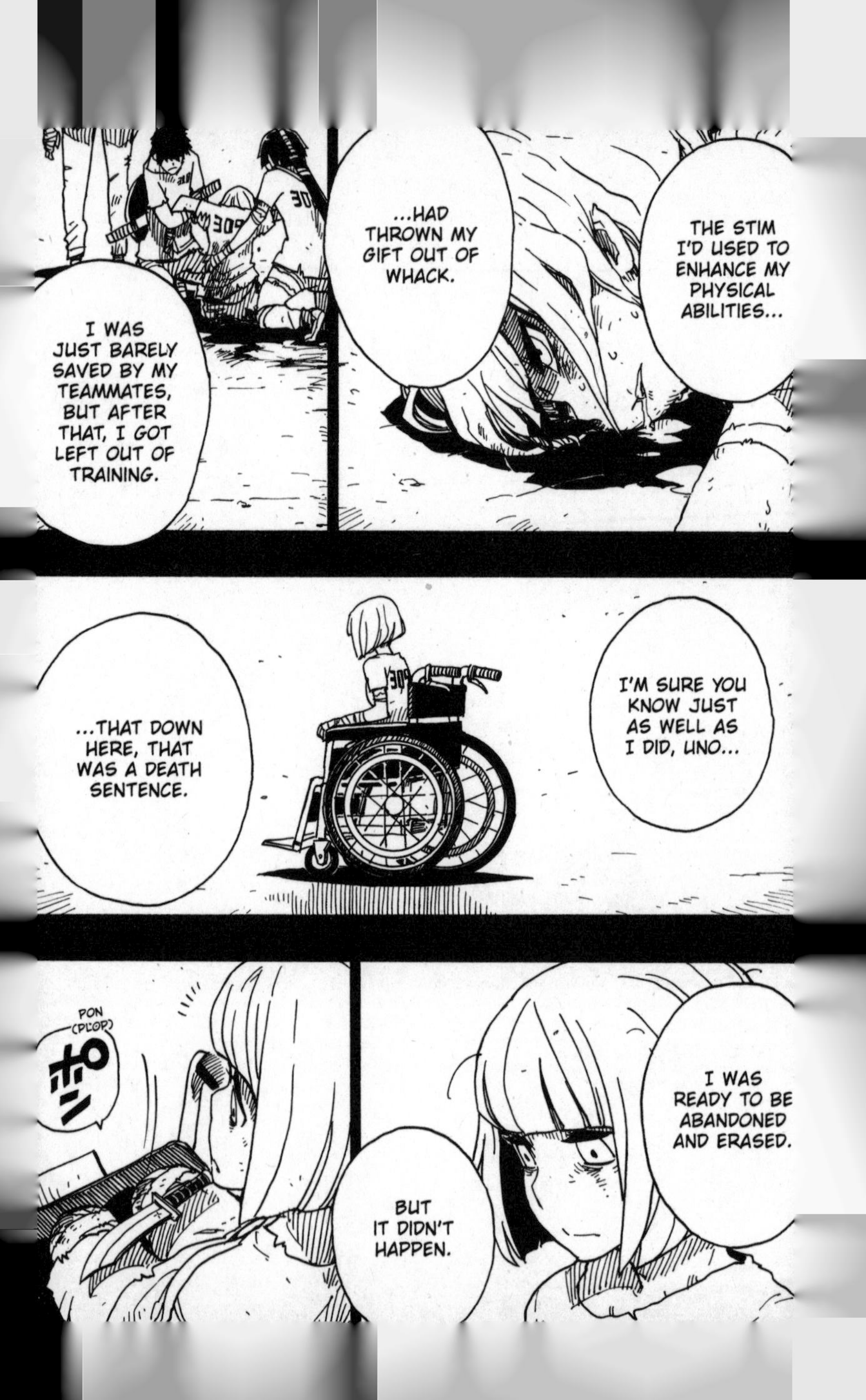
THE STIM I'D USED TO ENHANCE MY PHYSICAL ABILITIES...
...HAD THROWN MY GIFT OUT OF WHACK.
I WAS JUST BARELY SAVED BY MY TEAMMATES, BUT AFTER THAT, I GOT LEFT OUT OF TRAINING.
I'M SURE YOU KNOW JUST AS WELL AS I DID, UNO...
...THAT DOWN HERE, THAT WAS A DEATH SENTENCE.
I WAS READY TO BE ABANDONED AND ERASED.
BUT IT DIDN'T HAPPEN.
ポン
PON (PLOP)

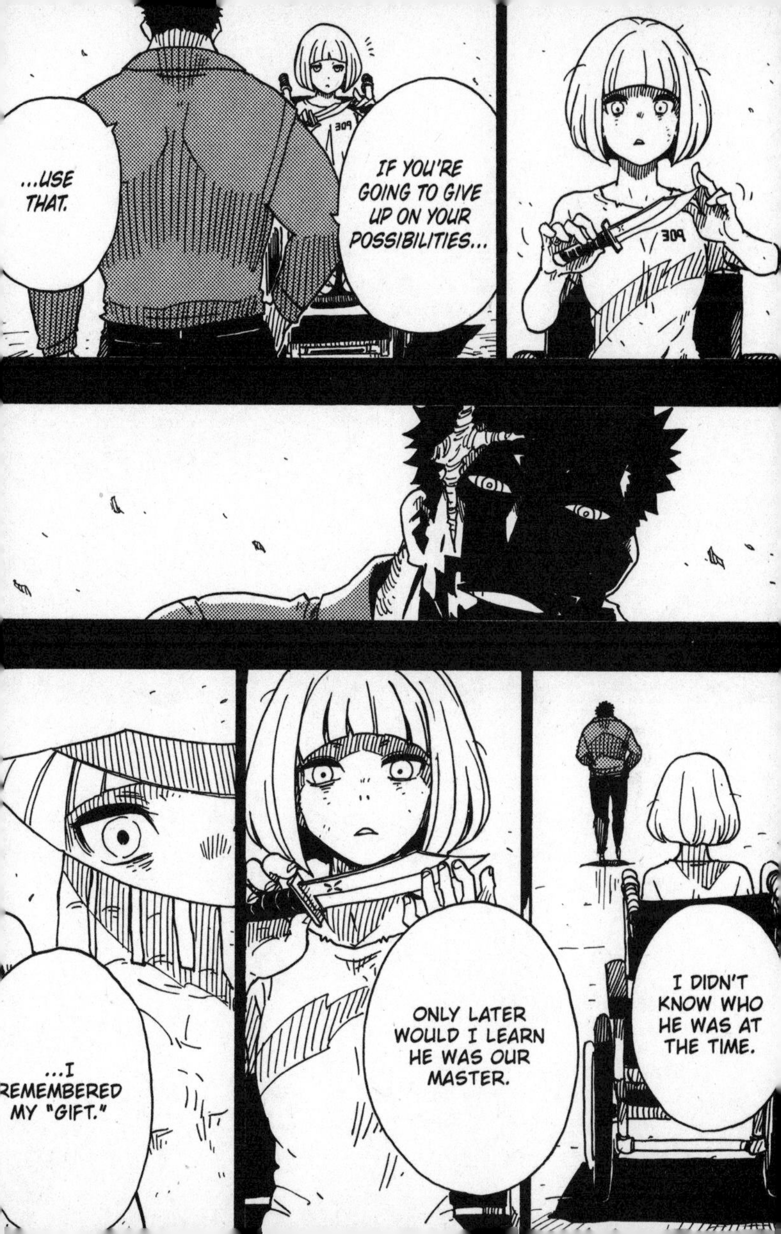
IF YOU'RE GOING TO GIVE UP ON YOUR POSSIBILITIES...
...USE THAT.
I DIDN'T KNOW WHO HE WAS AT THE TIME.
ONLY LATER WOULD I LEARN HE WAS OUR MASTER.
...I REMEMBERED MY "GIFT."

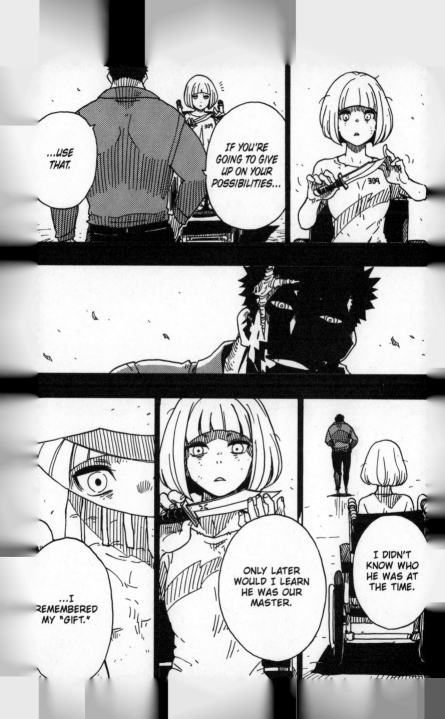

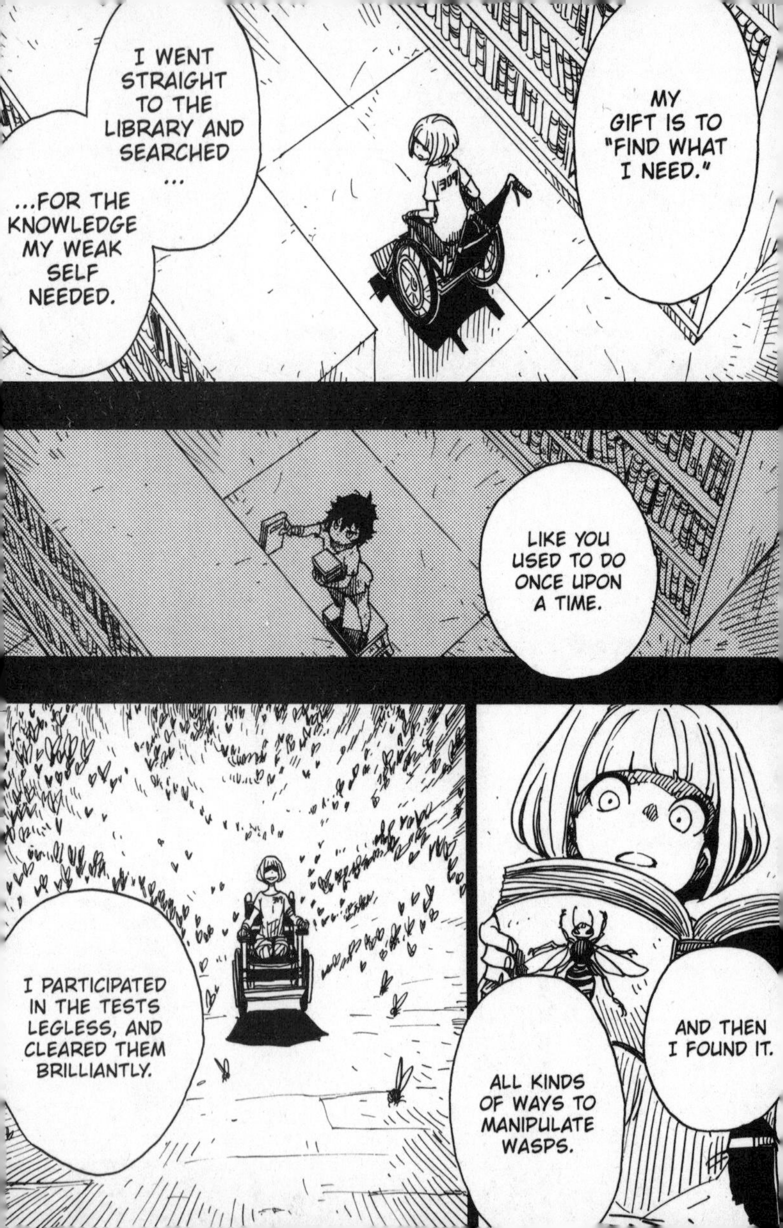
MY GIFT IS TO "FIND WHAT I NEED."
I WENT STRAIGHT TO THE LIBRARY AND SEARCHED ...
...FOR THE KNOWLEDGE MY WEAK SELF NEEDED.
LIKE YOU USED TO DO ONCE UPON A TIME.
AND THEN I FOUND IT.
ALL KINDS OF WAYS TO MANIPULATE WASPS.
I PARTICIPATED IN THE TESTS LEGLESS, AND CLEARED THEM BRILLIANTLY.

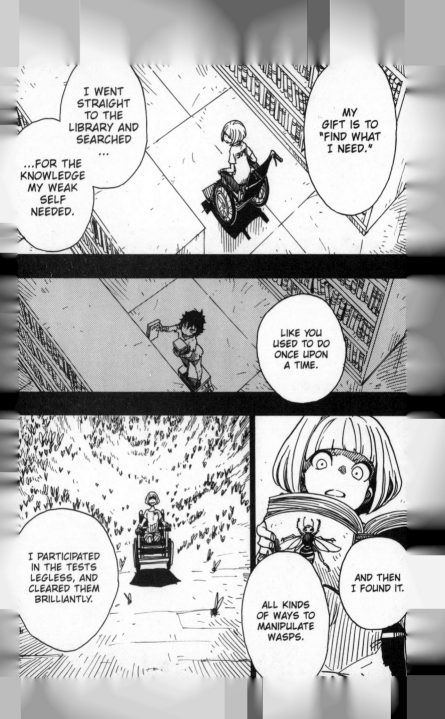

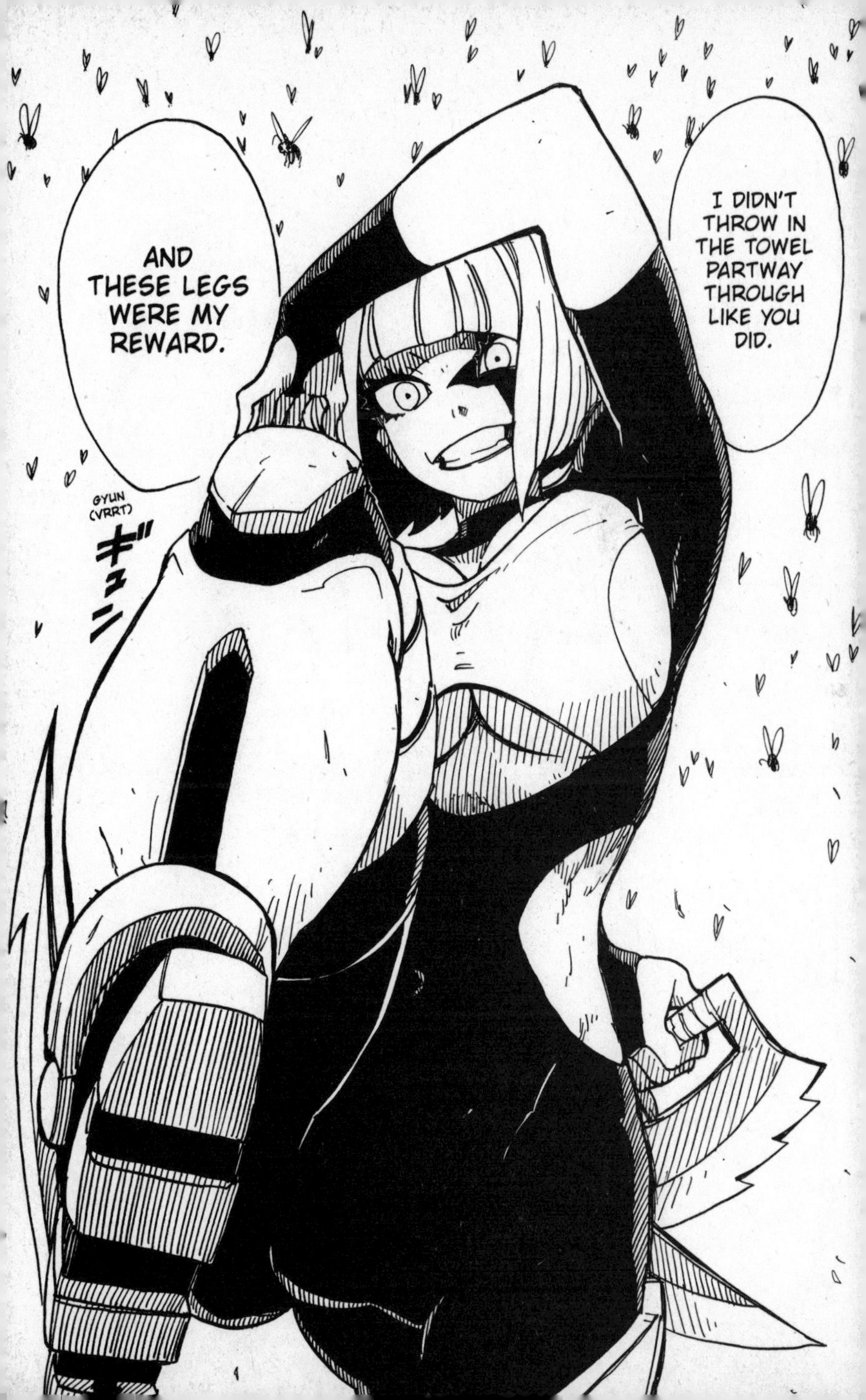
I DIDN'T THROW IN THE TOWEL PARTWAY THROUGH LIKE YOU DID.
AND THESE LEGS WERE MY REWARD.
GYUN (VRRT)
ギュン

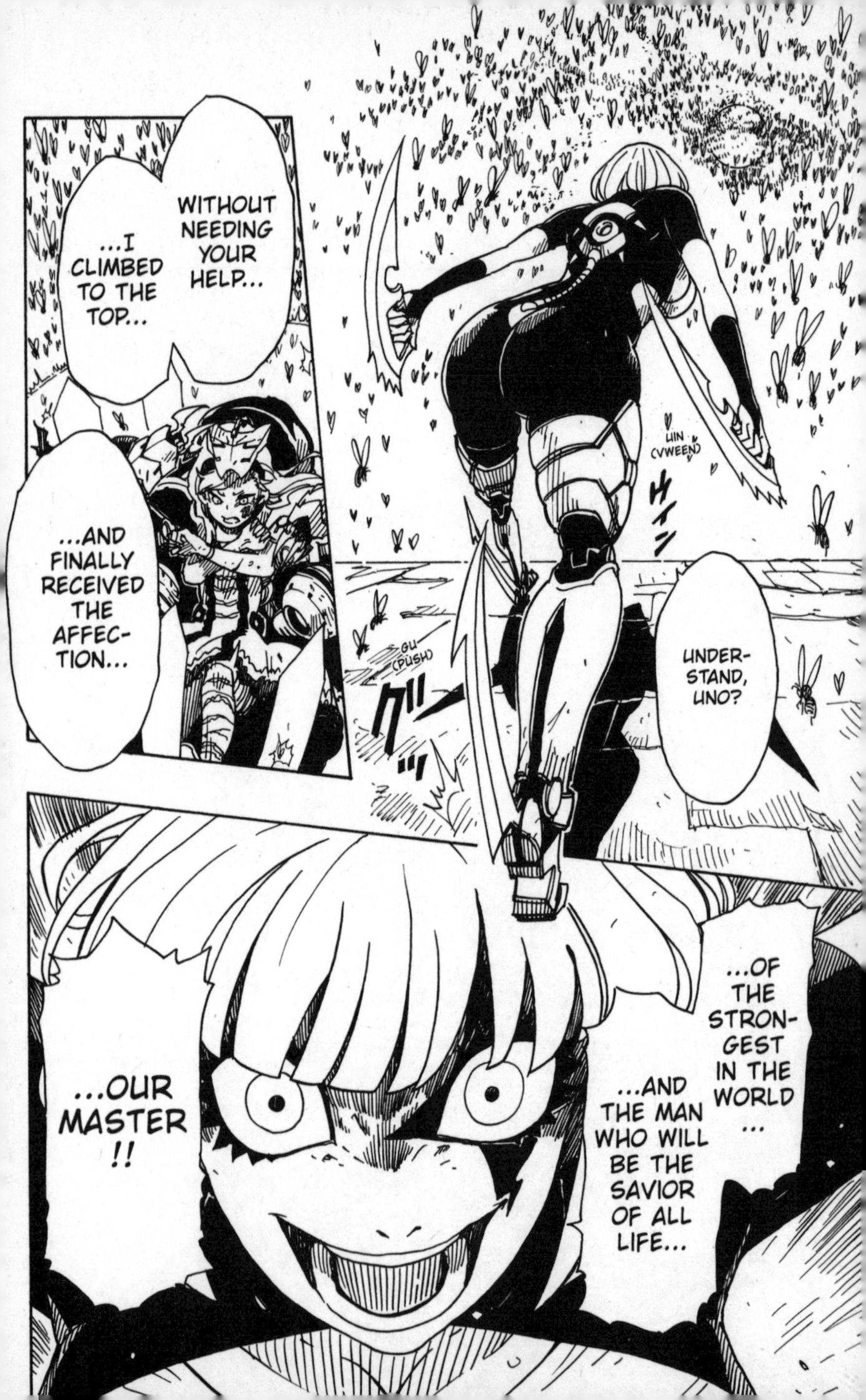

UIN (VWEEN)
UNDER-STAND, UNO?
GU (PUSH)
WITHOUT NEEDING YOUR HELP...
...I CLIMBED TO THE TOP...
...AND FINALLY RECEIVED THE AFFEC-TION...
...OF THE STRON-GEST IN THE WORLD...
...AND THE MAN WHO WILL BE THE SAVIOR OF ALL LIFE...
...OUR MASTER!!

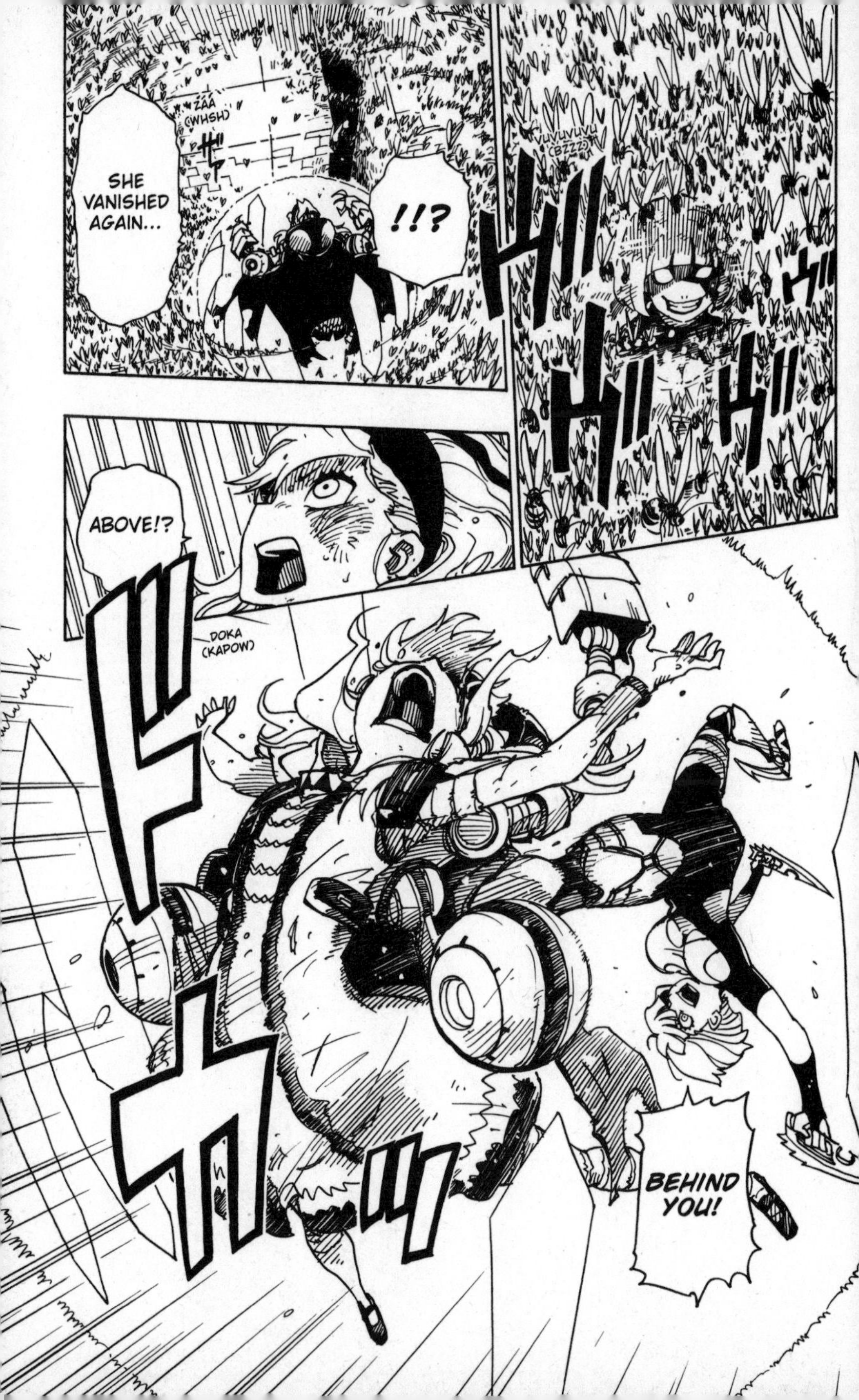
VUVUVUVU (BZZZ)
!!?
ZAA (WHSH)
SHE VANISHED AGAIN...
ABOVE!?
DOKA (KAPOW)
BEHIND YOU!

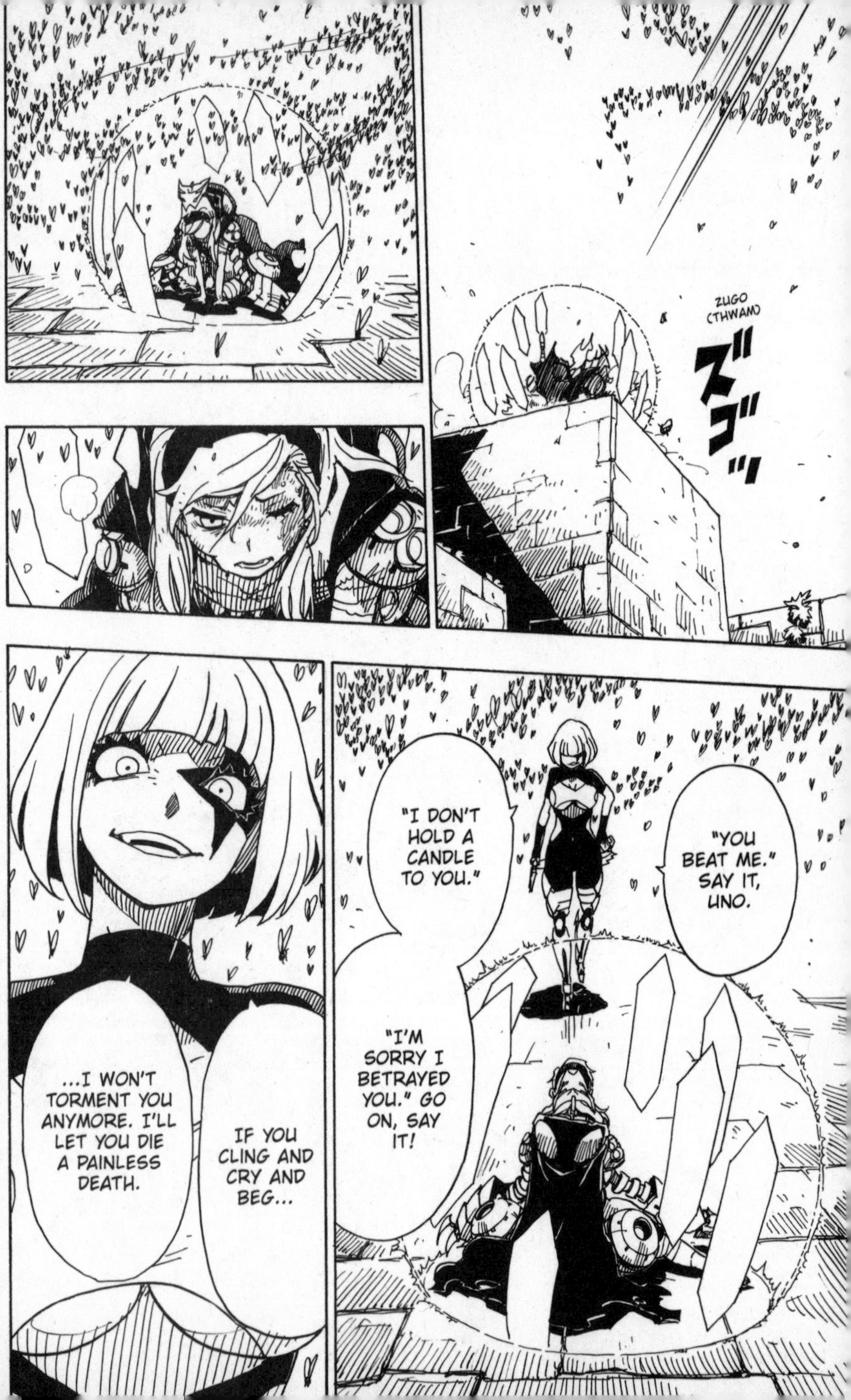
ZUGO (THWAM)
ズゴッ
"YOU BEAT ME." SAY IT, UNO.
"I DON'T HOLD A CANDLE TO YOU."
"I'M SORRY I BETRAYED YOU." GO ON, SAY IT!
IF YOU CLING AND CRY AND BEG...
...I WON'T TORMENT YOU ANYMORE. I'LL LET YOU DIE A PAINLESS DEATH.

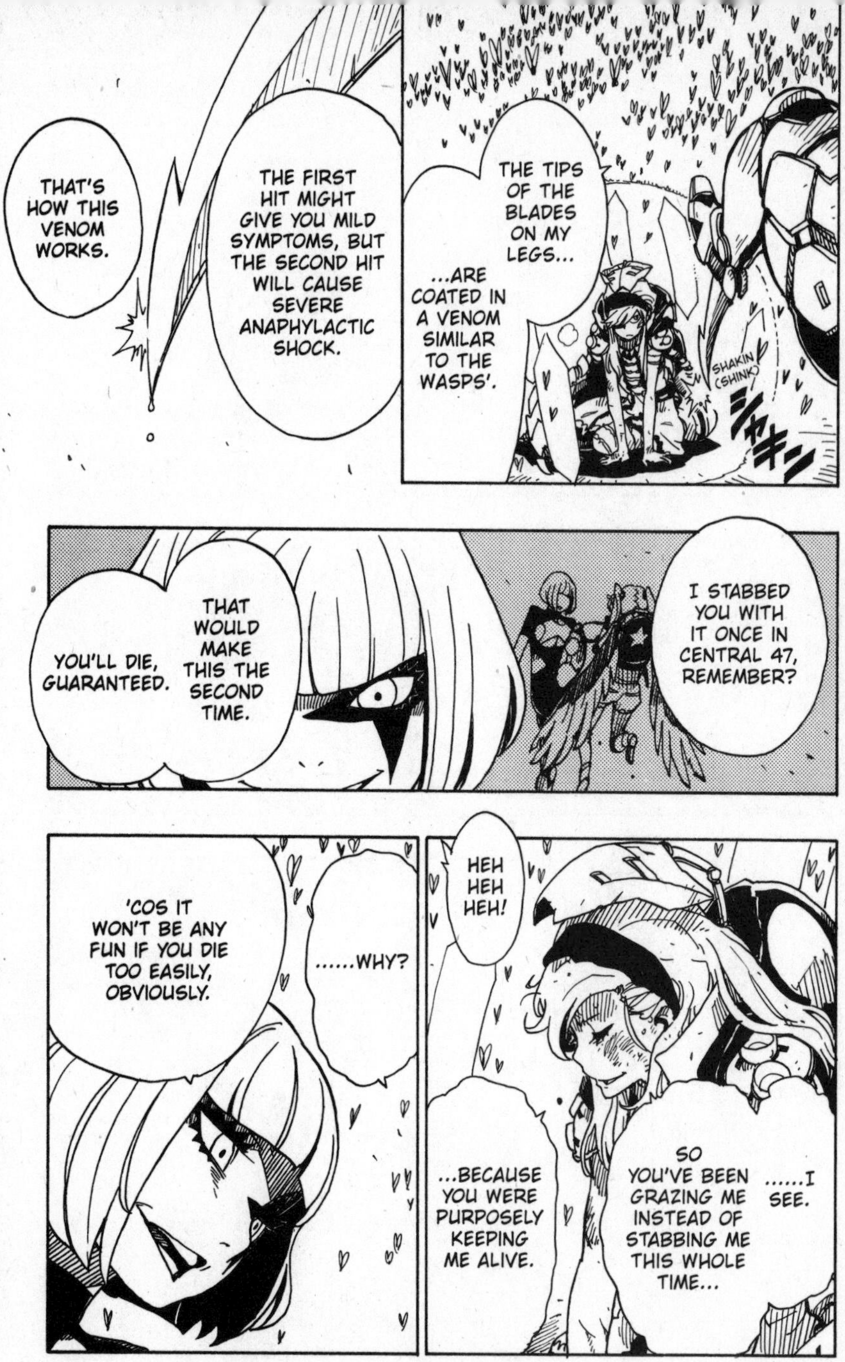
THE TIPS OF THE BLADES ON MY LEGS...
...ARE COATED IN A VENOM SIMILAR TO THE WASPS'.
SHAKIN (SHINK)
シャキン
THE FIRST HIT MIGHT GIVE YOU MILD SYMPTOMS, BUT THE SECOND HIT WILL CAUSE SEVERE ANAPHYLACTIC SHOCK.
THAT'S HOW THIS VENOM WORKS.
I STABBED YOU WITH IT ONCE IN CENTRAL 47, REMEMBER?
THAT WOULD MAKE THIS THE SECOND TIME.
YOU'LL DIE, GUARANTEED.
HEH HEH HEH!
......I SEE.
SO YOU'VE BEEN GRAZING ME INSTEAD OF STABBING ME THIS WHOLE TIME...
...BECAUSE YOU WERE PURPOSELY KEEPING ME ALIVE.
......WHY?
'COS IT WON'T BE ANY FUN IF YOU DIE TOO EASILY, OBVIOUSLY.

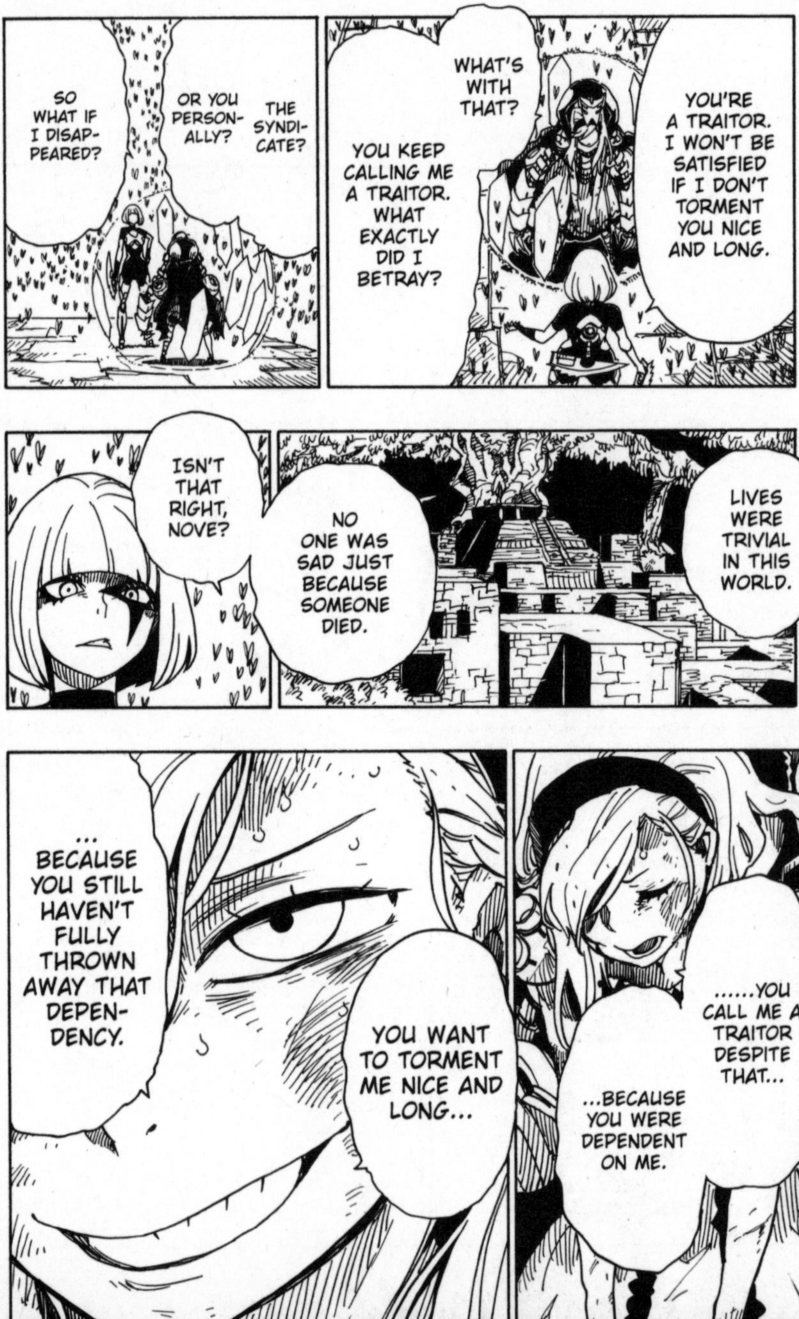
YOU'RE A TRAITOR. I WON'T BE SATISFIED IF I DON'T TORMENT YOU NICE AND LONG.
WHAT'S WITH THAT?
YOU KEEP CALLING ME A TRAITOR. WHAT EXACTLY DID I BETRAY?
THE SYNDICATE?
OR YOU PERSONALLY?
SO WHAT IF I DISAPPEARED?
LIVES WERE TRIVIAL IN THIS WORLD.
NO ONE WAS SAD JUST BECAUSE SOMEONE DIED.
ISN'T THAT RIGHT, NOVE?
......YOU CALL ME A TRAITOR DESPITE THAT...
...BECAUSE YOU WERE DEPENDENT ON ME.
YOU WANT TO TORMENT ME NICE AND LONG...
...BECAUSE YOU STILL HAVEN'T FULLY THROWN AWAY THAT DEPENDENCY.

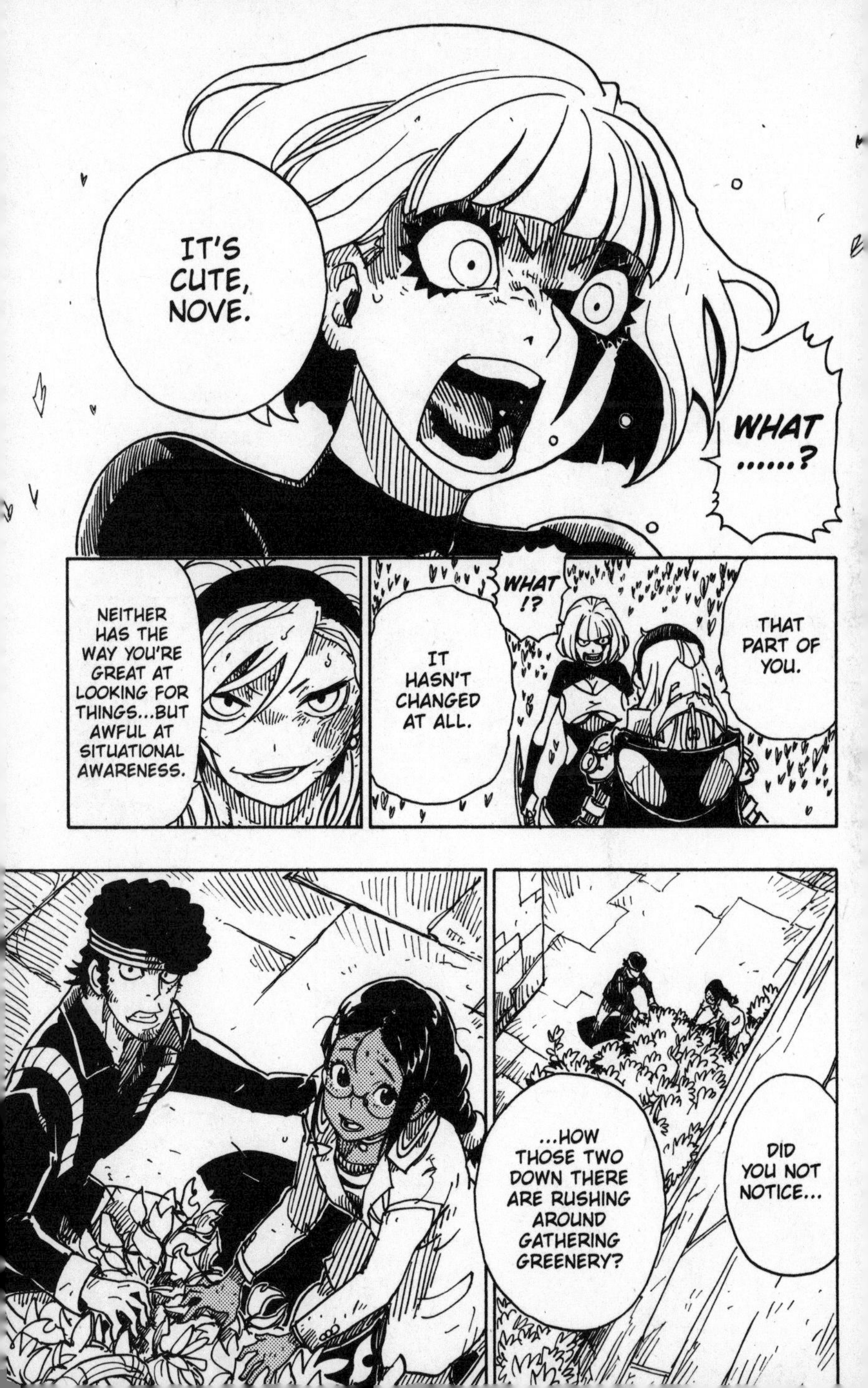
IT'S CUTE, NOVE.
WHAT......?
THAT PART OF YOU.
WHAT!?
IT HASN'T CHANGED AT ALL.
NEITHER HAS THE WAY YOU'RE GREAT AT LOOKING FOR THINGS...BUT AWFUL AT SITUATIONAL AWARENESS.
DID YOU NOT NOTICE...
...HOW THOSE TWO DOWN THERE ARE RUSHING AROUND GATHERING GREENERY?

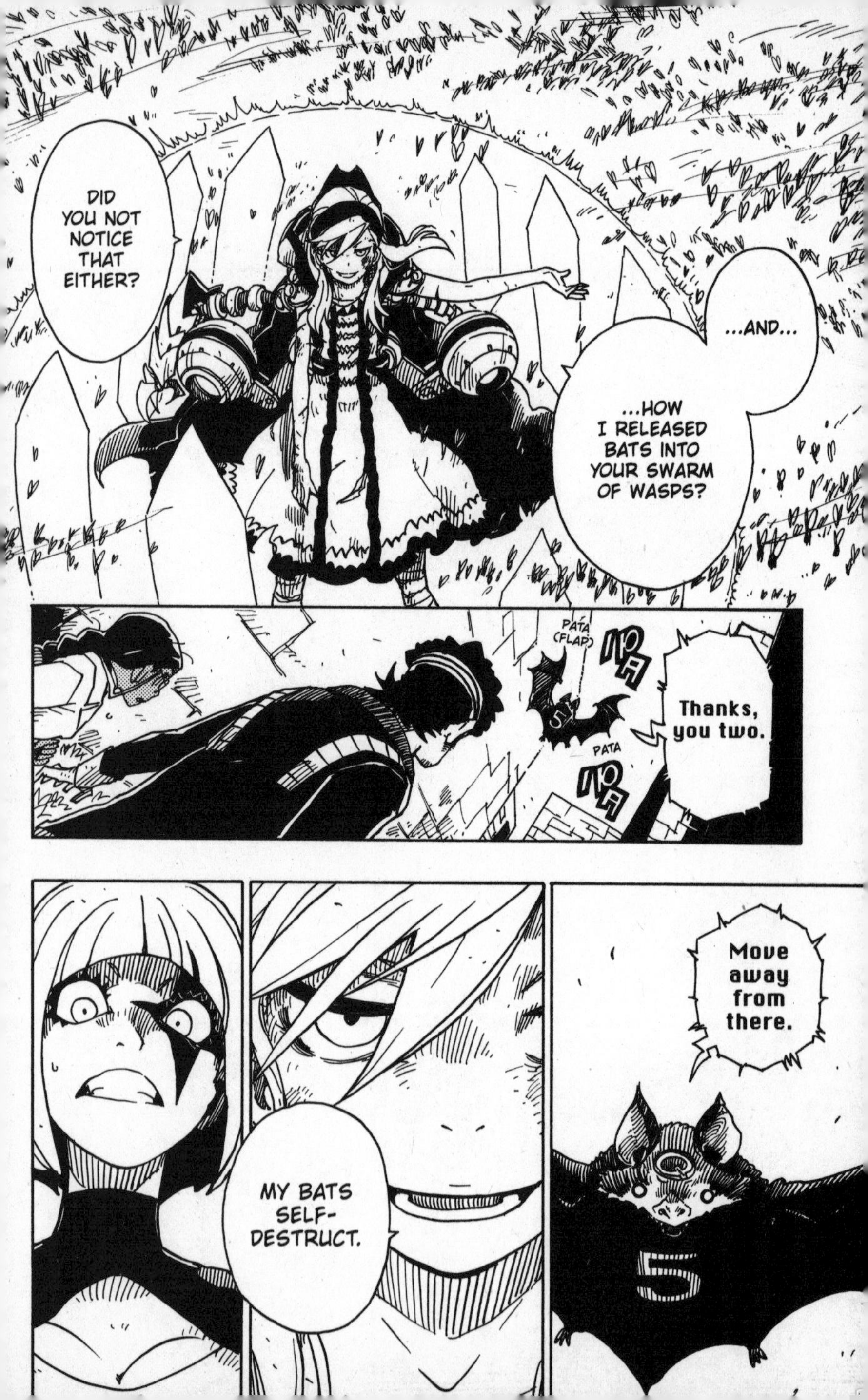
DID YOU NOT NOTICE THAT EITHER?
...AND...
...HOW I RELEASED BATS INTO YOUR SWARM OF WASPS?
PATA (FLAP)
PATA
Thanks, you two.
Move away from there.
MY BATS SELF-DESTRUCT.

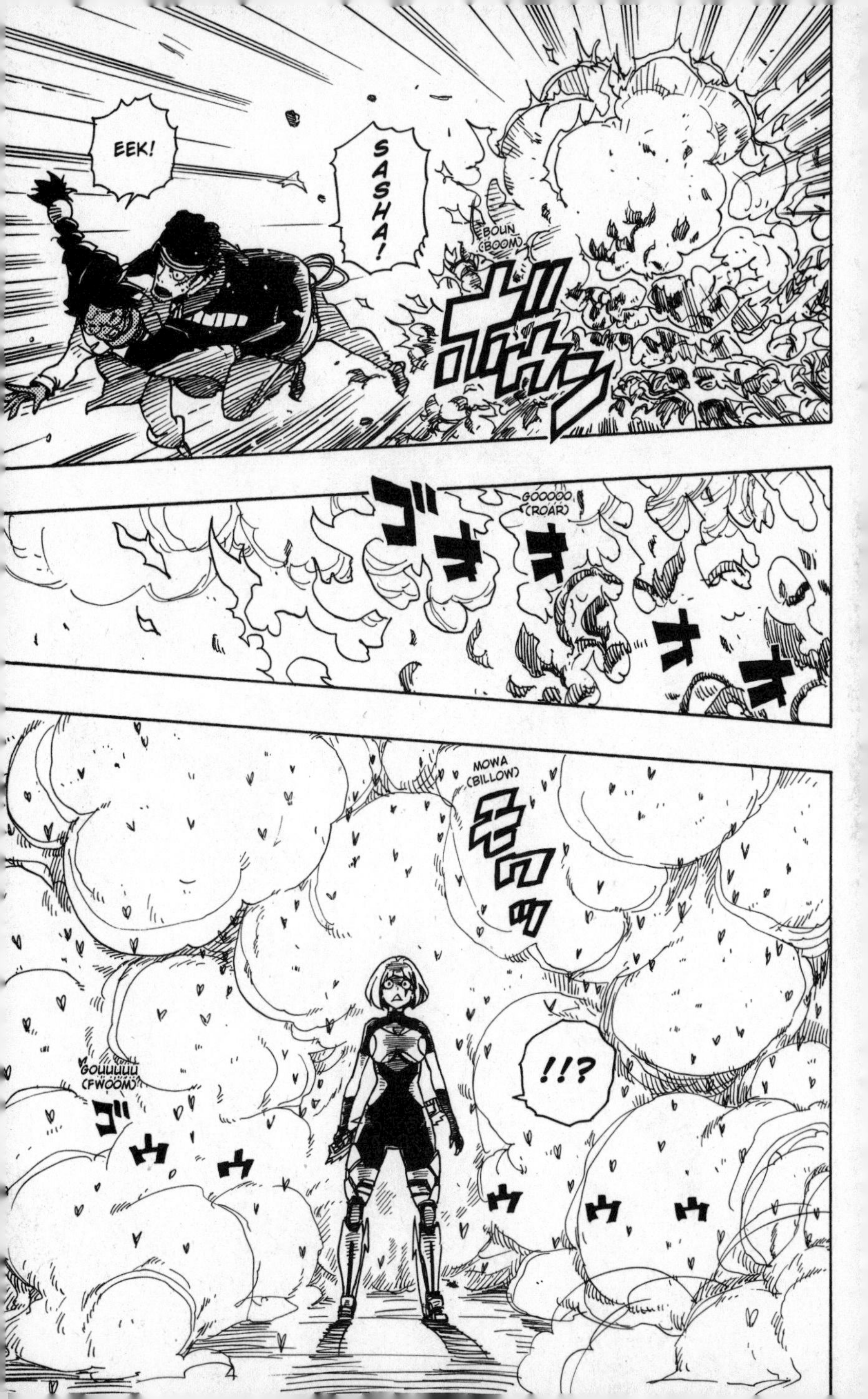
BOUN (BOOM)
SASHA!
EEK!
ゴオオオオ
GOOOOO (ROAR)
MOWA (BILLOW)
!!?
ゴウウウウウ
GOUUUUU (FWOOM)

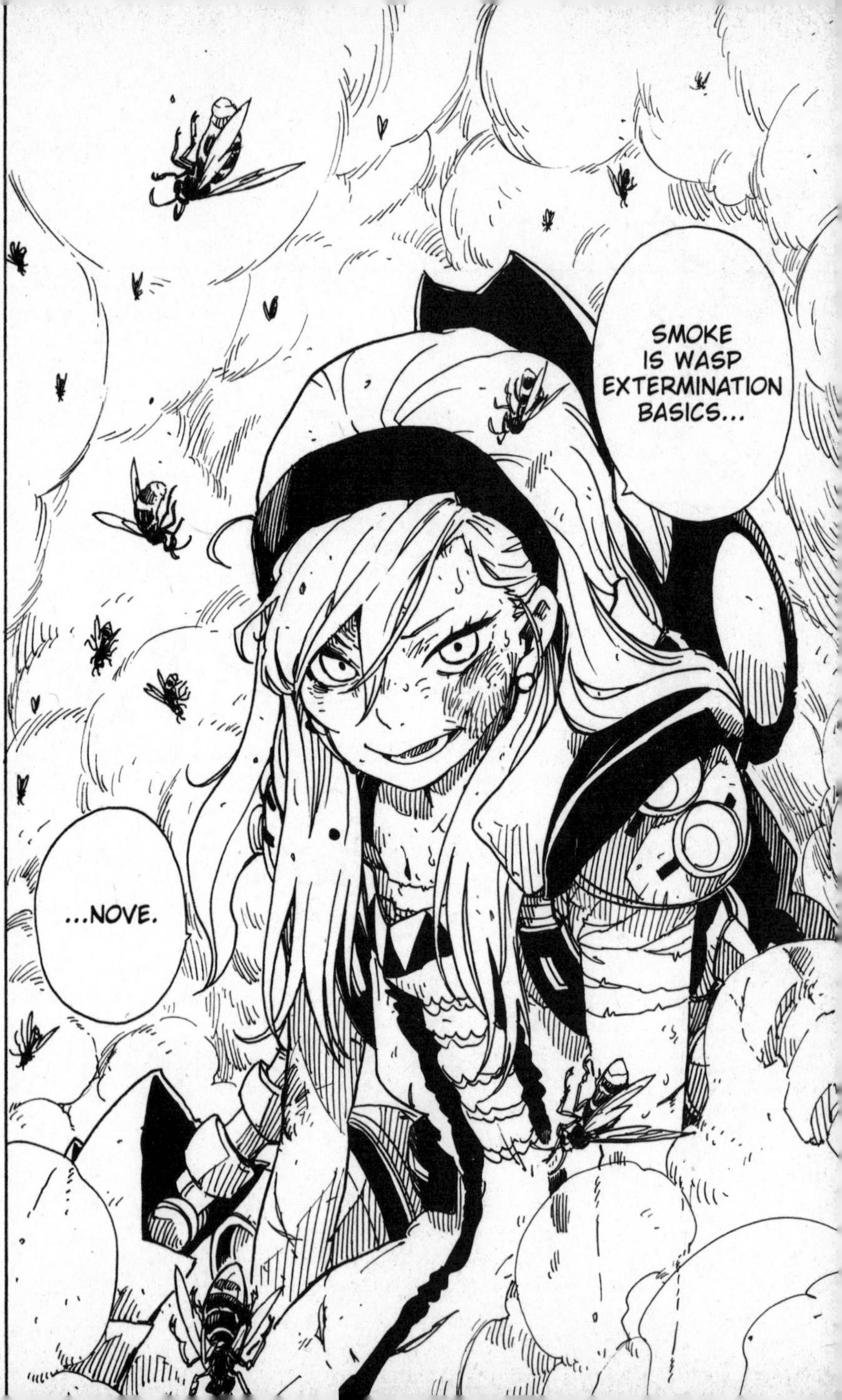
SMOKE IS WASP EXTERMINATION BASICS...
...NOVE.

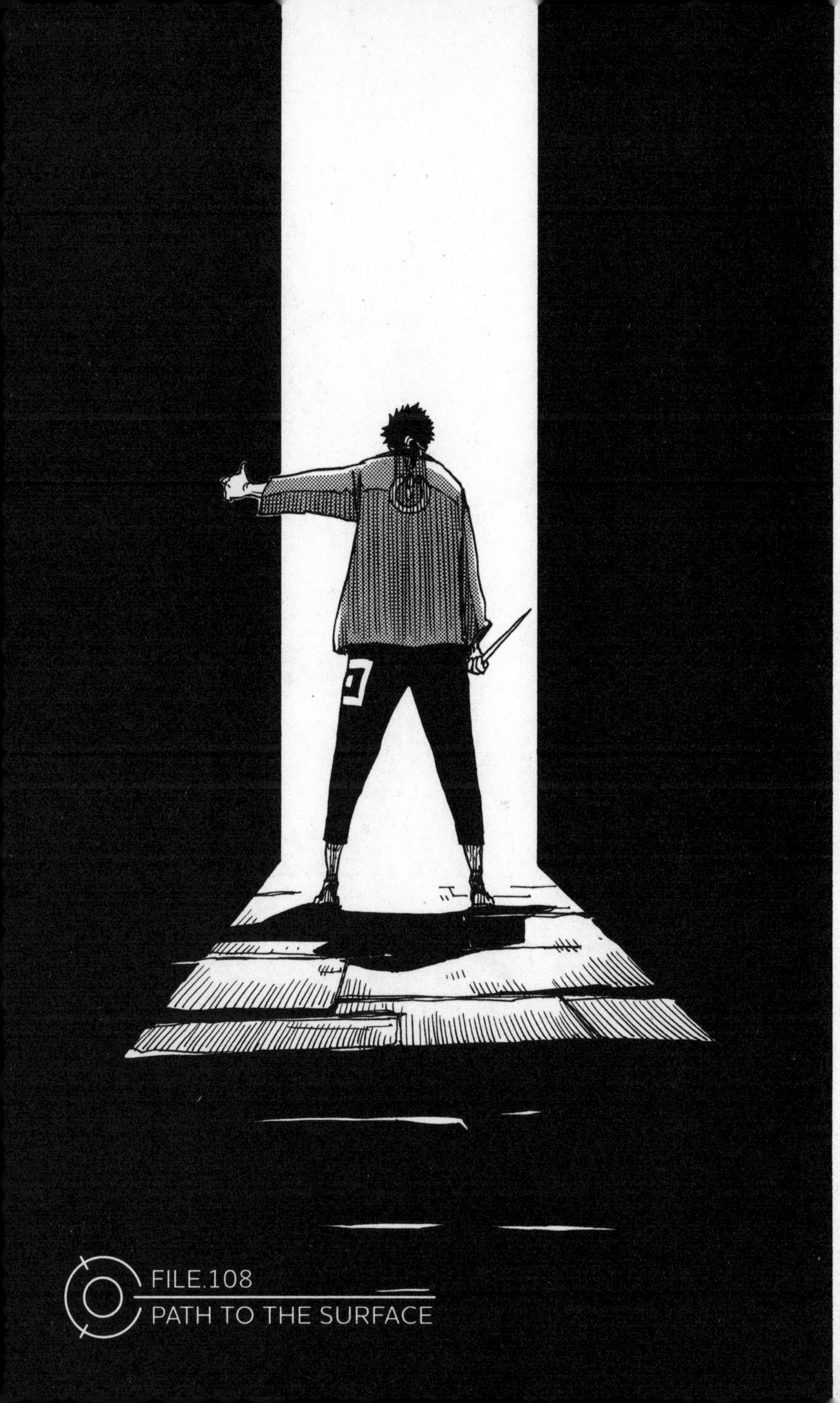
FILE.108
PATH TO THE SURFACE

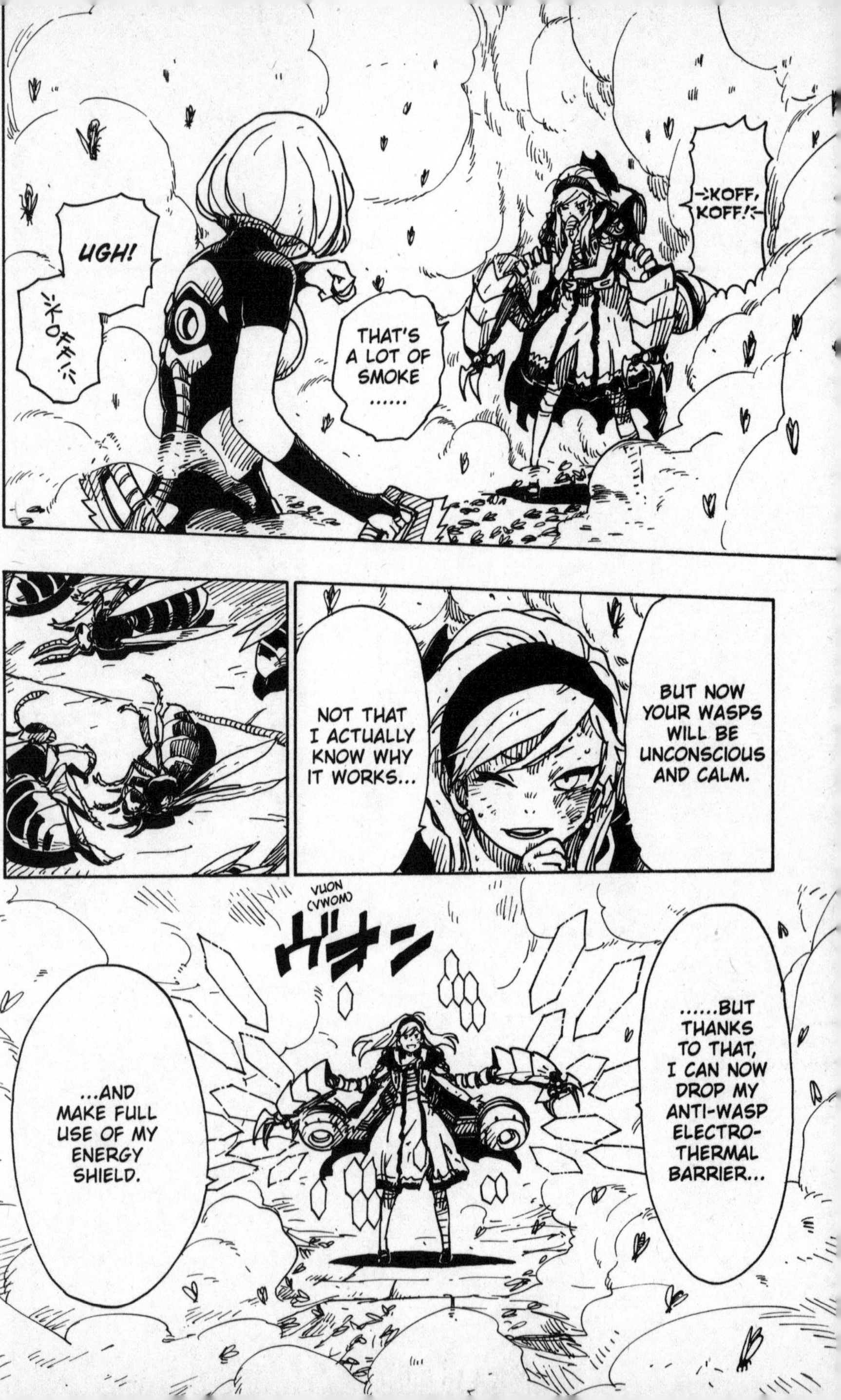
KOFF, KOFF!
THAT'S A LOT OF SMOKE ......
UGH!
KOFF!!
BUT NOW YOUR WASPS WILL BE UNCONSCIOUS AND CALM.
NOT THAT I ACTUALLY KNOW WHY IT WORKS...
ヴオン
VUON (VWOM)
......BUT THANKS TO THAT, I CAN NOW DROP MY ANTI-WASP ELECTRO-THERMAL BARRIER...
...AND MAKE FULL USE OF MY ENERGY SHIELD.

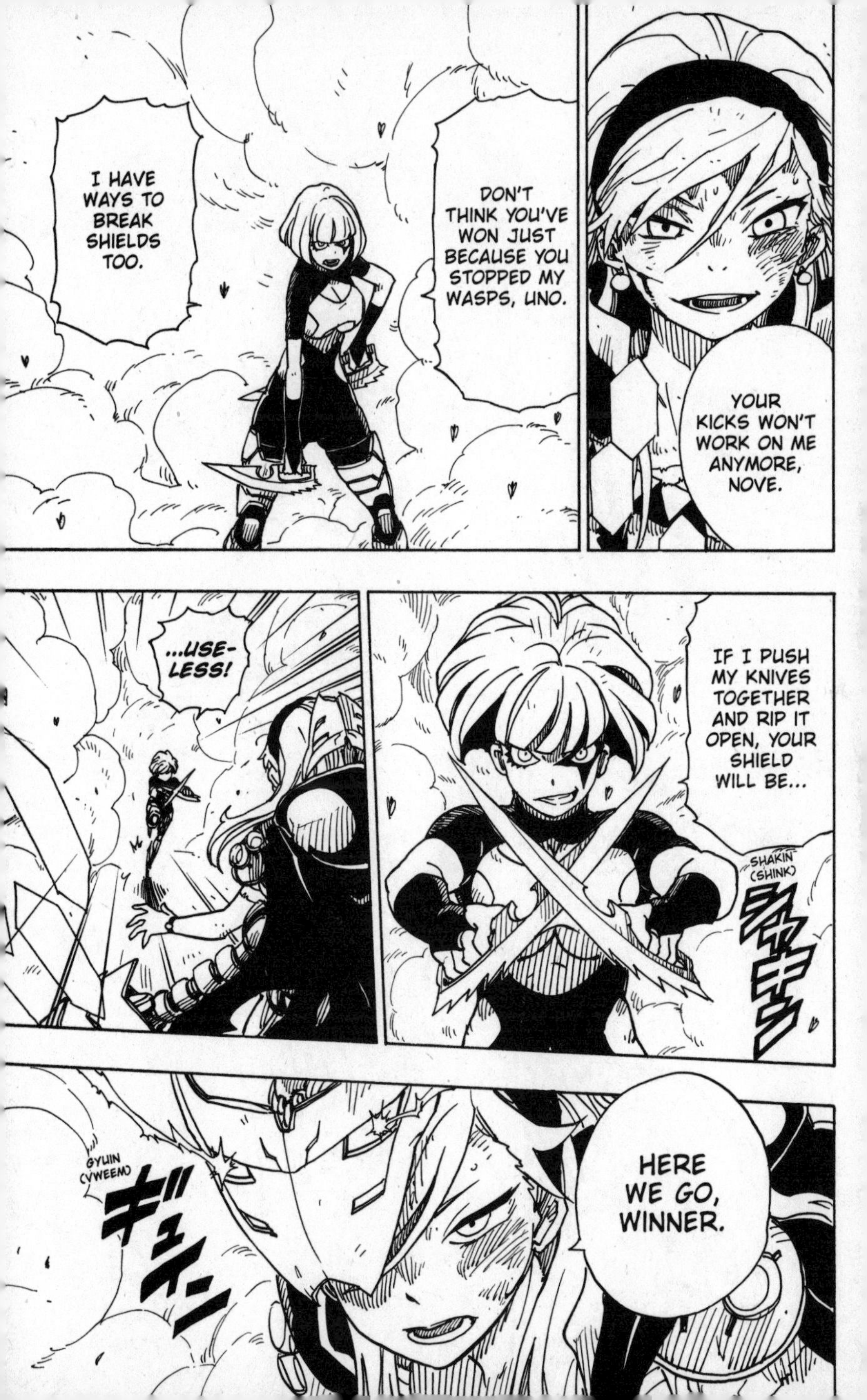
YOUR KICKS WON'T WORK ON ME ANYMORE, NOVE.
DON'T THINK YOU'VE WON JUST BECAUSE YOU STOPPED MY WASPS, UNO.
I HAVE WAYS TO BREAK SHIELDS TOO.
IF I PUSH MY KNIVES TOGETHER AND RIP IT OPEN, YOUR SHIELD WILL BE...
SHAKIN (SHINK)
シャキン
...USE-LESS!
HERE WE GO, WINNER.
GYUIN (VWEEM)
ギュイーン

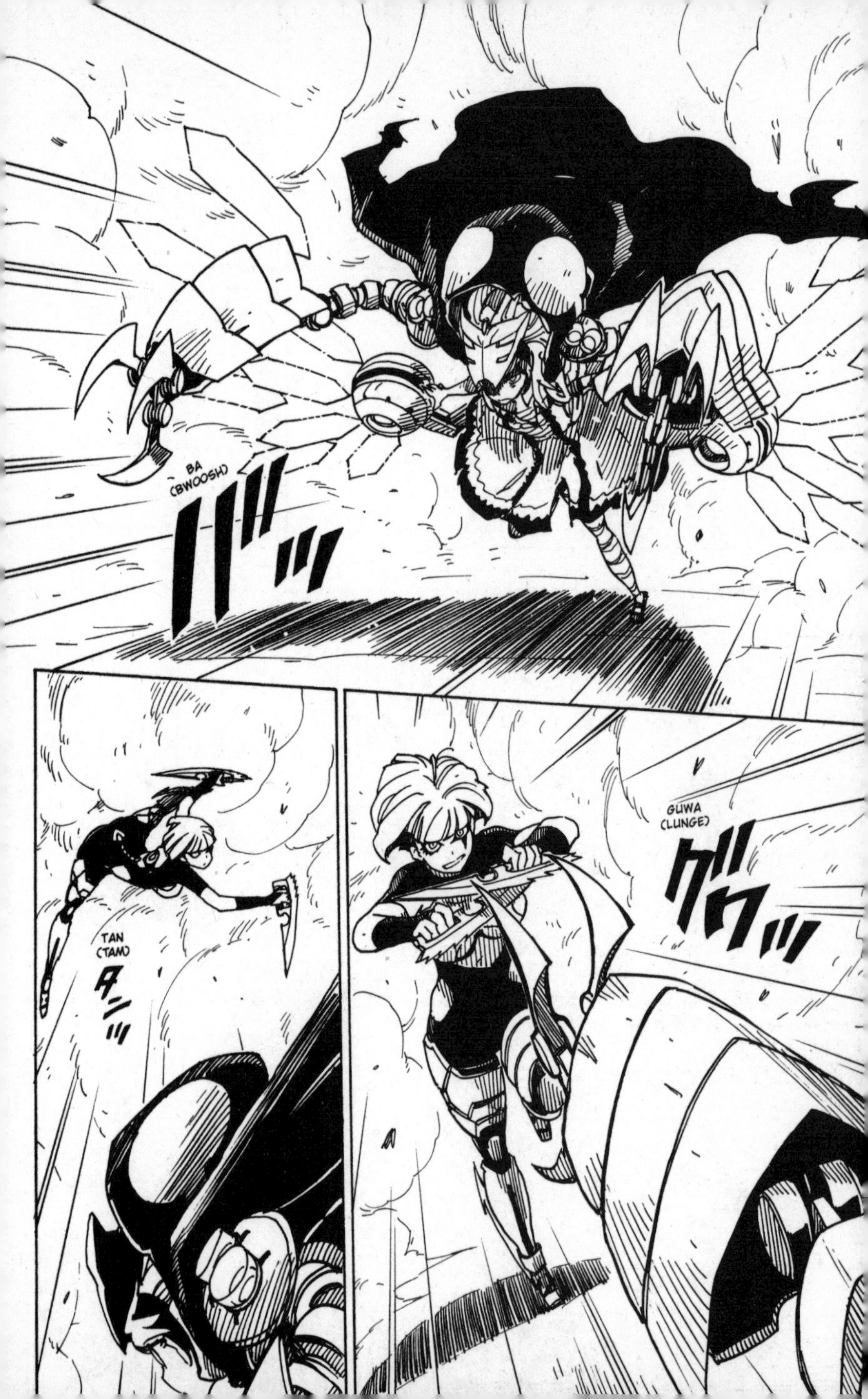
BA
(BWOOSH)
バッ
GUWA
(LUNGE)
グワッ
TAN
(TAM)
タンッ

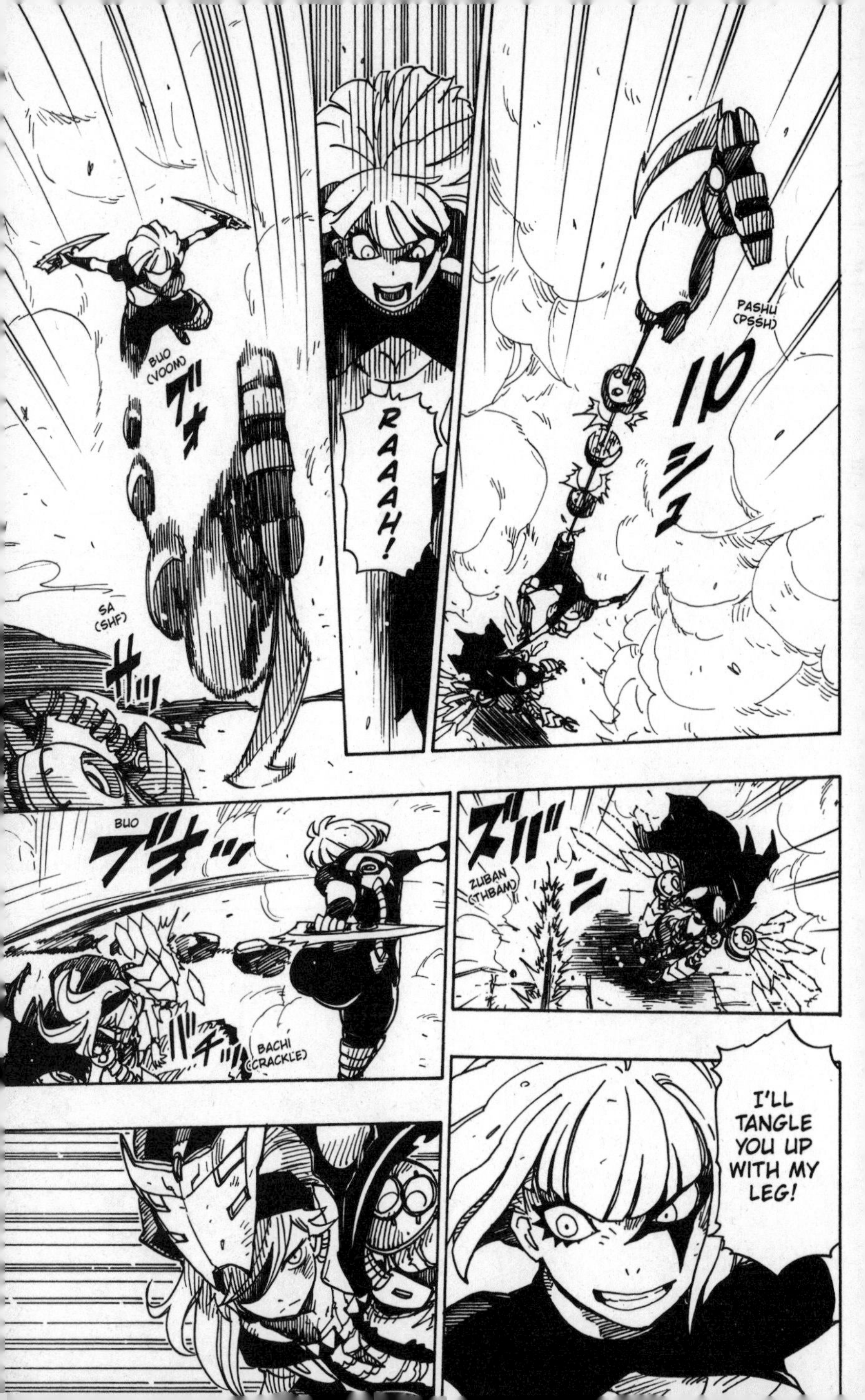
PASHU (PSSH)
パシュ
RAAAAH!
BUO (VOOM)
ブオ
SA (SHF)
サッ
ZUBAN (THBAM)
ズバン
BUO
ブオッ
BACHI (CRACKLE)
バチッ
I'LL TANGLE YOU UP WITH MY LEG!

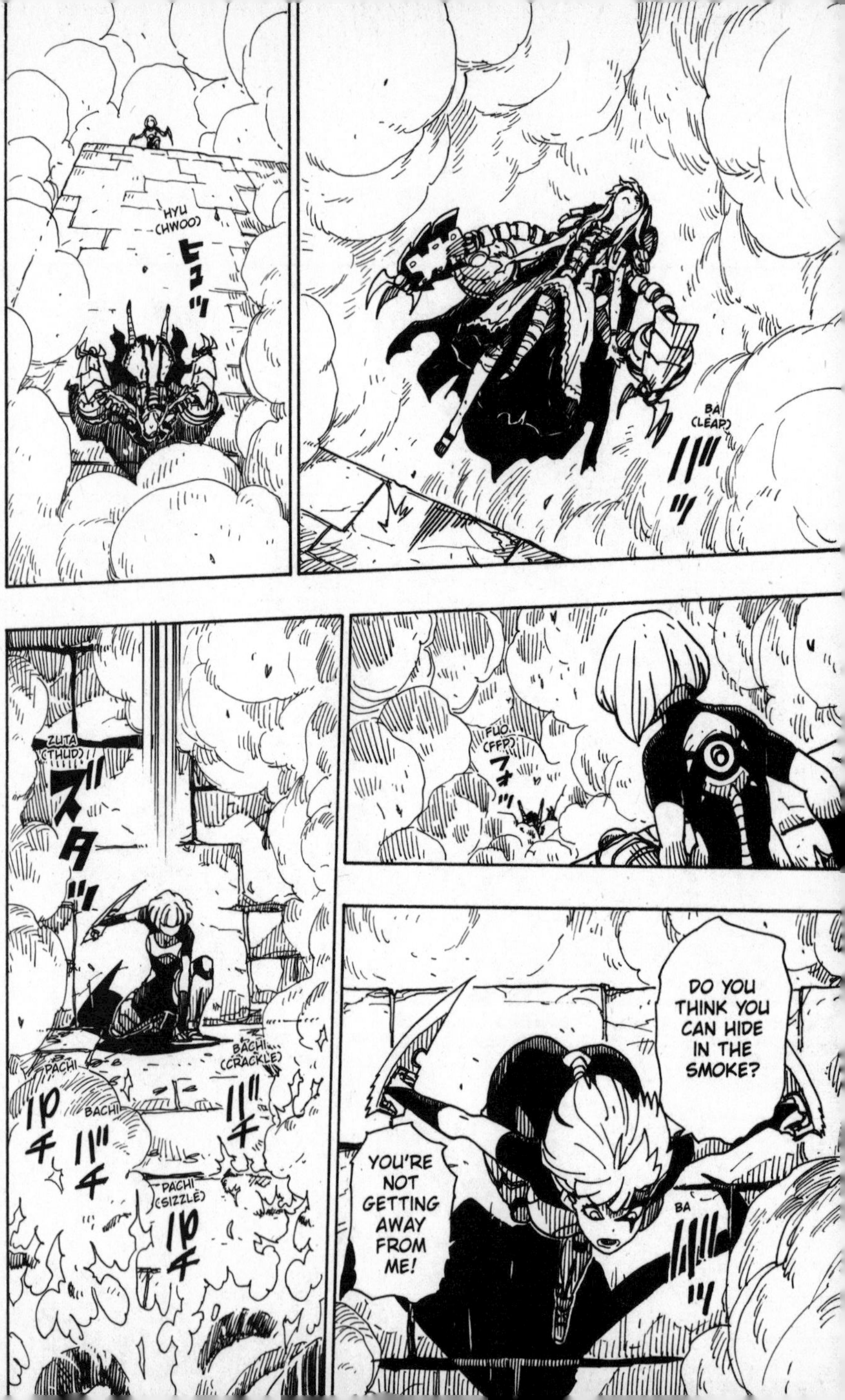
BA (LEAP)
バッ
HYU (HWOO)
ヒュッ
FUO (FFP)
フォッ
DO YOU THINK YOU CAN HIDE IN THE SMOKE?
YOU'RE NOT GETTING AWAY FROM ME!
BA
バッ
ZUTA (THUD)
ズタッ
BACHI (CRACKLE)
バチ
PACHI
パチ
BACHI
バチ
PACHI (SIZZLE)
パチ

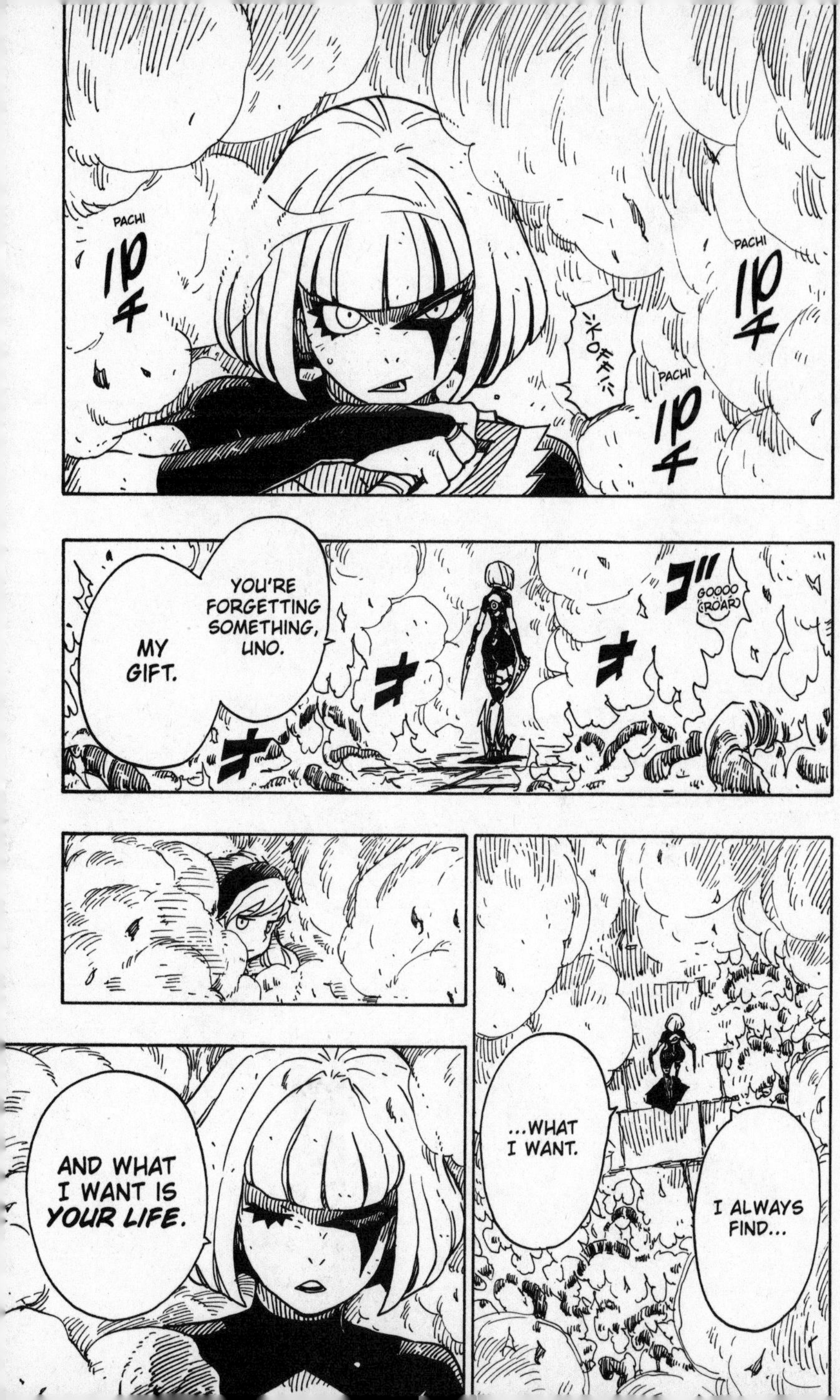
PACHI
PACHI
KOFF!!
PACHI
YOU'RE FORGETTING SOMETHING, UNO.
MY GIFT.
GOOOO (ROAR)
I ALWAYS FIND...
...WHAT I WANT.
AND WHAT I WANT IS *YOUR LIFE*.

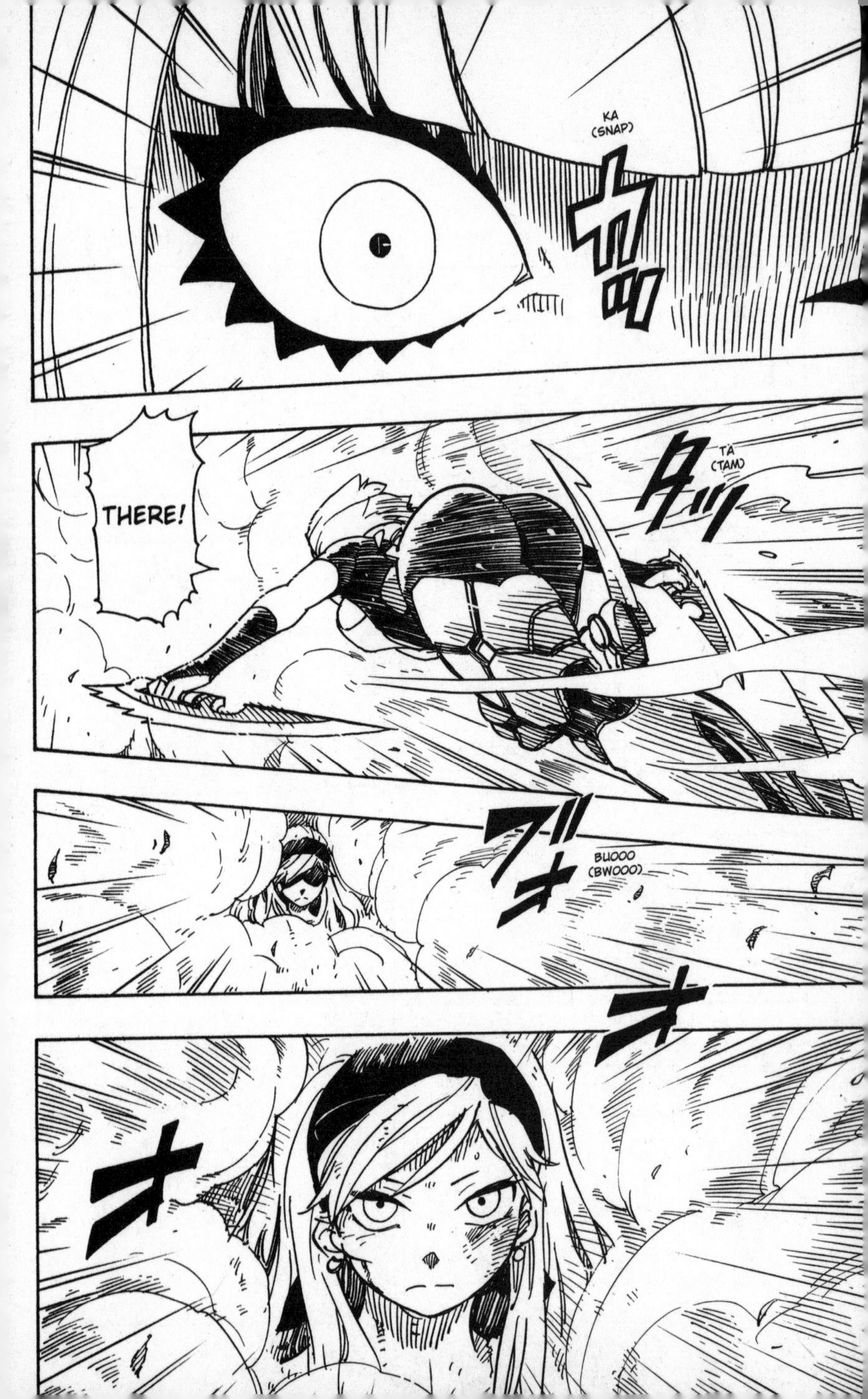
KA
(SNAP)
TA
(TAM)
THERE!
BUOOO
(BWOOO)

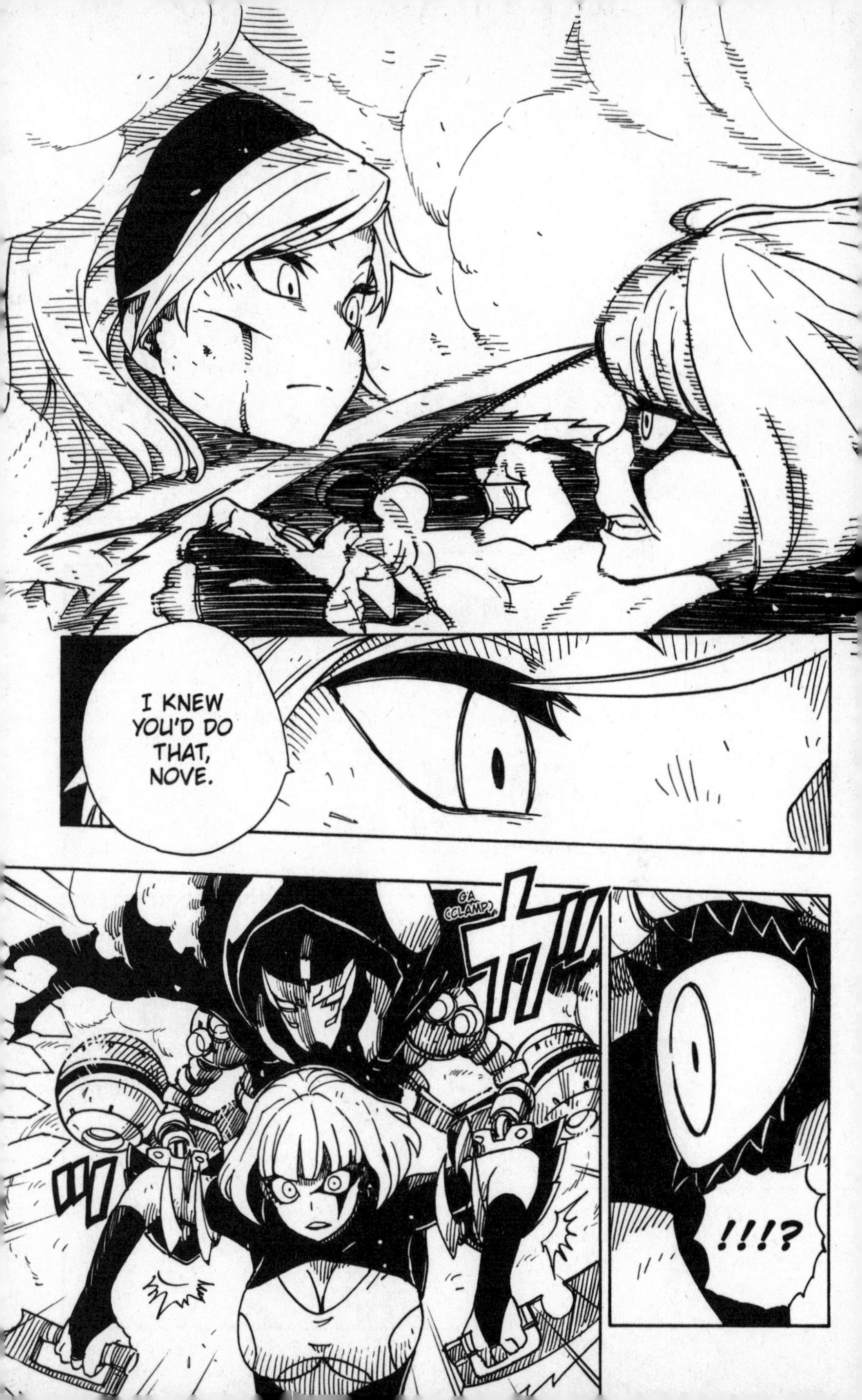
I KNEW YOU'D DO THAT, NOVE.
!!!?
GA (CLAMP)

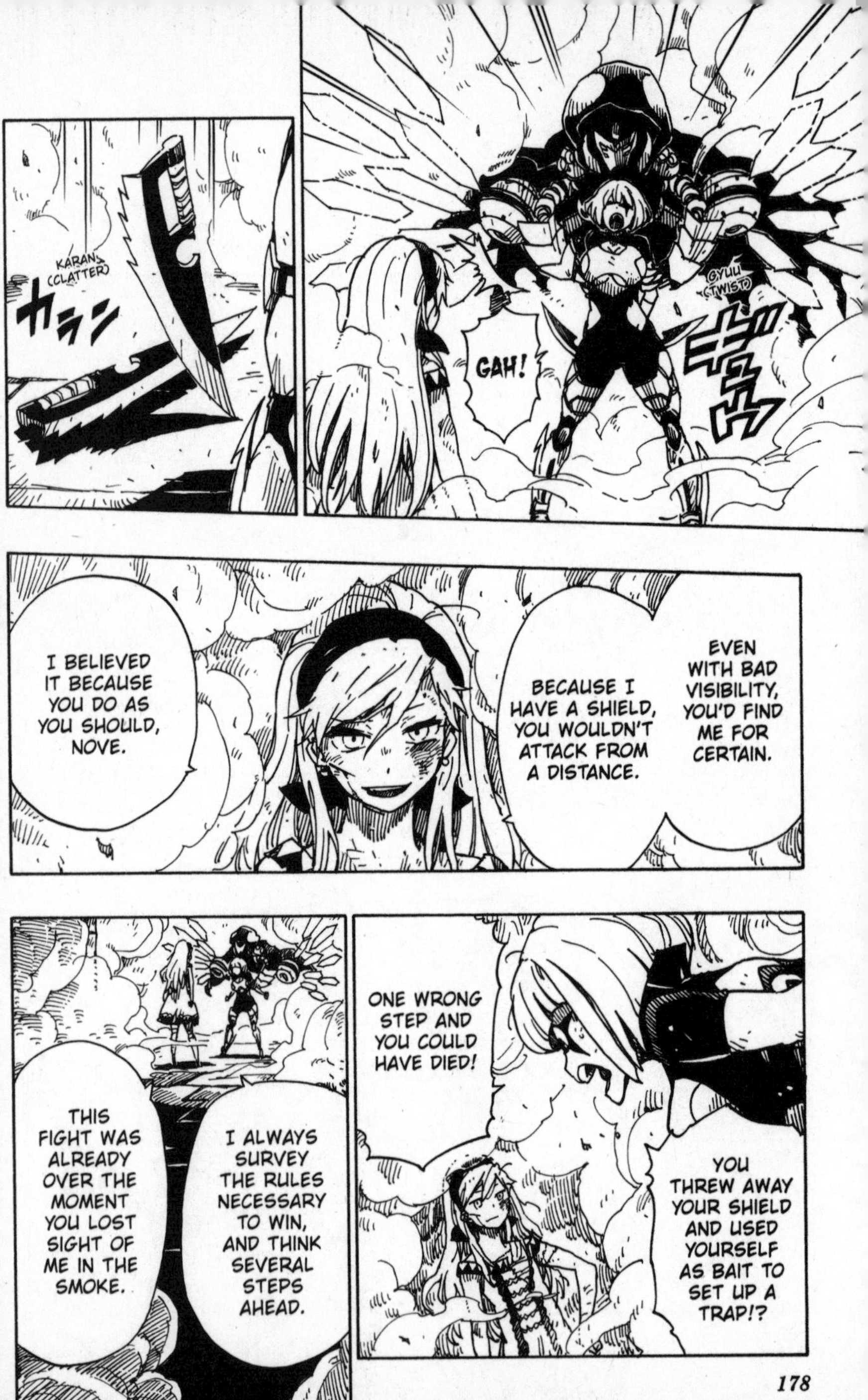
GAH!
GYUU (TWIST)
KARAN (CLATTER)
EVEN WITH BAD VISIBILITY, YOU'D FIND ME FOR CERTAIN.
BECAUSE I HAVE A SHIELD, YOU WOULDN'T ATTACK FROM A DISTANCE.
I BELIEVED IT BECAUSE YOU DO AS YOU SHOULD, NOVE.
ONE WRONG STEP AND YOU COULD HAVE DIED!
YOU THREW AWAY YOUR SHIELD AND USED YOURSELF AS BAIT TO SET UP A TRAP!?
I ALWAYS SURVEY THE RULES NECESSARY TO WIN, AND THINK SEVERAL STEPS AHEAD.
THIS FIGHT WAS ALREADY OVER THE MOMENT YOU LOST SIGHT OF ME IN THE SMOKE.

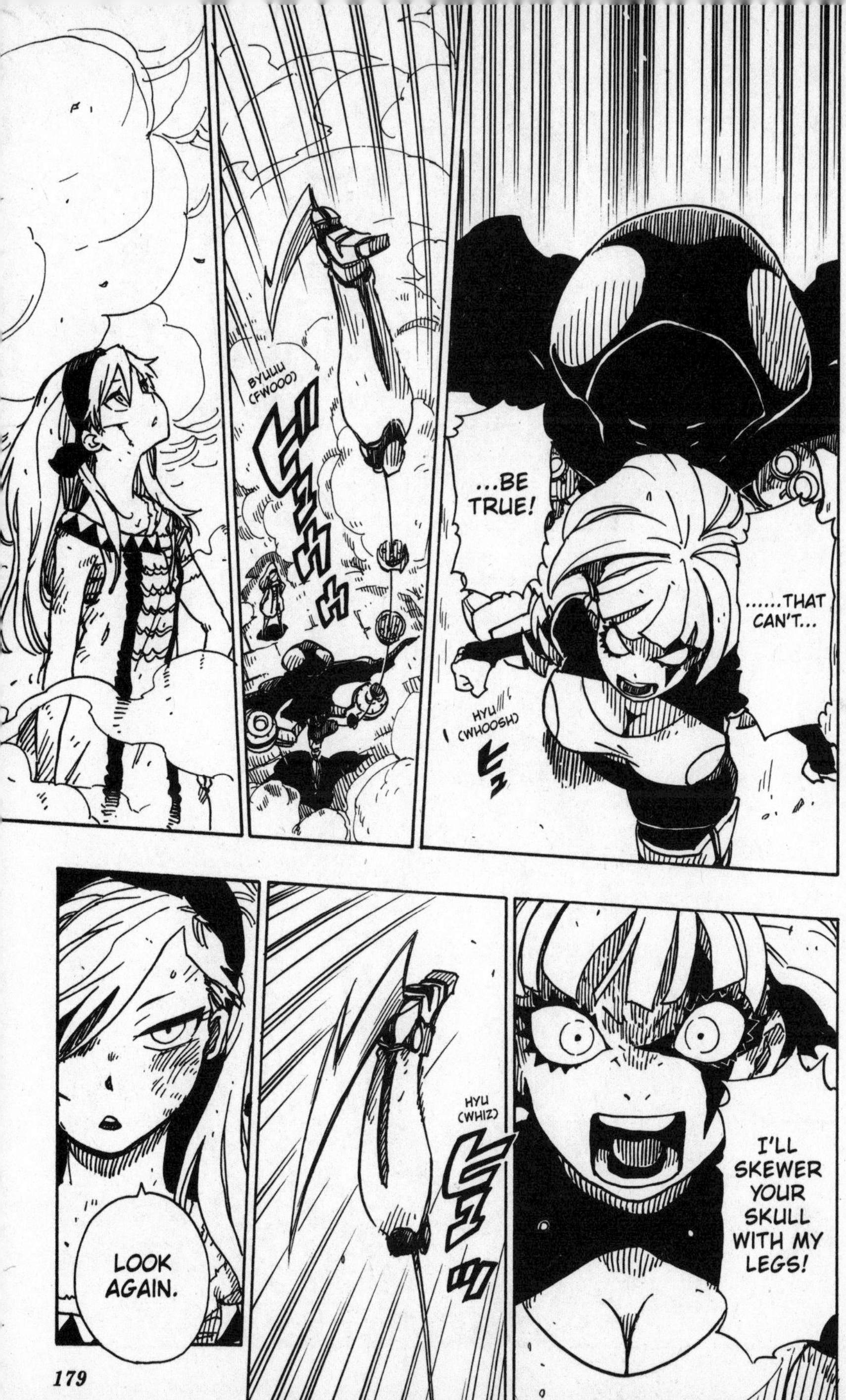
......THAT CAN'T...
...BE TRUE!
HYU (WHOOSH)
BYUUU (FWOOO)
I'LL SKEWER YOUR SKULL WITH MY LEGS!
HYU (WHIZ)
LOOK AGAIN.

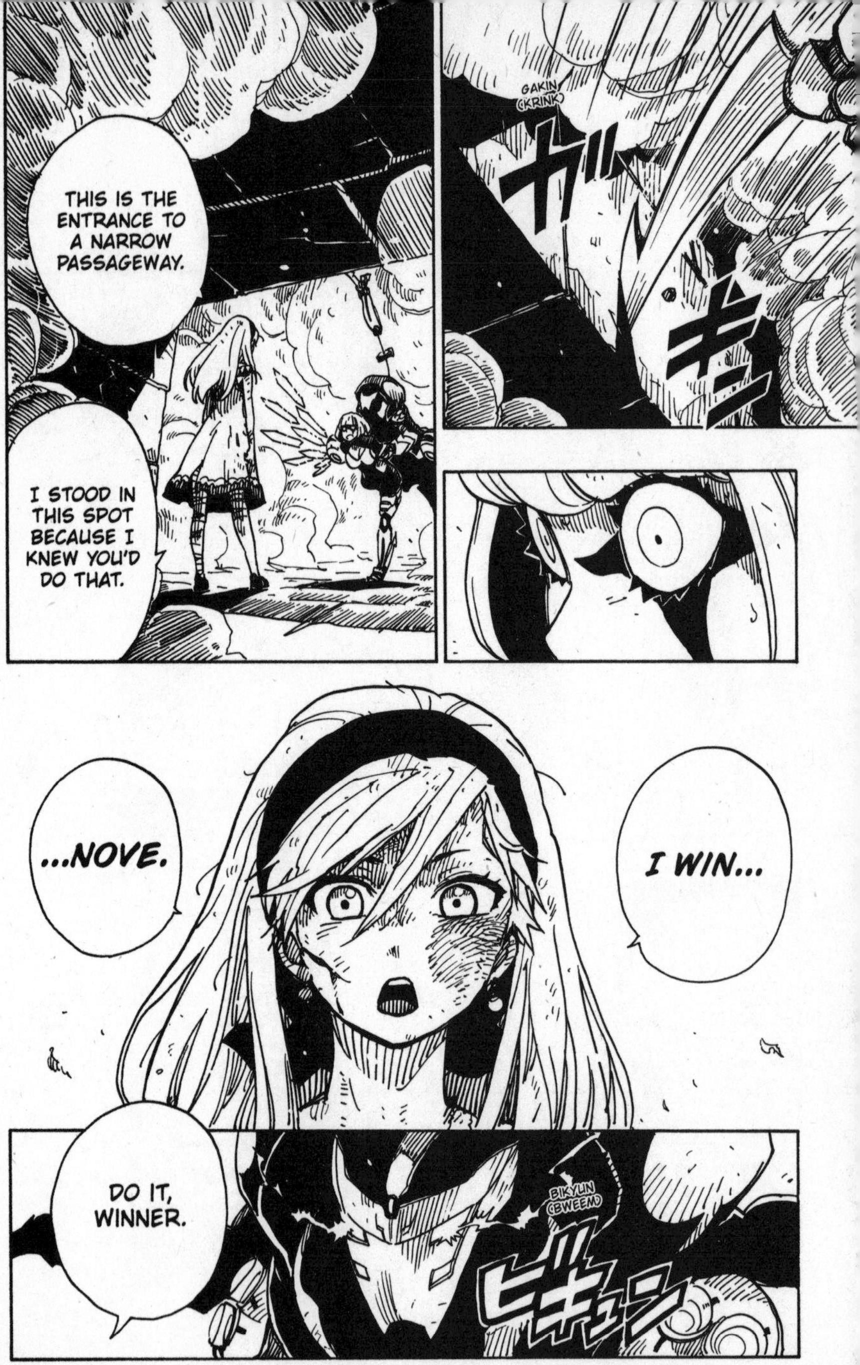
GAKIN (KRINK)
THIS IS THE ENTRANCE TO A NARROW PASSAGEWAY.
I STOOD IN THIS SPOT BECAUSE I KNEW YOU'D DO THAT.
I WIN...
...NOVE.
BIKYUN (BWEEM)
DO IT, WINNER.

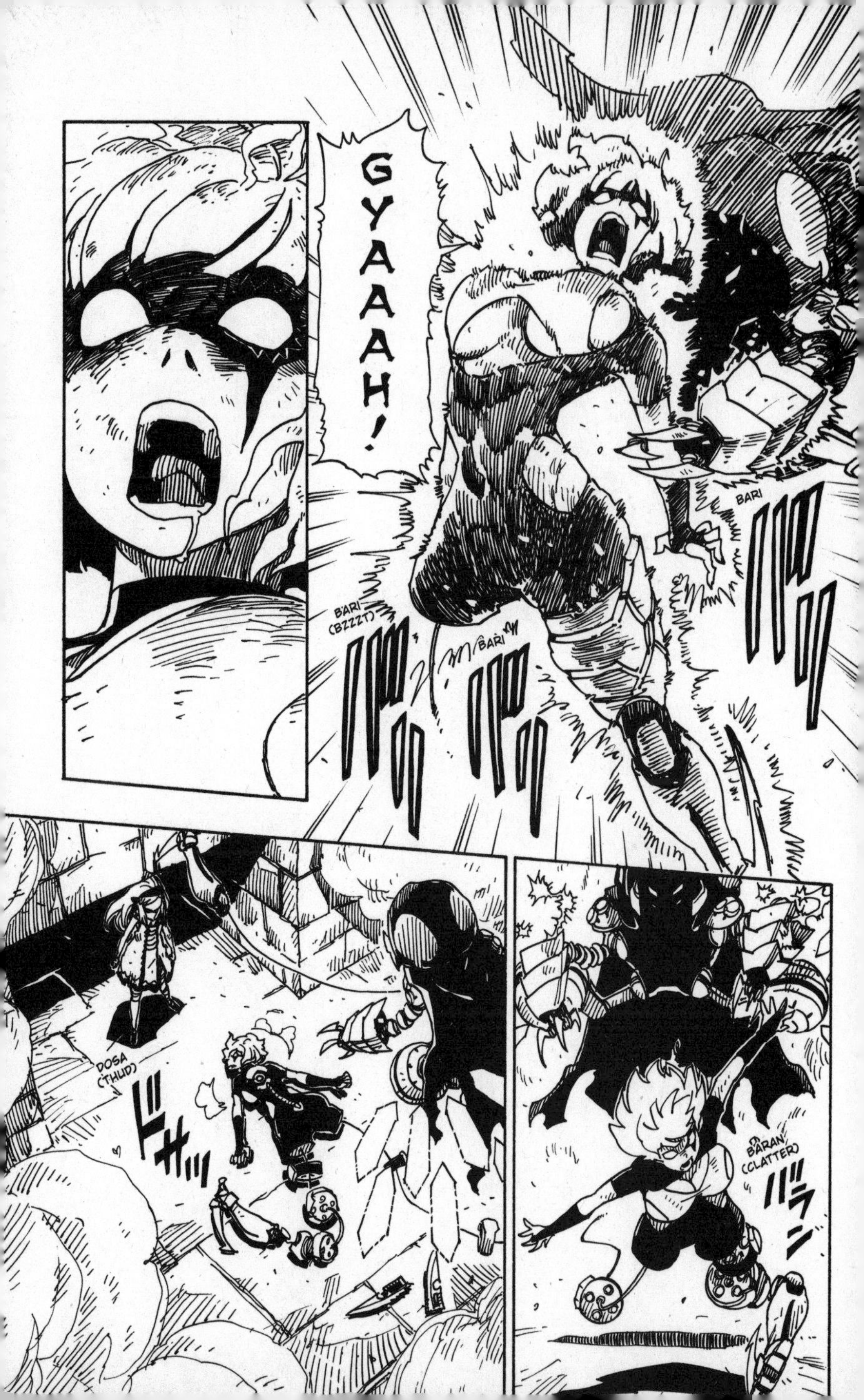

GYAAAH!
BARI
BARI
BARI (BZZZT)
BARAN (CLATTER)
DOSA (THUD)

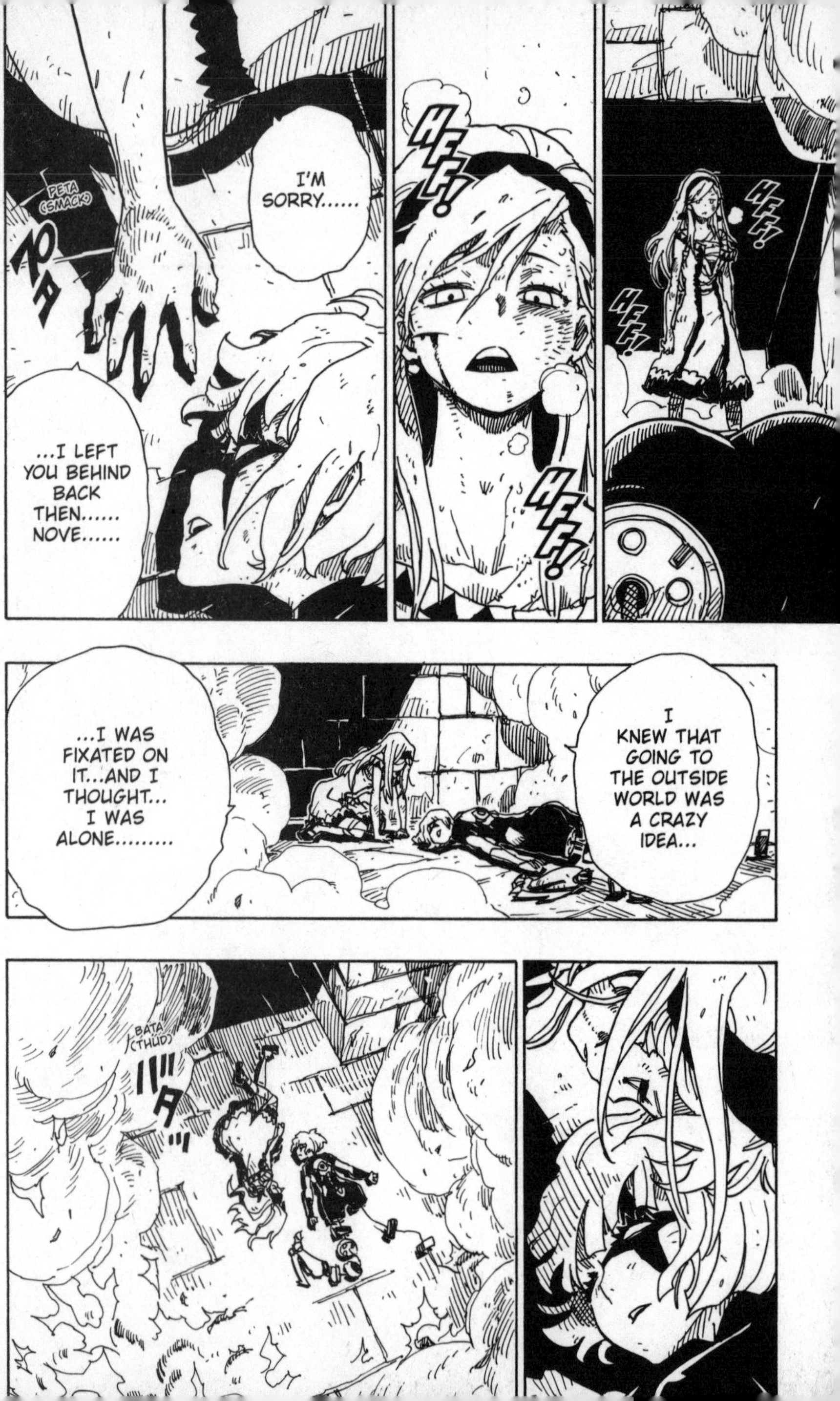
HFF!
HFF!
HFF!
HFF!
I'M SORRY......
PETA (SMACK)
...I LEFT YOU BEHIND BACK THEN...... NOVE......
I KNEW THAT GOING TO THE OUTSIDE WORLD WAS A CRAZY IDEA...
...I WAS FIXATED ON IT...AND I THOUGHT... I WAS ALONE.........
BATA (THUD)

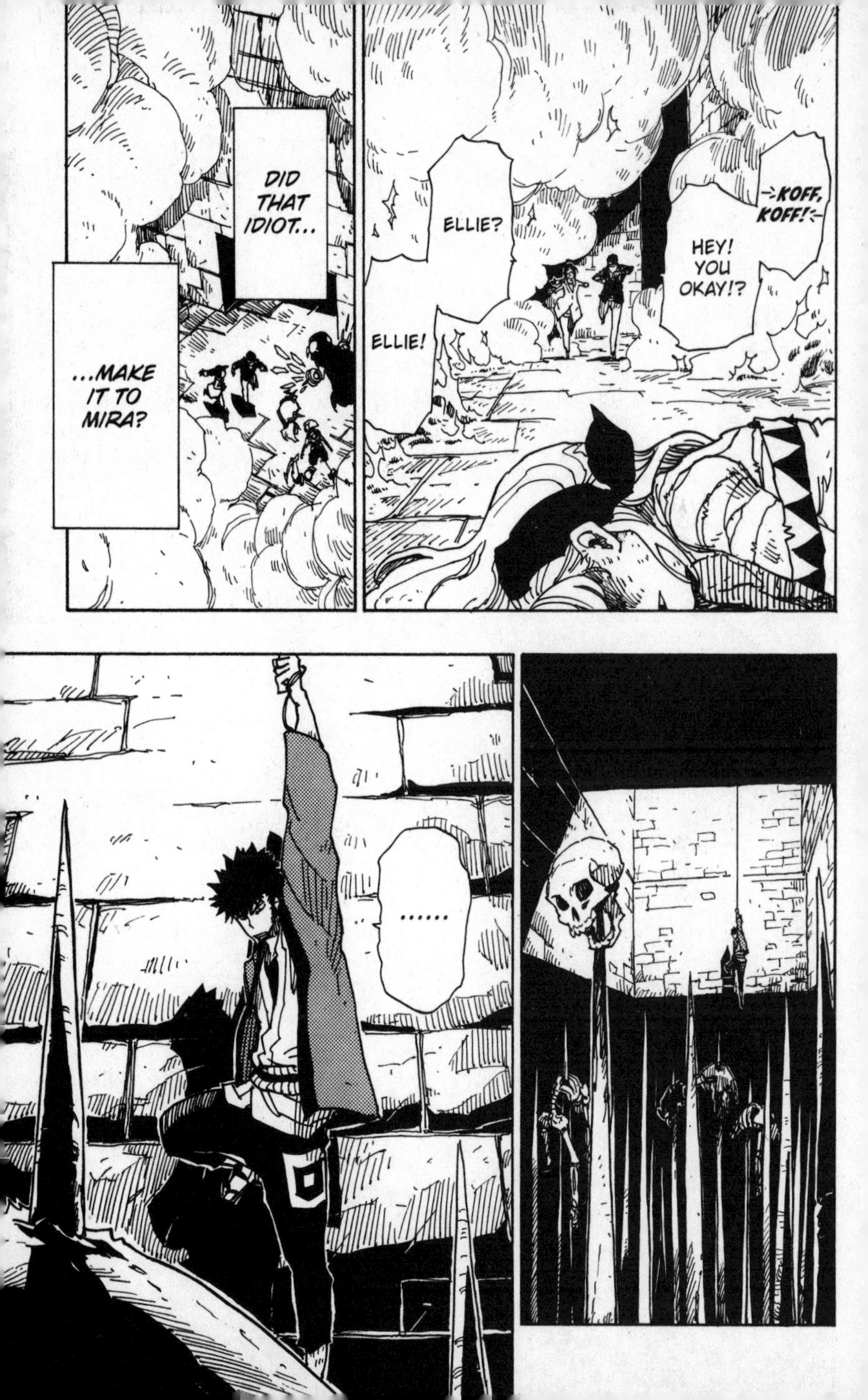
KOFF, KOFF!
HEY! YOU OKAY!?
ELLIE?
ELLIE!
DID THAT IDIOT...
...MAKE IT TO MIRA?
......

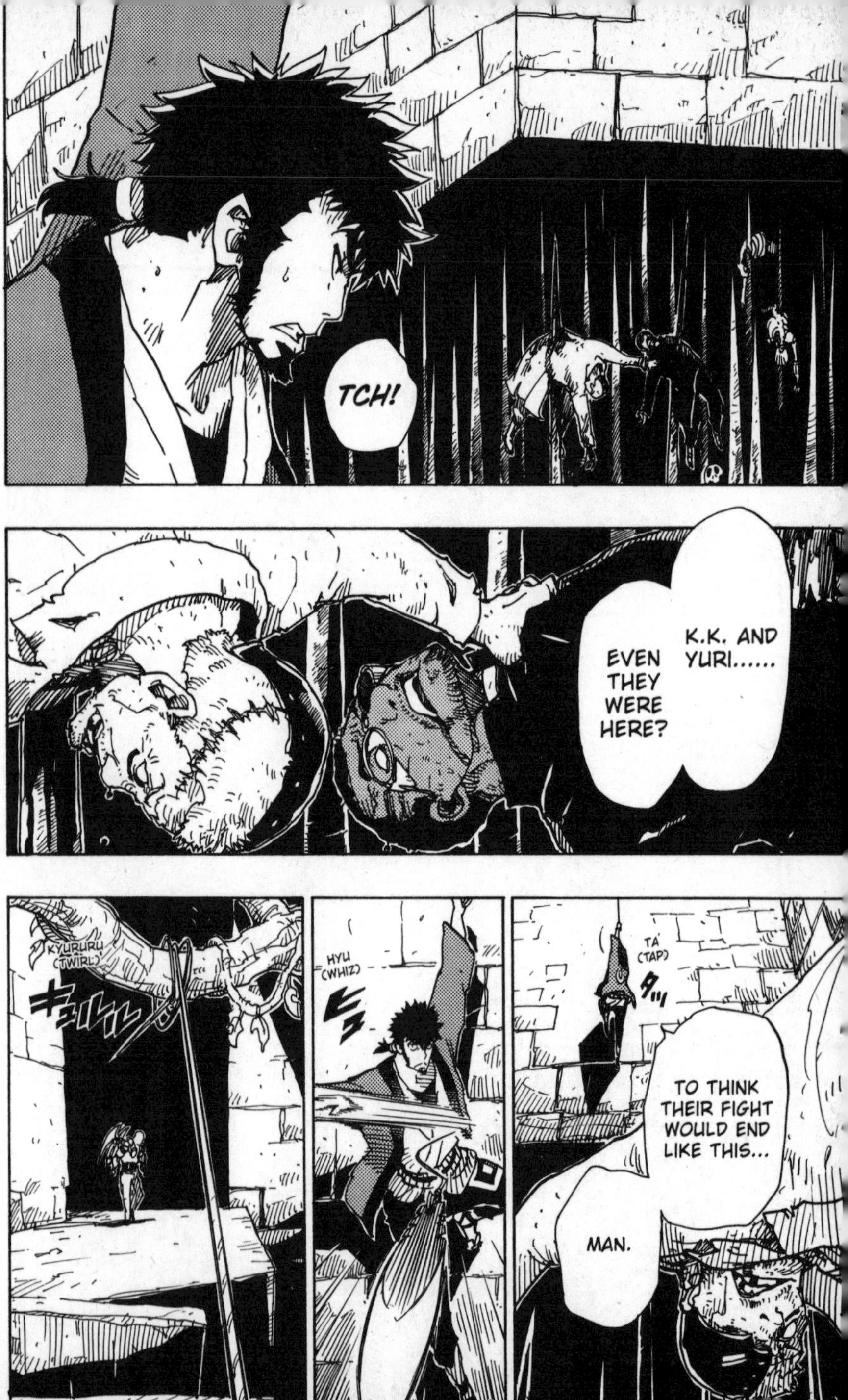
TCH!
K.K. AND YURI......
EVEN THEY WERE HERE?
タ
TA (TAP)
TO THINK THEIR FIGHT WOULD END LIKE THIS...
MAN.
ヒュ
HYU (WHIZ)
キュルル
KYURURU (TWIRL)

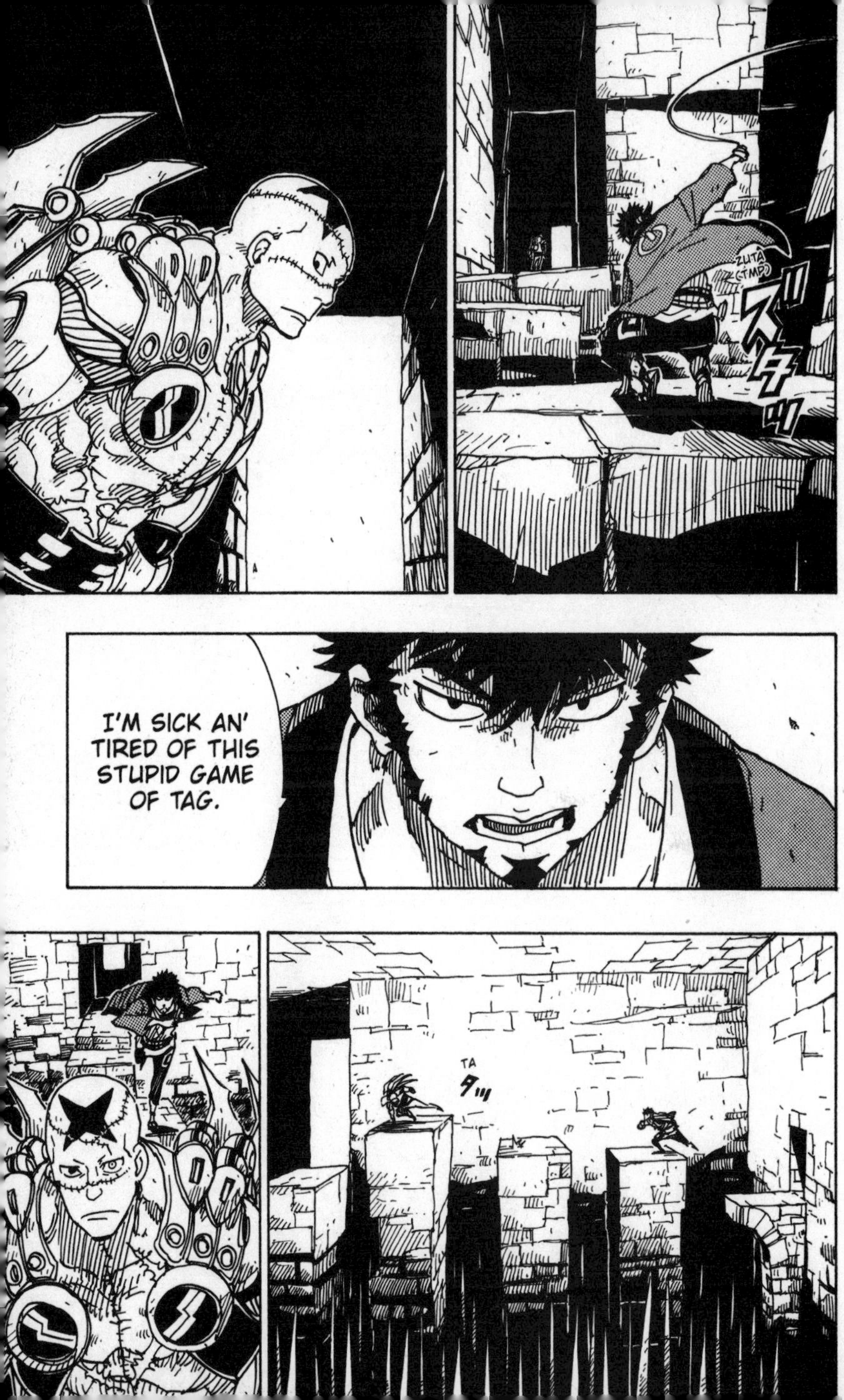
ZUTA (TMP)
I'M SICK AN' TIRED OF THIS STUPID GAME OF TAG.
TA

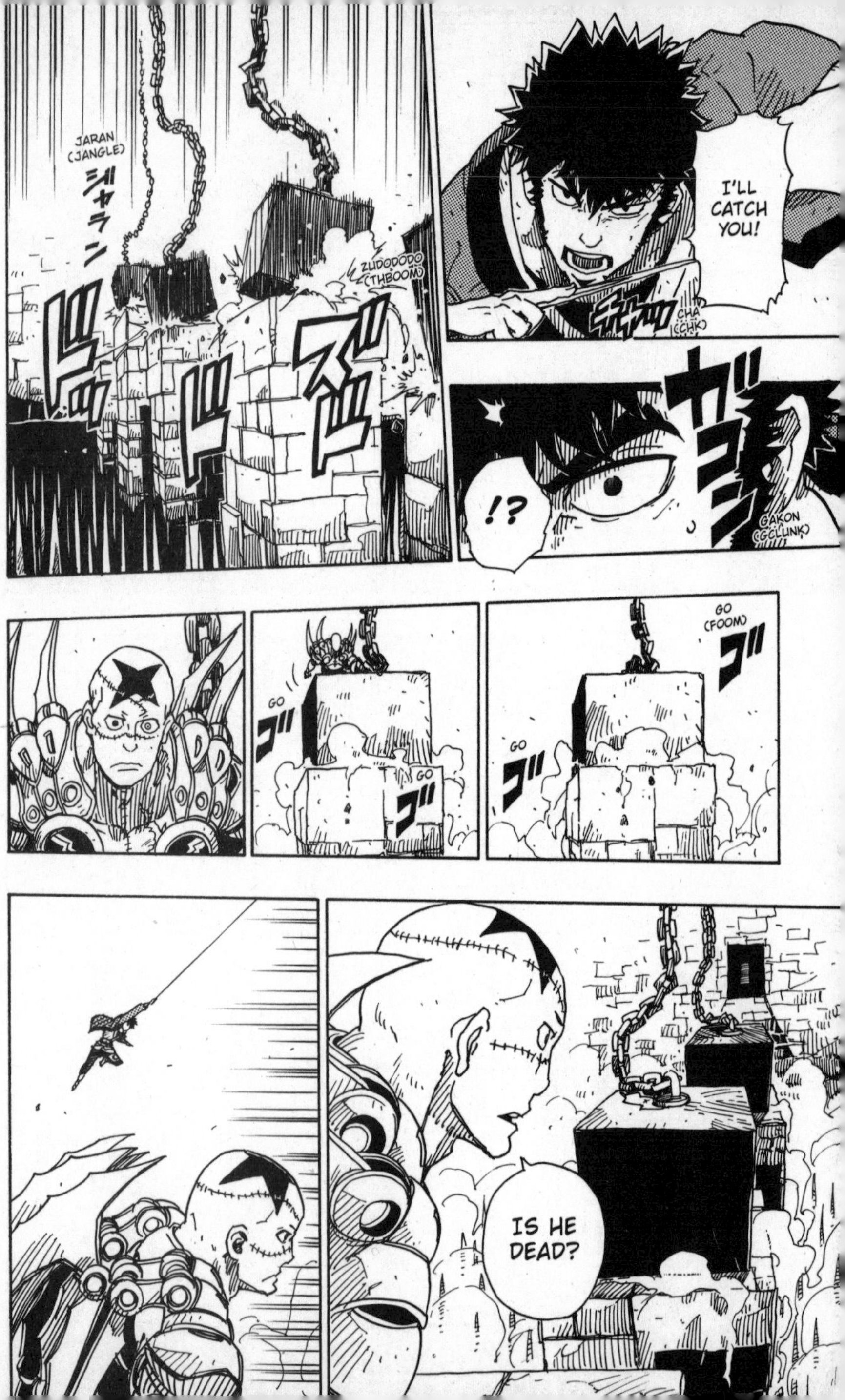
I'LL CATCH YOU!
CHA (CHK)
!?
GAKON (GCLUNK)
JARAN (JANGLE)
ジャラン
ZUDODODO (THBOOM)
GO (FOOM)
ゴ
GO
ゴ
GO
ゴ
GO
ゴ
IS HE DEAD?

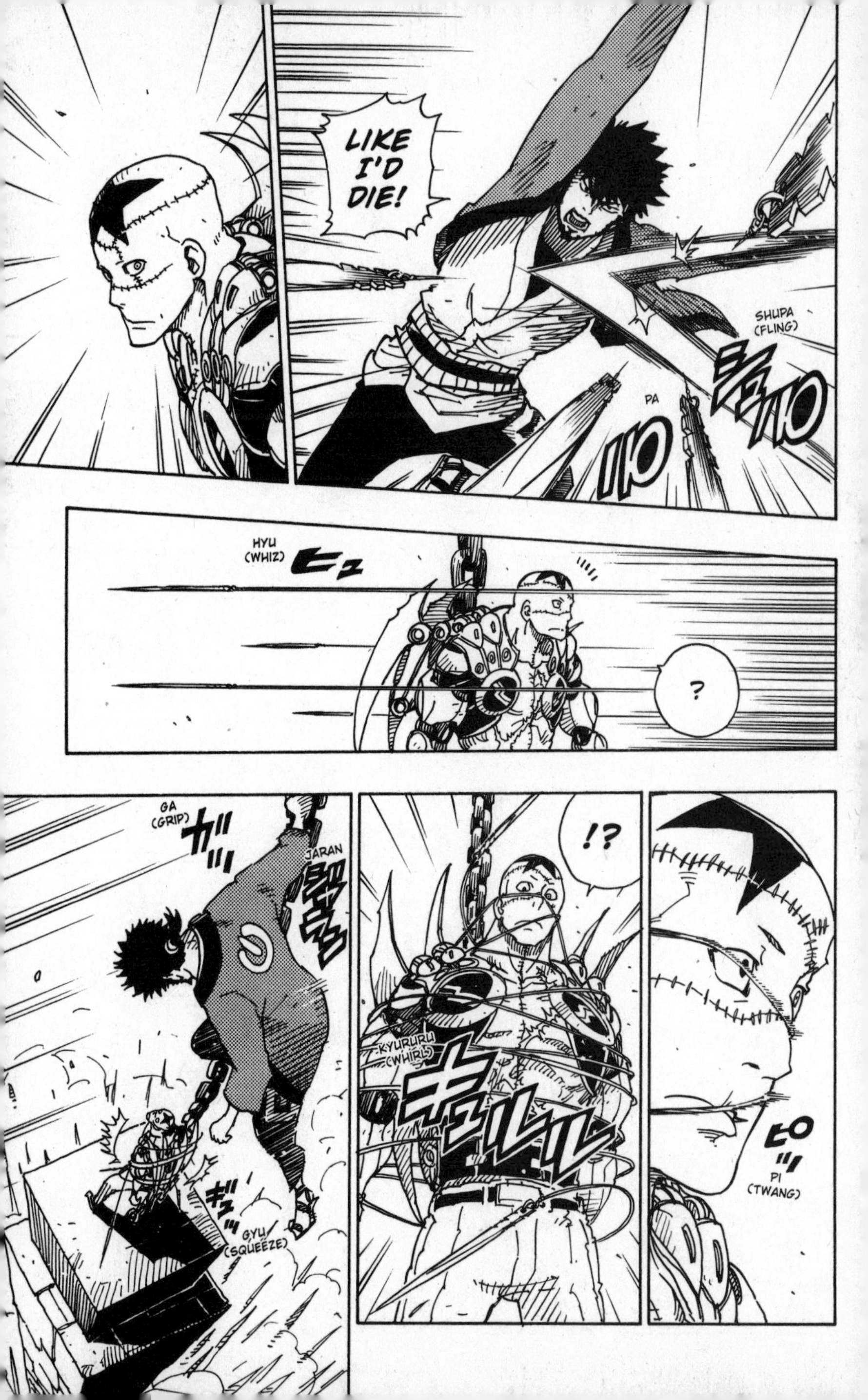
LIKE I'D DIE!
SHUPA (FLING)
PA
HYU (WHIZ)
?
PI (TWANG)
!?
KYURURU (WHIRL)
GA (GRIP)
JARAN
GYU (SQUEEZE)

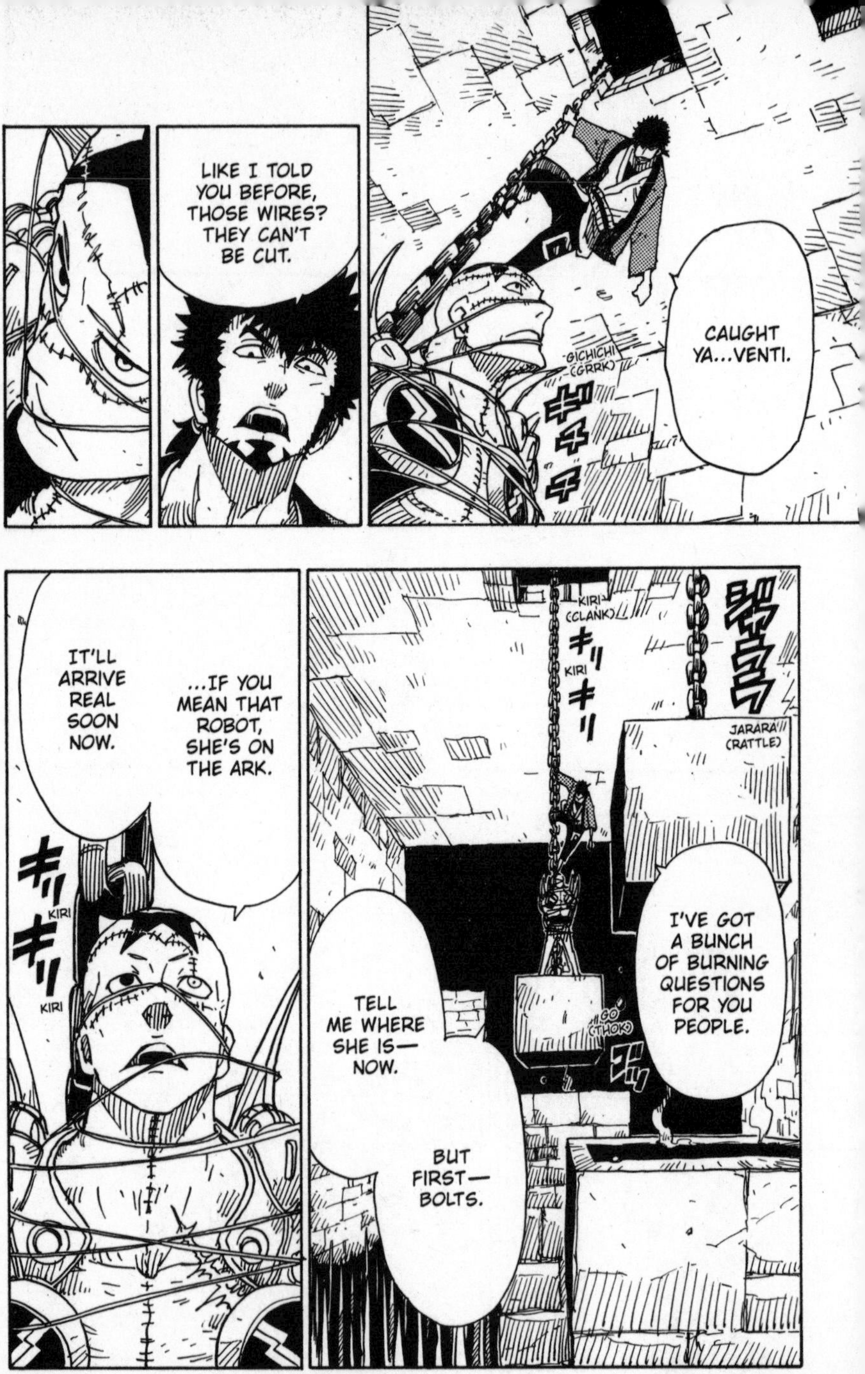
GICHICHI (GRRK)
CAUGHT YA...VENTI.
LIKE I TOLD YOU BEFORE, THOSE WIRES? THEY CAN'T BE CUT.
KIRI (CLANK)
KIRI
JARARA (RATTLE)
I'VE GOT A BUNCH OF BURNING QUESTIONS FOR YOU PEOPLE.
GO (THOK)
TELL ME WHERE SHE IS— NOW.
BUT FIRST— BOLTS.
...IF YOU MEAN THAT ROBOT, SHE'S ON THE ARK.
IT'LL ARRIVE REAL SOON NOW.
KIRI
KIRI

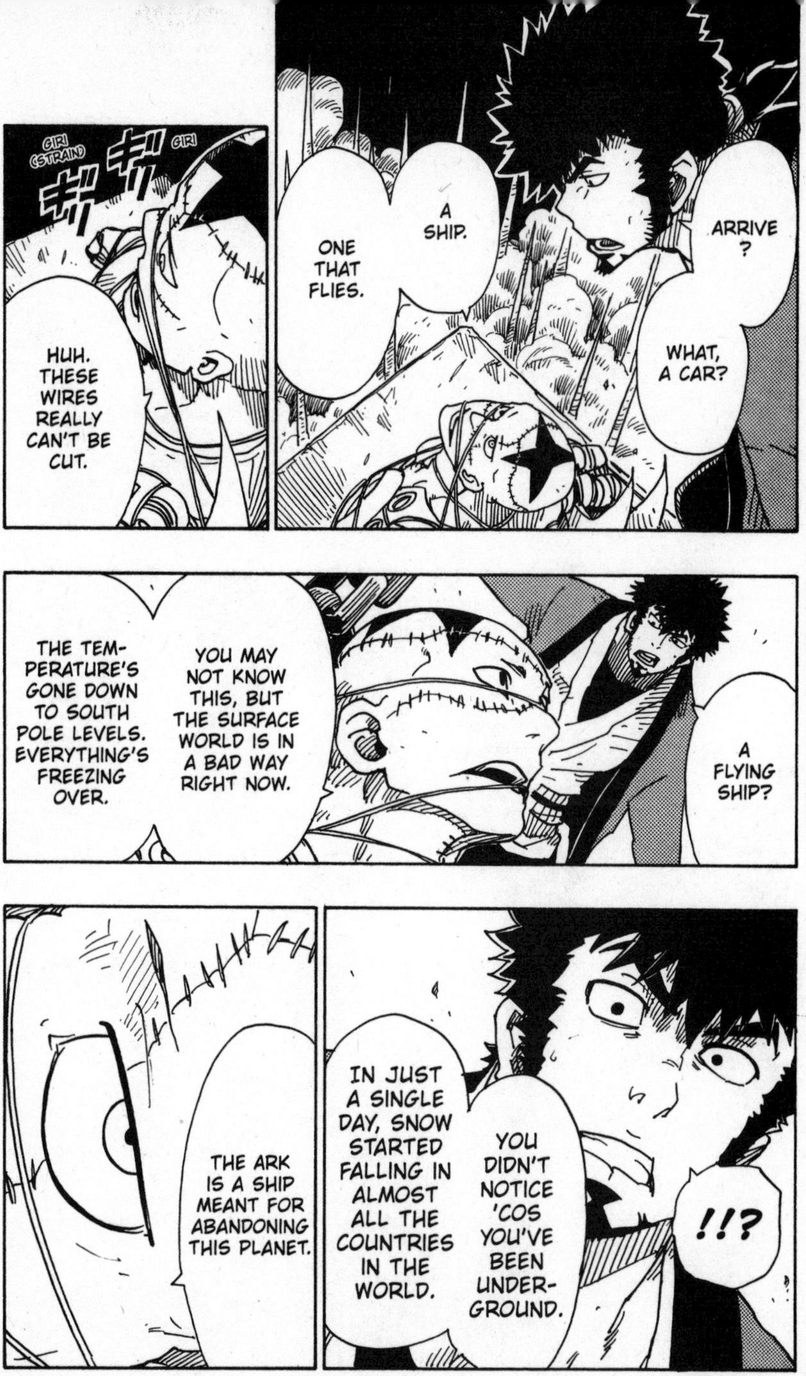
ARRIVE ?
WHAT, A CAR?
A SHIP.
ONE THAT FLIES.
GIRI (STRAIN)
GIRI
HUH. THESE WIRES REALLY CAN'T BE CUT.
A FLYING SHIP?
YOU MAY NOT KNOW THIS, BUT THE SURFACE WORLD IS IN A BAD WAY RIGHT NOW.
THE TEMPERATURE'S GONE DOWN TO SOUTH POLE LEVELS. EVERYTHING'S FREEZING OVER.
!!?
YOU DIDN'T NOTICE 'COS YOU'VE BEEN UNDERGROUND.
IN JUST A SINGLE DAY, SNOW STARTED FALLING IN ALMOST ALL THE COUNTRIES IN THE WORLD.
THE ARK IS A SHIP MEANT FOR ABANDONING THIS PLANET.

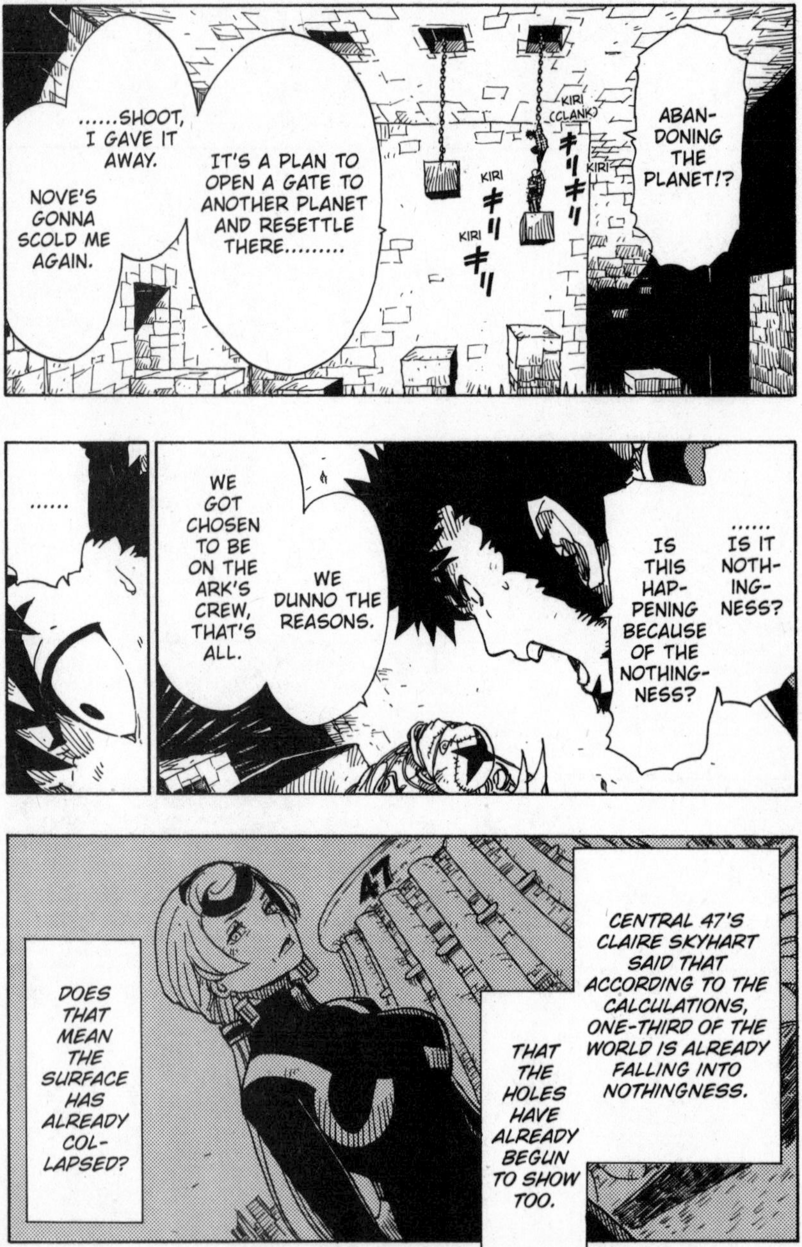
ABAN-DONING THE PLANET!?
KIRI (CLANK)
キリ
KIRI
キリ
KIRI
キリ
KIRI
キリ
IT'S A PLAN TO OPEN A GATE TO ANOTHER PLANET AND RESETTLE THERE.........
......SHOOT, I GAVE IT AWAY.
NOVE'S GONNA SCOLD ME AGAIN.
......IS IT NOTH-ING-NESS?
IS THIS HAP-PENING BECAUSE OF THE NOTHING-NESS?
WE DUNNO THE REASONS.
WE GOT CHOSEN TO BE ON THE ARK'S CREW, THAT'S ALL.
......
47
CENTRAL 47'S CLAIRE SKYHART SAID THAT ACCORDING TO THE CALCULATIONS, ONE-THIRD OF THE WORLD IS ALREADY FALLING INTO NOTHINGNESS.
THAT THE HOLES HAVE ALREADY BEGUN TO SHOW TOO.
DOES THAT MEAN THE SURFACE HAS ALREADY COL-LAPSED?

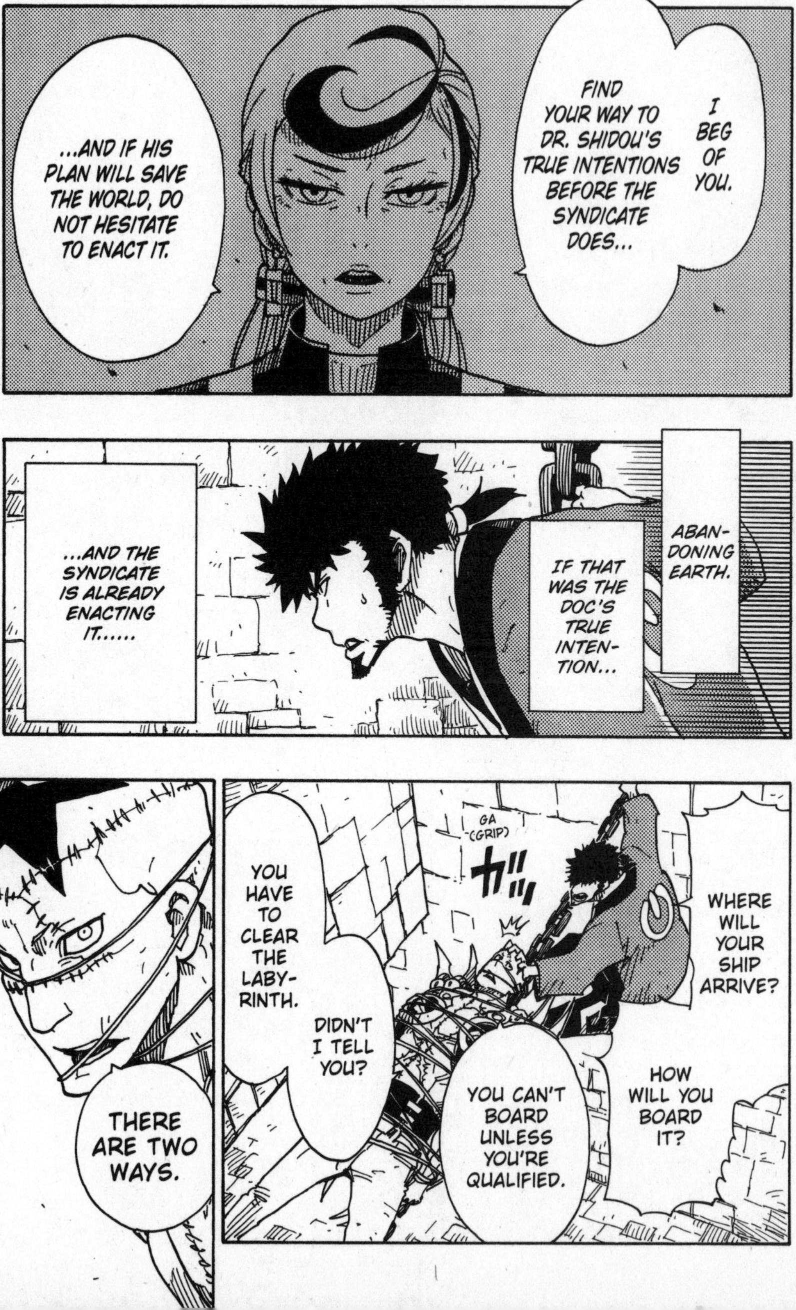
FIND YOUR WAY TO DR. SHIDOU'S TRUE INTENTIONS BEFORE THE SYNDICATE DOES...
I BEG OF YOU.
...AND IF HIS PLAN WILL SAVE THE WORLD, DO NOT HESITATE TO ENACT IT.
ABANDONING EARTH.
IF THAT WAS THE DOC'S TRUE INTENTION...
...AND THE SYNDICATE IS ALREADY ENACTING IT......
WHERE WILL YOUR SHIP ARRIVE?
HOW WILL YOU BOARD IT?
GA (GRIP)
YOU CAN'T BOARD UNLESS YOU'RE QUALIFIED.
YOU HAVE TO CLEAR THE LABYRINTH.
DIDN'T I TELL YOU?
THERE ARE TWO WAYS.

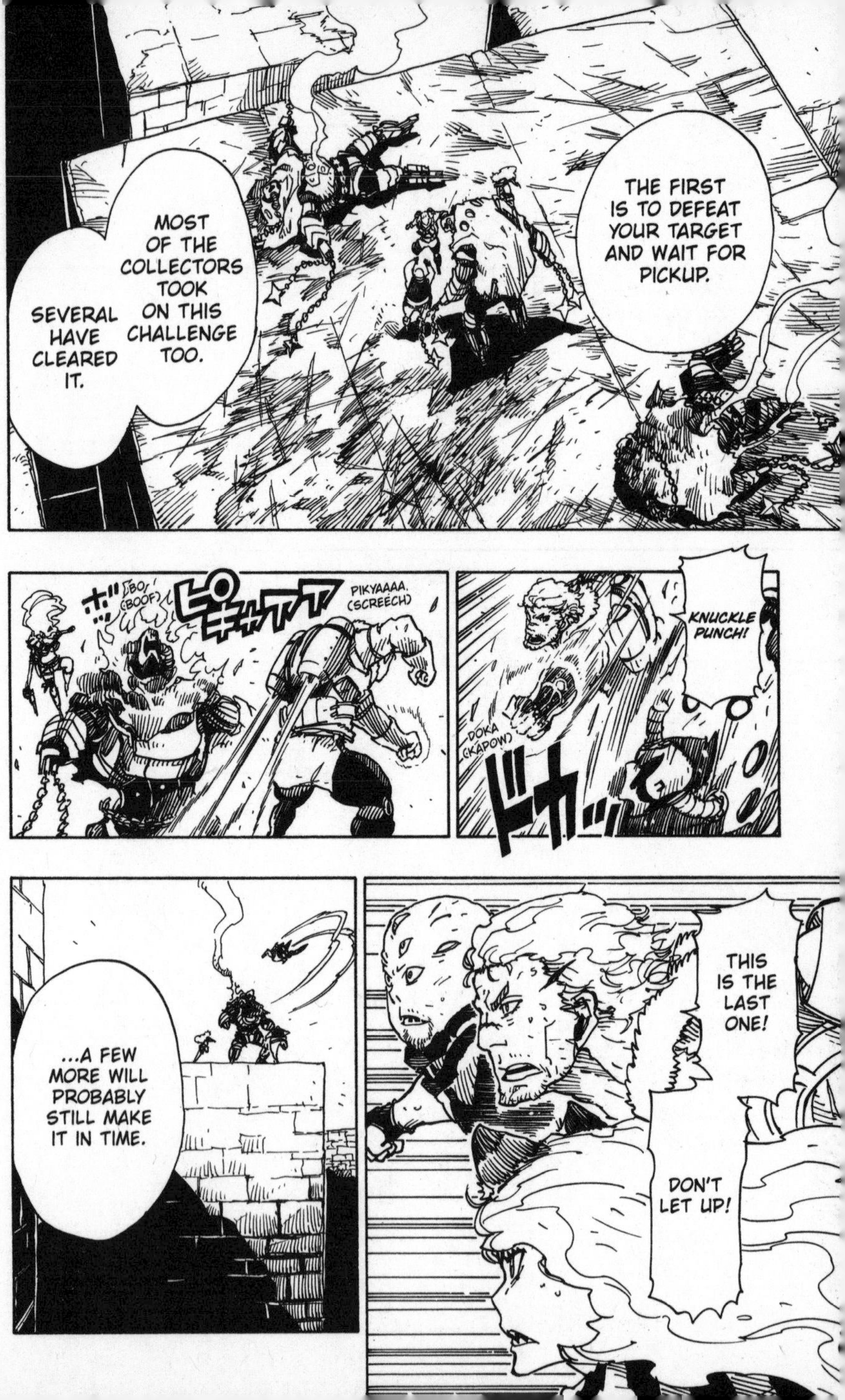
THE FIRST IS TO DEFEAT YOUR TARGET AND WAIT FOR PICKUP.
MOST OF THE COLLECTORS TOOK ON THIS CHALLENGE TOO.
SEVERAL HAVE CLEARED IT.
KNUCKLE PUNCH!
ドカッ
DOKA (KAPOW)
ピキャアア
PIKYAAAA. (SCREECH)
ボッ
BO! (BOOF)
THIS IS THE LAST ONE!
DON'T LET UP!
...A FEW MORE WILL PROBABLY STILL MAKE IT IN TIME.

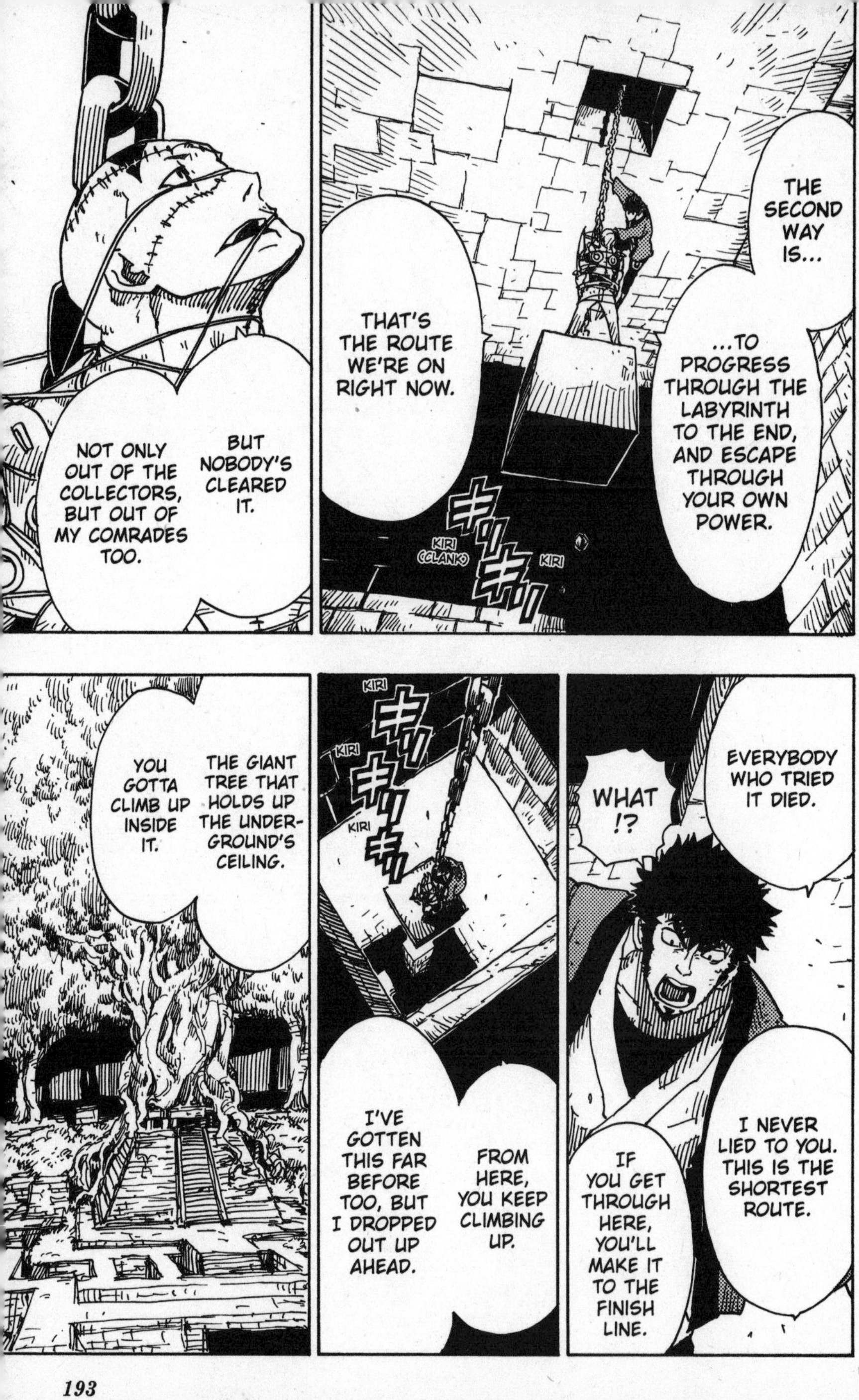
THE SECOND WAY IS...
...TO PROGRESS THROUGH THE LABYRINTH TO THE END, AND ESCAPE THROUGH YOUR OWN POWER.
THAT'S THE ROUTE WE'RE ON RIGHT NOW.
KIRI
KIRI (CLANK)
BUT NOBODY'S CLEARED IT.
NOT ONLY OUT OF THE COLLECTORS, BUT OUT OF MY COMRADES TOO.
EVERYBODY WHO TRIED IT DIED.
WHAT!?
I NEVER LIED TO YOU. THIS IS THE SHORTEST ROUTE.
IF YOU GET THROUGH HERE, YOU'LL MAKE IT TO THE FINISH LINE.
KIRI
KIRI
KIRI
FROM HERE, YOU KEEP CLIMBING UP.
I'VE GOTTEN THIS FAR BEFORE TOO, BUT I DROPPED OUT UP AHEAD.
THE GIANT TREE THAT HOLDS UP THE UNDERGROUND'S CEILING.
YOU GOTTA CLIMB UP INSIDE IT.

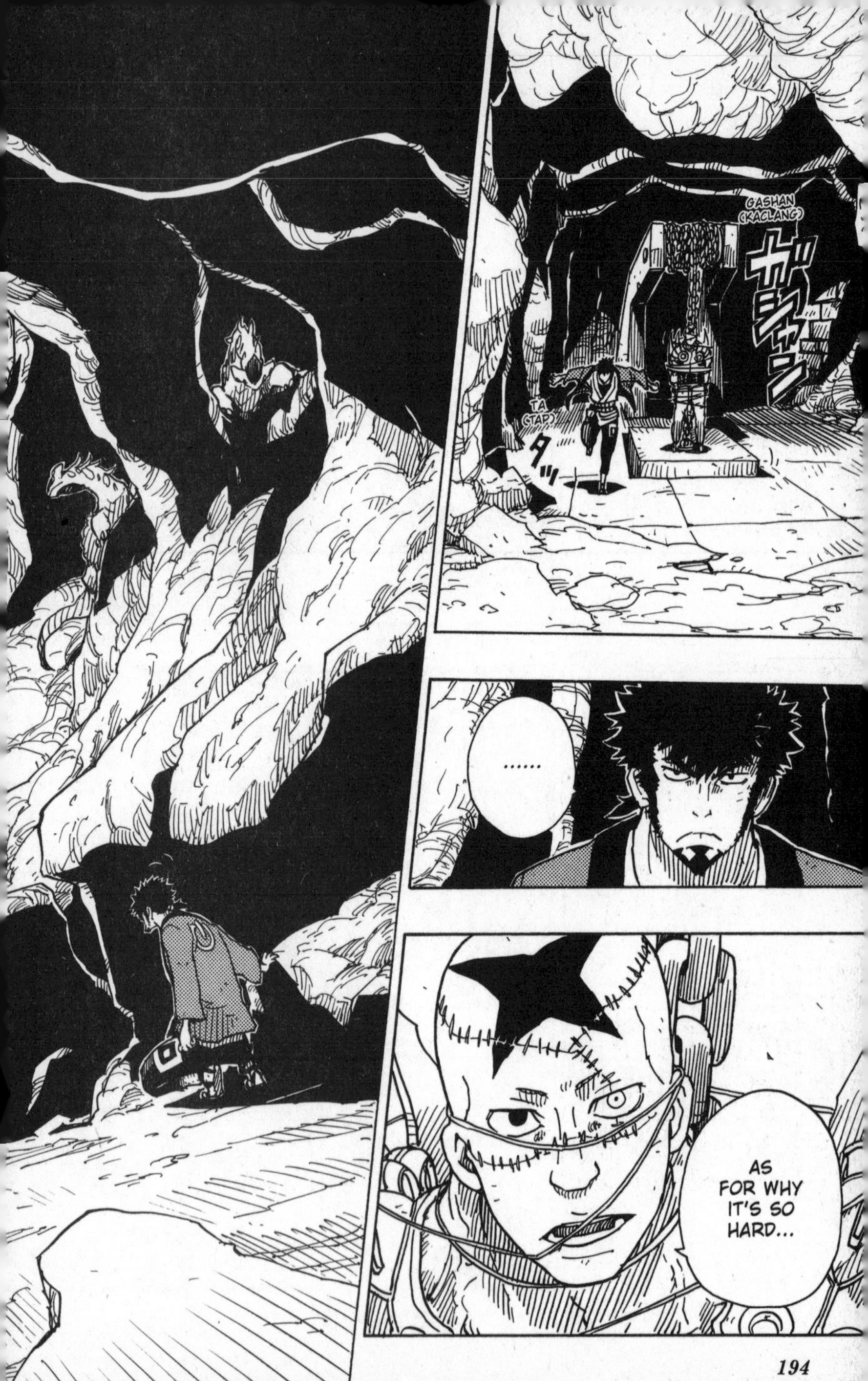
GASHAN
(KACLANG)
TA
(TAP)
......
AS FOR WHY IT'S SO HARD...

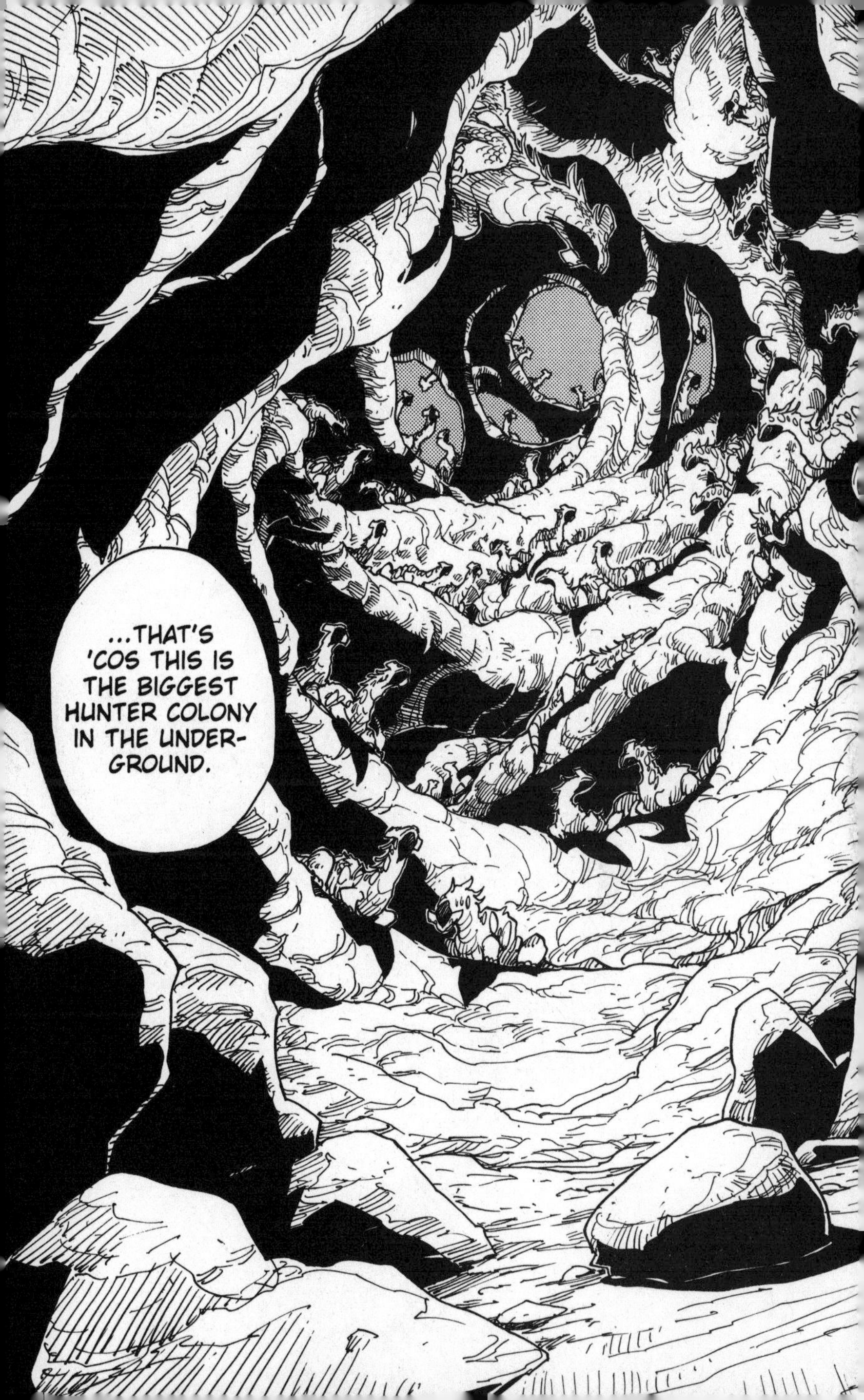
...THAT'S 'COS THIS IS THE BIGGEST HUNTER COLONY IN THE UNDER-GROUND.

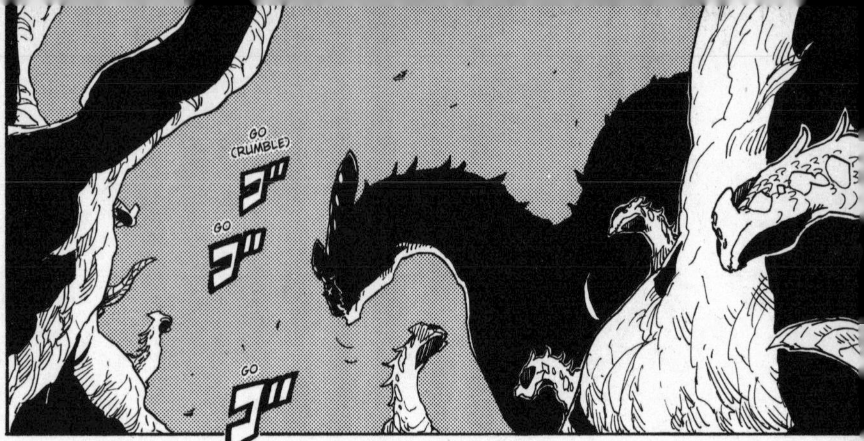
GO (RUMBLE)
ゴ
GO
ゴ
GO
ゴ

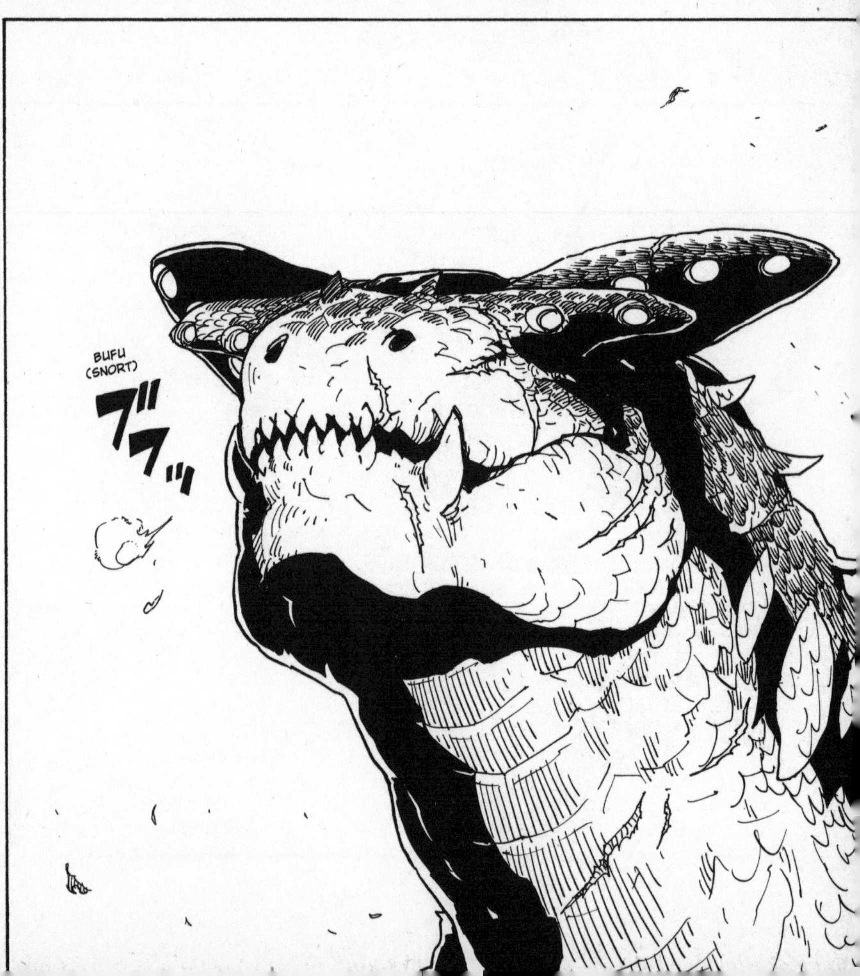
BUFU (SNORT)
ブフッ

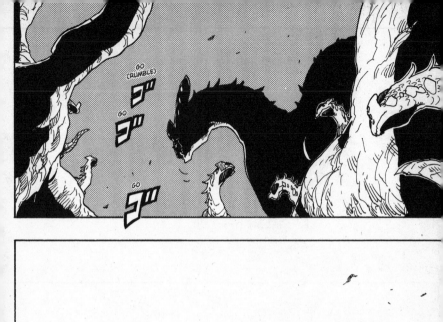

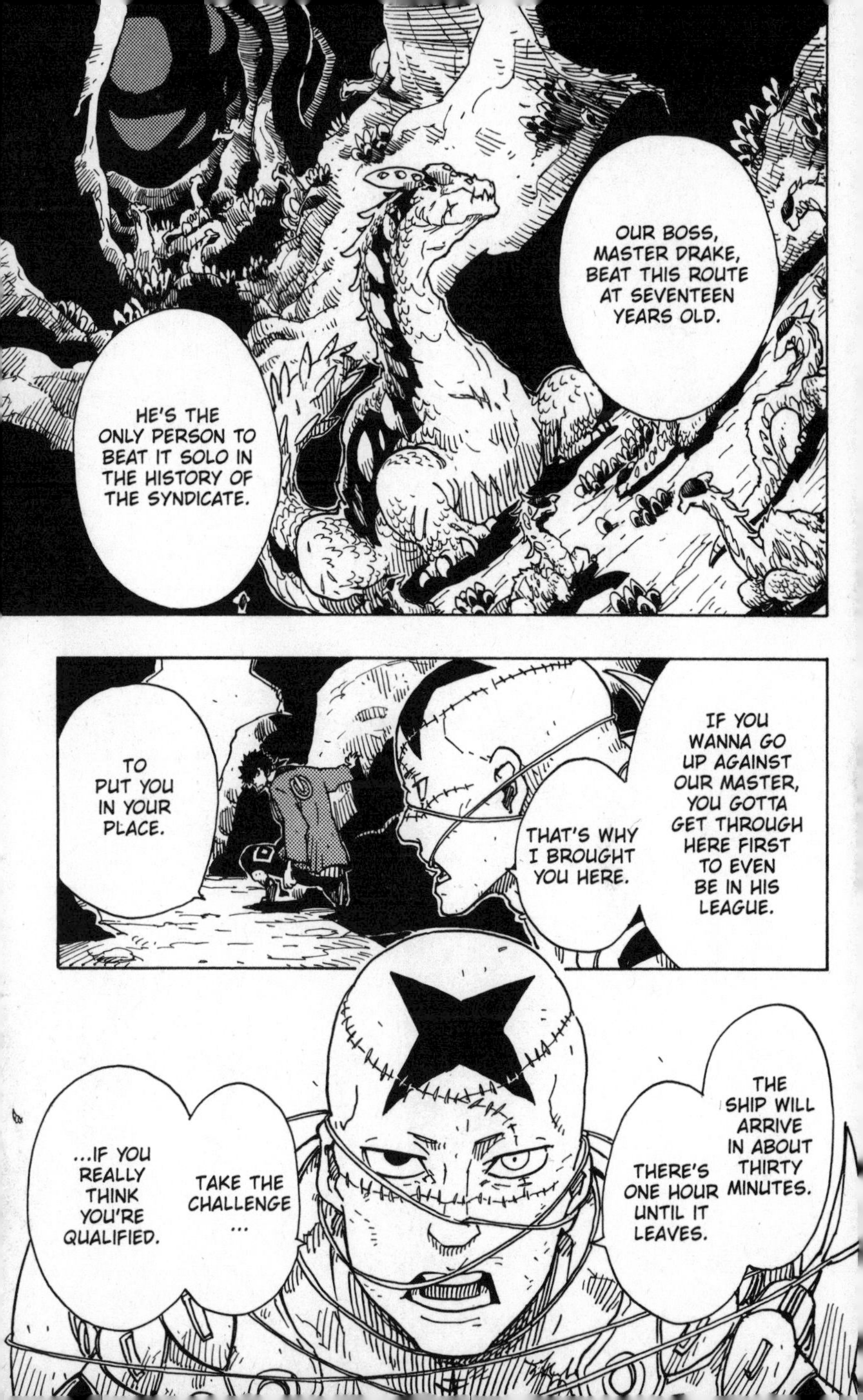
OUR BOSS, MASTER DRAKE, BEAT THIS ROUTE AT SEVENTEEN YEARS OLD.
HE'S THE ONLY PERSON TO BEAT IT SOLO IN THE HISTORY OF THE SYNDICATE.
IF YOU WANNA GO UP AGAINST OUR MASTER, YOU GOTTA GET THROUGH HERE FIRST TO EVEN BE IN HIS LEAGUE.
THAT'S WHY I BROUGHT YOU HERE.
TO PUT YOU IN YOUR PLACE.
THE SHIP WILL ARRIVE IN ABOUT THIRTY MINUTES.
THERE'S ONE HOUR UNTIL IT LEAVES.
TAKE THE CHALLENGE...
...IF YOU REALLY THINK YOU'RE QUALIFIED.

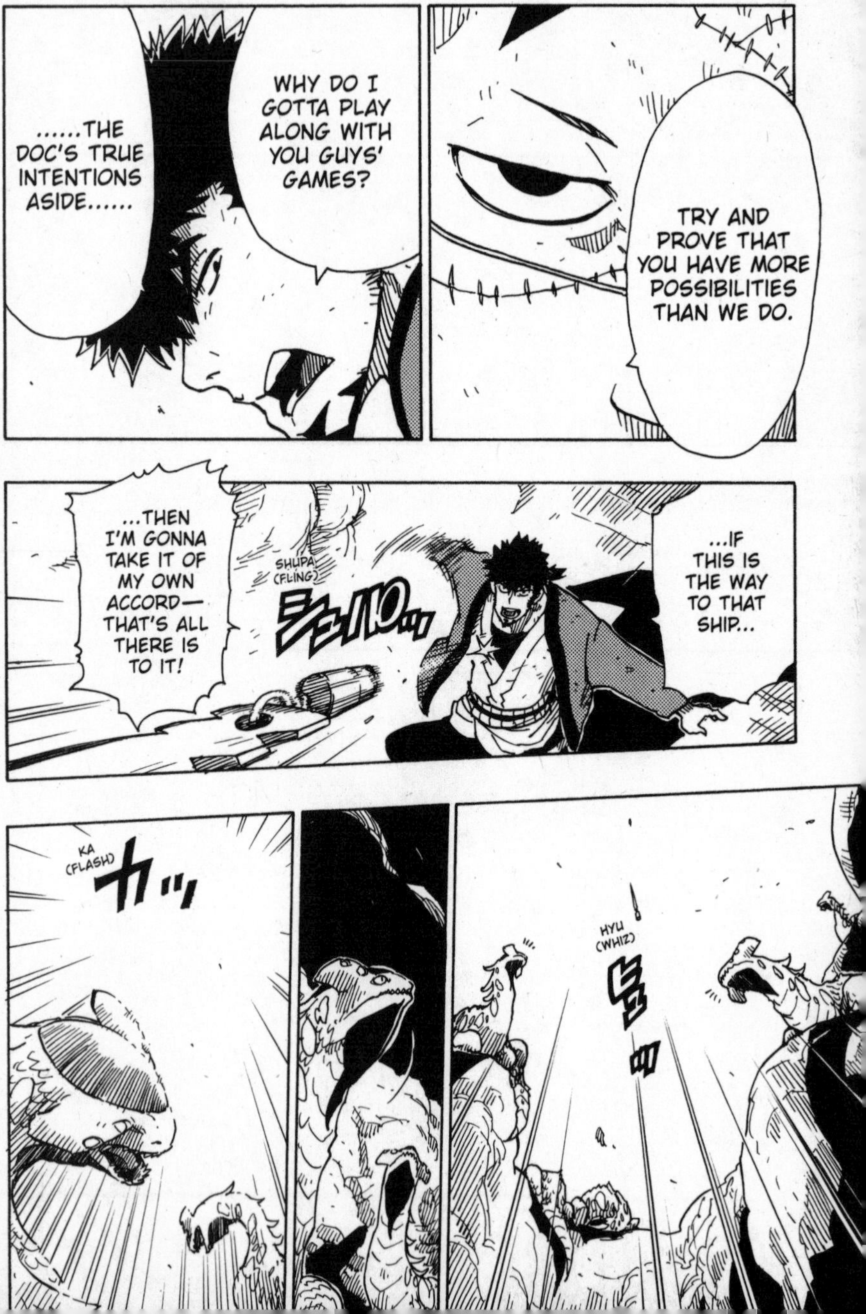
TRY AND PROVE THAT YOU HAVE MORE POSSIBILITIES THAN WE DO.
WHY DO I GOTTA PLAY ALONG WITH YOU GUYS' GAMES?
......THE DOC'S TRUE INTENTIONS ASIDE......
...IF THIS IS THE WAY TO THAT SHIP...
SHUPA (FLING)
...THEN I'M GONNA TAKE IT OF MY OWN ACCORD—THAT'S ALL THERE IS TO IT!
HYU (WHIZ)
KA (FLASH)

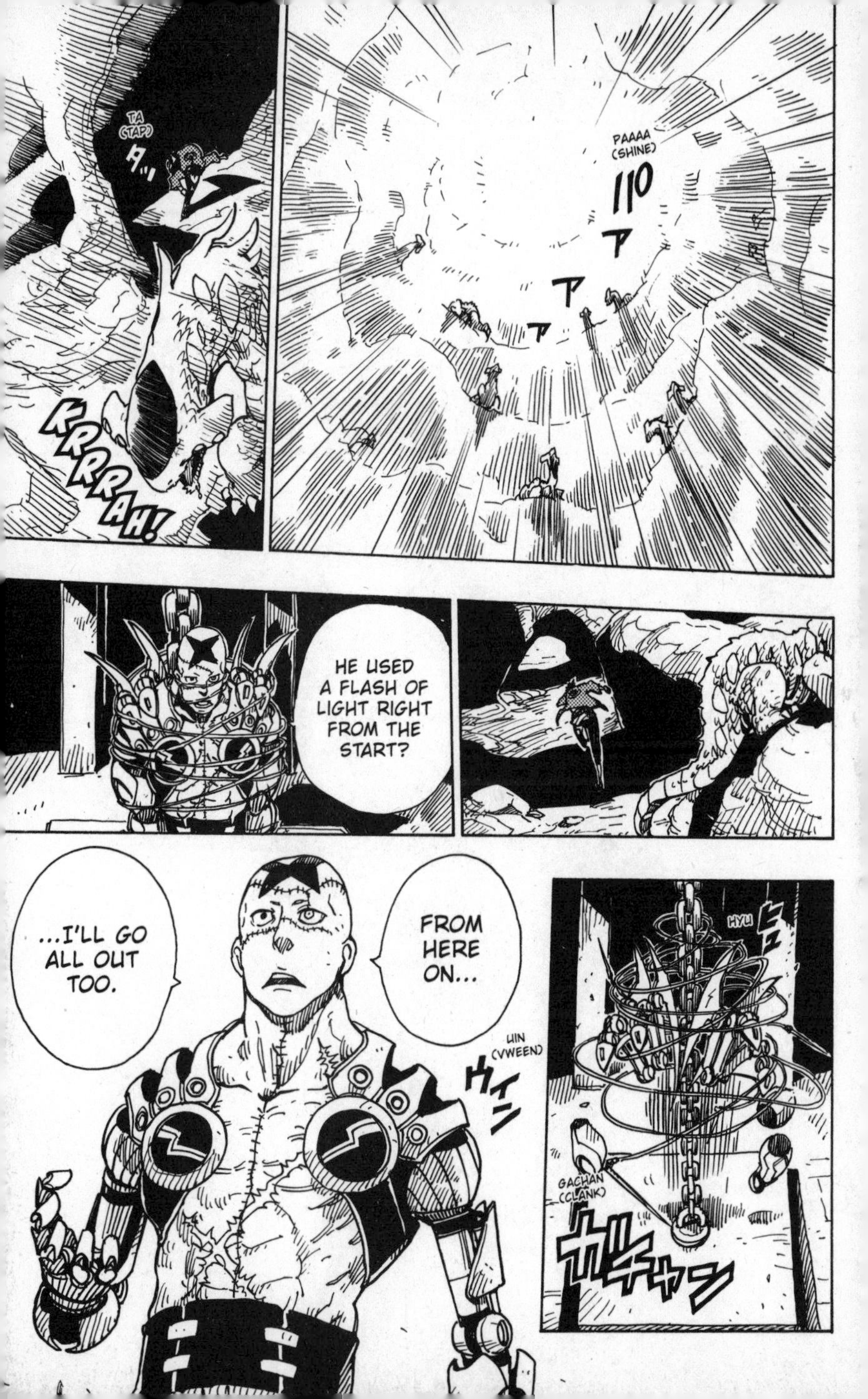
PAAAA (SHINE)
パァァァ
TA (TAP)
タッ
KRRRAH!
HE USED A FLASH OF LIGHT RIGHT FROM THE START?
HYU
ヒュ
GACHAN (CLANK)
ガチャン
UIN (VWEEN)
ウィン
FROM HERE ON...
...I'LL GO ALL OUT TOO.

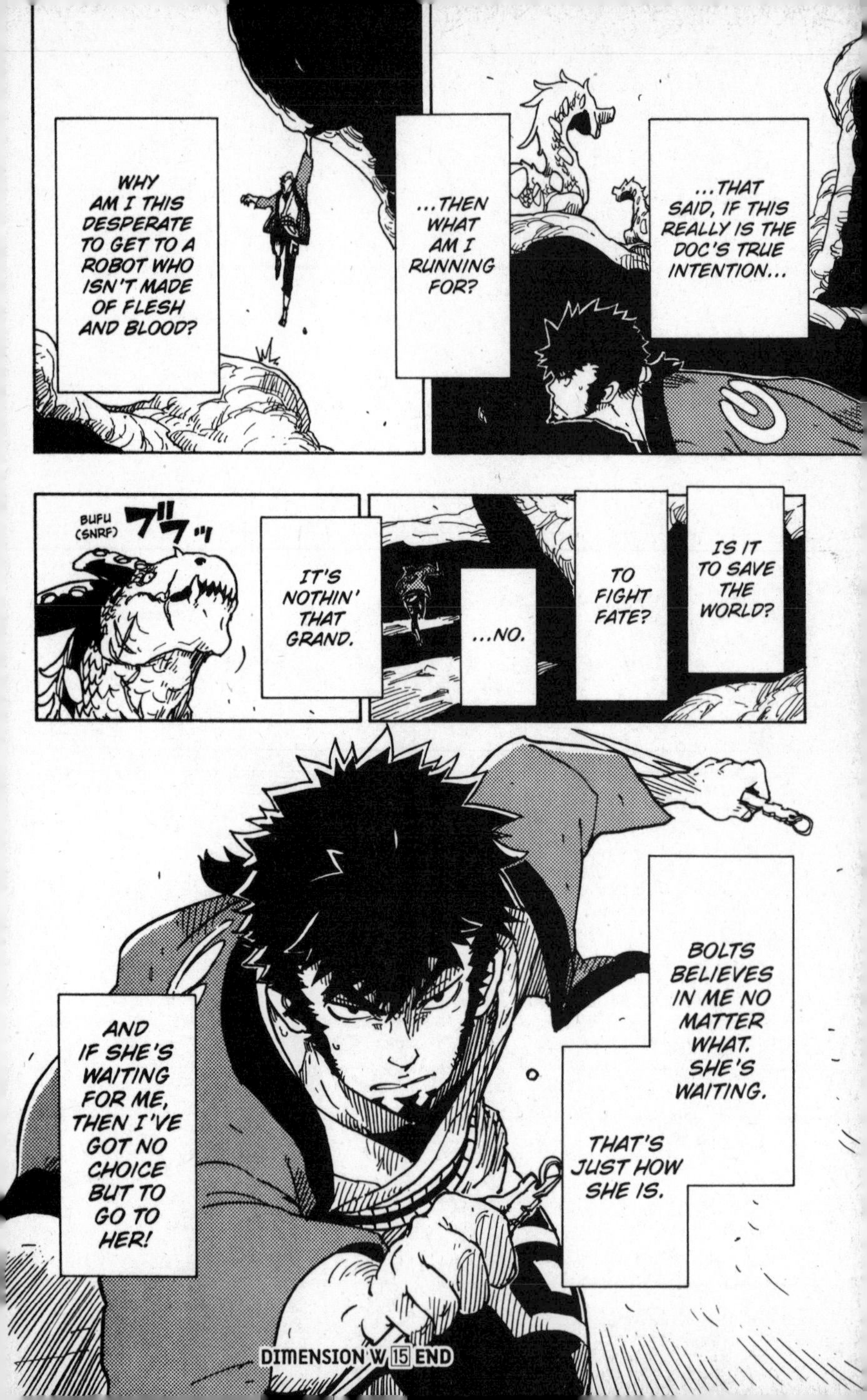
...THAT SAID, IF THIS REALLY IS THE DOC'S TRUE INTENTION...
...THEN WHAT AM I RUNNING FOR?
WHY AM I THIS DESPERATE TO GET TO A ROBOT WHO ISN'T MADE OF FLESH AND BLOOD?
IS IT TO SAVE THE WORLD?
TO FIGHT FATE?
...NO.
IT'S NOTHIN' THAT GRAND.
BUFU (SNRF)
ブフッ
BOLTS BELIEVES IN ME NO MATTER WHAT. SHE'S WAITING.
THAT'S JUST HOW SHE IS.
AND IF SHE'S WAITING FOR ME, THEN I'VE GOT NO CHOICE BUT TO GO TO HER!
DIMENSION W 15 END

Dimension W

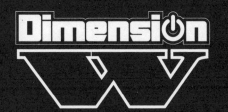

MINI CORNER

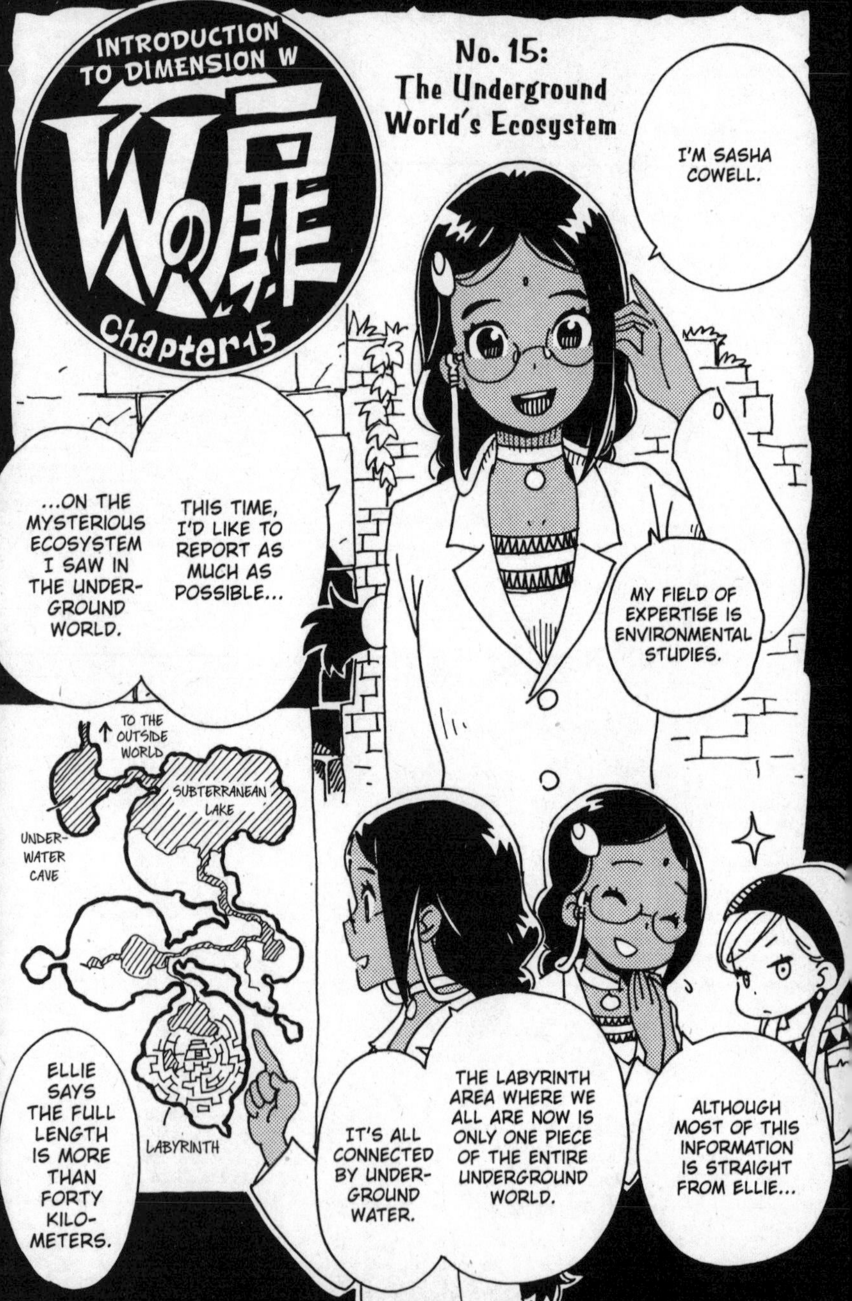
INTRODUCTION TO DIMENSION W
Wの扉
Chapter 15
No. 15: The Underground World's Ecosystem
I'M SASHA COWELL.
MY FIELD OF EXPERTISE IS ENVIRONMENTAL STUDIES.
THIS TIME, I'D LIKE TO REPORT AS MUCH AS POSSIBLE...
...ON THE MYSTERIOUS ECOSYSTEM I SAW IN THE UNDER-GROUND WORLD.
ALTHOUGH MOST OF THIS INFORMATION IS STRAIGHT FROM ELLIE...
THE LABYRINTH AREA WHERE WE ALL ARE NOW IS ONLY ONE PIECE OF THE ENTIRE UNDERGROUND WORLD.
IT'S ALL CONNECTED BY UNDER-GROUND WATER.
ELLIE SAYS THE FULL LENGTH IS MORE THAN FORTY KILO-METERS.
↑ TO THE OUTSIDE WORLD
SUBTERRANEAN LAKE
UNDER-WATER CAVE
LABYRINTH

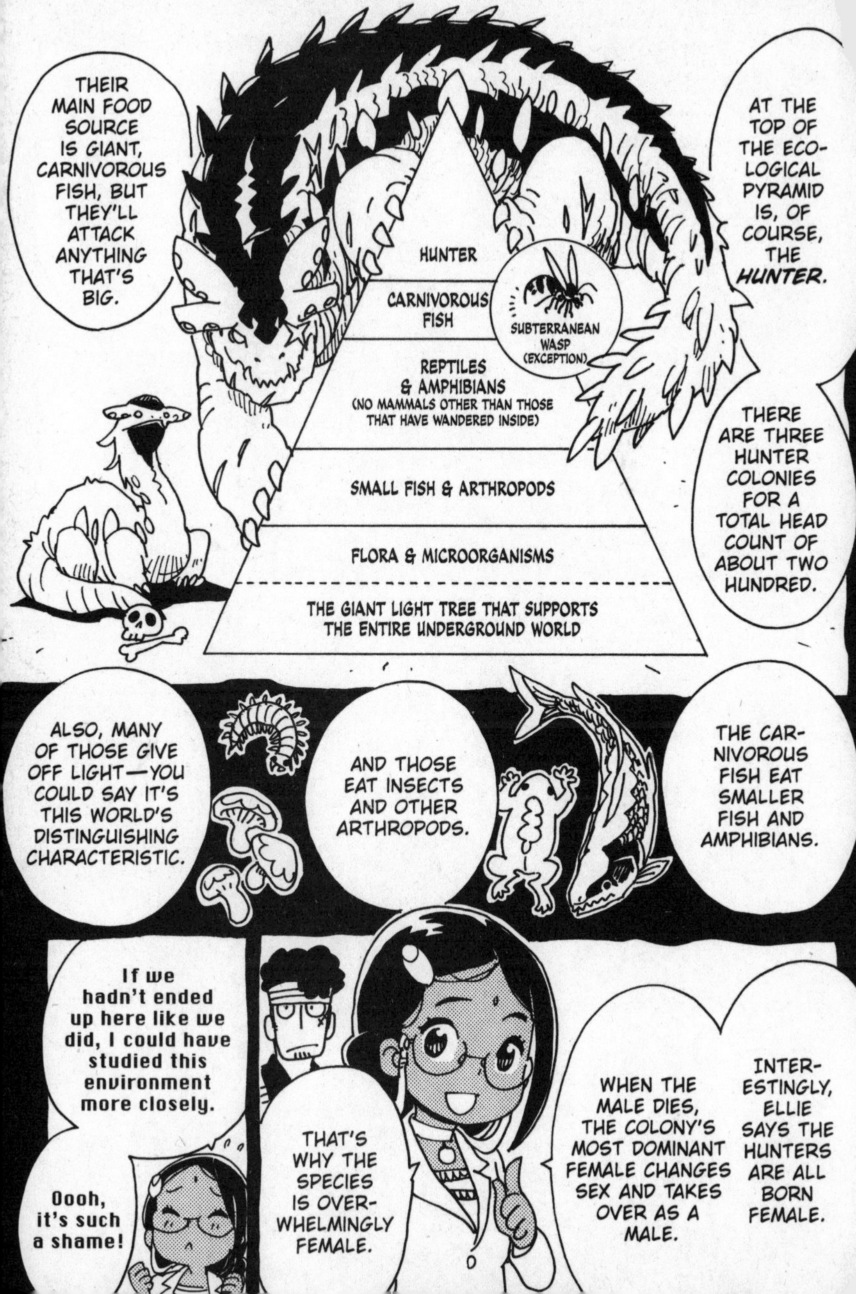
AT THE TOP OF THE ECOLOGICAL PYRAMID IS, OF COURSE, THE *HUNTER*.
THERE ARE THREE HUNTER COLONIES FOR A TOTAL HEAD COUNT OF ABOUT TWO HUNDRED.
THEIR MAIN FOOD SOURCE IS GIANT, CARNIVOROUS FISH, BUT THEY'LL ATTACK ANYTHING THAT'S BIG.
HUNTER
CARNIVOROUS FISH
SUBTERRANEAN WASP (EXCEPTION)
REPTILES & AMPHIBIANS (NO MAMMALS OTHER THAN THOSE THAT HAVE WANDERED INSIDE)
SMALL FISH & ARTHROPODS
FLORA & MICROORGANISMS
THE GIANT LIGHT TREE THAT SUPPORTS THE ENTIRE UNDERGROUND WORLD
THE CARNIVOROUS FISH EAT SMALLER FISH AND AMPHIBIANS.
AND THOSE EAT INSECTS AND OTHER ARTHROPODS.
ALSO, MANY OF THOSE GIVE OFF LIGHT—YOU COULD SAY IT'S THIS WORLD'S DISTINGUISHING CHARACTERISTIC.
INTERESTINGLY, ELLIE SAYS THE HUNTERS ARE ALL BORN FEMALE.
WHEN THE MALE DIES, THE COLONY'S MOST DOMINANT FEMALE CHANGES SEX AND TAKES OVER AS A MALE.
THAT'S WHY THE SPECIES IS OVERWHELMINGLY FEMALE.
If we hadn't ended up here like we did, I could have studied this environment more closely.
Oooh, it's such a shame!

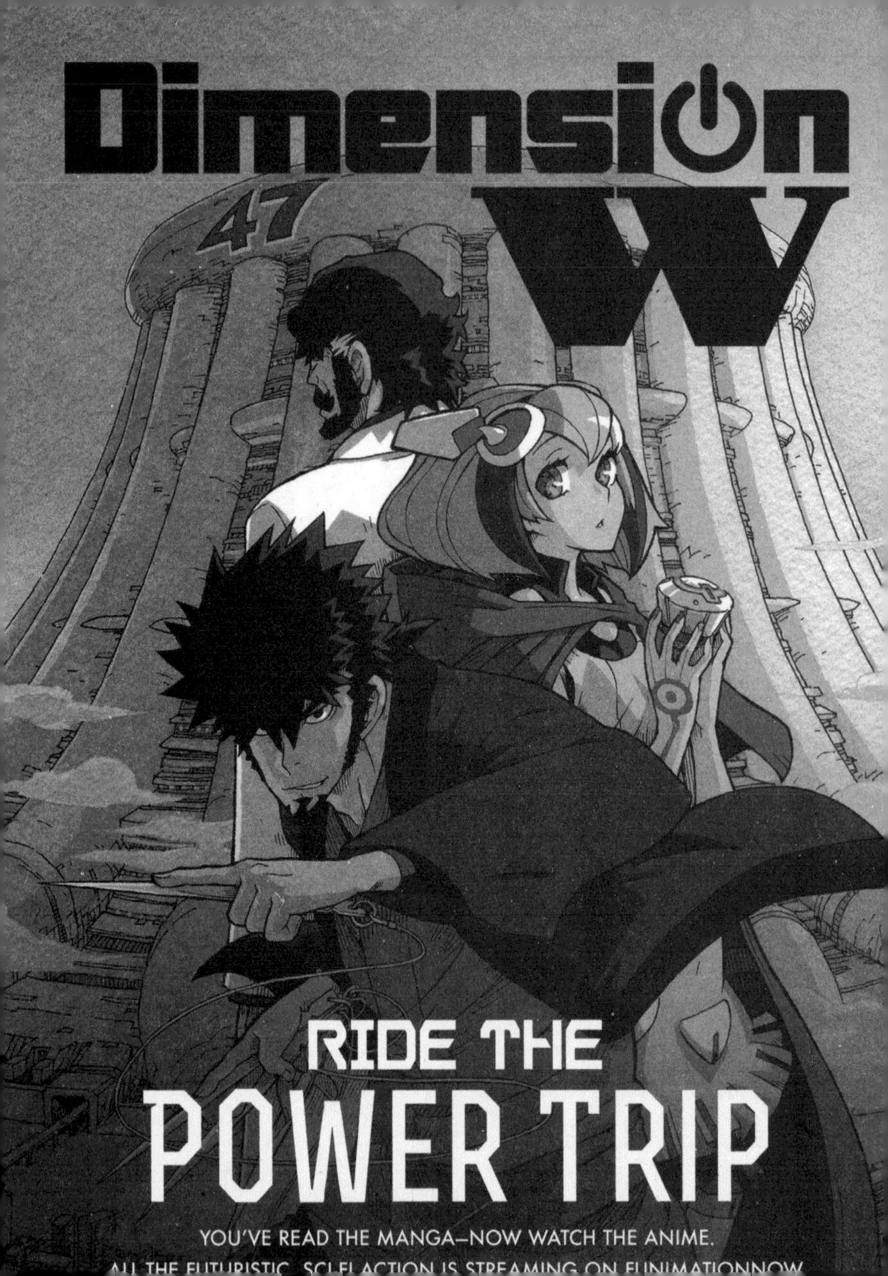
Dimension W
47
RIDE THE
POWER TRIP
YOU'VE READ THE MANGA—NOW WATCH THE ANIME.
[redacted]

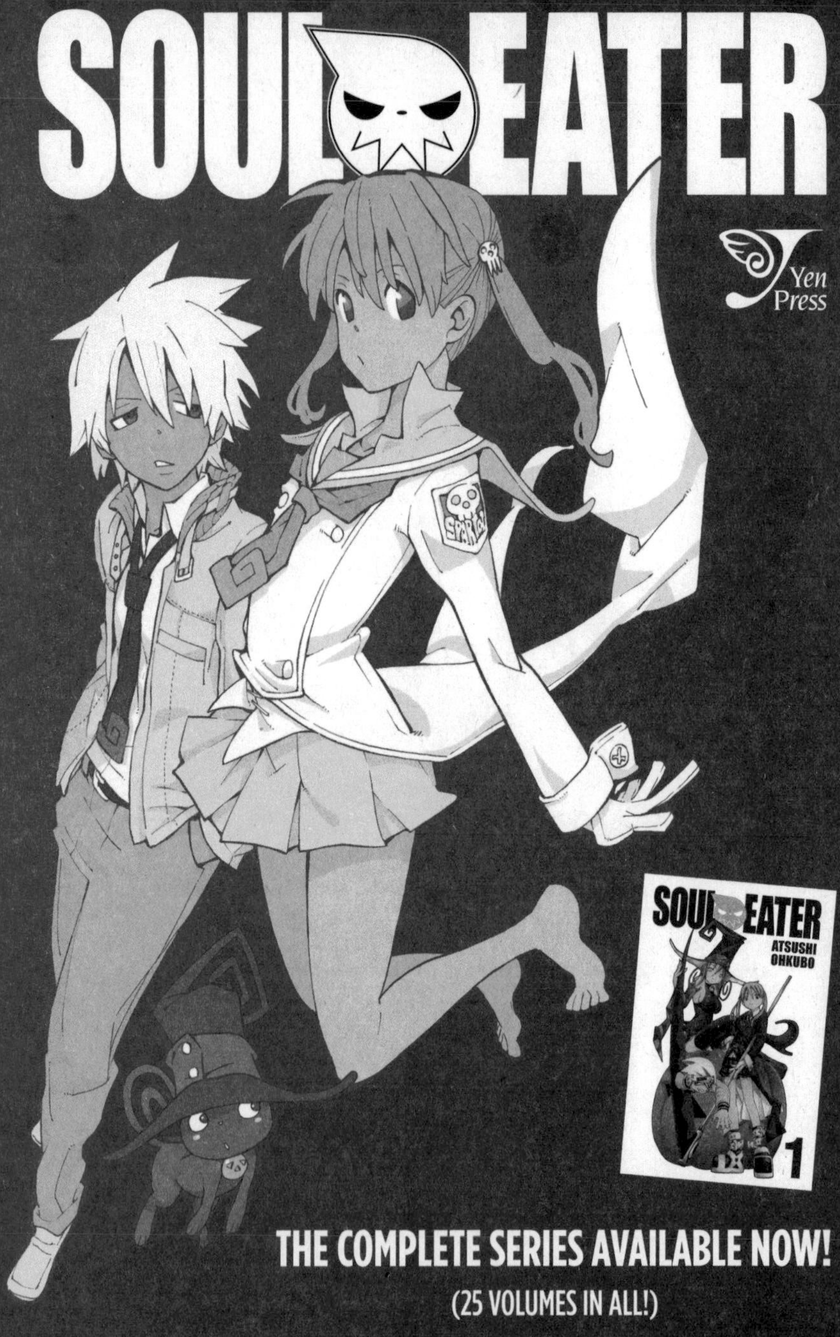
SOUL EATER
Yen Press
SOUL EATER
ATSUSHI OHKUBO
1
THE COMPLETE SERIES AVAILABLE NOW!
(25 VOLUMES IN ALL!)

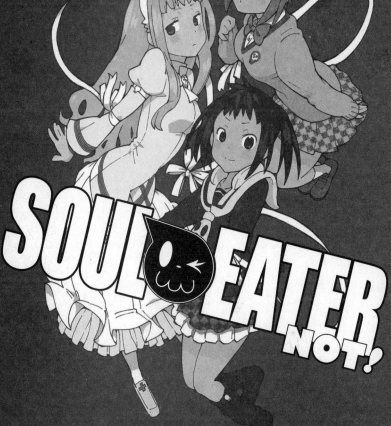

THE BEAT OF THE SOUL CONTINUES...

VOL. 1 – 5 AVAILABLE NOW!

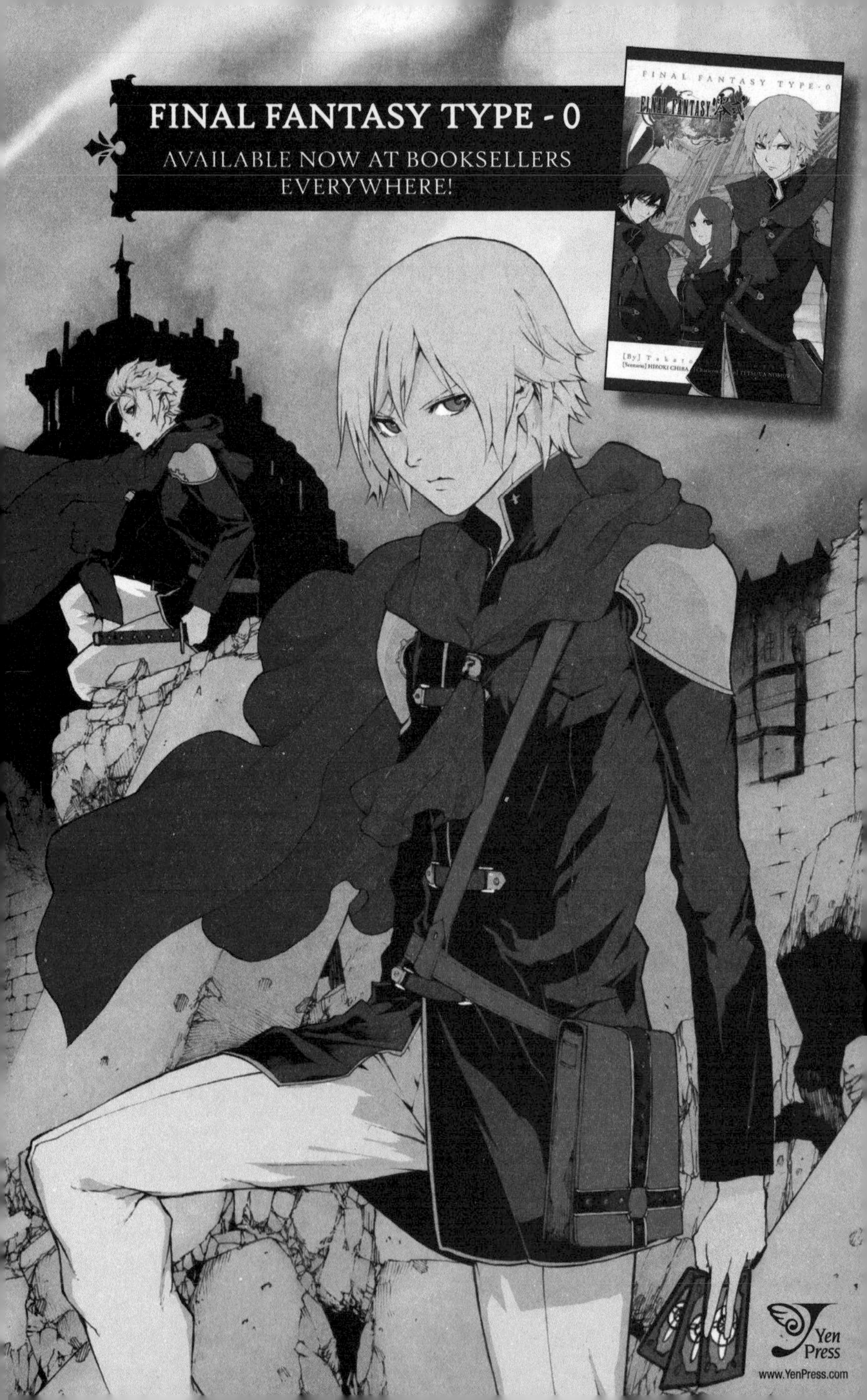
FINAL FANTASY TYPE - 0
AVAILABLE NOW AT BOOKSELLERS
EVERYWHERE!
FINAL FANTASY TYPE-0
Yen
Press
www.YenPress.com

FINAL FANTASY 零式 TYPE-0

Art: TAKATOSHI SHIOZAWA
Character Design: TETSUYA NOMURA
Scenario: HIROKI CHIBA

The cadets of Akademeia's Class Zero are legends, with strength and magic unrivaled, and crimson capes symbolizing the great Vermilion Bird of the Dominion. But will their elite training be enough to keep them alive when a war breaks out and the Class Zero cadets find themselves at the front and center of a bloody political battlefield?!

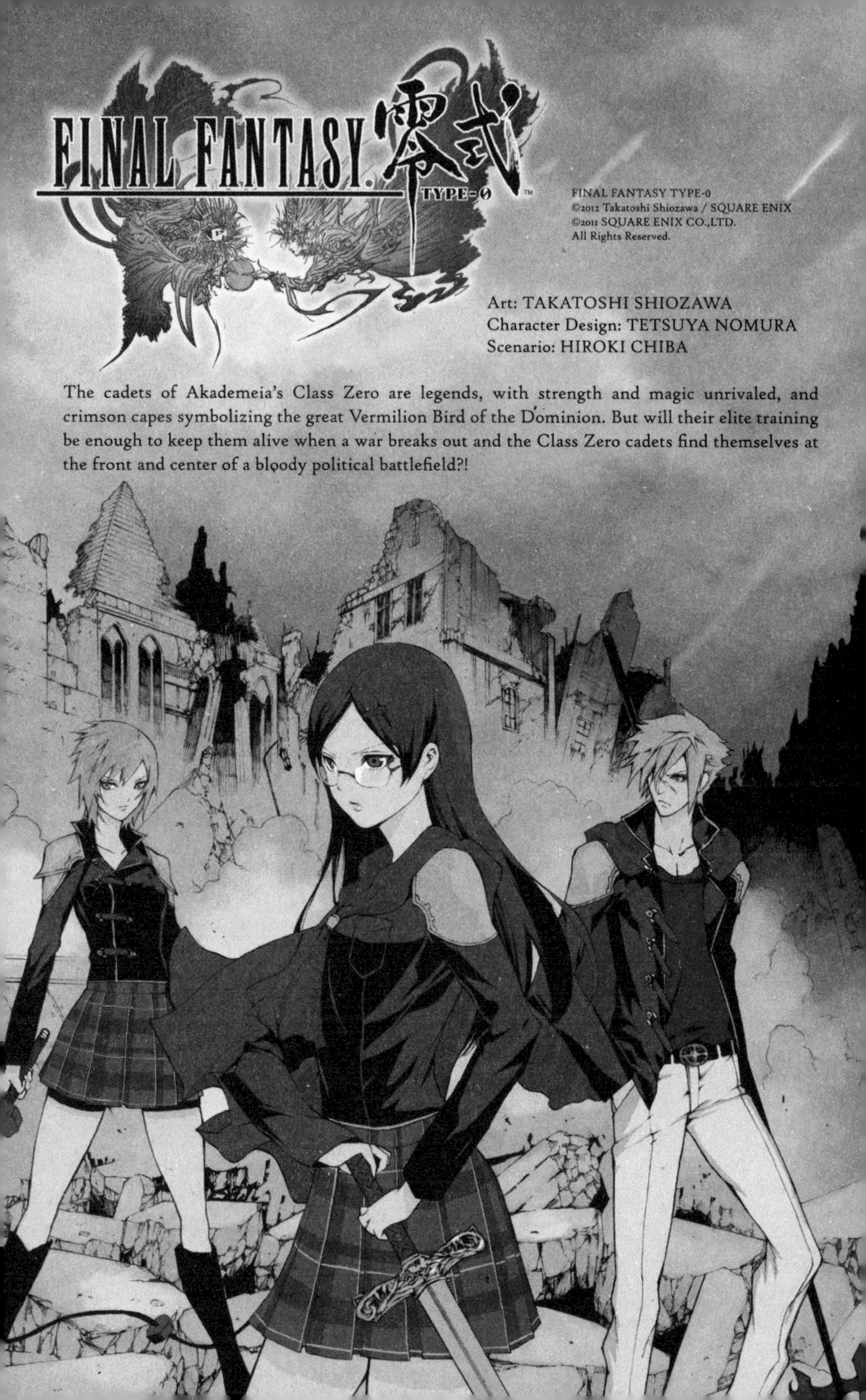

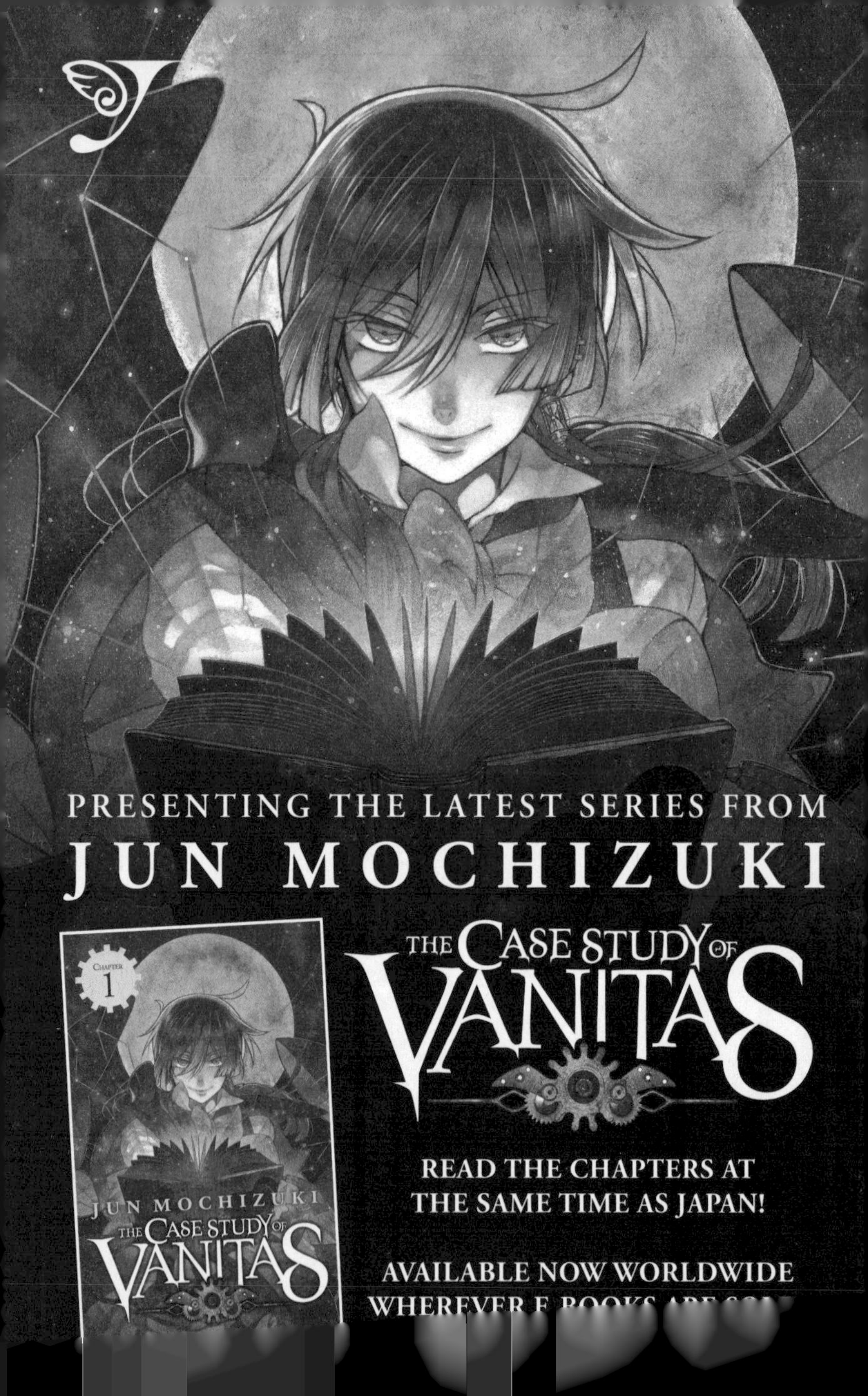
PRESENTING THE LATEST SERIES FROM
JUN MOCHIZUKI
CHAPTER 1
JUN MOCHIZUKI
THE CASE STUDY OF VANITAS
THE CASE STUDY OF VANITAS
READ THE CHAPTERS AT THE SAME TIME AS JAPAN!
AVAILABLE NOW WORLDWIDE
WHEREVER E-BOOKS ARE

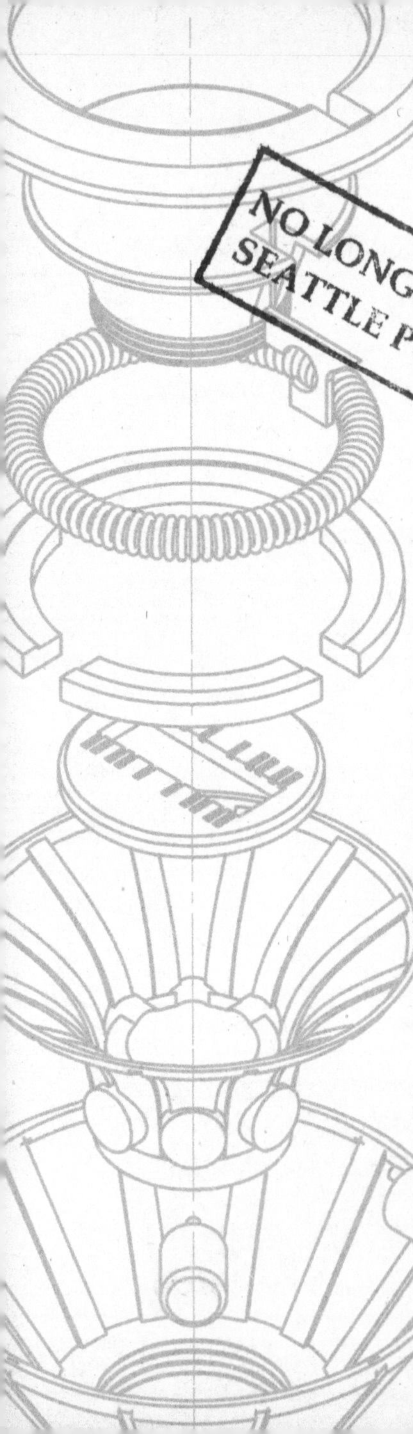

Dimensi⏻n W

by **YUJI IWAHARA**

Translation: Amanda Haley • Lettering: Phil Christie

DIMENSION W Volume 15 ©2018 YUJI IWAHARA/SQUARE ENIX CO., LTD. First published in Japan in 2018 by SQUARE ENIX CO., LTD. English translation rights arranged with Square Enix Co., Ltd. and Yen Press, LLC through Tuttle-Mori Agency, Inc.

English translation © 2019 by SQUARE ENIX CO., LTD.

Yen Press
150 West 30th Street, 19th Floor
New York, NY 10001

Visit us at yenpress.com
facebook.com/yenpress
twitter.com/yenpress
yenpress.tumblr.com
instagram.com/yenpress

First Yen Press Edition: August 2019

Yen Press is an imprint of Yen Press, LLC.
The Yen Press name and logo are trademarks of Yen Press, LLC.

The publisher is not responsible for websites (or their content) that are not owned by the publisher.

Library of Congress Control Number: 2015956889

ISBNs: 978-1-975-38495-1 (paperback)
       978-1-975-38496-8 (ebook)

10 9 8 7 6 5 4 3 2 1

WOR

Printed in the United States of America